McGraw-Hill Education

Beginning
Spanish
Grammar

Luis Aragonés and Ramón Palencia

New York   Chicago   San Francisco   Athens   London   Madrid
Mexico City   Milan   New Delhi   Singapore   Sydney   Toronto

Published by McGraw-Hill Global Education Holdings, LLC © 2014, under license from SM™.

  7 8 9 10   LHS   21 20 19

ISBN   978-0-07-184064-4
MHID   0-07-184064-8

e-ISBN 978-0-07-184065-1
e-MHID   0-07-184065-6

Library of Congress Control Number 2014940122

Proyecto editorial
Equipo de Idiomas de SM

Autores
Ramón Palencia
Luis Aragonés

Coordinación editorial
Yolanda Lozano Ramírez de Arellano
Pablo Fernández de Córdoba

Edición
María Álvarez Pedroso
Cristina Aparecida Duarte
Alejandro García-Caro García

Traducción y revisión lingüística
Gregory John Backes

Ilustración
Ángel Trigo

Diseño
Estudio SM

Maquetación
Preiscam, S. L.
Diego García Tirado

Dirección editorial
Pilar García García

What is this book?

McGraw-Hill Education: Beginning Spanish Grammar is addressed to beginner-level students. It is broken down into 107 units that deal with very concrete grammar points organized in double pages of theory and practice:

Presentation
of content in
drawings.

Exercises that work
on the material
presented on the
theory page.

THEORY   PRACTICE

Easy and
sequenced
grammar
explanations.

Reference
marks to other
units to clarify
or complete
concepts.

Be Careful tables
that indicate the
points that are
most difficult.

Sample answers
that make it
clearer how to
complete the
exercises.

Spaces to
indicate the
number of
correct answers
and to carry out
the self-test.

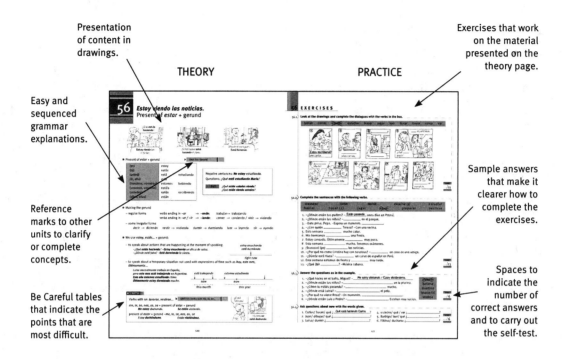

- A clear grammar explanation of the theoretical contents.
- Grammar practice that includes a large number of examples and exercises.
- Grammar usage with current and worthwhile vocabulary and contexualized examples of everyday situations.
- A grammar visual with clear structures, numerous illustrations, and colored references to indicate the most significant contents.

How is it used?

- The book can be used either in the classroom or as a self-taught instrument. For this reason, at the end of the book are an answer key with all of the answers to the exercises plus Spanish/English and English/Spanish glossaries with all the necessary vocabulary to understand the exercises.
- Each unit can be dealt with in an independent way: teacher or student can solve a specific question without having to follow the book from beginning to end.
- Each person can begin the book either at the Contents, where the units are organized by grammar points, or at the Index, where concepts and key words are included in alphabetical order.

A work proposal

- To work on new grammar aspects for the student:

  – Read the theory.

  – Do the exercises.

  – Review the exercises with the help of the answer key, highlighting the incorrect answers.

  – Read the theory again, focusing on finding new information that explains the mistakes made in the exercises.

  – Do the exercises again and then review them.

  – Repeat the previous step a few days later.

- To work on grammar points that the student already knows:

  Do the above-mentioned process starting on the second step. Read the grammar theory only to check the reasons for certain mistakes.

- To work on units that contain grammar points and common subjects and that are related to each other through rerference marks:

  – Remember previous contents necessary for the comprehension of a new unit or units by going back to the units indicated in a reference mark and reading the theory.

  – Advance and go into more detail in the grammar point or content by going to the unit or units indicated in the reference mark, reading the theory, and doing the exercises.

- To do a self-test for each unit, complete the table that appears in the margin of every exercise with the number of correct answers.

- To work on basic questions referring to Spanish grammar, two units are included at the back of the book that can be studied at any time, regardless of the itinerary chosen for the book units.

Contents

1 *el hijo, la hija*
Masculine, feminine (1)

padre, hijo = masculine   madre, hija = feminine

● In Spanish, **proper nouns** are either masculine or feminine.

 hombre = masculine   *mujer* = feminine

el hijo	*la hija*
el padre	*la madre*
el camarero	*la camarera*
el doctor	*la doctora*
el estudiante	*la estudiante*

● Masculine and feminine endings.

MASCULINE	FEMININE
-o, -e	**-a**
el niño	*la niña*
el cocinero	*la cocinera*
el dependiente	*la dependienta*
-consonante	**+a**
el profesor	*la profesora*
el bailarín	*la bailarina*
-ante, -ista	**-ante, -ista**
el estudiante	*la estudiante*
el taxista	*la taxista*
otras terminaciones	
el actor	*la actriz*
el rey	*la reina*
el príncipe	*la princesa*
formas diferentes	
*el **hombre***	*la **mujer***
*el **marido***	*la **mujer***
*el **padre***	*la **madre***

█ BUT:

el piloto	*la piloto*
el modelo	*la modelo*
el paciente	*la paciente*

█ BUT:

el joven	*la joven*

BE CAREFUL!

el tío ▸ *la* tía   *un* hombre alt**o** ▸ *una* mujer alt**a**   *ese* señor ▸ *esa* señora

---

▸ UNIT 2: Masculine, feminine (2)   UNIT 4: The indefinite article   UNIT 6: The definite article
  UNIT 13: Descriptive adjectives   UNIT 14: Adjectives of nationality

1.1 Write *M* (masculine) or *F* (feminine) in the box under each picture. Afterwards, label each picture using one of the words from the box with either *el* or *la*.

cantante	cocinero	estudiante	modelo	paciente
~~periodista~~	pianista	piloto	rey	taxista

① ② ③ ④ ⑤

| F | la periodista | ☐ _____ | ☐ _____ | ☐ _____ | ☐ _____ |

⑥ ⑦ ⑧ ⑨ ⑩

☐ _____ ☐ _____ ☐ _____ ☐ _____ ☐ _____

SCORE ..../10

1.2 Write the feminine form of the nouns.

1. señor _señora_
2. director _____
3. fotógrafo _____
4. artista _____
5. actor _____
6. pintor _____
7. abogado _____

8. turista _____
9. joven _____
10. tenista _____
11. rey _____
12. alumno _____
13. hombre _____
14. dependiente _____

15. doctor _____
16. paciente _____
17. marido _____
18. niño _____
19. escritor _____
20. príncipe _____
21. bailarín _____

SCORE ..../21

1.3 Look at the picture and complete each sentence with one word from the box.

abuela	abuelo	hermana	hermano
hija	hijo	madre	~~padre~~
	tía	tío	

1. Luis es mi _padre_.
2. Ana es mi _____.
3. Laura es mi _____.
4. Blanca es mi _____.
5. Pedro es mi _____.

6. Luis es mi _____.
7. Ana es mi _____.
8. Lucía es mi _____.
9. Julio es mi _____.
10. Raúl es mi _____.

SCORE ..../10

2 *el libro, la mesa*
Masculine, feminine (2)

El libro, el teléfono are masculine nouns.

La mesa, la silla are feminine nouns.

- In Spanish, **common nouns** are either masculine or feminine.
  - **Nouns ending in –o = masculine:**

    el li**bro**   el cuader**no**   el teléfo**no**   el va**so**   el muse**o**

  BUT: la mano   la foto (la fotografía)   la moto (la motocicleta)   la radio

  - **Nouns ending in –a = feminine:**

    la cas**a**   la sill**a**   la mes**a**   la guitar**ra**   la ros**a**

  BUT: el día   el idioma   el mapa   el programa   el problema   el sofá

  - **Nouns ending in –e or with a consonant = masculine or feminine.**
    - **Masculine:** el restaurant**e**   el coch**e**   el cin**e**   el hotel   el lápi**z**   el pan   el color
      - Days of the week: el lune**s**   el marte**s**
      - Compound nouns: el paragua**s**   el cumpleaño**s**
    - **Feminine:** la clas**e**   la noch**e**   la lech**e**   la sal   la flor   la lu**z**
      - Nouns ending in –**ción**, –**sión**: la can**ción**   la habita**ción**   la televi**sión**
      - Nouns ending in –**dad**, –**tad**: la ciu**dad**   la universi**dad**   la liber**tad**

    If in doubt, look it up in a dictionary.

- Some **names of animals** have a masculine form and a feminine form.

  el gato – la gata   el caballo – la yegua
  el perro – la perra   el toro   – la vaca
  el cerdo – la cerda   el gallo   – la gallina

  el león

  la leona

  But most have only one form, masculine or feminine:
  - These are **always masculine:** el canguro, el cocodrilo, el pingüino, el pájaro, el gorila, el chimpancé, el ratón, el pez
  - These are **always feminine:** la rata, la jirafa, la mariposa, la mosca, la araña, la ballena, la serpiente

  If in doubt, look it up in a dictionary.

▶ UNIT 1: Masculine, feminine (1)   UNIT 4: The indefinite article   UNIT 6: The definite article
   UNIT 13: Descriptive adjectives   UNIT 14: Adjectives of nationality

2 EXERCISES

2.1. Label the drawing with nouns from the box and *el* or *la*.

bolígrafo	cuaderno	foto	lapicero	libro
mapa	mesa	pizarra	silla	~~ventana~~

1. __la ventana__
2. _____
3. _____
4. _____
5. _____
6. _____
7. _____
8. _____
9. _____
10. _____

SCORE ...../10

2.2. Put the nouns from the box in the correct column.

~~árbol~~	autobús	avión	~~canción~~	cine	ciudad	cumpleaños	día	estación
habitación	hotel	idioma	lápiz	leche	luz	llave	mano	moto	noche
nariz	problema	programa	radio	sofá	televisión	tren	universidad	viernes

EL...		LA...	
árbol	_____	canción	_____
_____	_____	_____	_____
_____	_____	_____	_____
_____	_____	_____	_____
_____	_____	_____	_____
_____	_____	_____	_____

SCORE ...../28

2.3. Complete the boxes with the corresponding animals.

MASCULINE	FEMININE
el gato	la gata
el caballo	_____
el gallo	_____

MASCULINE	FEMININE
_____	la perra
el león	_____
_____	la vaca

SCORE ...../6

2.4. Complete with *el* for masculine and *la* for feminine. Use a dictionary if necessary.

①  ②  ③ ④ ⑤ ⑥

la mariposa   _____   _____   _____   _____   _____

chimpancé	gorila	jirafa	mariposa	pez	serpiente

SCORE ...../6

13

3 *libro, libros*
Singular, plural

libro   *reloj*

libro, reloj = **singular** (1)

libros   *relojes*

libros, relojes = **plural** (2, 3, 4, ...)

● How plurals are formed

SINGULAR	PLURAL	EXAMPLES
−a, −e, −i, −o, −u	+ s	*casa* ▸ *casas* *coche* ▸ *coches* *niño* ▸ *niños*
−consonant	+ es	*profesor* ▸ *profesores* *ciudad* ▸ *ciudades* *postal* ▸ *postales* *habitación* ▸ *habitaciones*
−s (words with one syllable)	+ es	*mes* ▸ *meses*
−ás, −és, −ís, −ós, −ús (words with two or more syllables)	+ es	*país* ▸ *países* *autobús* ▸ *autobuses*
−as, −es, −is, −os, −us (words with two or more syllabes)	without change	*(el) lunes* ▸ *(los) lunes* *(el) paraguas* ▸ *(los) paraguas*

> **BE CAREFUL!**
>
> −z ▸ −**ces**: *actriz* ▸ *actri**ces***
>
> *autobús* ▸ *autobuses*   *televisi**ón*** ▸ *televisi**ones***

● Some nouns have only a plural form.

gafas   *tijeras*   *pantalones*   *vaqueros*   *unas tijeras*   *tres tijeras*

● Masculine + feminine = plural masculine

padre + madre = padres   *hijo + hija = hijos*

Los padres de Miguel se llaman Antonio y Pilar.   **Julia tiene tres hijos.**

▶ UNIT 4: The indefinite article   UNIT 6: The definite article
    UNIT 13: Descriptive adjectives   UNIT 14: Adjectives of nationality

3 EXERCISES

3.1 Write the plural form of the nouns.

1. mujer	_mujeres_	11. niño	_____	21. cumpleaños	_____
2. pez	_____	12. hermana	_____	22. teléfono	_____
3. ventana	_____	13. león	_____	23. casa	_____
4. actriz	_____	14. día	_____	24. flor	_____
5. habitación	_____	15. clase	_____	25. vaqueros	_____
6. madre	_____	16. foto	_____	26. mes	_____
7. pantalones	_____	17. vaca	_____	27. médico	_____
8. hotel	_____	18. jueves	_____	28. país	_____
9. universidad	_____	19. actor	_____	29. jugador	_____
10. televisión	_____	20. estudiante	_____	30. ladrón	_____

SCORE ...... /30

3.2 Write the names of the objects that are in the drawing. Use the words from the box and the numbers 1, 2, 3, and 4.

En el dibujo hay...

_____ 1 mesa _____	_____ 2 botellas _____
_____	_____
_____	_____
_____	_____
_____	_____

botella	gafas	lámpara	lápiz	libro
~~mesa~~	postal	silla	tijeras	vaso

SCORE ...... /10

3.3 Look at the drawings and write the names of the objects in the correct form.

| autobús | ~~casa~~ | pantalones | paraguas | pez | reloj |

1. _casas_   2. _____   3. _____   4. _____   5. _____   6. _____

SCORE ...... /6

3.4 Change the underlined words as in the example.

1. Amalia tiene un hijo y dos hijas.
   Amalia tiene tres hijos.

2. El abuelo y la abuela de Marta viven en Caracas.
   Los _____ de Marta viven en Caracas.

3. Un amigo y una amiga míos están en Chile.
   Dos _____ míos están en Chile.

4. Mi hermano y mi hermana son médicos.
   Mis _____ son médicos.

5. Mi padre y mi madre son muy altos.
   Mis _____ son muy altos.

6. Voy a una fiesta con mis compañeros y compañeras.
   Voy a una fiesta con mis_____.

7. Es una compañía de ballet con un bailarín y dos bailarinas.
   Es una compañía de ballet con tres _____.

8. En mi escuela hay un profesor y dos profesoras.
   En mi escuela hay tres _____.

9. He mandado un correo electrónico a mi tío y a mi tía.
   He mandado un correo electrónico a mis _____.

10. En mi clase hay tres alumnos y cinco alumnas.
    En mi clase hay ocho _____.

SCORE ...... /10

4 *un, una, unos, unas*
The indefinite article

● Forms of the indefinite article

	MASCULINE	FEMININE
SINGULAR	un ***un** chico*, ***un** coche*	una ***una** chica*, ***una** casa*
PLURAL	unos ***unos** chicos*, ***unos** coches*	unas ***unas** chicas*, ***unas** casas*

> **BE CAREFUL!**
>
> Use *un* (not *una*) before singular feminine nouns that begin with *á*, *há*:
>
>   ***un águila***   ***un aula***   ***un hacha***   ***un ama de casa***
>
>   **BUT:**   ***unas** águilas*, ***una** buena aula*, ***una** pequeña hacha*, ***una** buena ama de casa*

● We use *un, una, unos, unas* + noun to identify something
or someone as part of a group.

    *–¿Qué es eso? –Es **un reloj**.*
    *–¿Quién es Chayanne? –Es **un cantante**.*
    *La papaya es **una fruta**.*

● We use *un, una, unos, unas* + noun to indicate amount.

  – *un, una* + singular countable nouns = 1

    *Necesito **un** lápiz.*
    ***Una** entrada, por favor.*

 un lápiz   *una entrada*

  – *unos, unas* + plural nouns with no singular form = 1

    *Necesito **unas** tijeras.*
    *Quiero **unos** vaqueros.*

 unas tijeras   *unos vaqueros*

  – *unos, unas* + countable plural nouns = some (3, 4, 5...)

    *He comprado **unas** flores.*
    *Hay **unos** libros en la mesa.*

 unas flores   *unos libros*

  – *unos, unas* + amount = approximately

    *Hay **unas veinte personas** en la clase.* = approximately twenty people.

▶   **UNIT 5: Absence of the article**   **UNIT 7: Contrasting the indefinite and definite article**

4 EXERCISES

4.1. Complete with *un, una, unos, unas.*

1. _una_ flor
2. _____ sillas
3. _____ relojes
4. _____ mesa
5. _____ alumnos

6. _____ cine
7. _____ habitación
8. _____ lápices
9. _____ chica
10. _____ aulas

11. _____ ciudad
12. _____ aula
13. _____ profesora
14. _____ pantalones
15. _____ camarero

4.2. Complete the answers using *un, una, unos, unas* and the words from the box.

ciudad	~~deporte~~	flor		actriz	cantante	cantante	escritora
fruta	isla	país	río	~~futbolista~~		jugador de golf	tenista

¿Qué es...

1. ... el balonmano? Es _un deporte_.
2. ... Sevilla? Es _____.
3. ... Colombia? Es _____.
4. ... una rosa? Es _____.
5. ... el mango? Es _____.
6. ... Tenerife? Es _____.
7. ... el Ebro? Es _____.

¿Quién es...

1. ... Ronaldinho? Es _un futbolista_.
2. ... Isabel Allende? Es _____.
3. ... Tiger Woods? Es _____.
4. ... Bruce Springsteen? Es _____.
5. ... María Sharapova? Es _____.
6. ... Penélope Cruz? Es _____.
7. ... Avril Lavigne? Es _____.

4.3. Write what you see in each drawing using *un, una, unos, unas* and the words from the box.

| árboles | caballo | casa | chicas | ~~coche~~ | gafas | gato | hacha | libros | niños | televisión | vacas |

1. _un coche_
2. _____
3. _____
4. _____

5. _____
6. _____
7. _____
8. _____

9. _____
10. _____
11. _____
12. _____

4.4. Complete the sentences with *un, una, unos, unas.*

1. _Un_ melón, por favor.
2. El Orinoco es _____ río.
3. ¡Cuidado, _____ serpiente!
4. ¡Mira, _____ águila!
5. Quiero _____ vaqueros, por favor.
6. –¿Qué es eso? –Es_____ radio.
7. ¿Tienes _____ mapa de Ecuador?
8. Rosa tiene _____ hija.
9. Necesitamos _____ tijeras.

10. Tenemos _____ cincuenta euros.
11. Necesito _____ diez plátanos.
12. Quieren _____ zapatos.
13. Susana tiene _____ treinta años.
14. Está lloviendo. Necesito _____ paraguas.
15. En mi colegio hay _____ quince aulas.
16. Quiero _____ habitación.
17. El tulipán es _____ flor.
18. En mi clase hay _____ diez chicas.

5 *un coche / coche*
Absence of the article

● We don't use *un, una, unos, unas* after *ser* with names of professions, religion, nationality or political ideology.

Soy profesora de español.
Chantal **es francesa**.
Lenin y Stalin **eran comunistas**.

Marta es abogada.

| **BUT:** | We use *un, una, unos, unas*: |

– when the noun goes with a description.

    Chantal es **una francesa muy simpática**.
    Es **un médico extraordinario**.

– when we identify someone because of his or her profession.

    –¿Quiénes son las Hijas del Sol? –Son **unas cantantes**.

▶ UNIT 4: The indefinite article

Es una actriz muy famosa.

Compare:

La hermana de Rosa es **profesora** de español. Almodóvar es **director de cine**.	Es **una profesora muy seria**. –¿Quién es Almodóvar? –Es **un director de cine**.

● We don't use *un, una, unos, unas* before the direct object of a verb when we refer to something in general.

    Lola colecciona **sellos**.
    El novio de Lali es escritor. Escribe **novelas**.
    Están buscando **piso**.
    ¿Tienes **teléfono**?
    No tengo **coche**.
    Luis y Juana no tienen **hijos**.

Luis siempre lleva corbata.

| **BUT:** | We use *un, una, unos, unas*: |

– when we speak about quantity.

    Quiero **un bolígrafo**, por favor. (= 1)
    Me han regalado **unos sellos**. (= 6, 8, 20... sellos)

– when the noun goes with a description.

    Tengo **unos sellos muy raros**.
    Buscan **un piso barato**.

Hoy lleva una corbata muy original.

Compare:

No tengo **coche**. Necesito **gafas**.	Me he comprado **un coche**. Necesito **unas gafas especiales**.

▶ UNIT 45: Present indicative of *haber* (impersonal)

5 EXERCISES

5.1 Look at the drawings and complete the sentences with the words from the box.

| abogada | actriz | camarera | cocinero | estudiante |
| fontanero | fotógrafo | médico | profesora | secretaria |

Eva es abogada. José Luis es _____ . Carla es _____ . Félix es _____ . Mar es _____ .

Mario es _____ . Adrián es _____ . Eloísa es _____ . Leonor es _____ . Roberto es _____ .

SCORE ..../10

5.2 Circle the correct answer for each one.

1. –¿Quién es Luis Miguel? –Es (*cantante* / *un cantante*); es (*mexicano* / *un mexicano*).
2. La doctora Ramírez es (*médica* / *una médica*) buenísima; es (*argentina* / *una argentina*).
3. El marido de Luisa es (*abogado* / *un abogado*). Es (*abogado* / *un abogado*) muy caro.
4. Mohamed es (*musulmán* / *un musulmán*).
5. Los tíos de Andrea son (*protestantes* / *unos protestantes*).
6. El hermano de Patricio es (*actor* / *un actor*) famoso.
7. –¿Quién es Vargas Llosa? –Es (*escritor* / *un escritor*); es (*peruano* / *un peruano*).
8. Alberto y Lola son (*estudiantes* / *unos estudiantes*). Son (*socialistas* / *unos socialistas*).
9. Sarita quiere ser (*bailarina* / *una bailarina*).
10. García Márquez es (*escritor* / *un escritor*) de éxito.
11. Kristina y Lotta son (*suecas* / *unas suecas*). Son (*suecas* / *unas suecas*) muy simpáticas.
12. –¿Qué es (*flauta* / *una flauta*)? –Es (*instrumento* / *un instrumento*) musical.

SCORE ..../19

5.3 Complete with *un, una, unos, unas* when necessary.

1. –¿Comes __∅__ carne? –No, soy __∅__ vegetariano.
2. Colecciono _____ monedas. Ayer me compré _____ monedas chinas.
3. Alberto tiene _____ piso en Benidorm.
4. –¿Tomas _____ café? –Solo _____ taza al día.
5. –¿Azúcar? –Gracias, no tomo _____ azúcar.
6. ¿Tenéis _____ hijos?
7. Chelo canta _____ ópera.
8. Ernesto es _____ músico. Escribe _____ canciones.
9. ¿Necesitas _____ dinero?
10. –¿Quieres _____ queso? –No, gracias; es _____ queso muy fuerte.
11. Carolina es _____ vendedora. Vende _____ enciclopedias.
12. ¿Tienes _____ hermanos?
13. No bebo _____ vino. No me gusta.
14. Necesito _____ diccionario de español.
15. ¿Tienen _____ plátanos?

SCORE ..../21

19

6 *el, la, los, las*
The definite article

Mira, **la madre** de Antonio.

Quiero ver **al director**.

Las rosas son mis flores preferidas.

● Forms of the definite article

	MASCULINE	FEMININE
SINGULAR	el *el padre, **el** libro*	la *la madre, **la** mesa*
PLURAL	los *los padres, **los** libros*	las *las madres, **las** mesas*

BE CAREFUL!

Use *el* (not *la*) before feminine singular nouns that begin with *a, ha*:

    el aula   ***el agua***   ***el hacha***   ***el águila***

   BUT: *la otra aula, **las** aulas, **las** hachas, **las** águilas*

a + el = al   *Juego **al** fútbol.*
de + el = del   *El hijo **del** profesor está en mi clase.*

● We use *el, la, los, las* + noun:

  – to speak about a person or something unique.
      La madre de Antonio es policía. (Antonio has one mother.)
      Buenos Aires es la capital de Argentina. (Argentina has only one capital.)
      ¿Quién es el presidente de Brasil? (Brasil has only one president.)

  – to speak about a person or something specific, when it is clear what person or thing we are talking about.
      Quiero ver al director. (the director of this bank)
      Enciende la luz, por favor. (the light in this room)
      Luis está en la cocina. (the kitchen in this house)

  – to speak about someone or something in a general manner.
      El tabaco es malo para la salud. (all types of tobacco)
      Los chilenos hablan español. (all the Chileans)

Cierra **la puerta**, por favor.

▶   UNIT 7: Contrasting the indefinite and definite article   UNIT 8: The definite article with proper nouns
     UNIT 9: The definite article with expressions of time   UNIT 10: Other uses of the definite article
     UNIT 11: Omitting the noun

6 EXERCISES

6.1. Complete with *el, la, los, las*.

1. __la__ casa
2. _____ médico
3. _____ naranjas
4. _____ coche
5. _____ habitación

6. _____ águila
7. _____ pantalones
8. _____ aula
9. _____ sillas
10. _____ lápices

11. _____ tijeras
12. _____ profesor
13. _____ perro
14. _____ hermana
15. _____ alumnos

6.2. Look at the drawing and complete the sentences with *el, la, los, las* and the words from the box.

Felipe Claudia Javier Lucía

Juan Marta Enrique Fernando Isabel

Irene Juana

abuela	abuelos	
hermana	hermanos	hijas
madre	marido	
~~padre~~	tía	tío

1. __El padre__ de Marta se llama Felipe.
2. _____ de Marta se llama Claudia.
3. _____ de Marta se llama Javier.
4. _____ de Marta se llama Lucía.
5. _____ de Juana se llaman Claudia y Felipe.
6. _____ de Marta se llaman Enrique y Fernando.
7. _____ de Marta se llama Isabel.
8. _____ de Marta se llama Juan.
9. _____ de Marta se llaman Irene y Juana.
10. _____ de Irene se llama Claudia.

6.3. Complete the sentences with the words from the box and *el, la, los, las*.

agua   diccionario   ~~jardín~~   luz   tijeras   ventana

① (Susana está en) __el jardín__

② Cierra _____

③ Pásame _____ por favor.

④ Déjame _____

⑤ Enciende _____

⑥ Pásame _____

6.4. Complete the following sentences with *el, la, los, las* (use *al* and *del* when necessary).

1. __Las__ águilas son aves.
2. Montevideo es ___ capital de Uruguay.
3. Queremos ver a ___ jefe de estudios.
4. ___ coche de Julio es blanco.
5. Cierra ___ puerta de ___ jardín, por favor.
6. ___ clase de español es en ___ aula 12.
7. ___ agua es mi bebida preferida.
8. ___ padres de Sofía viven en Lima.
9. ___ norteamericanos hablan inglés.
10. Me gustan ___ naranjas.
11. Escribe en ___ pizarra, por favor.
12. Ese coche es de ___ padre de Mónica.
13. ___ fresas son mi fruta preferida.
14. ___ novio de Julia es colombiano.
15. Vivimos cerca de ___ centro.

7 un perro / el perro
Contrasting the indefinite and definite article

Compare:

INDEFINITE ARTICLE	DEFINITE ARTICLE

INDEFINITE ARTICLE

- We use *un, una, unos, unas* when we speak for the first time about something new (new information).

DEFINITE ARTICLE

- We use *el, la, los, las* when we speak about something already mentioned (known information).

- We use *un, una, unos, unas* when we speak about a person, animal, or object that forms part of a group.

- We use *el, la, los, las* when we speak about a unique or specific person, animal, or object (unique in that situation).

Un hijo de Andrés es médico.
(Andrés has three children.)

Tucumán es una ciudad de Argentina.
(There are many cities in Argentina.)

Necesito alquilar un coche.
(any car)

La hija de Rosa es escritora.
(Rosa has only one daughter.)

Buenos Aires es la capital de Argentina.
(Argentina has only one capital.)

Necesito arreglar el coche.
(It's my car.)

- We use *un, una, unos, unas* to indicate quantity.

- We use *el, la, los, las* to speak about something in general.

He cortado unas rosas.
(3, 4,...)

Las rosas son mis flores preferidas.
(all roses)

▶ UNIT 4: The indefinite article   UNIT 6: The definite article

7 EXERCISES

7.1. Complete with *un, una, unos, unas* or *el, la, los, las*.

1. Mis hijos tienen <u>un</u> perro y ___ gato. ___ perro duerme en ___ jardín y ___ gato dentro de ___ casa.
2. –Natalia tiene ___ hijo y ___ hija. ___ hijo es ingeniero, y ___ hija es azafata.
   –¿Como se llama ___ hija?
3. –Clara tiene ___ tortuga y ___ peces de colores. ___ peces están en ___ pecera azul y ___ tortuga en ___ "piscina" de plástico.
4. Conozco ___ hotel muy bueno en Salamanca, pero ahora no recuerdo ___ nombre de ___ hotel.
5. –Ayer vimos ___ película china. Era sobre ___ chica que quería ser cantante.
   –¿Cómo se titula ___ película?
   –No recuerdo ___ título.
   –Y ¿qué le pasa a ___ chica?
   –Se enamora de ___ italiano y se casan.
6. –He comprado ___ naranjas y ___ fresas.
   –Y ¿dónde están ___ fresas?
7. –Me han regalado ___ pendientes y ___ pluma.
   –¿Quién te ha regalado ___ pendientes?

SCORE ..../32

7.2. Circle the correct answer in each case.

1. Chihuahua es (*la*/*una*) ciudad de México.
2. He visto (*la*/*una*) película muy buena. (*El*/*Un*) personaje principal era (*el*/*un*) asesino.
3. (*La*/*Una*) nueva película de Spielberg es muy buena.
4. Soy enfermero y trabajo en (*el*/*un*) hospital.
5. Estoy leyendo (*el*/*un*) libro sobre (*el*/*un*) rey Juan Carlos.
6. ¿Qué es eso? ¿Es (*la*/*una*) televisión portátil?
7. ¿Quién es (*el*/*un*) primer ministro?
8. Carmen trabaja en (*el*/*un*) hotel. Es recepcionista.
9. (*La*/*Una*) novia de Arturo es brasileña.
10. (*El*/*Un*) Sol es (*la*/*una*) estrella.
11. Paco es (*el*/*un*) nombre español.
12. –¿Dónde está Carlos? –En (*la*/*una*) cocina.
13. Vivo en (*el*/*un*) centro de Lima.
14. (*La*/*Una*) moto de Pedro es italiana.
15. (*La*/*Una*) Luna gira alrededor de (*la*/*una*) Tierra.

SCORE ..../20

7.3. Complete with *un, una, unos, unas* or *el, la, los, las*.

1. Me han regalado <u>unos</u> bombones.
2. No me gusta ___ chocolate.
3. ___ piña, por favor.
4. ___ piña es mi fruta preferida.
5. Me encantan ___ cuadros de Dalí.
6. ¿Te gustan ___ peras?
7. Me he comprado ___ vaqueros.
8. Te he comprado ___ margaritas.
9. Quiero ___ pantalones cortos.
10. Me encanta ___ agua.
11. ___ café, por favor.
12. No me gusta ___ café.

SCORE ..../12

8 *el señor Alonso, la calle Mayor*
The definite article with proper nouns

● *el*, *la*, *los*, *las* with proper nouns:
We use *el*, *la*, *los*, *las* + *señor, señora, señorita, doctor, doctora, presidente, presidenta...* + (noun) + last name.

> ***El señor Alonso*** *es mi jefe.*
> ***La señora Gómez*** *es muy amable.*
> ***La doctora Blanco*** *trabaja en este hospital.*

El señor Alonso es mi jefe.

BUT: – We don't use *el*, *la*, *los*, *las* when we speak directly to a person.

> *Buenos días,* ***señor Alonso.***
> *Una llamada para usted,* ***doctora Blanco.***

– We don't use *el*, *la*, *los*, *las* with last names or (*don/doña*) + first name.

> ***López*** *fue un buen director.*
> ***Julián*** *es mi primo.*
> ***Doña Rosa*** *es maestra.*

Buenos días, señor Alonso.

● *el*, *la*, *los*, *las* with names of places:
– We use *el*, *la* + names of streets, squares, avenues, boulevards...

> *Marga vive en* ***la avenida de América.***
> *Hay un cine nuevo en* ***el Paseo de Rosales.***

– We use *el*, *la*, *los*, *las* + names of movie theaters, theaters, hotels, museums...

el (hotel) **Ritz**	*el* (Museo del) **Prado**
el (cine) **Gran Vía**	*la* (Universidad) **Autónoma**
el (teatro) **Buenos Aires**	*el* (hospital) **Gregorio Marañon**

Y tú, ¿dónde estudias?

En la Autónoma.

– We use *el*, *la*, *los*, *las* + names of rivers, lakes, seas, oceans, groups of islands, mountains, deserts...

el (río) **Tajo,** *el* **Amazonas**	*las* (islas) **Canarias,** *las* **Antillas**
el (lago) **Titicaca**	*los* (montes) **Pirineos,** *los* **Andes**
el (mar) **Mediterráneo,** *el* **Caribe**	*el* (desierto del) **Sahara**
el (océano) **Pacífico,** *el* **Atlántico**	

BUT: We don't use *el*, *la*, *los*, *las* with names of only one island.

> **Mallorca**   **Sicilia**   **Santo Domingo**

BE CAREFUL!

We don't use *el*, *la*, *los*, *las* with names of most cities, regions, provinces, autonomous communities, countries, continents...

– Cities: *Valencia, París, Santiago de Chile, Buenos Aires.*
– Countries, regiones...: *España, Alemania, Bolivia, Francia; Galicia, Andalucía; California.*
– Continents: *África, América del Sur.*

BUT:

– Cities: *La Coruña, La Habana, El Escorial, La Paz, Las Palmas, Los Ángeles, El Cairo.*
– Countries and regions: *El Salvador, (la) India, (los) Estados Unidos, La Mancha, La Rioja, La Pampa.*

---

8 EXERCISES

8.1. Complete with *el*, *la*, *los*, *las* when necessary.

1. ¿Dónde vive _Ø_ don José?
2. _____ Rodríguez es muy simpático.
3. –Buenas tardes, _____ señor Alfonsín. –Buenas tardes, _____ Elena.
4. _____ doctora Castro está en la sexta planta.
5. –Esta es _____ Márquez, una compañera. –Encantada.
6. ¿Quién es _____ señora Jiménez?
7. _____ Presidente López es muy joven.
8. ¿En qué trabaja _____ doña Josefa?
9. _____ señorita Echevarría es secretaria.
10. –Buenos días, _____ doctor Rojo. –Buenos días, _____ María.

SCORE ...... /12

8.2. Look at the map and complete the sentences.

1. (*Hotel Central*) El Hotel Central está en la plaza de España.
2. (*Museo Botero*) _____ está en _____.
3. (*Banco Nacional*) _____ está en _____.
4. (*Teatro Lorca*) _____ está en _____.
5. (*Cine América*) _____ está en _____.
6. (*Hospital*) _____ está en _____.

SCORE ...... /12

8.3. Complete the sentences with the nouns and *el*, *la*, *los*, *las* when necessary.

1. (*Habana, Cuba*) La Habana es la capital de Cuba.
2. (*India, Asia*) _____ está en _____.
3. (*río Misisipi, Estados Unidos*) _____ está en _____.
4. (*Islas Galápagos, Ecuador*) _____ están en _____.
5. (*Salvador, Guatemala, Honduras*) _____ tiene frontera con _____ y _____.
6. (*Ángeles, California*) _____ está en _____.
7. (*Lago Titicaca, Perú, Bolivia*) _____ está entre _____ y _____.
8. (*Amazonas, América del Sur*) _____ es el río más largo de _____.
9. (*Jamaica, mar Caribe*) _____ está en _____.
10. (*Puerto Rico, islas Antillas*) _____ es una de _____.
11. (*Pampa, Argentina*) _____ es una región de _____.
12. (*Pirineos, España, Francia*) _____ separan _____ de _____.
13. (*Alemania, Europa*) _____ es un país de _____.
14. (*Cairo, Egipto*) _____ es la capital de _____.
15. (*Nilo*) _____ es el río más largo del mundo.

SCORE ...... /32

8.4. Circle the correct option in each case.

1. ¿Has estado en (el/Ø) Museo del Prado?
2. (El/Ø) Felipe estudia en (la/Ø) Universidad de Alcalá.
3. (La/Ø) doctora Soria trabaja en (el/Ø) Hospital Doce de Octubre.
4. El hermano de Ana vive en (La/Ø) Paz.
5. Veraneo en (La/Ø) Italia.
6. (El/Ø) Pancho vive en (El/Ø) Monterrey.
7. Este queso es de (La/Ø) Mancha.
8. (El/Ø) cine Cartago está en (la/Ø) calle Buenos Aires.
9. (El/Ø) Museo Picasso está en (la/Ø) Barcelona.
10. (El/Ø) Escorial está cerca de (El/Ø) Madrid.

SCORE ...... /16

9 *el seis de enero*
The definite article with expressions of time

● We use *la*, *las* + time.

la una y diez

las dos

las cuatro y cuarto

las cinco y media

las seis menos cuarto

*El partido es a **las nueve**.*

● We use *el* + days of the week when we talk about a specific day.
> *El domingo voy a una fiesta.* (this Sunday)
> *El sabado estuve con Luisa.* (last Saturday)

| BUT: | *–¿Qué día es hoy?* |
| | *–Lunes. Ayer fue **domingo**.* |

● We use *los* + days of the week when we talk about a habitual action.
> *Los miércoles tengo clases de español.* (every Wednesday)
> *Mariano trabaja **los domingos**.* (every Sunday)

● We use *el* + dates.
> *Me examino **el doce** de junio.*

| BUT: | *–¿Qué día es hoy?* |
| | *–**Cinco** de marzo. Ayer fue **cuatro** de marzo.* |

BE CAREFUL!

day of the week + date → only one article
> *El examen es **el jueves**. + El examen es **el veinte de junio**. = El examen es **el jueves, veinte de junio**.*

We don't use the article with months.
> *Rosa nació en **febrero**.*
> *Mi cumpleaños es el treinta y uno de **octubre**.*

● We use *por la* + parts of the day (*mañana, tarde, noche*).
> *Trabajo **por la mañana** y estudio **por la tarde**.*

BUT:	*A mediodía, a medianoche*
	*Voy a casa **a mediodía**.*
	*El camión de la basura pasa **a medianoche**.*

9 EXERCISES

9.1. **Write the time using the words from the box and *la* or *las*.**

cuatro menos diez	doce y cinco	dos	ocho y media	diez y cuarto
~~tres y veinte~~		una menos cuarto		una y veinticinco

① las tres y veinte

② _____

③ _____

④ _____

⑤ _____

⑥ _____

⑦ _____

⑧ _____

SCORE ....../8

9.2. **Complete with *el, la, los,* or *las* if necessary.**

1. __El__ miércoles es el cumpleaños de Antonio.
2. Nunca trabajo _____ domingos.
3. _____ jueves es fiesta.
4. Hoy es _____ jueves.
5. –¿Qué día fue ayer? –_____ martes.
6. _____ sábados voy a un gimnasio.
7. –_____ lunes no trabajo nunca. ¿Vamos al cine? –Bueno.
8. –¿Cuándo es el concierto, _____ sábado o _____ domingo? – _____ sábado.

SCORE ....../10

9.3. **Complete with *el, la, los,* or *las* if necessary.**

1. Hoy es _Ø_ siete de __ marzo.
2. El examen es __ quince de __ junio.
3. –¿Cuándo es tu cumpleaños? –__ doce de __ agosto.
4. Me caso __ sábado, __ diez de __ julio.
5. El concierto es __ día veinte.
6. Hoy es __ martes, __ dos de __ diciembre.
7. Me voy __ domingo, __ treinta de __ enero.
8. Ayer fue __ día nueve.

SCORE ....../17

9.4. **Complete with *el, la, los,* or *las* if necessary.**

1. Mi cumpleaños es _el_ doce de __ febrero.
2. __ martes tenemos clase de español.
3. Normalmente estudiamos por __ noche.
4. Me caso __ sábado, __ diez de __ julio.
5. La fiesta es __ domingo a __ siete.
6. Hoy es __ jueves, __ cuatro de__ octubre.
7. El partido es a __ diez.
8. Trabajo por __ tarde y estudio por __ mañana.
9. Nací __ dos de __ diciembre.
10. Diana sale siempre __ sábados.
11. Tengo vacaciones en __ agosto.
12. Tenemos un examen __ lunes.

SCORE ....../20

10 *tocar la guitarra*
Other uses of the definite article

- We use *el, la, los, las* in the following cases:

    – *tocar el piano, la guitarra...*
    *Ana está aprendiendo a **tocar el piano**.*

Juan **toca el piano** muy bien..., pero **necesita un piano** nuevo.

> **BUT:** *Tengo **una guitarra** española.*

    – *jugar al fútbol, al tenis, al ajedrez, al parchís, a las cartas...*
    *¿Sabes jugar **al ajedrez**?*
    ***Jugamos al fútbol** todos los domingos.*

> **BUT:** *hacer ejercicio, gimnasia, natación, alpinismo.*
> ***Hago gimnasia** todas las mañanas.*

*El **chino** es muy difícil.*

    – *las matemáticas, la lengua, el griego, el español...*
    *Mi asignatura preferida son **las matemáticas**.*
    ***El griego** es una lengua muy sonora.*

> **BUT:** Not with *hablar, saber, enseñar, estudiar...*
> *Claudia **estudia filosofía**.*
> *¿Andrés sabe **ruso**?*

    – *el cine, el teatro, la radio, la televisión, el periódico, las noticias...*
    *Juana es muy aficionada **al cine**.*
    *Me gusta escuchar música en **la radio**.*
    *¿Ves mucho **la televisión**?*
    *Siempre escuhamos **las noticias** de las nueve.*
    *¿Has leído **el periódico** hoy?*

*¿**Habla** usted **chino**?*

> **BUT:** *Me he comprado **una televisión**.* (un aparato de televisión)
> *Tengo **una buena noticia**.*

    – with expressions of place such as *ir, venir* or *estar*.

ir **al:** hospital, banco	ir a **la:** iglesia
venir **al/del:** cine, aeropuerto	venir de **la:** universidad
estar en **el:** teatro, lavabo, dentista, trabajo	estar en **la:** cárcel, oficina

    *¿Puedo **ir al lavabo**, por favor?*
    *La madre de Rosa **está en el hospital**.*
    *Mis padres **van** hoy **al teatro**.*

*Vengo **del dentista**.*

> **BUT:** ir a... casa
> venir a / de... correos
> estar en... clase
>
> ***Voy a correos** a enviar un paquete.*
> *Edgar **está en casa** desde las doce.*
> *Hoy han venido **a clase** pocos alumnos.*

10 EXERCISES

10.1. Look at the drawings and complete the sentences with the words from the box.

| ajedrez | cartas | fútbol | ~~guitarra~~ | piano | tenis | trompeta | violín |

① Santi toca __la guitarra__ .

② Elsa toca _____.

③ Rosa juega a _____.

④ Elena toca _____.

⑤ Inés juega a _____.

⑥ Pepe juega a _____.

⑦ Juan toca _____.

⑧ Miguel juega a _____.

SCORE /8

10.2. Complete with *el, la, los, las* or *un, una, unos, unas* if necessary.

1. __Las__ matemáticas son difíciles.
2. ¿Hablas __ø__ español?
3. ____ griego no es difícil.
4. Paco juega muy bien a ____ ajedrez.
5. ¿Has escuchado ____ noticias?
6. Susana estudia ____ Arquitectura.
7. Merche hace ____ gimnasia en el colegio.
8. Liebe enseña ____ español en una academia.
9. ____ Historia es una asignatura apasionante.
10. Nadim tiene ____ piano muy bonito.
11. Antonio tiene ____ guitarra eléctrica.
12. He comprado ____ televisión digital.
13. Escucho ____ radio por las mañanas.
14. Mi vecina habla ____ ruso.
15. Siempre leo ____ periódico después de desayunar.
16. Rodrigo está en ____ casa ahora.
17. Mis hijos ven mucho ____ televisión.
18. No vamos nunca a ____ clase por la tarde.
19. Me gusta mucho ____ teatro.
20. Tienes que hacer ____ ejercicio más a menudo.

SCORE /20

10.3. Look at the drawings and complete the sentences with the words from the box and *el, la* if necessary.

| cárcel | casa | cine | colegio | correos | hospital | iglesia | lavabo | médico | ~~universidad~~ |

① Va a __la universidad__ .

② Va a _____.

③ Lo llevan a _____.

④ Está en _____.

⑤ Viene de _____.

⑥ Está en _____.

⑦ Viene de _____.

⑧ Van a _____.

⑨ Están en _____.

⑩ Va a _____.

SCORE /10

29

el rojo, uno rojo
Omitting the noun

We can use *el, la, los, las* or *uno, una, unos, unas* rather than a previously mentioned noun when everyone knows what we are speaking about.

● *el, la, los, las* or *uno, una, unos, unas* + adjective

–*¿Qué camisa te gusta más?* –*La verde.* (the green shirt)
–*¿Qué tipo de zapatos quiere?* –*Quiero **unos cómodos**.* (some comfortable shoes)
–*¿Quién es don Tomás?* –*El delgado.* (the thin man)

Compare:

We use *el, la, los, las* when we speak about a specific person or object:	We use *uno, una, unos, unas* when we speak about a group of objects:
–*¿Quién es Susi?* –*La alta.* (the tall girl)	–*¿Qué tipo de coche busca?* –*Uno pequeño.* (a small car)

BE CAREFUL!

The form of the article and adjective (masculine, feminine, singular, or plural) is the same as the noun we are referring to.
–*¿Qué **zapatillas** te gustan más?* –*Las rojas.*

● *el, la, los, las* + *de* + noun = origin, possession, situation, material...

–*El de Valencia es muy trabajador.*
   (the man from Valencia)
*Mi coche es peor que **el de mi hermano**.*
   (my brother's car)
–*¿Quién es Alicia?* –*La del vestido blanco.*
   (the girl dressed in white)
*Esas gafas no me gustan. Prefiero **las de la derecha**.*
   (the glasses on the right)
–*¿Qué pendientes te vas a poner?* –*Los de oro.*
   (the gold earrings)

BE CAREFUL!

The form of the article (masculine, feminine, singular, or plural) is the same as the noun we are referring to.
–*No me gusta **la blusa** de lino. Prefiero **la de seda**.*

11.1. Complete the sentences with *el, la, los, las* or *uno, una, unos, unas* and the adjective in parentheses.

1. ¿Qué zapatos prefieres, (*negro, blanco*) <u>los negros</u> o <u>los blancos</u> ?
2. –¿Qué tipo de cuaderno quiere? – (*pequeño*) <u>Uno pequeño</u> .
3. –¿Te gustan estos sombreros? – Me gusta (*negro*) _____, pero no (*marrón*)_____.
4. –¿Qué pantalones prefieres? – (*rojo*) _____. (*blanco*) _____ son muy caros.
5. ¿Ves a esas dos chicas? (*alto*) _____ es Marta.
6. –¿Qué tipo de libro quieres leer? (*entretenido*) –_____.
7. ¿Qué manzanas prefiere, (*verde*) _____ o (*rojo*) _____?
8. Esta taza está sucia. Dame (*limpio*) _____, por favor.
9. –¿Qué clase de cámara quiere? –Quiero (*bueno*) _____, aunque sea cara.
10. –¿Tienes ordenador? –Sí, tengo (*portátil*) _____.

SCORE ..../14

11.2. Look at the drawings and complete the sentences with *el, la, los,* or *las;* with *de;* and with the given words.

① ¿Qué gafas le gustan?
<u>Las de la derecha.</u>
derecha

② ¿Quién es Alberto?
pelo corto

③ Me gusta más
izquierda

④ ¿Qué galletas te gustan más?
chocolate

⑤ ¿Cuál es tu padre?
bigote

⑥ ¿Qué zapatos le gustan más?
arriba

⑦ Quiero
Sandra Arenas

⑧ Me gusta más
Sevilla

⑨ ¿Quién es Rosi?
falda larga

⑩ ¿Cuál es tu hermano?
pantalones cortos

SCORE ..../10

11.3. Complete the sentences with *el, la, los, las, un, una, unos,* or *unas* and *de* if necessary.

1. Te gustan las camisas de pana? –Prefiero <u>las de</u> algodón.
2. No me gusta la sopa de pescado. Prefiero _____ verduras.
3. El coche es viejo. Yo quiero _____ nuevo.
4. Esas tijeras son pequeñas. Necesito _____ más grandes.
5. ¿Prefieres los guantes de lana o _____ cuero?
6. Prefiero el vino de Valdepeñas a _____ Rioja.
7. –¿Qué tipo de pendientes quieres? –_____ plata.
8. Estos vasos están sucios. Trae _____ limpios.
9. Mi coche no es muy bueno. Es mejor _____ mi padre.
10. No me gusta esta tarta. Prefiero _____ chocolate.

SCORE ..../10

12 *este, ese, aquel...*
Demonstrative adjectives

Este, ese, and *aquel* are demonstrative adjectives. They are used to point out or identify something or someone.

close to me	SINGULAR	PLURAL
MASCULINE	este	estos
FEMININE	esta	estas

¿Cuánto cuesta **esta** revista?

close to you	SINGULAR	PLURAL
MASCULINE	ese	esos
FEMININE	esa	esas

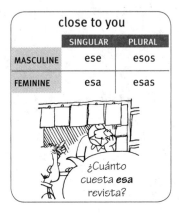

¿Cuánto cuesta **esa** revista?

far from you and me	SINGULAR	PLURAL
MASCULINE	aquel	aquellos
FEMININE	aquella	aquellas

¿Quiénes son **aquellas** chicas?

BUT: At times we use *ese, esa, esos, esas* to point out something that is far away from you and me.

Me gusta **esa** casa.

- *Este, esta, ese, esa, aquel, aquella...* can be used with nouns or on their own. They take the same form (masculine or feminine, singular or plural) as the noun that accompanies them or the noun that they refer to.

Esa chica es amiga de Ana.	*Estos zapatos son muy caros.*
Me gusta mucho este restaurante.	*Luis vive en aquella casa.*
¿Cuánto cuestan esas gafas?	*Este es Pedro, un amigo mío.*
–¿Es este tu abrigo? –No, ese no es.	*Aquel es Andrés, el profesor de Historia.*
–¿Cuál es tu maleta? –Aquella.	

- We also use *este, esta...* to refer to the present, the past, or the near future.

Esta semana tengo vacaciones.	*Este invierno ha llovido poco.*
Este verano vamos a ir a Chile.	

- *Esto, eso,* and *aquello* aren't used with nouns. We use them to point out something without mentioning it.

  – Because we don't know what it is.   – Because it isn't necessary to say it.

¿Qué es **esto**? No sé. Parece una lámpara.

¿De quién es **eso**?

12.1. Complete with *este, esta...*, *ese, esa...*, *aquel, aquella...* and the words from the box.

| árboles | bolso | cartera | gafas | llaves (2) | maleta | paraguas | pisos | revista |

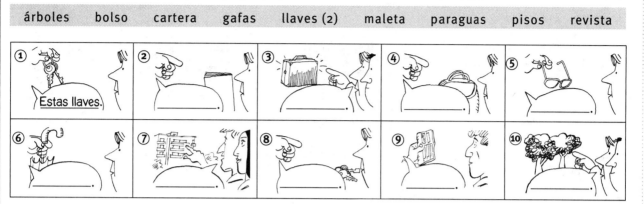

SCORE ....../10

12.2. Complete with *este, esta, ese, esa, aquel, aquella...*

SCORE ....../8

12.3. Complete with *este, ese, aquel...*

1. __Este__ verano vamos a ir a Ibiza.
2. _____ mes ha llovido mucho.
3. –¿Qué haces _____ noche? –Me quedo en casa. _____ semana tengo mucho trabajo.
4. _____ tarde tengo un examen.
5. ¿Qué haces _____ Navidades?
6. _____ meses son muy fríos.
7. Julián y Lola se casan _____ año.

SCORE ....../8

12.4. Complete with *esto, eso,* or *aquello.*

SCORE ....../5

13 un coche pequeño
Descriptive adjectives

un coche **pequeño**

una casa **pequeña**

Rosi es **alta**. 1'82m

Estamos **cansados**.

Pequeño, pequeña, alta, and *cansados* are descriptive adjectives: they express a trait or the state of a person, animal, or object.

● Adjectives: making the feminine and the plural

SINGULAR		PLURAL	
MASCULINE	FEMININE	MASCULINE	FEMININE
–o	**–a**	**–os**	**–as**
un coche pequeñ**o**	una casa pequeñ**a**	unos chicos alt**os**	unas chicas alt**as**
–e	**–e**	**–es**	**–es**
un chico inteligent**e**	una chica inteligent**e**	unos pantalones verd**es**	unas flores verd**es**
–consonant	**–consonant**	**+es**	**+es**
un chico jove**n**	una chica jove**n**	unos calcetines azul**es**	unas camisas azul**es**
–or	**+a**	**+es**	**+as**
un chico encantad**or**	una chica encantad**ora**	unos chicos encantad**ores**	unas chicas encantad**oras**

BE CAREFUL!

feli**z** ► feli**ces**	joven ► j**ó**venes	marr**ón** ► marr**ones**

● Adjectives take the same form (masculine or feminine, singular or plural) as the person, animal, or object that they refer to.

Yo soy **moreno**.

Yo soy **morena**.

*Me he comprado unos **zapatos negros**.*
*En Guatemala hay **ruinas** muy **antiguas**.*

***Susana y Elena** son muy **trabajadoras**.*

● Masculine noun + feminine noun = plural masculine adjective
> ***Antonio y Marta** son **altos** y **morenos**.*
> *Gabi lleva una **camisa** y un **pantalón negros**.*

● Placement of the adjective
> – *ser/estar* + adjective: *Roberto **es simpático**. **Está** muy **delgado**.*
> – noun + adjective: *María tiene los **ojos azules** y el **pelo largo**.*

BUT: *buen/buena* + noun: *Julio es un **buen escritor**.*
> *Luisa es una **buena profesora**.*
mal/mala + noun: *Felipe es un **mal ejemplo** para sus hijos.*
> *Tengo una **mala noticia**.*

13 EXERCISES

13.1. **Complete the sentences with the correct form of the adjective in parentheses.**

1. Vivo en un piso (*pequeño*) pequeño .
2. Rosa tiene los ojos (*verde*) _____. Es (*rubio*) _____ y tiene el pelo (*corto*) _____ y (*rizado*) _____. Es muy (*simpático*) _____ y (*alegre*) _____.
3. Gerardo y Ana son muy (*inteligente*) _____.
4. Me gustan las rosas (*blanco*) _____.
5. Don Santiago es una persona (*encantador*) _____.
6. Chus y Lolo no son (*feliz*) _____. Están siempre (*enfadado*) _____.
7. Me he comprado una camisa (*rojo*) _____ , unos pantalones (*gris*) _____ y unos zapatos (*blanco*) _____.
8. Eduardo es (*alto*) _____ y (*fuerte*) _____. Es (*moreno*) _____ y tiene los ojos (*negro*) _____. Es muy (*guapo*) _____, pero es un poco (*antipático*) _____.
9. Begoña lleva una falda (*verde*) _____ y una blusa (*amarillo*) _____.
10. Concha y Rodrigo son muy (*simpático*) _____ y muy (*trabajador*) _____. Además son muy (*amable*) _____.
11. Las hijas de Andrés son muy (*joven*) _____.
12. El metro es un transporte (*rápido*)_____ y (*barato*) _____ .

SCORE ...... /29

13.2. **Complete the sentences with the adjectives from the box in the correct form.**

| alegre | alto | cansado | contento | enfermo | feo | fuerte | gordo | ~~rubio~~ | triste |

① Somos rubias.
② Estoy muy _____
③ Elena es muy _____
④ Estamos _____
⑤ Esta gata está _____
⑥ Marga es muy _____
⑦ Estamos muy _____
⑧ Julia es muy _____
⑨ ¡Estamos _____!
⑩ Ese cuadro es muy _____

SCORE ...... /10

13.3. **Complete the sentences with a noun and an adjective from the box.**

1. Susana tiene los ojos azules .
2. La amapola es una _____.
3. El español es un _____.
4. Don Tomás es un _____.
5. La _____ de Peter es la tortilla de patatas.
6. Hoy tengo un _____. No me sale nada bien.
7. En Toledo hay muchos _____.
8. Esta camisa y estos pantalones están muy viejos. Necesito _____.
9. Mi _____ es el rojo.
10. Tengo una _____ para ti. Has suspendido.
11. Julia es una _____. Sus hijos la quieren mucho.
12. Me gustan las _____.

color	madre
comida	noticia
día	~~ojo~~
edificio	profesor
flor (2)	ropa
idioma	

antiguo	malo (2)
~~azul~~	nuevo
blanco	preferido (2)
bueno (2)	rojo
fácil	

SCORE ...... /12

35

14 *una amiga chilena*
Adjectives of nationality

Esta es Elsa, una **amiga chilena**.

¿De dónde sois?

Somos **cubanos**. ¿Y tú?

Yo soy **español**.

● Adjectives of nationality: making the feminine and the plural

SINGULAR		PLURAL	
MASCULINE	FEMININE	MASCULINE	FEMININE
–o	**–a**	**–os**	**–as**
chilen**o**, cuban**o**	chilen**a**, cuban**a**	chilen**os**, cuban**os**	chilen**as**, cuban**as**
Donoso es **un escritor chileno**. Isabel Allende es **una escritora chilena**.		Los puros **cubanos** son de gran calidad. Compré **unas empanadas chilenas** para cenar.	
–a, –e, –í, –ú	**–a, –e, –í, –ú**	**–as, –es, –ís (o –íes), ús (o –úes)**	**–as, –es, ís (o –íes), ús (o –úes)**
belg**a** canadiens**e** marroqu**í**	belg**a** canadiens**e** marroqu**í**	belg**as** canadiens**es** marroqu**ís**/marroqu**íes**	belg**as** canadiens**es** marroqu**ís**/marroqu**íes**
La capital **belga** es Bruselas. La bandera **canadiense** es roja y blanca. La capital **marroquí** es Rabat.		Me encantan **los bombones belgas**. Tengo dos **amigas canadienses**. Fez y Tetuán son **ciudades marroquíes**.	
–consonant	**+a**	**+es**	**+as**
portugu**és** alem**án** español	portugu**esa** alem**ana** español**a**	portugu**eses** alem**anes** español**es**	portugu**esas** alem**anas** español**as**
Bild es **una revista alemana**. A Carla le gusta mucho **la comida española**.		Faro y Oporto son **ciudades portuguesas**. Los **jugadores alemanes** son altos y rápidos.	

BE CAREFUL!

portugu**é**s ► portugu**e**sa, portugu**e**ses, portugu**e**sas   alem**á**n ► alem**a**na, alem**a**nes, alem**a**nas

● Adjectives take the same form (masculine or feminine, singular or plural) as the person, animal, or objects that they refer to.

> **Gabriela** es **mexicana**.
> Me encanta **el cine francés**.

● Masculine + feminine = plural masculine adjective

> Iván es **cubano**. Haydée es **cubana**. → Iván y Haydée son **cubanos**.
> Tengo **unos sellos** y **unas monedas rusos**.

● Placement of the adjective

> – *ser* + adjective: Gabriel García Márquez **es colombiano**.
> – noun + adjective: La **bandera argentina** es azul y blanca.

36

14.1 Complete the list.

SINGULAR		PLURAL	
MASCULINE	FEMININE	MASCULINE	FEMININE
1. brasileño	brasileña	_____	_____
2. costarricense	_____	_____	_____
3. escocés	_____	_____	_____
4. etíope	_____	_____	_____
5. francés	_____	_____	_____
6. iraní	_____	_____	_____
7. japonés	_____	_____	_____
8. mexicano	_____	_____	_____
9. nicaragüense	_____	_____	_____
10. sudanés	_____	_____	_____
11. venezolano	_____	_____	_____
12. vietnamita	_____	_____	_____

SCORE /36

14.2 Complete the sentences with the adjectives from the box.

belga   chino   egipcio   estadounidense   francés   indio   italiano   mexicano   ~~peruano~~   ruso

① Soy peruana.
② Somos _____
③ Somos _____
④ Soy _____
⑤ Somos _____
⑥ Soy _____
⑦ Somos _____
⑧ Somos _____
⑨ Soy _____
⑩ Somos _____

SCORE /10

14.3 Complete with a noun and an adjective from each box.

actriz   bandera (2)   cantante   capital (2)
ciudad (3)   escritor   futbolista
moneda (2)   nombre   periódico

argentino   belga   brasileño   canadiense
colombiano   escocés   español (2)   estadounidense
francés   griego   ~~japonés~~   marroquí   portugués   vietnamita

1. El yen es la ___moneda japonesa___ .
2. El dirham es la _____ .
3. Ewan y Moira son _____ .
4. Gabriel García Márquez es un _____ .
5. Plácido Domingo y Montserrat Caballé son unos _____ .
6. Burdeos es una _____ .
7. Scarlett Johansson es una _____ .
8. Robinho y Kaká son unos _____ .
9. Brujas es una _____ .
10. *La Nación* es un _____ .
11. Hanoi es la _____ .
12. Montreal y Edmonton son unas _____ .
13. La _____ es azul y blanca.
14. Lisboa es la _____ .
15. La _____ es roja y amarilla.

SCORE /15

15 *más caro, menos trabajador*
Comparative adjectives (1)

El Regina es **más caro** que el Relomátic.

Una jirafa es **más alta** que un oso.

Marta es **menos trabajadora** que Laura.

Más caro, más alta and *menos trabajadora* are comparative forms of the adjectives. We use them to compare two people, animals, or objects.

● Forming the comparative

SUPERIORITY (+)	INFERIORITY (–)
más + adjective (+ *que*)	*menos* + adjective (+ *que*)
*Felipe es **más alto** que su hermana. Y **más fuerte**. Necesitamos un piso **más grande**.*	*Clara es **menos trabajadora** que Gilberto y **menos inteligente**.*

Irregular forms		
+ *viejo* ▸ **mayor** – *viejo* ▸ **menor** + *bueno* ▸ **mejor** + *malo* ▸ **peor**	Eva, 24 Javi, 20 *Eva es **mayor** que Javi.* *Javi es **menor** que Eva.*	*El coche de Ana es **mejor** que el de Álvaro.* *El coche de Álvaro es **peor** que el de Ana.*

● The adjective takes the same **form** (masculine, or feminine, singular or plural) as the person, animal, or object it refers to.

Mis **hermanos** son más **altos** que yo.   **Marta** es menos **trabajadora** que Raúl.   Estas **camisas** son más **caras**.

▌ **BUT:** *mayor/menor/mejor/peor* → singular (masculine and feminine)
Eva es **mayor** que Javi, pero **Javi** es **mayor** que su hermano Ernesto.

mayores/menores/mejores/peores → plural (masculine and feminine)
Eva y **Javi** son **mayores** que su hermano Ernesto.

● Masculine and feminine = masculine comparative form

*¿Quién es más **alto**, Enrique o **su hermana**?*

● *más/menos... que* + subject pronoun   ▶ UNIT 28: Personal pronouns: subject

*Eres más fuerte **que mí**.* → *Eres más fuerte **que yo**.*

● At times it isn't necessary to mention the person or object to what we are comparing.

*Este piso es pequeño. Yo quiero uno **más grande**.*

Estas sillas son **más baratas** pero **menos cómodas**.

Este piso es pequeño.
Yo quiero uno **más grande**.

15 EXERCISES

15.1 Complete the sentences with the correct form of the comparative adjective.

1. ¿Quién es <u>más guapo</u> (+ *guapo*), Juan o su hermano?
2. ¿Quién es <u>menos caprichoso</u> (– *caprichoso*), Alberto o Luisa?
3. ¿Qué es _____ (+ *caro*), un coche o una moto?
4. ¿Qué ciudad es _____ (+ *antiguo*), Lima o Santiago?
5. ¿Quién es _____ (+ *bueno*), Ronaldo o Rivaldo?
6. ¿Qué país está _____ (– *poblado*), Venezuela o Colombia?
7. ¿Qué deporte es _____ (– *peligroso*), el esquí o el alpinismo?
8. ¿Qué es _____ (+ *malo*), estar enfermo o no tener dinero?
9. ¿Quién es _____ (+ *viejo*), Sofía o su esposo?
10. ¿Qué idioma es _____ (+ *fácil*), el chino o el japonés?

15.2 Write comparisons as in the example using the words from the box.

| ~~alto~~ | caro (2) | largo | lento | pequeño | poblado | potente | viejo |

1. (Luis, 1,90 cm; su hermano, 1,82 cm) Luis es <u>más alto que su hermano</u>.
2. (Uruguay, 176 220 km²; Argentina, 2 766 890 km²) Uruguay es _____.
3. (Paraguay, 5,5 millones de habitantes; Ecuador, 13 millones) Paraguay está _____.
4. (Luisa, 19 años; Clara, 25 años) Luisa es _____.
5. (fresas, 3,50 euros/kilo; plátanos, 1,75 euros/kilo) Las fresas son _____.
6. (Amazonas, 6 788 km; Paraná, 3 780 km) El Amazonas es _____.
7. (televisión, 345 euros; radio, 60 euros) Esta televisión es _____.
8. (Suiko, disco duro 20 GB; Misima, disco duro 80 GB) Los ordenadores Suiko son _____.
9. (león, 80 km/h; canguro, 50 km/h) El canguro es _____.

SCORE ..... /9

15.3 Complete the sentences with the correct comparative form.

1. Este piso es muy antiguo. Prefiero uno <u>menos antiguo</u> (*antiguo*).
2. Esta casa es muy cara. Prefiero una <u>más barata</u> (*barato*).
3. Estos pantalones son muy grandes. Necesito unos _____ (*pequeño*).
4. Esta cama es incómoda. Prefiero una _____ (*cómodo*).
5. Mi trabajo es muy malo. Quiero uno _____ (*bueno*).
6. Este postre está muy dulce. Prefiero los postres _____ (*dulce*).
7. Este libro es un poco aburrido. Prefiero uno _____ (*entretenido*).
8. Este trabajo es muy cansado. Prefiero uno _____ (*cansado*).
9. Esta falda es muy corta. Quiero una _____ (*largo*).
10. Jorge es un poco antipático. Prefiero los chicos _____ (*simpático*).

SCORE ..... /10

15.4 Complete the sentences with the comparative form of the adjectives from the box.

| alto | ~~fuerte~~ | inteligente | rápido | viejo |

① Soy <u>más fuerte que tú</u>.
② Soy _____.
③ Sois _____.
④ Eres _____.
⑤ Soy _____.

SCORE ..... /5

39

16 *tan alto*
Comparative adjectives (2)

Martín   Carlos

*Martín es **tan alto** como Carlos.*

*Un caballo no es **tan grande** como un elefante.*

Tan alto and *tan grande* are comparative expressions. We use these expressions to indicate whether or not a certain trait—tall, big—is the same in two people, animals, or objects.

> *Sonia es **tan guapa** como su **madre**.*
> *El tren no es **tan rápido** como **el avión**.*

● Making the comparisons of equality

EQUALITY (=)	
tan + adjective + *como*	*Soy **tan alto como** tú, pero no soy **tan fuerte**.* *Un toro no es **tan rápido como** un caballo.*

● The adjective takes the same **form** (masculine or feminine, singular or plural) as the person, animal, or object it refers to.

> *El **televisor** pequeño no es tan **caro** como el grande.*
> *Mi **hermana** es tan **alta** como yo.*
> *Los **hermanos** de Sandra no son tan **simpáticos** como ella.*
> *Las **hijas** de Sofía son tan **guapas** como su madre.*

● *como* + personal pronoun

▶ **UNIT 28:** Personal pronouns: subject

> *Los hijos de Andrés no son tan guapos **como él**.*
> *Tú no eres tan guapo **como yo**.*

Compare:

–Juani es simpática. –Pues Loli es ~~tan simpática~~. Pues Loli es **tan simpática** como ella.	– Felipe es muy trabajador. – Pues sus hermanos no son **tan trabajadores**. Pues sus hermanos no son **tan trabajadores** como él.

BE CAREFUL!

At times we prefer *no tan* + positive adjective, rather than *más* + negative adjective or *menos* + positive adjective.

> *Adolfo es **más feo** que Jorge.* → *Adolfo **no es tan guapo** como Jorge.*
> *Luisa es **menos fuerte** que Ana.* → *Luisa **no** es **tan fuerte** como Ana.*

16 EXERCISES

16.1 **Complete the comparisons of equality with the adjectives from the box.**

| alto | bueno | entretenido | ~~fácil~~ | famoso (2) | fuerte | grande | malo | peligroso | rápido (2) |

1. El italiano es _tan fácil como_ _____ el español.
2. Un coche no es _tan rápido como_ _____ un avión.
3. Un gorila no es _____ una jirafa.
4. Un oso es _____ un gorila.
5. Chile no es _____ Argentina.
6. Antonio Banderas no es _____ Tom Cruise.

7. El café de Brasil es _____ el de México.
8. El teatro es _____ el cine.
9. La natación no es _____ el alpinismo.
10. El tabaco no es _____ el alcohol.
11. Una jirafa no es _____ un león.
12. Maribel Verdú no es _____ Penélope Cruz.

SCORE ...../12

16.2 **Complete the sentences with the comparison of equality and the words from the box.**

| alegre | alto (2) | barato | caro (2) | elegante | inteligente | ~~joven~~ | rápido |

1. (David, 52 años; Alonso, 40 años) David _no es tan joven como Alonso_ _____.
2. (Ana, 1,72 m; María, 1,72 m) Ana es _____.
3. (ordenador Suiko, 1200 euros; ordenador Misima, 1875 euros) El Suiko _____.
4. (reloj Relomátic, 300 euros; reloj Victorio, 300 euros) El Relomátic _____.
5. (naranjas, 2,20 euros el kilo; manzanas, 1,90 euros el kilo) Las naranjas _____.
6. (Paco, 100 m / 9,5 segundos; Antonio, 100 m / 9,5 segundos) Paco _____.
7. (Esther, alegre ++; Pilar, alegre +) Pilar _____.
8. (Darío, 90/100; Margarita, 90/100) Darío _____.
9. (Álvaro, elegante + ; Fermín, elegante, ++) Álvaro _____.
10. (Fermín, 1,75 m; Álvaro, 1,78 m) Fermín _____.

SCORE ...../10

16.3 **Complete the dialogues with the comparison of equality.**

1. –Luis es muy listo. –Pues su hermano es _tan listo como él_ _____.
2. –Rosario es muy elegante. –Pues sus hijas no son _tan elegantes como ella_ _____.
3. –Jesús es muy simpático. –Pues su hermana no es _____.
4. –Los peruanos son muy amables. –Pues los colombianos son _____.
5. –Esta cama es muy cómoda. –Pues la mía no es _____.
6. –Juan es muy amable. –Pues sus hijos son _____.
7. –Este piso es viejo. –Pues el mío no es _____.
8. –Elvira es muy guapa. –Pues sus hermanas son _____.

SCORE ...../8

16.4 **Rewrite the sentences with the comparison of equality.**

1. Jorge es más feo que yo.
2. Elio es más bajo que su padre.
3. La silla es más incómoda que el sillón.
4. Vosotras sois más simpáticas que Hugo.
5. Eres más vago que yo.

Jorge _no es tan guapo como yo_ _____.
Elio _____.
La silla _____.
Hugo _____.
(Tú) _____.

| alto |
| cómodo |
| ~~guapo~~ |
| simpático |
| trabajador |

SCORE ...../5

41

17 *mi, tu, su...*
Possessives (1)

Te presento a **mi hermana**.

¿Cuál es **tu coche**?
Ese pequeño.

Mira, ese es **nuestro profesor**.

Mi, tu, and *nuestro* are possessives. We use them to indicate possession and other types of relationships (family, origin, etc.) with people, animals, or objects.

> **Mi madre** *trabaja en un laboratorio.*
> *–¿Dónde es la fiesta? –En* **mi casa**.

> *Jimena tiene un pequeño chalé en* **su pueblo**.
> *–¿Cuál es* **tu color** *preferido? –El blanco.*

● Forms of the possessives (1)

OWNER	POSSESSIVES (1)			
	SINGULAR		PLURAL	
	MASCULINE	FEMININE	MASCULINE	FEMININE
yo	mi	mi	mis	mis
tú	tu	tu	tus	tus
usted	su	su	sus	sus
él, ella	su	su	sus	sus
nosotros, nosotras	nuestro	nuestra	nuestros	nuestras
vosotros, vosotras	vuestro	vuestra	vuestros	vuestras
ustedes	su	su	sus	sus
ellos, ellas	su	su	sus	sus

● We use *mi, tu, su...* + nouns.

> *¿Quién es* **tu profesor**?   *Ayer vi a Ignacio con* **sus primas**.   *¿Dónde están* **vuestras cosas**?

● *Mi, tu, su...* take the same form (masculine or feminine, singular or plural) as the noun that accompanies it.

> *Este es* **mi hermano** *y estas son* **mis hermanas**.
> *Ese es* **nuestro profesor** *de Matemáticas y esa es* **nuestra profesora** *de Ciencias.*

BE CAREFUL!

su, sus = de él, de ella, de usted, de ellos, de ellas, de ustedes

Jorge y **sus** *hijas.*

Alicia en **su** *coche.*

Los señores Puebla en **su** *casa.*

Abel, es **su** *mujer.*

In general, the situation indicates who *su* and *sus* refer to.

> *Mire, don Raúl. Ahí va Jorge con* **sus** *hijas.* (Raúl knows whose daughters they are, his or Jorges's.)

● We use *el, la, los, las* or *un, una, unos, unas,* not *mi, tu...* with parts of the body, clothes, and other personal objects.

> *Me duele ~~mi~~ cabeza.*   →   *Me duele la cabeza.*
> *Quítate ~~tu~~ abrigo.*   →   *Quítate el abrigo.*
> *Tengo que lavar ~~mi~~ coche.*   →   *Tengo que lavar el coche.*
> *Me he roto ~~mi~~ dedo.*   →   *Me he roto un dedo.*

17 EXERCISES

17.1. **Look at the family trees and complete the sentences with *mi, tu, su*...**

Familia Suárez

Lucas – María

Rosa   Begoña – Alfonso

Arturo   Carlota

Familia Salina

Julio – Rosario

Carmelo – Justa   Lupe

Blanca   Lucía   Emilio

1. ARTURO: –¿Cómo se llaman <u>tus</u> padres, Blanca? –Carmelo y Justa.
2. EMILIO: –_____ hermanas se llaman Blanca y Lucía.
3. –¿Cómo se llama _____ mujer, don Carmelo? –Justa.
4. BLANCA y LUCÍA: _____ abuela se llama Rosario.
5. –Arturo, Carlota, ¿cómo se llaman _____ abuelos? –Lucas y María.
6. ALFONSO: _____ madre se llama María.
7. –¿Cómo se llama _____ tía, Arturo? –Rosa.
8. –¿Cómo se llaman _____ hijos, don Julio? –Carmelo y Lupe.
9. CARMELO y LUPE: _____ padres se llaman Julio y Rosario.
10. –Blanca, Lucía, ¿cómo se llama _____ madre? –Justa.
11. –¿Cómo se llama ___ hermano, Lucía? –Emilio.

SCORE ..../11

17.2. **Complete the sentences with *mi, tu, su*...**

1. –¿Cuál es <u>tu</u> color preferido, Berta? –El azul.
2. Mi hermano y yo jugamos mucho al tenis. Es _____ deporte preferido.
3. La señora Valverde y _____ hijas son muy simpáticas.
4. –¿Dónde están Sol y Rocío? –En _____ casa, están enfermas.
5. Anoche fui al cine con _____ padre y _____ hermanos.
6. Jorge, Juan, ¿dónde están _____ trabajos?
7. –¿Cuál es _____ comida preferida, Enrique? –La paella.
8. Ayer conocí a _____ padres, Verónica. Son muy simpáticos.
9. He invitado a cenar a don Blas y a _____ señora.
10. Ayer estuve en _____ casa, estudiando con _____ hermano, pero vosotras no estabais.

SCORE ..../12

17.3. **Circle the correct answer in each case.**

1. Me estoy lavando (*mi*/*el*) pelo.
2. Átate (*tus*/*los*) zapatos.
3. Rodrigo trabaja con (*su*/*el*) padre.
4. Tenéis (*vuestros*/*los*) ojos rojos.
5. (*Mis*/*Los*) tíos viven en Puerto Rico.
6. Le di (*mi*/*la*) mano.
7. (*Su*/*La*) abuela tiene 85 años.
8. Tienes una mancha en (*tu*/*la*) nariz.
9. Quitaos (*vuestras*/*las*) chaquetas.
10. Al señor Alfonsín se le ha estropeado (*su*/*el*) coche.
11. Tengo (*mi*/*una*) mano rota.
12. Me duele (*mi*/*la*) cabeza.
13. Me limpio (*mis*/*los*) dientes todas las noches.
14. Tienes algo en (*tu*/*la*) cara.
15. (*Mi*/*La*) casa tiene cinco habitaciones.

SCORE ..../15

18 *mío, tuyo, suyo...*
Possessives (2)

Mía, mío, tuyo, and *nuestro* are possessives. We use them to indicate possession and other types of relationships (family, origin, etc.) with people or objects.

–¿De quién es este cuaderno? –Es **mío**.   –Mi pueblo es muy bonito y moderno. –Pues **el nuestro** es muy antiguo.
–Mi madre trabaja en un banco. ¿Y **la tuya**? –**La mía** trabaja en una agencia de viajes.

● *Mía, mío, tuyo...* are never used with a noun.

> UNIT 17: Possessives (1)

~~El mío coche~~ es muy viejo. → Mi coche es muy viejo.

● Forms of the possessives (2)

OWNER	POSSESSIVES (2)			
	SINGULAR		PLURAL	
	MASCULINE	FEMININE	MASCULINE	FEMININE
yo	mío	mía	míos	mías
tú	tuyo	tuya	tuyos	tuyas
usted	suyo	suya	suyos	suyas
él, ella	suyo	suya	suyos	suyas
nosotros, nosotras	nuestro	nuestra	nuestros	nuestras
vosotros, vosotras	vuestro	vuestra	vuestros	vuestras
ustedes	suyo	suya	suyos	suyas
ellos, ellas	suyo	suya	suyos	suyas

● We use *ser + mío, tuyo...* to express possession.

Esta bolsa no es **mía**. ¿Es **tuya**, Amparo?   –¿Es esto **vuestro**?

● We use *el, la, los, las + mío, tuyo...* rather than *mi, tu, su...* + noun when it isn't necessary to repeat the noun.

–Mi **padre** habla dos idiomas. –Pues **el mío** (mi padre) habla cuatro.
–¿Es tuya esa **bolsa**? –No, **la mía** (mi bolsa) es más pequeña.
–¿Vamos en el **coche** de Jaime? –No, vamos en **el nuestro** (nuestro coche).

● We also use *un, una, unos, unas, dos, tres...* + noun + *mío, tuyo...* when speaking about something or someone as part of a group.

–¿Conoces a Julián? –Sí, hombre. Es **amigo mío**. (He's one of my friends.)
Te voy a regalar **un cuadro mío**. (one of my paintings)   **Dos tías nuestras** viven en Panamá. (two of our aunts)

● *Mío, tuyo,* and *suyo...* take the same form (masculine or feminine, singular or plural) as the noun that accompanies them or they refer to.

¿Son **tuyas** estas **maletas**?   Quiero presentarte a una **hermana mía**.
Estos son nuestros **asientos**. ¿Dónde están los **vuestros**?

BE CAREFUL!

> suyo, suya, suyos, suyas = de él, de ella, de usted, de ellos, de ellas, de ustedes
>
> In general, the situation indicates who *suyo, suya, suyos,* and *suyas* refer to.
>
> –¿Son estas las maletas de Felisa? –No, **las suyas** son azules. (las de Felisa)
> –¿Son estas mis maletas? –No, **las suyas** son más pequeñas. (las de usted)

● To ask about possession we use *¿de quién?*

–¿**De quién** es esta maleta? –Es mía.   –¿**De quién** son estos libros? –Son nuestros.

44

18 EXERCISES

18.1. Complete the sentences with *mío, tuyo, suyo...* as in the example.

① ¿De quién son estas llaves?
Son _mías_.

② ¿De quién es este libro?
Es _____.

③ ¿De quién es este paraguas?
Es _____.

④ ¿De quién son estos cedés?
Son _____.

⑤ ¿Son _____ estos libros?

⑥ ¿Son _____ estas maletas?

⑦ ¿Es _____ este reloj?

⑧ ¿Es _____ esta bufanda?

SCORE ....../8

18.2. Complete the sentences with *el mío, el tuyo, el suyo...* as appropriate.

1. Estas llaves no son mías. _Las mías_ son más pequeñas.
2. –¿Es ese vuestro coche? –No, _____ es más grande.
3. Este abrigo no es de Pedro. _____ es azul.
4. –Perdona, ¿es este mi asiento? –No, _____ está más atrás.
5. –¿Es ese nuestro profesor? –No, _____ es más viejo.
6. –Mi deporte preferido es el fútbol. ¿Y _____ ? –_____ es el esquí.
7. –Mis hijos practican muchos deportes. ¿Y _____, Manuel? –_____ solo juegan al tenis.
8. –¿Son esos los padres de Arturo? –No, _____ son más jóvenes.
9. –Mi profesora es peruana. –Pues _____ es argentina.
10. –Nuestros hijos son muy trabajadores. –_____ son un poco vagos.
11. –¿Es este tu diccionario? –No, _____ es más pequeño.
12. –Mi hermana tiene 22 años. ¿Y _____? –_____ tiene 24.

SCORE ....../15

18.3. Complete with *mío, tuyo, suyo...* and *un, una, unos,* or *unas* if necessary.

1. (*amigo, yo*) _Un amigo mío_ es pintor.
2. (*amiga, yo*) _____ ha ganado un premio.
3. Ayer estuve con (*primo, vosotros*) _____.
4. El director del banco es (*amigo, ellos*) _____.
5. Raquel es (*prima, nosotros*) _____.
6. ¿Es Alicia (*tía, tú*) _____?
7. –¿Conocéis a Mariano? –Sí, es (*amigo, nosotros*) _____.
8. El domingo conocimos a (*familiares, ustedes*) _____.
9. He visto a Hans con (*dos amigas, vosotros*) _____.
10. (*dos tíos, yo*) _____ viven en Australia.
11. Han llegado (*amigos, tú*) _____.
12. He visto a Lola con (*compañero, ella*) _____.

SCORE ....../12

19 uno, dos, tres...
Cardinal numbers (1)

● Cardinal numbers 0–29

0	cero				
1	uno/un, una	11	once	21	veintiuno/veintiún, veintiuna
2	dos	12	doce	22	veintidós
3	tres	13	trece	23	veintitrés
4	cuatro	14	catorce	24	veinticuatro
5	cinco	15	quince	25	veinticinco
6	seis	16	dieciséis	26	veintiséis
7	siete	17	diecisiete	27	veintisiete
8	ocho	18	dieciocho	28	veintiocho
9	nueve	19	diecinueve	29	veintinueve
10	diez	20	veinte		

● Cardinal numbers can be used on their own or with nouns.

> –¿Cuántos años tienes? – **Veinticinco**.
>
> En mi clase hay **catorce alumnos**.

● *Uno/un*, *una* take the same form (masculine or feminine) as the noun they refer to.

  – without a noun: *uno, veintiuno* (masculine), *una, veintiuna* (feminine)

  – ¿Cuántos años tiene tu hijo? –**Uno**.

  – ¿Cuántas alumnas hay en tu clase? –**Veintiuna**.

  – *un, veintiún* + masculine noun

  Tengo **un hijo**.   En mi oficina hay **veintiún hombres**.

  – *una, veintiuna* + feminine noun

  Solo tengo **una libra**.   Necesito **veintiuna rosas**.

  – *un, veintiún* + feminine noun starting with á-, há-.

  He visto **un águila**.   Hay **veintiún aulas** en la academia.

● Cardinal numbers are used to indicate:

  – quantity. *En mi clase hay **veinte alumnos**.*

  – math calculations. ***Tres** por **nueve** son **veintisiete**.*

  – price. *–¿Cuánto cuesta esto? –**Quince pesos**.*

  – height, weight, and distance. *Mide **dos metros**.*

                    *Quiero **un kilo** de patatas.*

  – age. *Elisa tiene **veinticuatro años**.*

  – dates. *Hoy es **cuatro** de febrero. La boda es el día **trece**.*

  – time. *–¿Qué hora es? –Las **tres** y **veinte**.*

la **una** en punto   las **tres y diez**   las **cuatro** y cuarto   las **cinco** y media   las **cinco** menos cuarto

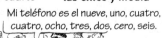

Mi teléfono es el nueve, uno, cuatro, cuatro, ocho, tres, dos, cero, seis.

  – telephone numbers.

    902 35 46 57 = nueve, cero, dos; tres, cinco; cuatro, seis; cinco, siete.

19.1. Complete with the correct form of *uno, un, una, veintiuno, veintiún, veintiuna*.

1. Las entradas cuestan (21) ___veintiún___ euros.
2. –¿Cuántos euros tienes? –(21) ___Veintiuno___.
3. –¿Qué día es hoy? –(1) _____ de mayo.
4. En esta clase hay (21) _____ alumnas.
5. Tengo (21) _____ libras.
6. –¿Cuántas hermanas tienes? –(1) _____.
7. El periódico cuesta (1) _____ euro.
8. Miguel tiene (21) _____ años.
9. –¿Cuántos kilos quiere? (1) _____.
10. Solo hay (1) _____ aula.
11. Julián mide (1) _____ metro y (21) _____ centímetros.
12. En mi clase hay (21) _____ alumnos.

SCORE ..../13

19.2. Write the following numbers in words.

1. 10 de enero. ___Diez de enero___.
2. 15 de diciembre _____.
3. 25 años _____.
4. 28 de febrero _____.
5. 5 de agosto _____.

SCORE ..../10

19.3. Complete the following calculations.

1. tres x cuatro = ___doce___.
2. cinco + ocho = _____.
3. diecinueve – quince = _____.
4. cuatro x cuatro = _____.
5. veinticinco ÷ cinco = _____.

6. doce + doce = _____.
7. dos x diez = _____.
8. trece + catorce = _____.
9. veintitrés – trece = _____.
10. siete + siete = _____.

SCORE ..../10

19.4. Write the time in words.

1. ___las tres y veinte___
2. _____
3. _____
4. _____
5. _____

6. _____
7. _____
8. _____
9. _____
10. _____

SCORE ..../10

19.5. Write the telephone numbers as in the example.

1. Jorge: 91 357 86 04
2. Andrea: 96 826 17 30
3. Nicolás: 93 327 20 14
4. Federico: 809 20 27 31
5. Dolores: 606 09 30 15

1. ___nueve uno, tres cinco siete, ocho seis, cero cuatro___
2. _____
3. _____
4. _____
5. _____

SCORE ..../5

47

20 *treinta, cuarenta...*
Cardinal numbers (2)

● Cardinal numbers 30-99

		1	uno/un, una			
30	treinta	2	dos			
40	cuarenta	3	tres			
50	cincuenta	4	cuatro			
60	sesenta + y +	5	cinco			
70	setenta	6	seis			
80	ochenta	7	siete			
90	noventa	8	ocho			
		9	nueve			
31	treinta y uno	43	cuarenta y tres	87	ochenta y siete
	treinta y un	54	cincuenta y cuatro	98	noventa y ocho
	treinta y una	65	sesenta y cinco	99	noventa y nueve
32	treinta y dos	76	setenta y seis		

● Cardinal numbers can be used on their own or with nouns.

> –¿Cuántos kilómetros hay a Colmenar? –**Veinticinco**.
>
> Esa camisa cuesta **treinta y seis** euros.

● *Uno/un, una* take the same form (masculine or feminine) as the noun they refer to.

> –without a noun: *uno* (masculine), *una* (feminine)
>> –¿Cuántos **años** tienes? –Cincuenta y **uno**.
>> –¿A qué hora llega el tren? –A las doce y **cuarenta y una**.
> –*un* + masculine noun
>> Peso **setenta y un** kilos.
> –*una* + feminine noun
>> Necesitamos **cuarenta y una** sillas.
> –*un* + feminine noun starting with á-, há-
>> Este instituto tiene **treinta y un** aulas.

● Cardinal numbers are used to indicate:

> – quantity. *En este instituto hay **cincuenta y seis profesores**.*
>
> – price. *Las entradas cuestan **treinta euros**.*
>
> – height, weight, and distance.
>> Rosa mide **un metro setenta centímetros**.
>> Peso **sesenta y cinco kilos**.
> – age. *Elisa tiene **cuarenta y cuatro** años.*
>
> – dates. *Mi cumpleaños es el (día) **treinta y uno** de octubre.*
>
> – time. *El tren sale a las **quince cuarenta**.*

De Madrid a Toledo
hay **ochenta kilómetros**.

| las trece horas | las dieciséis quince | las diecisiete treinta | las diecinueve cuarenta y cinco | las veinte cincuenta y ocho |

> –telephone numbers. *91 447 82 63 = noventa y uno, cuatro, cuarenta y siete, ochenta y dos, sesenta y tres*

▶ UNIT 19: Cardinal numbers (1)   UNIT 21: Cardinal numbers (3)

20 EXERCISES

20.1 **Write the numbers in parentheses in words.**

1. (31) _treinta y uno_ de enero
2. (41) _____ pesos
3. (51) _____ dólares
4. (71) _____ sillas

5. (91) _____ kilómetros
6. (61) _____ euros
7. (81) _____ alumnas
8. (41) _____ grados

SCORE ...../8

20.2 **Write the following numbers in words.**

1. 34 metros _treinta y cuatro metros_
2. 45 kilómetros _____
3. 36 meses _____
4. 49 kilos _____
5. 53 años _____
6. 92 kilos _____

7. 88 centímetros _____
8. 40 días _____
9. 57 euros _____
10. 32 alumnos _____
11. 55 años _____
12. 76 años _____

SCORE ...../12

20.3 **Write the time in words.**

1. las dieciocho cincuenta y dos
2. _____
3. _____
4. _____
5. _____
6. _____
7. _____
8. _____
9. _____
10. _____

SCORE ...../10

20.4 **Write the telephone numbers in words as in the example.**

PILAR 935478902
ELVIRA 924478901
TOMÁS 532 44 96
JOSÉ LUIS 91 4643358
ANTONIA 96 3526361
VIRGINIA 955 887941

1. _noventa y tres, cinco, cuarenta y siete, ochenta y nueve, cero, dos_
2. _____
3. _____
4. _____
5. _____
6. _____

SCORE ...../6

49

21 *cien, mil, un millón...*
Cardinal numbers (3)

● Cardinal numbers: 100, 1 000...

100	cien	1 000	mil
101	ciento uno/un, ciento una	2 000	dos mil
125	ciento veinticinco	10 000	diez mil
200	doscientos, doscientas	100 000	cien mil
300	trescientos, trescientas		
400	cuatrocientos, cuatrocientas		
500	quinientos, quinientas		
600	seiscientos, seiscientas	1 000 000	un millón
700	setecientos, setecientas	2 000 000	dos millones
800	ochocientos, ochocientas	200 000 000	doscientos millones
900	novecientos, novecientas	1 000 000 000	mil millones

137	ciento treinta y siete
2 079	dos mil setenta y nueve
821 325	ochocientos veintiún mil trescientos veinticinco
1 537 982	un millón quinientos treinta y siete mil novecientos ochenta y dos
10 410 212	diez millones cuatrocientos diez mil doscientos doce

– *cien* + masculine/feminine noun → *cien euros, cien personas*

   doscientos, trescientos... + masculine noun → *doscientos euros*

   doscientas, trescientas... + feminine noun → *doscientas personas*

– *millón/millones* + *de* + noun → *un millón **de** euros, tres millones **de** habitantes*

▌ BUT:

▸ *un millón doscientos mil euros*
  tres millones cien mil habitantes

▸ *~~un millón~~ dólares* → *un millón de dólares*

  un millón cien mil de habitantes → *un millón cien mil habitantes*

¡Un millón de pesos!

● Cardinal numbers can be used to indicate:

– quantity. *Jorge gana **ciento veinticinco mil pesos** al mes.*
    *Este piso cuesta cerca de **ciento cincuenta mil euros**.*

– measurements, weights, and distances. *Esta mesa mide **ciento cincuenta centímetros**.*
    *De Barcelona a Madrid hay más de **seiscientos kilómetros**.*
    *Quiero **doscientos gramos** de jamón.*

– age. *El hombre más viejo del mundo tiene **ciento veintisiete años**.*
    *La catedral de Lima tiene más de **cuatrocientos años**.*

– years. 1989 ***mil novecientos ochenta y nueve***
    2002 ***dos mil dos***

2008
MARZO

L	M	Mi	J	V	S	D
					1	2
3	4	5	6	7	8	9
10	11	12	13	14	15	16
17	18	19	20	21	22	23

Doce de marzo
*de **dos mil ocho***

▶ UNIT 19: Cardinal numbers (1)   UNIT 20: Cardinal numbers (2)

21 EXERCISES

21.1 **Write the numbers.**

1. Ciento uno _____101_____
2. Tres mil diecisiete _____
3. Diez mil cien _____
4. Trece mil quinientos ocho _____
5. Cincuenta mil doscientos siete _____

6. Cien mil uno _____
7. Cuatrocientos mil ciento veinte _____
8. Un millón cien mil _____
9. Dos millones trescientos quince mil _____
10. Mil trescientos millones _____

21.2 **Write the numbers in words.**

1. 100 _____cien_____
2. 102 _____
3. 183 _____
4. 349 _____
5. 1 070 _____
6. 3 561 _____
7. 62 201 _____
8. 115 100 _____

9. 416 252 _____
10. 933 344 _____
11. 1 231 758 _____
12. 3 050 947 _____
13. 22 891 604 _____
14. 101 712 413 _____
15. 200 034 027 _____
16. 1 000 615 105 _____

21.3 **Write the following prices in words.**

1. $ 205 ____doscientos cinco dólares____
2. € 301 _____
3. ¥ 2 612 _____
4. € 83 195 _____
5. DKK 1 421 _____
6. BRL 568 _____
7. TRL 833 _____
8. MXN 471 950 _____

1 $	= un dólar
1 €	= un euro
1 ¥	= un yen
1 BRL	= un real
1 DKK	= una corona danesa
1 TRL	= una lira turca
1 MXN	= un peso mexicano

21.4 **Complete the sentences with the numbers in parentheses.**

1. La Habana tiene (*2 000 000*) _____dos millones_____ de habitantes.
2. María gana (*2 085*) _____ euros al mes.
3. –¿Cuántas mariposas tienes? –Más de (*300*) _____ .
4. La mujer más vieja del mundo tiene (*121*) _____ años.
5. –¿Cuántos kilómetros hay de Cartagena a Bogotá? –(*1 274*) _____ kilómetros.
6. Alberto pesa (*108*) _____ kilos.
7. Machu Picchu tiene más de (*500*) _____ años.
8. Esta televisión cuesta (*310*) _____ bolívares.
9. –¿Qué desea? –(*250*) _____ gramos de queso, por favor.
10. Mi piso tiene (*100*) _____ metros cuadrados.

21.5 **Write the dates in words.**

1. ___veintiuno de enero de mil ochocientos doce___
2. _____
3. _____
4. _____
5. _____
6. _____

22 *primero, segundo, tercero...*
Ordinal numbers

Yo vivo allí, en **el cuarto piso**.

Ángeles tiene siete hermanos.
Ella es **la segunda**.

Cuarto and *segunda* are ordinal numbers. We use them to indicate the order, ranking, or sequence.

> Javier acabó **sexto** en el maratón.   Ana es mi **tercera** profesora de español.

● Ordinal numbers

1.º/1.ª *primero/primer, primera*	6.º/6.ª *sexto, sexta*
2.º/2.ª *segundo, segunda*	7.º/7.ª *séptimo, séptima*
3.º/3.ª *tercero/tercer, tercera*	8.º/8.ª *octavo, octava*
4.º/4.ª *cuarto, cuarta*	9.º/9.ª *noveno, novena*
5.º/5.ª *quinto, quinta*	10.º/10.ª *décimo, décima*

BE CAREFUL!

primero, tercero + singular masculine noun = *primer, tercer*

> El **primer tren** sale a las 7.20.   Hoy es nuestro **tercer día** en Bolivia.

– When we write ordinal numbers, we add º to the numbers for the masculine, and ª for the feminine, or we use Roman numerals.

Fernando **III** (tercero)
Capítulo **VIII** (octavo)
Siglo **VI** (sexto)

Peluquería Rodolfo
1º dcha.

– From 11 on the cardinal numbers are usually used.

► **UNIT 19**: Cardinal numbers (1)

> Alfonso **XIII** (trece) *es el abuelo de Juan Carlos* **I** (primero).
> La oficina de Maribel está en el piso **diecisiete**.
> Federico García Lorca nació a finales del siglo **XIX** (diecinueve).

– Ordinal numbers take the same form (masculine or feminine, singular or plural) as the noun they refer to.

> Las oficinas de Intersa están en la **tercera planta**.
> **Chus y yo** quedamos **segundos** en un campeonato de tenis.

– Ordinal numbers often go before the noun.

> Vivo en el **segundo piso**.

BUT: Not with proper nouns.
> Carlos **V** (quinto)

– Ordinal numbers can be on their own when it is clear what they refer to.

> El Boca Juniors va **primero** en la liga.
> –¿Por qué capítulo vas? –Por el **quinto**.

22 EXERCISES

22.1. **Look at the drawings and complete the sentences with the corresponding numbers.**

Antonio Oliva 2º C	Servicios de Gas 11º A	Sastrería MODERNA 10º D	Moreno-Arribas ABOGADOS 3º D	Molina Cardoso 12º A
Gestoría Salvado 1º A	Hispanosa 14º D	Academia Cervantes 4º B	Julia Salinas 7º C	Editorial Mundisa 9º D

1. Antonio Oliva vive en el __segundo__ piso.
2. Las oficinas de Servicios de Gas están en el piso _____.
3. La sastrería Moderna está en la _____ planta.
4. Hay un despacho de abogados en el _____ piso.
5. La familia Molina Cardoso vive en el piso _____.
6. La gestoría Salvado está en el _____ piso.
7. Las oficinas de Hispanosa están en el piso _____.
8. La academia Cervantes está en la _____ planta.
9. Julia Salinas vive en el piso _____.
10. La editorial Mundisa está en el _____ piso.

SCORE __ /10

22.2. **Write the names of the people in words.**

1. Juan Carlos I __Juan Carlos primero__.
2. Isabel I _____.
3. Juan XXIII _____.
4. Alfonso XII _____.
5. Luis XV _____.

6. Iván IV _____.
7. Margarita II _____.
8. Pío XI _____.
9. Juana III _____.
10. Juan Pablo II _____.

SCORE __ /10

22.3. **Write the numbers in parentheses in words.**

1. Estudio (2.º) __segundo__ curso de Arquitectura.
2. Enero es el (1.º) _____ mes del año.
3. Estoy leyendo un libro con (15) _____ capítulos. Voy por el capítulo (11.º) _____.
4. El Valencia es el (1.º) _____ en la Liga de fútbol.
5. Javi es el (3.º) _____ de sus hermanos. Yo soy la (5.ª) _____ de seis hermanas.
6. Las hijas de Carlos son las (1.ª) _____ de la clase.
7. La ñ es la letra (15.ª) _____ del alfabeto.
8. En la (1.ª) _____ planta hay muchas oficinas, pero el despacho de José está en el (8.º) _____ piso.
9. Tuerza por la (2.ª) _____ calle a la izquierda.
10. Nos vamos de vacaciones la (3.ª) _____ semana de agosto; es el (3.º) _____ año que vamos a España.
11. El siglo 18º _____ fue el Siglo de las Luces.
12. Tina y Carla acabaron (4.ªs) _____ en el campeonato de tenis.
13. Los (1.º) _____ platos son muy buenos.

SCORE __ /17

22.4. **Write in ordinal numbers (1º, 2º, 3º....) or Roman numerals (I, II, III).**

1. (Segundo) __2.º__ izquierda.
2. Siglo (quince) _____.
3. Alfonso (primero) _____.
4. (Cuarto) _____ interior.

5. Isabel (segunda) _____.
6. Siglo (veintiuno) _____.
7. Capítulo (sexto) _____.
8. Margarita (primera) _____.

SCORE __ /8

23 *todo, toda, todos, todas*
Indefinite reference (1)

Se han comido **toda** la tarta.

Todas las tartas cuestan 12 euros.

We use *todo*, *toda*, *todos*, and *todas* to refer to all or whole.

    todo, toda = the whole group
               all the parts

*Ayer estuve en casa **todo el día**.*

    todos, todas = the whole group

Toda mi familia

Todos mis amigos *hablan español.*

● *todo, toda, todos, todas*

todo + el
    + mi, tu..., nuestro...   + masculine singular noun
    + este, ese

*He trabajado **todo el día**.*
*Hemos perdido **todo nuestro dinero**.*
*¿De quién es **todo ese dinero**?*

toda + la
    + mi, tu..., nuestra...   + feminine singular noun
    + esta, esa

*He dormido **toda la noche**.*
*Anoche salí con **toda mi clase**.*
*¿De dónde es **toda esa gente**?*

todos + los
    + mis, tus..., nuestros... + masculine plural noun
    + estos, esos

*Voy a México **todos los veranos**.*
Todos tus cuadros *son preciosos*
*Tira **todos esos papeles**.*

todas + las
    + mis, tus..., nuestras... + feminine plural noun
    + estas, esas

*Voy al gimnasio **todas las tardes**.*
Todas mis hermanas *hablan francés.*
*Conozco a **todas esas chicas**.*

Compare:

todos los días

*Toco el piano **todos los días**.*
*Me gustan **todos los libros**.*

todo el día

*Ayer no salí. Estuve en casa **todo el día**.*
*He leído **todo el libro**. Es muy interesante.*

● *Todo, toda, todos,* and *todas* can be used on their own when what we are talking about is clear.
    *No hay pan. Te lo has comido **todo**.* (all the bread)
    *Nicolás tiene tres hermanas, y son **todas** muy simpáticas.* (all of his sisters)

● *todo* = everything

Desde aquí lo veo **todo**.

    *–¿Qué te gusta más de España? –**Todo**.* (everything)

● *todo el mundo, todos, todas*

    todo el mundo, todos = everyone

*A **todo el mundo** le gusta París.*
*A **todos** nos gusta vivir bien.*

    todos, todas = all of us (in a group)

*En mi clase, **todos** somos buenos estudiantes.*
*Somos tres hermanas y a **todas** nos gusta viajar.*

BE CAREFUL!

todo el mundo + singular verb →	***Todo el mundo quiere** ser feliz.*
todos, todas + plural verb →	***Todos queremos** ser felices.*

23 EXERCISES

23.1 **Complete with *todo*, *toda*, *todos*, or *todas*.**

1. Sofía no está bien. Ayer estuvo en la cama _todo_ el día.
2. No he visto a Luis en _____ la semana.
3. Voy al cine _____ las semanas.
4. Conozco _____ las canciones de Aute.
5. _____ mis hermanas viven en Caracas.
6. Vamos al campo _____ los fines de semana.
7. Hemos visto _____ el museo.
8. He ordenado _____ mis cedés.
9. Sé _____ esa canción de memoria.
10. Ha llovido poco por _____ la zona.
11. _____ las casas del pueblo son antiguas.
12. ¿De quién son _____ esos libros?

SCORE _____/12

23.2 **Complete the sentences with *todo*, *toda*, *todos*, *todas*, and *el, la, los, las* and the words from the box.**

| bolsillo | ~~caja~~ | dinero | leche | niño | queso | tienda |

① ② ③ ④ ⑤ ⑥

____ ____ ____ ____ ____ ____

1. _Todas las cajas_ están vacías.
2. Se han comido_____.
3. _____ están contentos.
4. _____ está en la nevera.
5. _____ están cerradas.
6. Se ha gastado_____.

SCORE _____/6

23.3 **Complete with *todos*, *todas* and *mi, tu, su...***

1. Conozco a _toda tu_ familia, Pedro.
2. _____ maletas están ya en el coche, don Manuel.
3. Lucas gasta _____ dinero en novelas.
4. –¿Dónde están _____ alumnos, Srta. Hernández? –Están en la biblioteca.
5. _____ amigos nos quieren mucho.
6. –¿Dónde están _____ hijos, Sr. Ramírez? –Están de vacaciones en la playa.

SCORE _____/6

23.4 **Complete the sentences with *todo*, *toda*, *todos*, or *todas*.**

1. Me encantan las mariposas. _Todas_ tienen alas muy bonitas.
2. –¿Dónde están tus hermanos? –Están _____ en el jardín.
3. –¿Dónde está la tarta? –Se la han comido _____.
4. –¿Qué libro prefieres? –Es igual. Me gustan _____.
5. No hay leche. Se la han bebido _____.
6. No tengo dinero. Lo he perdido _____.

SCORE _____/6

23.5 **Complete with *todo*, *todos*, *todas*, or *todo el mundo*.**

1. Lo sé _todo_.
2. _____ somos altas.
3. _____ buscamos la felicidad.
4. _____ quiere a Marta.
5. _____ ha venido a la fiesta.
6. _____ es más barato en esta tienda.
7. _____ están de acuerdo conmigo.
8. Conozco algunas calles del pueblo, no _____.
9. Somos cuatro hermanos y_____ somos rubios.
10. Francisco es muy egoísta. Lo quiere _____ para él.

SCORE _____/10

24 *un, otro*
Indefinite reference (2)

● *un, una, unos, unas*

un, una = an undetermined object; which one is unknown.

> *He visto a Juan con **una amiga**.*

unos, unas = identity and quantity are not determined; we don't say which ones or how many.

> *Mañana voy al cine con **unos amigos**.*

Necesito **un** móvil nuevo

un + masculine singular noun	*Necesito **un móvil** nuevo.*
una + feminine singular noun	*Conozco **a una chica** muy interesante.*
unos + masculine plural noun	***Unos chicos** quieren verte.*
unas + feminine plural noun	*Rosa está estudiando con **unas compañeras**.*

● *otro, otra, otros, otras*

= plus the same type of object

> *Toma **otra galleta**.* (another cookie)
> ***Otros dos bocadillos**, por favor.* (two more sub sandwiches)
> *Hazlo **otra vez**.* (again)

= different objects

> *Déjame **otro libro**. Este no me gusta.* (a different book)
> *Luisa ya no sale con Luis. Tiene **otro novio**.* (a different boyfriend)

Otro zumo, por favor.

otro + masculine singular noun	*Gloria está esperando **otro hijo**.*
otra + feminine singular noun	*Tráiganos **otra cuchara**, por favor.*
otros + (*dos, tres...*) masculine plural noun	*Enséñeme **otros zapatos**. Estos no me gustan.*
otras + (*dos, tres ...*) feminine plural noun	*Necesitamos **otras dos jugadoras**.*

● *Uno* (not *un*), *una, unos, unas, otro, otra, otros,* and *otras* can be used on their own when who or what we are speaking about is clear.

> *–Necesitamos **sillas** nuevas. –He visto **unas** preciosas.* (some chairs)
> *Hay muchos **bocadillos**. Toma **otro**.* (another sub sandwich)

BE CAREFUL!

–No tengo bolígrafo. –Yo tengo ~~un~~. → *–No tengo bolígrafo. –Yo tengo **uno**.*

● We use *el/la + otro/otra + día, mañana, tarde...* to refer to a past moment.

> ***El otro día** vi a Jesús.*
> ***La otra tarde** estuve con Lola.*

24 EXERCISES

24.1. Look at the situations and complete the sentences with *un, una, unos, unas* or *otro, otra, otros, otras*.

① Una tónica, por favor.

② Deme ___ bolsa, por favor. Esta está rota.

③ Préstame ___ libro, por favor.

④ ___ tónica, por favor.

⑤ Préstame ___ libros. Estos los he leído.

⑥ Deme ___ bolsa, por favor.

⑦ Tráiganos ___ cucharas. Estas están sucias.

⑧ ¡Qué rica estaba! ¿Me das ___ manzana?

24.2. Complete the sentences with *un, una, unos, unas* or *otro, otra, otros, otras*.

1. –¿Dónde estabas? –Con __unas__ amigas.
2. –¿Vamos al cine? –Hoy no puedo, pero podemos ir _____ día.
3. Tengo _____ dos hermanas en Argentina.
4. He pasado _____ días en Medellín.
5. Han llegado _____ libros para la biblioteca.
6. He recibido una postal de _____ alumnas.
7. Hoy estoy ocupado. Ven _____ día.
8. Tráiganos _____ botella, por favor. Esta está vacía.
9. Ponte _____ zapatos. Esos están muy viejos.
10. Necesito _____ coche. Este tiene muchos años.

SCORE /10

24.3. Complete the sentences with *uno, una, unos, unas* or *otro, otra, otros, otras*.

1. –¿Le gustan estos zapatos? –No, enséñeme __otros__, por favor.
2. No he encontrado mis llaves, pero Juan tiene _____.
3. He perdido el tren a Cuzco. ¿Cuándo hay _____?
4. –¿Le gustan estos plátanos? –No, deme _____. Esos están muy verdes.
5. Esta tienda está cerrada hoy, pero hay _____ muy cerca.
6. Este bolígrafo no escribe. ¿Tienes _____?
7. ¿Te gustan las galletas? Coge _____. Lleva _____ a tu hermano.
8. Hay muchos bocadillos. Coge _____.
9. Tienes muchas revistas. Préstame _____.
10. No me gustan estas gafas. Enséñeme _____, por favor.

SCORE /11

24.4. Complete the sentences with *otro, otra* and *el, la* if necessary.

1. –¿Cuándo viste a Raquel? –__La otra__ noche.
2. _____ día conocimos a una familia de Colombia.
3. Lo he pasado muy bien. Podemos salir _____ día.
4. _____ tarde fui al cine con Luis.
5. Esta noche no puedo salir, pero podemos salir _____ noche.
6. _____ noche nos divertimos muchísimo.

SCORE /6

mucho, poco, demasiado, suficiente...
Indefinite reference (3)

mucho dinero

poco dinero

demasiado dinero

suficiente dinero

Mucho, poco, demasiado, and *suficiente* are used to indicate quantity.

mucho = a large amount	*demasiado* = more than is necessary
poco = a small amount	*suficiente* = the necessary amount

● *mucho, poco, demasiado, suficiente*

mucho, mucha poco, poca demasiado, demasiada suficiente	+ uncountable singular noun	*Ana sabe **mucha informática**.* *Martín tiene **poco tiempo** libre.* *Rodri come **demasiado chocolate**.* *No tengo **suficiente dinero** para el avión.*
muchos, muchas pocos, pocas demasiados, demasiadas suficientes	+ plural noun	*Mis hijos duermen **muchas horas**.* *Marcela tiene **pocas amigas**.* *Tenemos **demasiadas horas** de clase.* *Tenemos **suficientes patatas** para hoy.*

BE CAREFUL!

suficiente(s) + noun → *Hay **suficiente agua**.*	noun + *suficiente(s)* → *Hay **agua suficiente**.*

● *bastante, bastantes*

= a large amount, but not a lot

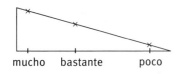

mucho   bastante   poco

mucha gente

bastante gente

= the necessary amount, enough

  *–¿Crees que hay **bastante comida**?* (enough food) *–Sí, solo somos tres.*
  ● *bastante* + singular noun   *Felipe gana **bastante dinero**.*
  ● *bastantes* + plural noun   *Ernestina no está nunca sola. Tiene **bastantes amigos**.*

● *Mucho, poco, demasiado, suficiente,* and *bastante* can be on their own when what we are speaking about is clear. They take the same form (masculine or feminine, singular or plural) as the noun they refer to.

  *–¿Cuántos **huevos** hay? –Tres. Son **suficientes** para una tortilla.   –¿Tienes **tiempo**? –No **mucho**. Me voy en diez minutos.*
  *–Solo tengo **diez** euros. –Es **bastante** para ir al cine. La entrada cuesta seis.*

● *un poco de* + uncountable noun (*inglés, pan, agua*...) = some
    *Sé **un poco de** francés.* (a little French)

Compare:

poco, poca (small amount)	*un poco de* (some)
*Sé **poco español**. No puedo comunicarme.*	*Sé **un poco de español**. Puedo comunicarme.*

– We can use *un poco* only when the noun that we refer to is mentioned previously.

    *–¿Quieres pan? –Sí, dame **un poco**.*

25 EXERCISES

25.1. **Replace the underlined amounts with *mucho/a/os/as* or *poco/a/os/as*.**

1. Sonia tiene <u>unos dos mil</u> libros. _Sonia tiene muchos libros_____.
2. Alberto tiene <u>dos</u> amigos. _____.
3. Necesito <u>tres mil</u> dólares. _____.
4. Ayer dormimos <u>diez</u> horas. _____.
5. Bebo <u>tres litros</u> de agua al día. _____.
6. Hemos comprado <u>diez litros</u> de aceite. _____.
7. Quedan <u>dos</u> patatas. _____.
8. Luisa toma <u>media cucharada</u> de azúcar en el café. _____.

25.2. **Write whether these amounts seem to be enough or too much.**

1. Javier trabaja doce horas todos los días. _Trabaja demasiadas horas_____.
2. Enrique duerme cuatro horas todos los días. _No duerme suficientes horas_____.
3. Jacinta bebe un vaso de agua al día. _____.
4. Como cinco plátanos al día. _____.
5. Óscar bebe diez tazas de café al día. _____.
6. Inés bebe litro y medio de agua al día. _____.
7. Gabriel come medio kilo de carne todos los días. _____.
8. Tenemos una patata para hacer una tortilla. _____.

25.3. **Describe what is in each drawing using *mucho/a/os/as*, *poco/a/os/as*, or *bastante/s*.**

agua	árboles (2)	~~coches~~	comida	dinero	gente (3)	ruido

muchos coches _____ _____ _____ _____

_____ _____ _____ _____ _____

25.4. **Complete the sentences with *mucho, poco, demasiado, suficiente, bastante...***

1. –¿Tienes hambre? –No tengo _mucha_. Puedo esperar.
2. –¿Cuántas manzanas tienes? –Tres. Son _____ para una tarta.
3. –He invitado a unas cuarenta personas. –Son _____. Aquí solo caben veinte.
4. –¿Cuánto dinero tienes? –Veinticinco euros. Es _____. Las entradas cuestan veinte.
5. –¿Tenemos tiempo? –Tenemos muy _____. El tren sale dentro de cinco minutos.
6. –¿Cuánta gente hay? –No hay _____. Unas diez personas.

25.5. **Complete the sentences with *poco, poca, un poco*, or *un poco de*.**

1. No quiero comer. Tengo _poca_ hambre.
2. Quiero comer. Tengo _____ hambre.
3. –¿Sabes inglés? –Sí, _____. Me entiendo con la gente.
4. Dame _____ agua, por favor. Tengo sed.
5. No puedo salir esta noche. Tengo _____ dinero.
6. Ponme _____ sopa. No tengo mucha hambre.
7. Necesito _____ pan para el bocadillo.

26 *alguien, algo, nadie, nada*
Indefinite reference (4)

   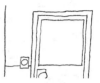

*Hay **alguien** detrás de la puerta.*

*No hay **nadie** detrás de la puerta.*

*Hay **algo** detrás de la puerta.*

*No hay **nada** detrás de la puerta.*

We use *alguien, algo, nadie,* and *nada* to refer to people or objects that are unknown.

  alguien = a person (or several), but we don't know who. *nadie* = no one
  algo = an object (or several), but we don't know what. *nada* = nothing

● *alguien, algo, nadie, nada*

	PEOPLE	OBJECTS
Affirmative sentences and questions	alguien ***Alguien** ha roto la silla.* *¿Hay **alguien** ahí dentro?*	algo *Hay **algo** en la sopa.* *¿Has dicho **algo**?*
Negative sentences	nadie *No hay **nadie** en casa.*	nada *No hay **nada** en la nevera.*

BE CAREFUL!

nadie, nada + affirmative verb	***Nadie** me ha visto.*	***Nada** le importa.*
negative verb + *nadie, nada*	***No** me ha visto **nadie** en casa.*	***No** le importa **nada**.*

● We use *algo de, nada de* + uncountable nouns (*agua, queso, español*...) to indicate quantity.

 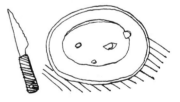

*Hay **algo de queso** en la nevera.* (a little cheese)

*Sé **algo de árabe**.* (a little Arabic)

*No hay **nada de queso**.*

*No sé **nada de árabe**.*

–We can use *algo* and *nada* on their own to indicate quantity when the noun we refer to has been mentioned previously.

*–¿Tienes **dinero**? –Tengo **algo**. –Pues yo no tengo **nada**.*

*–¿Sabes **informática**? –**Algo**.*

▶ UNIT 88: Adverbs of quantity   UNIT 91: Negative adverbs

26.1 Look at the drawings and complete the sentences with *hay, no hay* + *alguien, algo, nadie,* or *nada.*

① ② ③ ④

⑤ ⑥ ⑦ ⑧

1. __No hay nada__ en la mesa.
2. _____ en mi habitación.
3. _____ detrás del árbol.
4. _____ en el salón.
5. _____ en el libro.
6. _____ en la piscina.
7. _____ en la caja.
8. _____ en el árbol.

SCORE /8

26.2 Complete the sentences with *alguien, algo, nadie,* or *nada.*

1. Hay _alguien_ esperándole en recepción. Ha traído _____ para usted.
2. _____ huele mal en la cocina.
3. Hoy no he hecho _____.
4. ¿Ha cogido _____ mi bolígrafo?
5. _____ quiere acompañarme al cine.
6. Necesito que _____ me ayude con este ejercicio.
7. –Hay mucha gente en la calle. ¿Ha pasado _____? –No ha pasado _____. Ha sido una falsa alarma.
8. No hay _____ en casa de Tomás. No contestan el teléfono.
9. –¿Hay _____ interesante en la TV? –No. No hay _____ interesante.
10. –¿Hay _____ en el aula? –Sí, dos alumnos.
11. Mis abuelos necesitan _____ en casa.
12. –¿Quieres _____? –No, gracias. No quiero _____.

SCORE /16

26.3 Write sentences with the words given.

1. me quiere, nadie ___Nadie me quiere___.
2. me quiere, nadie, no _____.
3. pasa, nada, no _____.
4. le gusta, nada _____.
5. tengo, nada, no _____.
6. sé, nada, no _____.
7. veo, a nadie, no _____.
8. habla, nadie _____.

SCORE /8

26.4 Answer the questions using *algo, nada, algo de,* or *nada de.*

1.–¿Hay _algo de_ comida?　–No hay _____ queso, pero hay _____ jamón.

2.–¿Hay _____ pan?　–Hay _____, pero poco.

3.–¿Y leche?　–No hay _____, pero hay _____ zumo.

4.–Necesitamos comprar comida. ¿Tenéis dinero?　–Tenemos _____, pero poco.

5.–¿Qué podemos comprar?　–Bueno, podemos comprar _____ pan y _____ queso.

6.–¿Y fruta?　–No podemos comprar _____ fruta. No tenemos suficiente dinero.

SCORE /11

26.5 Complete the sentences with *algo, nada, algo de,* or *nada de.*

1. –¿Sabes _algo de_ chino? – No, no sé _____.
2. –¿Tienes _____ de dinero? –Tengo _____, pero poco.
3. No tengo _____ hambre.
4. Yo no sé _____ inglés, pero Marta sabe _____. Puede entenderse.
5. Necesito _____ ayuda.
6. –¿Sabes _____ informática? –Bueno, sé _____. ¿Qué quieres?

SCORE /10

27 *más, menos, tanto*
Comparisons with nouns

Belén tiene
más libros
que yo.

Ahora tengo **menos pelo**
que cuando era joven.

Hoy no tengo
tanto trabajo
como ayer.

Más, menos, and *tanto* are used to make comparisons with nouns.

   más = greater amount (+)

   menos = smaller amount (–)

   tanto = same amount (=)

● Comparisons with nouns

> **+** *más* + noun (+ *que*)
>
>   *Ernesto tiene **más alumnos** que Guadalupe.*
>   *Pedro tiene **más amigos** que Antonio.*
>
> **–** *menos* + noun (+ *que*)
>
>   *Antes había **menos coches** que ahora.*
>   *Ahora tengo **menos sueño** (que antes).*
>
> **=** *tanto, tanta, tantos, tantas* + noun (+ *como*)
>
>   *Hoy no hay **tanta gente** como ayer.*
>   *No tengo **tantos amigos** como mi hermana.*

– The form (masculine or feminine, singular or plural) is the same as the noun.

   *Hoy no tengo **tanto tiempo** como ayer.*   *Trabajo **tantas horas** como tú.*

– *que, como* + personal pronoun of the subject   ▶ UNIT 28: Personal pronouns:subject

   *Rodolfo tiene más vacaciones **que tú**, pero tú haces más viajes **que él**.*
   *¿Tienes tanta hambre **como yo**?*

– We usually don't use *que, como* + comparison element when it is clear what we are comparing.

   *Ahora tengo **menos hambre**.* (than before the meal)
   *Hoy no hay **tanta gente**.* (than yesterday)

● *Más, menos, tanto...* can be used on their own when the noun we refer to is mentioned previously.

   *–Sonia tiene cerca de cien **cedés**. –Yo tengo **más**. –Pues yo no tengo **tantos**.*

> **BUT:** In affirmative sentences *tanto, tanta, tantos,* and *tantas* always go with *como* + comparison element.
>
>   *–Elisa tiene una gran colección de cedés.*
>
>   *–Yo ~~tengo tantos~~.*   *–Yo tengo **tantos como ella**.*

27.1 Complete the sentences with *más, menos* or *tanto, tanta, tantos, tantas* and the word in parentheses.

1. Buenos Aires tiene (+ habitantes) _más habitantes_ que Madrid.
2. Ahora bebo (– leche) _____ que cuando era pequeño.
3. Los chinos comen (= arroz) _____ como los indios.
4. Sol ha leído (+ libros) _____ que yo.
5. No tengo (= amigas) _____ como mi hermana.
6. En Canarias no hace (= calor) _____ como en Cuba.
7. Un policía gana (– dinero) _____ que un médico.
8. Tenemos (= prisa) _____ como tú.
9. Samuel tiene (+ ropa) _____ que yo.
10. En La Paz hace (+ frío) _____ que en Caracas.

SCORE ...... /10

27.2 Complete the sentences comparing the information given in parentheses. Use the words from the box.

años	calor	corbatas	~~dinero~~	estudiantes	frío	habitantes	hambre	leche	postales

1. (Roberto tiene 200 pesos. Clara tiene 20.) Clara tiene _menos dinero que Roberto_ .
2. (Elsa bebe 1/2 litro de leche al día. Eloy bebe 1 litro.) Elsa no bebe _____ .
3. (Hoy hace 30°. Ayer hizo 25°.) Hoy hace _____ .
4. (Rosario tiene un millón de habitantes. Mendoza tiene un millón y medio de habitantes.)
   Rosario no tiene _____ .
5. (Simón tiene 30 años. Yo tengo 28.) Simón tiene _____ .
6. (Ayer vinieron doce estudiantes. Hoy han venido diez.) Hoy no han venido _____
   _____ .
7. (Ayer hizo 5°. Hoy hace 10°.) Hoy no hace _____ .
8. (Son las 3 de la tarde; todavía no he comido. Irene tampoco ha comido todavía.)
   Irene tiene _____ .
9. (Tengo dos corbatas. Tú también tienes dos corbatas.) Tengo _____
   _____ .
10. (Habéis recibido cinco postales este verano. Yo he recibido tres.) He recibido
   _____ .

SCORE ...... /10

27.3 Complete the answers as in the examples.

1. –Felipe tiene dos hijos. –Yo tengo _más_. Tengo cuatro.
2. –Tengo siete hermanos. –Yo tengo casi _tantos como tú_. Tengo seis.
3. –Aurora tiene 30 días de vacaciones. –Yo tengo _____. Tengo 22.
4. –Tengo unos quinientos libros. –Yo no tengo _____. Tengo unos trescientos.
5. –Tengo sueño. He dormido solo cuatro horas. –Yo tengo _____. He dormido solo dos horas.
6. –Hoy hay cerca de doscientos espectadores. –Ayer había _____. Había solo cincuenta.
7. –Hemos estado en diez países diferentes. –Yo he estado en _____. He estado en doce.
8. –Trabajo ocho horas al día. –Yo trabajo _____. También trabajo ocho.
9. –Maite hace ejercicio dos veces por semana. –Yo hago _____. Hago ejercicio todos los días.
10. –Voy a clase cinco veces por semana. –Yo voy _____. Voy tres.

SCORE ...... /10

28 *yo, tú, él...*
Personal pronouns: subject

BE CAREFUL!

tú + yo = nosotros, nosotras

(tú +) él/ella + yo = nosotros, nosotras

– masculine + feminine = masculine plural

       *ella, él y yo = **nosotros***   *ella, él y tú = **vosotros***

       *ella y él = **ellos***

● *tú, usted; vosotros, vosotras, ustedes*

  – We use *tú*, *vosotros*, and *vosotras* with family, friends, workmates, or young people.

  – We use *usted*, *ustedes* with people we don't know, superiors, or elderly people.

● We use *yo, tú, él...* + verb to refer to the person who does action of the verb. (subject).

    Usted trabaja *en un banco, ¿verdad?*   ***Nosotras somos*** *muy alegres.*

● It isn't usually necessary to use *yo, tú, él...* with verbs.

    ~~Yo~~ *vivo en Bogotá.*   *¿Dónde trabajas* ~~tú~~*?*

BUT:

  – *Usted, ustedes* are used with more frequency.

    *Don Ricardo, ¿dónde vive **usted**?*   *–**Usted** no es peruano, ¿verdad? –No, soy boliviano.*

    *–**Ustedes no son** franceses, ¿verdad? –No, somos belgas.*

  – We use *yo, tú, él...* + verb:

    • to indicate contrast. ***Yo** soy de Alicante, ¿y tú?*

    • to emphasize. ***Yo** quiero trabajar, pero mis padres no quieren.*

    • to make clear who we are speaking about.

        *Mira, allí van Silvia y Jorge. Son peruanos. **Él** es de Arequipa y **ella** es de Lima.*

    • when used with other people.

        ***Alicia y tú** parecéis hermanas.*   ***Mi padre y yo** somos buenos amigos.*

● *Yo, tú, él...* can be used on their own to identify someone.

    *–¿Quién es Hans Liebe? – (Soy) **Yo**.*   *–¿Quién quiere ir a la excursión? – **Nosotras**.*

    *–¿Quién es Marina? –**Ella**.*

▶ UNIT 34: Personal pronouns with prepositions

28.1 Write the correct pronoun.

① Ellas ② ___ ③ ___ ④ ___ ⑤ ___ ⑥ ___

⑦ ___ ⑧ ___ ⑨ ___ ⑩ ___ ⑪ ___ ⑫ ___

SCORE ..../12

28.2 Write the personal pronoun of the corresponding subject.

1. Sofía y Alberto: _ellos_
2. Tú, Juan y yo: _____
3. Sofía y Luisa: _____
4. Juan y tú: _____
5. Luis y Andrés _____
6. Luis, mis amigos y yo _____
7. Mis padres y tú _____
8. Mi madre y mi novia _____

SCORE ..../8

28.3 Read the information and complete the sentences with *yo, tú*... only if necessary.

	Pep	Concha	Adriana	Gabriel	Rosita
nacionalidad	española	española	argentina	mexicana	mexicana
ciudad	Barcelona	Murcia	Córdoba	Monterrey	Mérida
ocupación	periodista	estudiante	enfermera	periodista	estudiante

1. PEP: Concha y _yo_ somos españoles. ____ es de Murcia y ____ soy de Barcelona.
2. CONCHA: Gabriel y Rosita son mexicanos. ____ es de Mérida y ____ es de Monterrey.
3. ADRIANA: ¿De dónde son Pep y Concha? GABRIEL: ____ son españoles. ____ es estudiante y ____ es periodista.
4. ROSITA: Concha y ____ somos estudiantes. ____ es española y ____ soy mexicana.
5. GABRIEL: ¿De dónde es Adriana? PEP: ____ es argentina.

SCORE ..../12

28.4 Complete the sentences with the personal pronoun if necessary.

1. –¿De dónde sois Adolfo y _tú_? –____Ø____ somos de Uruguay.
2. –¿Dónde vives _____? –_____ vivo en Murcia. ¿Y _____? –_____ vivo en Granada.
3. –Perdone, ¿de dónde son _____? –_____ somos de Arequipa.
4. _____ estudiamos Medicina.
5. _____ quiero un café, y _____ ¿qué queréis?
6. Mira, Lucía y Ana. _____ son amigas de Blanca.
7. _____ quiero ser abogada, pero mis padres quieren que estudie Medicina.
8. _____ trabajo todo el día y _____ no hacéis nada.
9. ¿Quiere _____ algo, Sr. Hernández?
10. –¿Dónde está Alberto? –_____ está en su habitación.
11. –¿Quién tiene mi diccionario? –_____. Lo necesito unos minutos.
12. Te felicito. _____ eres la ganadora.

SCORE ..../19

29 *Te amo.*
Personal pronouns: direct object

Me, te, lo, and *las* are personal pronouns of the direct object. They are used to refer to people, animals, or objects that are directly affected by the action of the verb (direct object).

- Personal pronouns of the direct object

SINGULAR		PLURAL	
(yo)	me	(nosotros, nosotras)	nos
(tú)	te	(vosotros, vosotras)	os
(usted - hombre) (él) (una cosa masculina)	lo	(ustedes - hombres) (ellos) (cosas masculinas)	los
(usted - mujer) (ella) (una cosa femenina)	la	(ustedes - mujeres) (ellas) (cosas femeninas)	las

BE CAREFUL!

masculine + feminine = masculine plural

*¿Veis mucho **a Almudena y a Luis**? –No, no **los** vemos mucho.*

- We use *me, te, lo...* to refer to people who are present...

    – ***Me** amas, Lola? –Sí, Carlos, te amo.*
    *¿Quién eres? No **te** conozco.*
    – *¿**Nos** recuerdas? **Nos** conocimos en Mallorca. – ¡Ah, sí! Ahora **los** recuerdo.*

... or to people, animals, or objects mentioned previously.

    *¿Dónde está **el pan**? No **lo** encuentro.*
    *–¿Amas **a Ana**? –Sí, **la** amo.*
    *–¿Quieres **este libro**, Héctor? –No, no **lo** quiero. Gracias.*
    *–¿Amas **a tus padres**? –Sí, **los** amo.*

- Placement

  (*no*) *me, te, lo...* + personal form of the verb

    *Yo **os conozco**. Vosotros sois los hermanos de Lucía.*
    *¿Dónde está Marisa? No **la veo**.*
    *–¿Quieres una raqueta? –No, gracias. No **la necesito**.*

29 EXERCISES

29.1 **Complete the sentences with *lo, la, los, las.***

1. ¿Dónde está Andrés? No __lo__ veo.
2. ¿Dónde están las cucharas? No _____ veo.
3. ¿Dónde están tus amigos? No _____ veo.
4. ¿Dónde está el teléfono? No _____ veo.
5. ¿Dónde está Julia? No _____ veo.
6. ¿Dónde están tus padres? No _____ veo.
7. ¿Dónde está la entrada? No _____ veo.
8. ¿Dónde están las naranjas? No _____ veo.

29.2 **Complete with *me, te, lo...***

1. Yo __te__ conozco. Tú eres amigo de Ana.
2. Yo _____ conozco. Ustedes son los padres de Jesús.
3. Yo _____ conozco. Vosotros sois compañeros de Ramón.
4. Yo _____ conozco. Usted es la madre de Rosario.
5. Yo _____ conozco. Ustedes son las tías de Pepe.
6. Yo _____ conozco. Vosotras sois amigas de Raquel.
7. Yo _____ conozco. Usted es el padre de Pedro.
8. Yo _____ conozco. Tú vives en la calle Arenal.
9. Yo _____ conozco. Esa chica es compañera de Pamelita.
10. Yo _____ conozco. Ese hombre trabaja en mi empresa.

29.3 **Complete the answers with *me, te, lo...***

1. –¿Amas a Luis? –Sí, __lo__ amo.
2. –¿Quieres esta foto? –No, no __la__ quiero.
3. –¿Has comprado el periódico? –No, no _____ he comprado.
4. –¿Nos quieres, mamá? –Sí, _____ quiero mucho.
5. –¿Has visto mis zapatillas? –No, no _____ he visto.
6. –¿Me recuerdas? –Sí, _____ recuerdo.
7. –¿Ves mucho a Pepe y a Luisa? –Sí, _____ veo mucho.
8. –¿Te quiere Elena? –No, no _____ quiere.
9. –¿Conoces a los Sres. Pardo? –No, no _____ conozco.
10. –¿Te conocen en esta tienda? –Sí, _____ conocen mucho.
11. –¿Quieres a tus hermanos? –Sí, _____ quiero.
12. –¿Quieres esta corbata? –No, no _____ quiero.
13. –¿Me amas? –Sí, _____ amo.
14. –¿Nos recuerdas? –No, no _____ recuerdo.

29.4 **Order the words to make sentences.**

1. te/no/conozco __No te conozco__.
2. ¿Dónde está Luis? veo/lo/no _____.
3. conozco/yo/os _____.
4. ella/quiere/nos _____.
5. tú/me/necesitas _____.
6. nos/no/llaman _____.
7. la/no/ayudo/yo _____.
8. encuentro/no/lo/ _____.
9. quieren/me/no _____.
10. os/veo/no _____.

67

Me ha regalado un reloj.
Personal pronouns: indirect object

Me, te, and *le* are personal pronouns of the indirect object. They are used to refer to people, animals, or objects that are indirectly affected by action of the verb (indirect object).

*Luis ha regalado un reloj **a Chus**.*
(***A Chus*** is the indirect object.)

*Luis **le** ha regalado un reloj.*

● Personal pronouns of the indirect object

SINGULAR		PLURAL	
(yo)	me	(nosotros/nosotras)	nos
(tú)	te	(vosotros/vosotras)	os
(usted - hombre o mujer)		(ustedes - hombres o mujeres)	
(él, ella)	le	(ellos, ellas)	les
(una cosa masculina o femenina)		(cosas masculinas o femeninas)	

● We use *me, te, le...* to refer to people who are present...

   *–¿Qué **te** ha regalado Luis? –**Me** ha regalado un reloj.*
   *–¿Qué **os** ha preguntado Leonor? –**Nos** ha preguntado dónde vivimos.*

   ...or to replace the people, animals, or objects mentioned previously.

   *–Ayer hablé con **el director**. –¿Qué **le** dijiste?*
   *–¿Has hablado con **Ana**? –Sí, y **le** he preguntado por su padre.*
   *–¿Qué haces con **el perro**? –**Le** estoy cortando el pelo.*
   *Ya funciona **la radio**. **Le** he puesto pilas nuevas.*

● Placement

   (no) me, te, le... + personal form of the verb

   *–¿Qué **te ha dicho** el médico? –**Me ha dicho** que estoy bien.*
   *–¿Qué **te ha preguntado** Charo? –No **me ha preguntado** nada.*

BE CAREFUL!

We usually use *le* or *les* in addition to the name of the person we are referring to when the indirect object is mentioned for the first time.

   *–¿Qué **le** has regalado **a Pedro**? –**Le** he regalado una cartera.*

   *–¿Qué **le** pasa **al gato**? –No **le** pasa nada.*

   ***Les** he comprado unos bombones **a mis hermanas**.*

   *–¿Qué **le** pasa **a la radio**? –No funciona.*

---

30 EXERCISES

30.1. Complete with *me, te, le...*

① ¿Qué **te** ha regalado?
___ ha regalado un pañuelo.
② ___ ha regalado unos libros.
③ ___ ha regalado una bufanda.
④ ¿Qué ___ ha regalado a usted?
⑤ ___ ha regalado perfume.
⑥ ¿Qué ___ ha regalado?
⑦ ___ ha regalado un paraguas.

SCORE ...../8

30.2. Answer as in the example.

1. ¿Qué te han dicho? __No me han dicho nada__.
2. ¿Qué le ha dicho a usted? _____.
3. ¿Qué os ha dado? _____.
4. ¿Qué le han preguntado a Susana? _____.
5. ¿Qué me ha dicho? _____.
6. ¿Qué nos han preguntado? _____.
7. ¿Qué te ha vendido? _____.
8. ¿Qué les han dado a ustedes? _____.
9. ¿Qué le han preguntado a Alberto? _____.
10. ¿Qué les han regalado a tus hijas? _____.
11. ¿Qué le pasa a la televisión? _____.
12. ¿Qué les pasa a estas flores? _____.

SCORE ...../12

30.3. What has Don Ernesto given to his employees? Use the words from the box.

unos bombones   una bufanda   un perfume   una pluma   unos reproductores de MP3

1. __A Rosa le ha dado una bufanda__.
2. _____.
3. _____.
4. _____.
5. _____.

SCORE ...../5

69

31 Se lo he dado.
Indirect and direct object pronouns

At times there are two objects in the sentence, a direct object (OD) and an indirect object (OI). Look at the forms and the order when two object pronouns are used.

¿**Le** has dado **tu teléfono a Rafa**? → ¿**Se lo** he dado?
OI   OD   OI   OI OD

● Forms and order of the pronouns in the sentence

PRONOUNS - INDIRECT OBJECT		PRONOUNS - DIRECT OBJECT
(yo)	me	
(tú)	te	
(usted)	se	lo (singular masculine)
(él, ella)	se	la (singular feminine)
(nosotros, nosotras)	nos	los (plural masculine)
(vosotros, vosotras)	os	las (plural feminine)
(ustedes)	se	
(ellos, ellas)	se	

(indirect + direct)

– ¿**Les** has presentado **tu novia a tus padres**? – No, no **se la** he presentado.
                     OD   OI   OI OD

– ¿**Me** dejas **el coche**? – Lo siento, no **te lo** dejo.
     OI   OD   OI OD

> **BE CAREFUL!**
>
> We use *se* (not *le* or *les*) for *usted, ustedes, él, ella, ellos,* and *ellas.*
> ~~Le~~ *lo he dado.* → **Se** *lo he dado.*

● We use *se* in addition to the noun that we refer to when the indirect object is mentioned for the first time.
   –¿*Qué has hecho con el coche? ¿**Se lo** has regalado a Pepe?* –No, **se lo** he vendido.
   –¿*Dónde está el pollo? –**Se lo** he echado a la sopa.*

31 EXERCISES

31.1▷ **Replace the underlined nouns with pronouns.**

1. He dado la <u>sortija</u> <u>a Andrés</u>. <u>Se la he dado</u>.
2. Han traído <u>los libros</u> <u>a Marta</u>. _____.
3. Han alquilado <u>el piso</u> <u>a Ana y Luci</u>_____.
4. Han hecho <u>un traje</u> <u>a Pedro</u>. _____.
5. He escrito <u>dos cartas</u> <u>a Rosa</u>. _____.
6. Ella ha vendido <u>la moto</u> <u>a Raúl</u>. _____.
7. No has dado <u>las naranjas</u> <u>a Pilar</u>. _____.
8. Habéis roto <u>las gafas</u> <u>al profesor</u>. _____.
9. Han echado <u>agua</u> <u>a las plantas</u>. _____.
10. Han curado <u>la pata</u> <u>al perro</u>. _____.

SCORE ....../10

31.2▷ **Complete the answers with *me, te, se...* and *lo, la, los, las*.**

1. –¿Quién te ha regalado esos bombones? –<u>Me</u> <u>los</u> ha regalado Anita.
2. –¿Quién les ha prestado el dinero a tus padres? –_____ _____ ha prestado Juan.
3. –¿Quién os ha enviado ese paquete? –_____ _____ ha enviado mi tía Rosa.
4. –¿Quién me envía estas flores? –_____ _____ envía Raúl.
5. –¿Quién le ha comprado ese libro a Elvirita? –_____ _____ ha comprado su padre.
6. –¿Quién le ha regalado esa corbata, Antonio? –_____ _____ ha regalado mi mujer.
7. –¿Quién les ha enseñado el museo a ustedes? –_____ _____ ha enseñado un guía turístico.
8. –¿Quién le ha regalado esos pendientes, doña Julia? –_____ _____ ha regalado mi marido.
9. –¿Quién os ha vendido el mueble? _____ _____ ha vendido Ramón.
10. –¿Quién nos ha hecho la sopa? _____ _____ ha hecho Alberto.

SCORE ....../20

31.3▷ **Answer the questions.**

1. –¿Te ha dado Pepe el regalo? –<u>No, no me lo ha dado</u>.
2. –¿Os ha prestado Pablo el dinero? –Sí, _____.
3. –¿Les ha presentado Sara su novio a sus padres? –No, _____.
4. –¿Le ha enseñado a usted su casa? –Sí, _____.
5. –¿Nos ha traído el camarero la comida? –Sí, _____.
6. –¿Les ha presentado sus amigos a sus padres? –Sí, _____.
7. –¿Te ha presentado a sus padres? –No, _____.
8. –¿Le ha vendido Jesús su coche a Antonia? –No, _____.
9. –¿Les ha enseñado a ustedes los cuadros? –Sí, _____.
10. –¿Me ha traído Rita las entradas? –Sí, _____.
11. –¿Le has cortado el pelo al perro? –Sí, _____.
12. –¿Le has echado sal a la sopa? –No, _____.

SCORE ....../12

31.4▷ **Write sentences with the words given and the necessary pronouns.**

1. –¿Qué has hecho con el diccionario? (¿has dejado, a Marta?) <u>¿Se lo has dejado a Marta?</u>.
   –(sí, he dejado) <u>Sí, se lo he dejado</u>.
2. –¿Qué has hecho con tus apuntes? (¿has dejado, a Pablo?) _____
   –(no, no he dejado) _____.
3. –¿Qué has hecho con el piso? (¿has alquilado, a unos amigos?) _____.
   –(sí, he alquilado) _____.
4. –¿Dónde están los huesos? (¿has dado, al perro?) _____.
   –(sí, he dado) _____.
5. –¿Qué pasa con tu novia? (¿has presentado, a tus padres?) _____.
   –(no, no he presentado) _____.

SCORE ....../10

71

32 *lo/la/le*
Contrasting the personal pronouns

- *Lo, la, los,* and *las* are used as direct objects of the verb to refer to people, animals, or objects mentioned previously.

> ¿Me dejas el coche?
> No puedo. **Lo** necesito.

▶ UNIT 29: Personal pronouns: direct object

	SINGULAR	PLURAL
MASCULINE	*lo*	*los*
FEMININE	*la*	*las*

–¿Me dejas **el diccionario**? –No puedo. **Lo** necesito.

–¿Amas a **Juan**? –Sí, **lo** amo.

–¿Me dejas **la pluma**? –No puedo. **La** necesito.

–¿Quieres a **tus padres**? –Sí, **los** quiero.

BUT: Some people use *le* and *les* rather than *lo* and *los* to refer to people.

> –¿Amas a **Juan**? –Sí, **le** amo.
> –¿Quieres a **tus padres**? –Sí, **les** quiero.

BE CAREFUL!

> –¿Me dejas el diccionario? –No puedo. ~~Le~~ necesito. → –¿Me dejas el diccionario? –No puedo. **Lo** necesito.
> –Di a Sofía que ~~le~~ llaman por teléfono. → –Di a Sofía que **la** llaman por teléfono.

- *Le* (singular) and *les* (plural) are used as an indirect object of a verb to refer to people (men or women), animals, or objects (masculine or feminine).

> ¿Qué le pasa?
> **Le** duelen las muelas.

▶ UNIT 30: Personal pronouns: indirect object

–¿Qué **le** has regalado **a Pedro**? –**Le** he regalado una cartera.

–¿Y **a María**? –**Le** he regalado unos pendientes.

A **Elena le** duele la cabeza.

BE CAREFUL!

> A María ~~la~~ he regalado unos pendientes. → A María **le** he regalado unos pendientes.
> A Juan ~~lo~~ han regalado un disco. → A Juan **le** han regalado un disco.
> Ya funciona la radio. ~~La~~ he puesto pilas nuevas. → Ya funciona la radio. **Le** he puesto pilas nuevas.

– *le, les* → *se* when there are two pronouns.

> –¿**Le** has dado la carta a Joaquín? –Sí, **se la** he dado.
> –¿**Les** has enseñado las notas a tus padres? –Sí, **se las** he enseñado.

BE CAREFUL!

> –¿Le has prestado el diccionario a Lu? –Sí, ~~le~~ lo he prestado. → –Sí, **se** lo he prestado.

- *Lo* is also used as a direct object of a verb to refer to an idea or a fact.

> –¿Dónde vive Juan? –No **lo** sé.
> –Aurora se casa. –Se **lo** he dicho a Pili.

32.1 **Circle the correct answer in each case.**

1. –¿Quieres este libro? –No, no (*le*/*lo*) quiero. Gracias.
2. –¿Me dejas el lápiz? –No puedo. (*Le/Lo*) necesito.
3. –¿Quieres a Ana? –Sí, (*la/le*) quiero.
4. –¿Ha visto usted mis gafas? –No, no (*las/les*) he visto.
5. –¿(*La/Le*) has regalado tu chaqueta a Luisa? –No, no (*se/le*) (*la/le*) he regalado. (*Se/Le*) (*la/le*) he vendido.
6. –¿Han visto ustedes a mis padres? –No, no (*les/los*) hemos visto.
7. (*Le/La*) he prestado cien euros a Ivana.
8. –¿(*Les/Los*) has dejado el coche a tus hermanos? –No, no (*se/les*) (*le/lo*) he dejado.
9. –¿Has visto a mis hermanas? –Sí, (*las/les*) he visto.
10. Inés, (*la/le*) llaman por teléfono.
11. –¿Quieres ver a Andrés? –No, no (*le/lo*) quiero ver.
12. (*Les/Los*) he comprado una televisión a mis padres.
13. (*La/Le*) dije a Juana que no tengo dinero.
14. Ayer (*la/le*) vi en el parque, Elisa.
15. –¿Qué (*la/le*) pasa a Elsa? –(*La/Le*) duele la cabeza.

SCORE ....../22

32.2 **Indicate if the sentence is correct (C) or incorrect (I). Correct the wrong ones.**

1. –¿Has visto a Lola? –Sí, le he visto. __I__ __Sí, la he visto__
2. –¿Necesitas el diccionario? –No, ahora no le necesito. ____ _____.
3. –¿Tienes el periódico? –No, hoy no lo he comprado. ____ _____.
4. –¿Dónde está Andrés? –No sé. No le he visto. ____ _____.
5. –Sra. Hernando, le llaman por teléfono. ____ _____.
6. –¿Quieres mis gafas? –No, gracias. No las necesito. ____ _____.
7. –¿Qué sabes de Marta y Antonio? –Están bien. Ayer los vi en la universidad. _____ _____.
8. –¿Dónde están Inés y María? Hoy no les he visto. ____ _____.
9. –¿Conoces a mis padres? –Sí, les conocí en una fiesta. ____ _____.
10. –Déjame los libros de Griego. –No puedo. Les necesito. ____ _____.

SCORE ....../10

32.3 **Complete the sentences with *lo, la, los, las, le, les*, or *se*.**

1. –¿Has visto a Juana? –Sí, __la__ he visto.
2. _____ he regalado unos bombones a Sarita.
3. –¿Has llamado a tu padre, Héctor? –Sí, _____ he llamado.
4. ¿Qué _____ has dicho a la profesora?
5. –¿_____ has regalado tus discos a Enrique? –Sí, _____ _____ he regalado.
6. –¿Has visto a Concha? –No, hoy no _____ he visto.
7. A Pili _____ duelen las muelas.
8. –¿Qué _____ has comprado a tus padres? –A mi padre _____ he comprado un libro y a mi madre _____ he comprado un pañuelo.

SCORE ....../12

32.4 **Use the correct pronouns to complete the sentences.**

1. –¿__Le__ has dicho a Juan que necesito el coche? –Sí, ____ ____ he dicho, pero él también ____ necesita.
2. –¿Sabes que me voy a Colombia? –No, no ____ sabía.
3. –¿Es verdad que Ángela es muy inteligente? –____ es, pero no ____ parece.
4. –¿Sabe papá que necesito dinero? –____ sabe, pero dice que ____ ____ pidas luego.
5. No ____ entiendo. ____ he ofrecido ayuda a Teresa, pero no ____ ha aceptado.
6. –¿Sabes que Ana es escritora? –Sí ____ sé.
7. –Juan y Lola se van a casar. – ____ sabía. Él ____ quiere mucho.
8. –Se ha muerto el perro de Nati. –____ siento. Yo ____ quería mucho.

SCORE ....../18

33 *me ducho*
Reflexive pronouns

Me ducho todos
los días.

Ricardo se afeita
todas las mañanas.

Me and *se* are reflexive pronouns. They are used to indicate that the action of the verb (*ducharse, afeitarse*) is received by:

– the same person that does it.

Me ducho.

– a part of the body or a person's clothes.

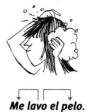

Me lavo el pelo.

Nos ponemos una bata para trabajar.

● Reflexive pronouns

(yo)	me	(nosotros, nosotras)	nos
(tú)	te	(vosotros, vosotras)	os
(usted)	se	(ustedes)	se
(él, ella)	se	(ellos, ellas)	se

Compare:

Me afeito todas
las mañanas.

Ruth se viste después de desayunar.
Antón y yo nos quemamos con unas cerillas.

Afeito a unas
veinte personas
todas las
mañanas.

Ruth viste a los niños después de desayunar.
Ayer **quemamos unos troncos** en la chimenea.

33 EXERCISES

33.1. **Circle the correct answer in each case.**

1. (Me/Ø) ducho todos los días.
2. Mi profesora (se/Ø) pone una bata en clase.
3. Luisa (se/Ø) baña a los niños por la noche.
4. Roberto y Pablo (se/Ø) acuestan siempre tarde.
5. ¿A qué hora (te/Ø) acuestas a los niños?
6. No (nos/Ø) levantamos nunca temprano.
7. Los domingos (me/Ø) lavo el pelo a Ana.
8. ¿Dónde (os/Ø) bañasteis ayer?
9. María (se/Ø) mira mucho al espejo.
10. ¿Cuándo (te/Ø) afeitas?

SCORE ....../10

33.2. **Complete the sentences with *me, te, se*... only when necessary.**

1. Rosa _se_ cortó con un cuchillo ayer.
2. Sandra ___ mira mucho al espejo.
3. Juan ___ cortó el pan con su cuchillo.
4. No ___ mires tanto al espejo, Saúl.
5. ¿Cuándo ___ duchan los niños?
6. Mi hermana y yo ___ quemamos cocinando.
7. Roberto ___ ha quemado las cartas de Aurora.
8. Alicia ___ rompió una pierna esquiando.
9. ¿Quién ___ ha tirado mis gafas a la basura?
10. ¿Por qué ___ pone usted el sombrero?
11. Mira. (Yo) ___ veo en el agua.
12. ¿Qué ___ ves en el agua?
13. ¿Cuándo ___ lavas el pelo, Sonia?
14. ¿Vosotros ___ afeitáis todos los días?
15. Alicia ___ ha roto la silla.

SCORE ....../15

33.3. **Complete the sentences with *me, te, se*... when necessary.**

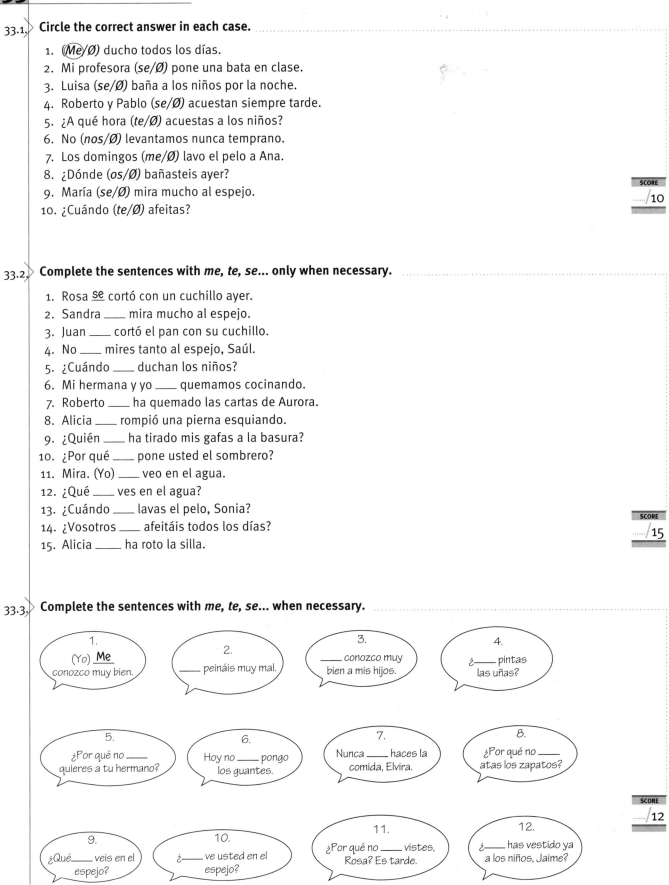

1. (Yo) _Me_ conozco muy bien.

2. ___ peináis muy mal.

3. ___ conozco muy bien a mis hijos.

4. ¿___ pintas las uñas?

5. ¿Por qué no ___ quieres a tu hermano?

6. Hoy no ___ pongo los guantes.

7. Nunca ___ haces la comida, Elvira.

8. ¿Por qué no ___ atas los zapatos?

9. ¿Qué ___ veis en el espejo?

10. ¿___ ve usted en el espejo?

11. ¿Por qué no ___ vistes, Rosa? Es tarde.

12. ¿___ has vestido ya a los niños, Jaime?

SCORE ....../12

34 *para mí, conmigo...*
Personal pronouns with prepositions

Toma. Es **para ti**.
¿**Para mí**? Gracias.

Irene, ¿quieres venir al cine **conmigo**?

¿Has visto a Luis? Quiero hablar **con él**.

● Prepositions + pronouns

PREPOSITIONS		PRONOUNS
a		mí
con		ti
de		usted
en	+	él, ella
para		nosotros, nosotras
por		vosotros, vosotras
sin		ustedes
...		ellos, ellas

BUT:

con + mí→ conmigo
con + ti → contigo

*No pueden vivir **sin mí**.*
*Estamos hablando **de ti**.*
*Hay una llamada **para usted**.*
*¿Has visto a Luis? Quiero hablar **con él**.*
*¿Dónde está Dana? Esto es **para ella**.*
***A nosotras** no nos gusta.*
*¿Puedo jugar **con vosotros**?*
*Tengo algo **para ustedes**.*
*¿Dónde están los gatos? Tengo algo de comida **para ellos**.*

*¿Quieres venir al cine **conmigo**?*
*Soy muy feliz **contigo**.*

● Remember that the pronouns are used to refer to a person who is present...

Mi perro viaja siempre **conmigo**.

Es un paquete **para usted**.

... or to replace a person, animal, or object mentioned previously.

*–Ya no tengo **coche**. –¿Qué has hecho **con él**?*
*Arregla **la televisión**, por favor. Me aburro **sin ella**.*

BE CAREFUL!		
entre		
excepto	+	yo
menos		tú

Todos hablan idiomas **menos yo**.

*Siéntate aquí, **entre Ivana y yo**.*
*Saben nadar todos **excepto yo**.*

34 EXERCISES

34.1 Complete the sentences using pronouns.

① Para _ti_.
② Para _____.
③ Estoy enfadada con _____.
④ Para _____.
⑤ ¿Está Carolina con _____?

⑥ ¿Es para _____? Gracias.
⑦ Buenos días, don Salvador. Me gustaría hablar con _____
⑧ Está hecha por _____
⑨ ¿Para _____? Gracias.
⑩ ¿Quieres venir al cine con _____?

34.2 Complete the sentences with the correct pronoun.

1. ¿Has visto a Adolfo? Quiero hablar con _él_.
2. ¿Has visto a Petra? Quiero hablar con _____.
3. ¿Has visto al señor Carmona? Tengo algo para _____.
4. Antonio te está buscando. Quiere hablar con _____.
5. ¿Dónde están Pepe y Susana? Mercedes quiere hablar con _____.
6. Aurora nos está buscando. No puede estar un momento sin _____.
7. Mi jefe me necesita. No sabe hacer nada sin _____.
8. Felipe me está buscando. Tiene algo para _____.

34.3 Complete the sentences with yo, mí, –migo or tú, ti, –tigo.

1. Estoy triste. Luisa no quiere salir con _migo_.
2. Lo siento, Jaime. Han aprobado todos menos _____.
3. Toma, un regalo para _____ de parte de Ana.
4. El perro viene con _____ a todas partes.
5. ¿Quién va a ir con _____ al médico, Lucas?
6. ¿Esto es para _____? Gracias.
7. Ven con _____, por favor. Necesito ayuda.
8. ¿Está Berta con _____, María?

34.4 Circle the correct answer in each case.

1. Se divierten todos excepto (mí/**yo**).
2. Toma. Este disco es para (ti/tú).
3. Ven. Siéntate junto a (mí/yo).
4. Luisa se sienta entre Jorge y (mí/yo).
5. ¿Quieres venir (conmigo/con yo), Sonia?
6. Sebastián se sienta delante de (mí/yo).
7. A todos les gusta el pescado menos a (mí/yo).
8. Han leído todos el Quijote menos (mí/yo).
9. Jorge siempre se pone detrás de (ti/tú)
10. En casa cocinan todos menos (tú/ti).

35 *que, donde*
Relative pronouns

Que is a relative pronoun. It is used to **add information** about a previous noun without mentioning it again.

Tengo una amiga. Mi amiga vive en Canadá.
↓
*Tengo **una amiga que vive en Canadá**.*

Mira los cuadros. Los cuadros los ha pintado Miguel.
↓
*Mira **los cuadros que ha pintado Miguel**.*

Conozco a un médico. El médico trabaja en el Hospital Internacional.
↓
*Conozco a **un médico que trabaja en el Hospital Internacional**.*

– In some cases, the information is used to **identify** the noun that we are referring to.

*– ¿Quién es Begoña? –Es **la chica que está bailando** con Pedro.*

***El coche que está delante del banco** es el mío.*

– In other cases, it is used to **define** the noun that we are referring to.

*Un carnicero es **una persona que vende carne**.*

● *Que* is used to refer to people, animals, or objects.

***Las chicas que** conocimos ayer son de Córdoba.*

*El cóndor es **un ave que** procede de América del Sur.*

*No me gusta **el libro que** estoy leyendo.*

● We can use *donde* (= en el que, en la que, en los que, en las que) to refer to places.

*Ese es **el banco donde** trabaja Alfonso.*

*Hemos visitado **el pueblo donde** veranea Helga.*

BUT: *Ese es **el hotel d̶o̶n̶d̶e̶** recomienda la guía.* → *Ese es **el hotel que** recomienda la guía.*

78

35.1. **Join the two sentences with *que*.**

1. Tengo un perro. Juega al fútbol. _____Tengo un perro que juega al fútbol_____.
2. Me gusta mucho el libro. Lo estoy leyendo. _____Me gusta mucho el libro que estoy leyendo_____.
3. Conozco a unos actores. Dan clases de teatro. _____.
4. Estamos comiendo una paella. La ha preparado Marisa. _____.
5. No me gustó la película. La vimos ayer. _____.
6. Tengo un amigo. Vive en Guatemala. _____.
7. Usa el bolígrafo. Está en la mesa. _____.
8. Paco sale con una chica. La chica es piloto. _____.
9. Trabajo en una tienda. Está en el centro de Madrid. _____.
10. Tengo una tortuga. Tiene doce años. _____.
11. Alicia trabaja en una empresa. Exporta guitarras. _____.
12. Ayer se estropeó la lavadora. La compré el año pasado _____.
13. Tengo una vecina. Es enfermera _____

SCORE ...... /13

35.2. **Identify the people in the drawing. Use *chico* or *chica*.**

1. _____Elisa es la chica que_____ está tocando el piano.
2. _____ está cantando.
3. _____ está viendo la tele.
4. _____ está bailando.
5. _____ está leyendo.
6. _____ está escuchando música.

SCORE ...... /6

35.3. **Write the answers with the words in parentheses and *que*.**

1. ¿Quién es Roberto? (Un chico. Lo conocí en el parque.) _____Un chico que conocí en el parque_____.
2. ¿Qué es un abstemio? (Una persona. No bebe alcohol.) _____.
3. ¿Qué le has regalado a Cristóbal? (Un cuadro. Lo he pintado yo.) _____.
4. ¿Quién hace tanto ruido? (Unos obreros. Están arreglando la calle.) _____.
5. ¿Quién es Hans? (Un chico. Vive en el sexto.) _____.
6. ¿Qué es un ateo? (Una persona. No cree en Dios.) _____.
7. ¿Qué es un "canguro"? (Una persona. Cuida niños) _____.
8. ¿Qué es una llama? (Un animal. Procede de los Andes) _____.
9. ¿Qué es un políglota? (Una persona. Habla muchos idiomas) _____.

SCORE ...... /9

35.4. **Circle the correct answer in each case.**

1. ¿Cómo se llama el hotel (*que*/*donde*) os alojáis?
2. Ese es el hotel (*que*/*donde*) nos recomendó la agencia.
3. Una farmacia es un lugar (*que*/*donde*) venden medicinas.
4. La farmacia (*que*/*donde*) está en la esquina está cerrada.
5. El banco (*que*/*donde*) trabaja Fredi es árabe.
6. Vivo en una casa (*donde*/*que*) tiene tres pisos.

SCORE ...... /6

35.5. **Complete the sentences with *que* or *donde*.**

1. Esta es la calle _____donde_____ tuve el accidente.
2. Ese es el hotel _____ está Albert.
3. Quiero un piso _____ tenga tres habitaciones.
4. Estamos en un hotel _____ tiene cuatro estrellas.
5. Esa es la agencia _____ compré los billetes.
6. Esa es la agencia _____ nos recomendó Juan.

SCORE ...... /6

36 ¿quién?, ¿qué?
Interrogatives (1)

¿**Quién** vive en esa casa?

Un actor famoso.

¿**Qué** va a tomar?

Un café, por favor.

¿Quién? and *¿qué?* are interrogatives. They are used to ask for information about people, animals, or objects.

(preposition: *a, con, de...* +)	*quién, quiénes* *qué*

> –¿**Quién** ha llamado por teléfono? –Alfonso.
> –¿**Quiénes** son los ganadores? –Marisa y José.
> –¿**De quién** es el diccionario? –De James.
> –¿**Para quién** es esta carta? –Para Marta.
> –¿**Con quién** vives? –Con unas amigas.
> –¿**Qué** vende esa señora? –Fruta.
> –¿**De qué** es la mesa? –De madera.
> –¿**Con qué** has hecho el caldo? –Con pescado.

● We use *¿quién?* (singular) or *¿quiénes?* (plural) to ask about people.

> –¿**Quién** es esa señora? –Es mi profesora de piano.
> –¿**Quiénes** son los hermanos de Mercedes? –Los que están en la mesa del centro.
> –¿**Quién** ha roto el cristal? –Jesús.
> –¿**Con quién** está hablando Pablo? –Con un vecino.

● We use *¿qué?* to:
   – ask about objects, actions, or situations.

> –¿**Qué** tienes en la mano? –Unas monedas.
> –¿**Qué** hacéis? –Estamos estudiando un poco.
> –¿**De qué** están hablando? –De fútbol, como siempre.
> –¿**Qué** pasa? –Ha habido un accidente.

   – ask about the **definition** of a person, animal, or object.

> –¿**Qué** es un políglota? –Una persona que habla muchos idiomas.
> –¿**Qué** es una llama? –Es un animal originario de los Andes.
> –¿**Qué** es un termómetro? –Es un instrumento para medir la temperatura.

BE CAREFUL!

Notice the word order in the questions:

¿(*a, con, de...* +) *quién, quiénes, qué* + verb (+ subject) (+ objects)?

¿**Qué** pasa?	¿**De qué** habláis?
¿**Qué** quiere Raúl?	¿**Quién** es tu hermano?
¿**De quién** es este boli?	¿**A quién** dio Paco la llave?
¿**Quién** vive aquí?	¿**Quién** ha roto el cristal?
¿**Con quién** fuiste al cine?	¿**Qué** hiciste ayer?

36.1. Complete the questions with *quién, quiénes,* or *qué.*

1. ¿_Qué_ quieres?
2. ¿_____ es tu profesor?
3. ¿_____ son las amigas de Ana?
4. ¿_____ llevas en la bolsa?
5. ¿_____ tiene mi diccionario?
6. ¿_____ te dijo Sofía?
7. ¿_____ estás leyendo?
8. ¿_____ fueron los aztecas?
9. ¿_____ significa "mechero"?
10. ¿_____ vive en el quinto?
11. Perdonen, no los conozco ¿_____ son ustedes?
12. ¿_____ van a jugar el domingo?
13. ¿_____ viste anoche en la tele?
14. ¿_____ es Jacinto?
15. ¿_____ estáis haciendo?
16. ¿_____ te ha hecho ese regalo?

36.2. Make questions about the underlined information.

1. −Ayer estuve con Águeda. −¿_Con quién_ estuviste ayer?
2. −Esa silla es de plástico. −¿_____ es esa silla?
3. −Alfonso quiere comprarse un cedé. −¿_____ quiere comprarse Alfonso?
4. −Estas gafas son de Pablo. −¿_____ son esas gafas?
5. −Georgina está trabajando con su madre. −¿_____ está trabajando Georgina?
6. −Han ganado Eduardo y Marisa. −¿_____ han ganado?
7. −Mira. Esos chicos están bailando. −¿_____ están haciendo esos chicos?
8. −Belinda no quiere a Ariel. −¿_____ no quiere Belinda?
9. −Estas flores son para mi abuela. −¿_____ son esas flores?
10. −Ayer vino Adela. −¿_____ vino ayer?

36.3. Order the words in the questions.

1. ¿tiene / en la mano / Julián / qué? _¿Qué tiene Julián en la mano?_
2. ¿quién / este abrigo / es / de? _¿De quién es este abrigo?_
3. ¿ese anillo / para / es / quién? _____
4. ¿anoche / pasó / qué? _____
5. ¿quién / esa bolsa / de / es? _____
6. ¿lleva / qué / en la cabeza / Luis? _____
7. ¿la puerta / qué / has abierto / con? _____
8. ¿está escribiendo / una novela / quién? _____
9. ¿vio / quién / el accidente? _____
10. ¿es / la sopa / qué / de? _____

36.4. Make questions to ask more information.

1. Juan ha invitado a alguien. _¿A quién ha invitado Juan?_
2. Luis ha comprado algo. _____
3. Alguien ha llamado. _____
4. Ayer pasó algo. _____
5. Rosa va a ver a alguien. _____
6. Están hablando de algo. _____
7. Juan está estudiando con alguien. _____
8. Los niños tienen algo. _____
9. Sofía está hablando con alguien. _____
10. María está buscando algo. _____

37 ¿cuál?, ¿qué?
Interrogatives (2)

¿**Cuál** es tu coche?

El que tiene muchas pegatinas.

¿**Cuáles de estos países** no tienen costa: Uruguay, Paraguay, Bolivia...?

¿Cuál? and ¿cuáles? are interrogatives. They are used to ask for information about people, animals, or objects.

(preposition: *a, con, de...* +)	cuál, cuáles	
	cuál, cuáles + de +	estos, estas, esos... (+ noun)
		mis, tus + noun
		los + noun
		nosotros, vosotras, ustedes, ellos...

–¿**Cuál** es tu color preferido? –El blanco. –¿**Cuáles** son tus deportes preferidos? –El tenis y la natación.
–Tengo cuatro hermanas. –¿A **cuál** quieres más?
–¿**Cuál de estas ciudades** está en Argentina: Tucumán, Guayaquil o Arequipa? –Tucumán.
–¿**Cuál de tus hermanos** vive en La Habana? –Iván.   –¿**Cuál de vosotros** habla ruso? –Yo.

● We use ¿cuál? (singular) and ¿cuáles? (plural) to ask for information about a specific group of people or objects. The question allows us to choose among the objects in that group.

–¿Tienes un boli? –Sí. Tengo uno azul y otro negro. ¿**Cuál** prefieres? –El negro.
–¿**Cuál de esas chicas** es la hermana de Toni? –La del pelo largo.
–¿**Cuál** es el río más largo del mundo? –El Nilo.
–¿**Por cuál de estas ciudades** pasa el Ebro: Barcelona, Zaragoza o Valencia? –Por Zaragoza.
–¿**Cuál** es tu profesión? –Soy contable.

– We can also use *qué* + noun to ask for information about a specific group of people or objects.

¿**Qué libro** prefieres: el de Borges o el de Cortázar?
–¿**Qué médico** te ha visto? –La doctora Martín.
–¿**De qué color** es? –Azul.

¿**En qué ciudad española** está la Puerta de Alcalá?

Compare:

¿cuál, cuáles + de + estos, mis, los + noun?	¿Qué + noun?
¿**Cuál de estos países** tiene frontera con Colombia: Panamá, Bolivia o Costa Rica?	¿**Qué país** centroamericano tiene frontera con Colombia?
¿**Qué de estos países** tiene frontera con Colombia: Panamá, Bolivia o Costa Rica?	¿**Cuál país** centroamericano tiene frontera con Colombia?

● We also use *qué* + noun with the meaning of ¿qué clase de...?, ¿qué tipo de...?

–¿**Qué queso** habéis comprado? / ¿**Qué tipo de queso** habéis comprado? –Queso manchego.
–¿**Qué música** te gusta? / ¿**Qué clase de música** te gusta? –Toda.

BE CAREFUL!

Notice the word order in questions:

¿(a, con, de...+) interrogative + verb (+ subject) (+ objects)?

¿**Cuál de estos libros** quieres?   ¿**Qué camisa** prefieres?
¿**En qué capital sudamericana** está La Casa Rosada?   ¿**Qué poeta famoso** nació en Chile?

37.1. **Join the interrogatives with the rest of the questions.**

Cuál...
Cuáles...
Cuál de...
Cuáles de...

1. ¿ __Cuál de__ esos chicos es el hijo de Guillermo?
2. ¿ _____ es tu bebida preferida?
3. ¿ _____ tus padres nació en Panamá?
4. ¿ _____ tus hermanos nacieron en Ecuador?
5. ¿ _____ ustedes ha estado en la Patagonia?
6. ¿ _____ los dos diccionarios prefieres?
7. ¿ _____ es la montaña más alta del mundo?
8. ¿ _____ son las cinco ciudades más pobladas de América?
9. En _____ estas calles vive Santiago?
10. ¿ _____ son nuestros libros?

SCORE ...... /10

37.2. **Complete the sentences with ¿cuál?, ¿cuáles?, ¿cuál de?, ¿cuáles de?, or ¿qué?**

1. –¿ __Cuál de__ tus hermanos trabaja en Aerolíneas? –Jaime.
2. –¿ _____ es tu comida preferida? –El pescado.
3. –¿ _____ son tus deportes preferidos? –El baloncesto y el tenis.
4. –¿ _____ deportes practicas? –Tenis y natación.
5. ¿A _____ hora empieza el concierto? –A las siete.
6. –¿ _____ es tu película preferida? –*Casablanca*.
7. –¿ _____ tus hermanas vive en Rosario? –Cecilia.
8. –¿En _____ ciudad de México vive María? –En Tijuana.
9. –¿Con _____ líneas aéreas va a viajar Sol? –Con Iberia.
10. –¿ _____ son nuestras habitaciones? –Las tres de la derecha.
11. –¿ _____ vino prefieres? –No bebo.
12. –¿ _____ color te gusta más, el rojo o el verde? –El rojo.
13. ¿En _____ estas ciudades está el Coliseo?
14. –¿Tienes un diccionario? –Sí, tengo estos dos. ¿ _____ quieres?
15. ¿ _____ estos libros son tuyos?

SCORE ...... /15

37.3. **Make questions about the underlined information with ¿qué?, ¿qué tipo de?, ¿qué clase de?, ¿cuál?, or ¿cuál de?**

1. A Juan le gusta la música <u>clásica</u>. ¿ __Qué música / Qué tipo de música / Qué clase de música__ le gusta a Juan?
2. Mi hermano <u>Roberto</u> vive en California. ¿ __Cuál de tus hermanos__ vive en California?
3. Sara prefiere el jersey <u>verde</u>. ¿ _____ prefiere Sara?
4. Mi hermana <u>Isabel</u> es abogada. ¿ _____ es abogada?
5. Alejandro prefiere los coches <u>grandes</u>. ¿ _____ prefiere Alejandro?
6. Mi tío <u>Paco</u> está en Bogota. ¿ _____ está en Bogota?
7. A Lola le gusta el queso <u>holandés</u> ¿ _____ le gusta a Lola?
8. Me gusta el cuadro <u>de la derecha</u>. ¿ _____ te gusta?
9. La entrenadora <u>de hockey</u> es argentina. ¿ _____ es argentina?
10. Me gusta la comida <u>india</u>. ¿ _____ te gusta?

SCORE ...... /10

37.4. **Order the words of the following questions.**

1. ¿tus padres / cuál / habla / de / español? ¿ __Cuál de tus padres habla español__ ?
2. ¿hora / empieza / a / la película / qué? _____
3. ¿de / esas chicas / cuál / es / Sofía? _____
4. ¿escritor famoso / en Alcalá / qué / nació? _____
5. ¿ciudad española / está / en qué / la Giralda? _____
6. ¿instrumento / toca / qué / Mario? _____

SCORE ...... /6

38 ¿dónde?, ¿cuándo?, ¿cuánto/a/os/as?
Interrogatives (3)

- We use *¿dónde?* to ask for information about a place.

  > –*¿Dónde* vive Graciela?
  > –*En Rosario.*
  >
  > –*¿De dónde* es Amelia?
  > –*De Santander.*

¿Dónde estás trabajando ahora?

En un banco holandés.

  – We use *¿adónde?* when asking about the place where someone or something is going to.

  > –*¿Adónde* vais a ir este verano? –*A Punta del Este.*
  > –*¿Adónde* va este autobús? –*A Argüelles.*

¿Adónde vas?

A la playa.

- We use *¿cuándo?* to ask for information about the time or moment of doing an action.

  > –*¿Cuándo* es tu cumpleaños? –*En enero.*
  > –*¿Cuándo* se casa Sebastián? –*El mes que viene.*

- We use *¿cuánto?*, *¿cuánta?*, *¿cuántos?*, and *¿cuántas?* to ask for information about quantity.

  > –*¿Cuántos años* tiene Rosario? –*Doce.*
  > –*Necesitamos doscientos euros.* –*¿Y cuántos tenemos?*

¿Cuántas horas duerme al día?

Ocho o nueve.

  – *¿Cuánto?*, *¿cuánta?*, *¿cuántos?*, and *¿cuántas?* take the same form (masculine or feminine, singular or plural), as the noun they accompany.

  > *¿Cuánto dinero* necesitas?   *¿Cuánta leche* compro?
  > *¿Cuántos hermanos* tienes?   *¿Cuántas horas* estudias?

  – *¿Cuánto?*, *¿cuánta?*, *¿cuántos?*, *¿cuántas?* can be used on their own when the noun they are referring to has been mentioned previously. They take the same form (masculine or feminine, singular or plural) as the noun they refer to.

  > –*Quiero café.* –*¿Cuánto quiere?*
  > –*¿Cuántos años* tienes? –*Veintitrés. Y tú, ¿cuántos tienes?*
  > –*Necesito pilas para la radio.* –*¿Cuántas necesitas?*

  – We can use *¿cuánto?* on its own when what we are speaking about is clear.

  > –*¿Cuánto vale esa revista?* (= how much money?) –*Cinco pesos.*
  > –*¿Cuánto dura la película?* (= how much time?) –*Hora y media.*
  > –*¿Cuánto pesas?* (= how much weight?) –*Sesenta y cinco kilos.*

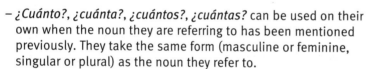

Notice the word order in questions:

   ¿(preposition +) interrogative + verb (+ subject)?

   ¿De dónde eres?   *¿Adónde* vais en verano?   *¿Dónde* vive Graciela?
   ¿Cuándo llegó Gema?   *¿Cuánto dinero* necesitas?

38 EXERCISES

38.1 **Make questions about the underlined information with ¿dónde?, ¿adónde?, or ¿cuándo?**

1. El año pasado estuve en Antigua. −¿ _Cuándo_ estuviste en Antigua?
2. El domingo vamos a ir al campo. −¿_____ vais a ir el domingo?
3. Ese autobús va al centro. −¿_____ va ese autobús?
4. Nos casamos en junio. −¿_____ os casáis?
5. Normalmente estudio por la tarde. −¿_____ estudias normalmente?
6. Ramón está en la playa. −¿_____ está Ramón?
7. Santiago vive en Quito. − ¿_____ vive Santiago?
8. La Giralda está en Sevilla. ¿_____ está la Giralda?
9. Voy a la playa por la mañana. −¿_____ vas a la playa?
10. Martina es de Bolivia. −¿De_____ es Martina?

38.2 **Complete the questions with ¿cuánto?, ¿cuánta?, ¿cuántos?, or ¿cuántas?**

1. −¿ _Cuántos_ años tienes? −Veinticuatro.
2. −¿_____ tiempo necesitas para hacer la comida? −Una hora.
3. −¿_____ semanas tiene un año? −Cincuenta y tres.
4. −¿_____ habitantes tiene Madrid? −Cuatro millones.
5. −¿_____ dinero tienes? −Cincuenta euros.
6. −¿_____ leche hay en la nevera? −Un litro.
7. −¿_____ gente ha venido a la conferencia? −Unas treinta personas.
8. −¿_____ alumnas hay en tu clase? −Doce.
9. −¿_____ monedas antiguas tienes? −Ciento doce.
10. −¿_____ hermanos tienes? −Un hermano y una hermana.

SCORE ___/10

38.3 **Complete the questions with ¿cuánto?, ¿cuánta?, ¿cuántos?, or ¿cuántas?**

1. −Ese reloj cuesta 50 euros. −¿ _Cuánto_ cuesta ese reloj?
2. −Necesito dinero para la compra. −¿_____ quieres?
3. −En mi clase hay muy pocas chicas. −¿_____ hay?
4. −¿_____ se tarda en hacer el test? −Media hora.
5. −Quiero plátanos. −¿_____ quiere?
6. −¿_____ mides? −Un metro setenta.
7. −Necesito entradas para el concierto. −¿_____ quieres?
8. −¿_____ dura el concierto? −Dos horas.
9. −Necesitamos leche. −¿_____ compro?
10. −Teresa tiene muchos hijos. −¿_____ tiene?

SCORE ___/10

38.4 **Order the words to make a question.**

1. ¿los domingos / vais / adónde? _¿Adónde vais los domingos?_
2. ¿está / dónde / mi bolígrafo? _____
3. ¿cuántos / vives / hermanos / con? _____
4. ¿has recibido / postales / cuántas? _____
5. ¿vale / este libro / cuánto? _____
6. ¿trabaja / Sebastián / dónde? _____
7. ¿vive / Alicia / dónde? _____
8. ¿dónde / Peter / de / es? _____
9. ¿personas / hay / en la conferencia / cuántas? _____
10. ¿cuándo / Rocío / se casa? _____
11. ¿para / cuántos / esa / paella / es? _____

SCORE ___/11

39 ¿cómo?, ¿por qué?, ¿para qué?
Interrogatives (4)

● We use *¿cómo?*:

– to ask for information about the way or manner that an action is done.

–*¿**Cómo** conduce Alberto?* –*Bastante mal.*
–*¿**Cómo** has abierto la puerta?* –*Con la llave de Marcela.*

¿Cómo vienes a la academia?

En autobús.

– to ask for information about the state of someone or something.

–*¿**Cómo** está la madre de Susi?* –*Ya está mejor.*

– to ask for information about the characteristics of someone or something.

–*¿**Cómo** es Ivan?* –*Es alto y rubio.*
–*¿**Cómo** son los padres de Aurora?* –*Son muy simpáticos.*
–*¿**Cómo** es la casa de Arturo?* –*Es muy grande. Tiene diez habitaciones.*
–*¿**Cómo** te llamas?* –*Alicia.*

– We can use *¿qué tal?* to ask for information about the way to do an action or the state or characteristics of someone or something.

*¿**Qué tal** conduce Alberto?*   *¿**Qué tal** está la madre de Susi?*   *¿**Qué tal** es la casa de Arturo?*

● We use *¿por qué?* to ask for information about the causes or motives of an action.

–*¿**Por qué** no viniste ayer?* –*Estaba un poco cansada.*
–*¿**Por qué** se ha ido Hugo?* –*Porque tenía prisa.*

Por la cebolla.

¿Por qué lloras?

BE CAREFUL!

In the explanation of the answer we use *porque*.

*¿**Por qué** corres?* –*Porque llego tarde a clase.*

– We can also use *¿por qué no?* to make suggestions.

–*¿**Por qué no** vamos al cine?* –*De acuerdo. ¿Qué quieres ver?*

● We use *¿para qué?*:
– to ask for information about the objective or the purpose of the action.

–*¿**Para qué** quieres la plancha?* –*Quiero plancharme una corbata.*

Para descongelar.

¿Para qué sirve este botón?

– to ask for information about what an object is used for.

–*¿**Para qué** sirve esa máquina?* –*Para moler café.*

● Placement: ¿interrogative + verb (+ subject)?

*¿**Por qué** corres?*   *¿**Por qué** se ríe Juanjo?*   *¿**Para qué** quieres ese libro?*

39 EXERCISES

39.1. **Complete with ¿cómo? and/or ¿qué tal?**

1. ¿__Cómo / Qué tal__ es la novia de Arturo?
2. ¿_____ se llama?
3. ¿_____ has abierto la ventana?
4. ¿_____ canta Susana?
5. ¿_____ está tu padre?
6. ¿_____ vas a la universidad?

39.2. **Complete with ¿por qué?, ¿para qué?, or porque.**

1. –¿__Por qué__ estás en la cama? –__Porque__ no me siento bien.
2. –¿_____ es ese cuchillo? –Para cortar queso.
3. –¿_____ estás cansado? –_____ he trabajado mucho.
4. –¿_____ sonríes? –_____ estoy contenta.
5. –¿_____ quieres dinero? –Para comprar un cuaderno.
6. –¿_____ sirve un CD? –Para guardar datos.

39.3. **Make suggestions with ¿por qué no? and the ideas from the box.**

abrir una ventana	comprar un bocadillo	coger el metro	estudiar más
hacer más ejercicio	mirar en internet	ponerse las gafas	tomar una aspirina

1. Hace calor. _____¿Por qué no abres la ventana?_____
2. Tengo un poco de hambre. _____
3. Estoy un poco gordo. _____
4. Me duele la cabeza. _____
5. Voy a suspender Física. _____
6. No veo la pizarra. _____
7. Hay mucho tráfico. _____
8. Necesito reservar un hotel. _____

39.4. **Make questions about the underlined information.**

1. –Hemos venido en taxi –¿_____Cómo_____ habéis venido?
2. –Mi mujer está mejor. –¿_____ está su mujer, Don Julio?
3. –El novio de Carla es muy vago. –¿_____ es el novio de Carla?
4. –Pilar viene porque quiere hablar. –¿_____ viene Pilar?
5. –No salgo porque hace bastante frío. –¿_____ no sales?
6. –He hecho el examen muy bien. –¿_____ has hecho el examen?
7. –Necesito un cuchillo para pelar la fruta –¿_____ necesitas un cuchillo?
8. –No pude venir anoche. Estaba muy resfriado –¿_____ no pudiste venir anoche?
9. –Mara conduce muy deprisa. –¿_____ conduce Mara?
10. –He venido para ayudarte. –¿_____ has venido?

39.5. **Make questions with ¿por qué?, ¿qué tal?, ¿cómo?, or ¿para qué?**

1. Juan viste muy bien. _____¿Cómo viste Juan? / ¿Qué tal viste Juan?_____
2. Veo a Iván muy enfadado. _____
3. No viajo porque no tengo tiempo. _____
4. Esos pinceles son para pintar. _____
5. No salen porque tienen exámenes. _____
6. Voy al trabajo en metro. _____
7. Necesito dinero para comprar el billete. _____
8. Andrés no viene porque está ocupado. _____

¡qué!
Exclamatories

¡Qué! is an exclamatory. It is used to express different feelings: joy, surprise, admiration, annoyance...

¡Qué bien! He aprobado todo.   **¡Qué divertido** es esquiar!
¡Qué alta es Sarah!
¡Qué grosero es ese chico!   **¡Qué aburrida** es la tele!

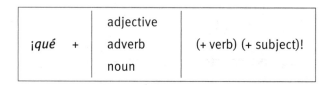

¡qué +	adjective adverb noun	(+ verb) (+ subject)!

¡Qué inteligente!   **¡Qué inteligente** es!   **¡Qué inteligente** es Ana!
¡Qué mal!   **¡Qué mal** conduces!   **¡Qué mal** conduce Pedro!
¡Qué hambre!   **¡Qué hambre** tengo!   **¡Qué hambre** tienen tus hijos!

- We use *¡qué* + adjective (+ verb) (+ subject)! to express feelings:

  – about the characteristics of someone or something: **¡Qué caro!**   **¡Qué inteligente** eres!   **¡Qué agradables** son tus padres!

  – about a state: **¡Qué cansado** estoy!

    • The adjective takes the same form (masculine or feminine, singular or plural) as the person, animal, or object that it refers to.

      ¡Qué alto es **Juan!**   **¡Qué alta** es **Lola!**
      ¡Qué caro es ese **reloj!**   **¡Qué caros** son esos **pantalones!**

- We use *¡qué* + adverb (+ verb) (+ subject)! to express feelings about the way something is done.

    ¡Qué mal!   **¡Qué bien** conduces!   **¡Qué rápido** habla Pedro!

- We use *¡qué* + noun (+ verb) (+ subject)! to express feelings about a situation.

    ¡Qué calor!   **¡Qué sueño** tengo!

- We use *¡qué* + noun + *tan/más* + adjective (+ verb) (+ subject)! to express feelings about the characteristics of someone or something.

    ¡Qué pendientes tan/más caros!   **¡Qué chico tan/más listo!**
    ¡Qué casa tan/más bonita tiene Lola!

- It isn't necesssary to mention the verb or the subject when it is clear who or what we are speaking about.

–A *Pablo le ha tocado la lotería.* –**¡Qué** *suerte (tiene Pablo)!*

40 EXERCISES

40.1. Complete with *¡qué!* and the correct form of the adjectives from the box.

altobarato caliente ~~caro~~ grande guapo largo sucio

1. ¡ _Qué cara_ !
2. _____
3. _____
4. _____

5. _____
6. _____
7. _____
8. _____

SCORE ..../8

40.2. Look at the drawings and write the exclamatory with *¡qué!* and the words from the box.

bien calor frío hambre ~~mal~~ rápido sueño tarde

1. ¡ _Qué mal_ juega!
2. ¡_____ habla!
3. ¡_____ corre!
4. ¡_____ es!

5. ¡_____ hace!
6. ¡_____ hace!
7. ¡_____!
8. ¡_____ tengo!

SCORE ..../8

40.3. Look at the drawings from exercise 40.1 and the nouns from the box and write the exclamatories with *¡qué!* + *más/tan.*

1. ¡ _Qué camisa más/tan cara_ !
2. ¡_____!
3. ¡_____!
4. ¡_____!
5. ¡_____!
6. ¡_____!
7. ¡_____!
8. ¡_____!

~~camisa~~	niños
chica	relojes
chico	sandías
coche	sopa

SCORE ..../8

40.4. Make exclamatories as in the example.

1. Es una chica muy elegante. _¡Qué elegante es!_
2. Hoy hace mucho calor. _____
3. Felipe habla muy bien. _____
4. Tengo mucha sed. _____
5. Arturo conduce muy rápido. _____
6. La vida está cara. _____
7. Isabel es muy tacaña. _____
8. La calle está sucia. _____
9. Iliana cocina mal. _____
10. Ricardo está muy delgado. _____
11. El ejercicio era fácil. _____
12. El camarero es muy lento. _____

SCORE ..../12

soy, eres, es...
Present indicative of *ser*

● *Ser*: present indicative

	ser
(yo)	**soy**
(tú)	**eres**
(usted)	**es**
(él, ella)	**es**
(nosotros, nosotras)	**somos**
(vosotros, vosotras)	**sois**
(ustedes)	**son**
(ellos, ellas)	**son**

¿De dónde eres?
Soy peruana.

¿Qué es eso?
Es un sombrero.

● We use *ser*:

– to identify or define people or objects.
> *Mira. Ese es Andrés.*
> *–¿Qué es eso? –Es una cámara digital.*
> *Cuba es un país americano.*

– to state profession, nationality, or ideology.
> *Soy estudiante.*   *El hermano de Ana es médico.*
> *Chelo es peruana.*   *Laika y yo somos musulmanes.*

– to indicate the relationship between people.
> *Luis y María son amigos.*   *Pedro y yo somos primos.*

¿Quién es Alberto?
Soy yo.

– to express qualities.
> *Diana es muy inteligente.*
> *Estos libros no son muy interesantes.*
> *El coche de Eduardo es rojo.*
> *Ana es rubia.*

– to indicate time, quantity, or price.
> *–¿Qué día es hoy? –Es martes.*
> *En mi clase somos veintidós.*
> *–¿Cuánto es esto? –Son sesenta euros.*

¿Qué hora es, por favor?
Son las cinco.

BE CAREFUL!

Es *la una.*	**Son** *las dos.*

– to say the place or the moment of an event.
> *¿Dónde es la fiesta?*   *El partido es a las diez.*

● We use *ser* + *de* + noun to indicate origin, material, or possession.
> – origin: *–¿De dónde son ustedes? –Somos de Santander.*
> – material: *Esta silla es de plástico.*
> – possession: *–¿De quién es el perro? –Es de Eduardo.*

● In negative sentences, we place *no* before the verb.
> **No somos** *hermanos.*   *Elsa* **no es** *argentina. Es chilena.*

● In questions, we usually place the subject after the verb.
> *¿De dónde es Alicia?*   *¿Qué es eso?*
> *¿Son tus padres de Salamanca?*   *¿De dónde eres (tú)?*

41.1. **Look at the drawings and complete the sentences with *soy, eres, es*...**

① ¿De dónde _sois_? — _____ mexicanos.

② ¿Quién _____ Liz? — _____ yo.

③ _____ hermanas.

④ ¿_____ ustedes médicos? — No, _____ enfermeros.

⑤ ¿De dónde _____? — _____ de Barcelona.

⑥ _____ 25 euros.

ACIERTOS ...../10

41.2. **Complete the questions and answers with *soy, eres, es*...**

1. ¿De dónde _eres_ (tú)?
2. ¿De dónde _____ tus padres?
3. ¿Cuántos _____ en tu familia?
4. ¿_____ profesor?
5. ¿Qué hora _____?
6. ¿Qué día _____ hoy?
7. ¿_____ Rosa y tú hermanos?
8. ¿A qué hora _____ la clase?
9. ¿Cuántos _____ en clase?
10. ¿De quién _____ estos libros?

1. _____ de Quito.
2. _____ de Guayaquil.
3. _____ cuatro.
4. No, _____ estudiante.
5. _____ las tres.
6. _____ jueves.
7. No, _____ primos.
8. _____ a las ocho.
9. _____ doce.
10. _____ de la profesora.

ACIERTOS ...../20

41.3. **Write sentences with *soy, eres, es*... Add *de* if necessary.**

1. Elsa y Tomás / chilenos _Elsa y Tomás son chilenos._
2. Juan y Elisa / Zamora _____.
3. Yo/alto y moreno _____.
4. Esa mesa / cristal _____.
5. Mis padres / jóvenes _____.
6. Mi coche / blanco _____.
7. Mi hermana y yo / no / morenos _____.
8. La fiesta / en mi casa _____.
9. La boda / a las cinco _____.
10. Ese libro / Marta _____.
11. Hoy / no / domingo _____.
12. En clase / doce _____.

ACIERTOS ...../12

41.4. **Complete the sentences with *soy, eres, es*, ... in the affirmative or negative, as needed.**

1. En mi clase _somos /no somos_ diez.
2. Mis amigos y yo _____ estudiantes.
3. Mi cama _____ de madera.
4. (yo) _____ arquitecto.
5. Hoy _____ jueves.
6. Mi profesor/a _____ español/a.
7. La clase _____ a las siete.
8. Mis amigos _____ simpáticos.

ACIERTOS ...../8

41.5. **Write sentences with the given words in the correct order and the correct form of the present of *ser*.**

1. ¿Hoy / qué día? _¿Qué día es hoy?_
2. Sofía / estudiante _____.
3. ¿Tus padres / de Granada? _____.
4. Mis amigos / españoles _____.
5. Ana / no / abogada _____.
6. ¿Lieve / belga? _____.
7. ¿De dónde / Julián y Rosa? _____.
8. ¿Cuándo / tu cumpleaños? _____.

ACIERTOS ...../8

42 estoy, estás, está...
Present indicative of estar

Estoy en Sevilla.

¿Dónde **están** mis llaves?

Están encima de la televisión.

Luis **está** en la cama.
Está enfermo.

● *Estar*: present indicative

	estar
(yo)	**estoy**
(tú)	**estás**
(usted)	**está**
(él, ella)	**está**
(nosotros, nosotras)	**estamos**
(vosotros, vosotras)	**estáis**
(ustedes)	**están**
(ellos, ellas)	**están**

● We use *estar*:

– to indicate the physical situation of someone or something.

> *Mis padres **están** en Caracas.*
> *–¿Dónde **está** Monterrey? –Está en el norte de México.*

> **BE CAREFUL!**

> *estar* + name of person = to be here or there (in the place where the person we are asking about is)
> *¿**Está** Miguel? (Is Miguel here / at home?)*
> *Buenos días. ¿**Está** la señora Vasconcelos? (Is Mrs. Vasconcelos here / in the office?)*

– to indicate some physical temporary states:
sick, cold, tired, exhausted, happy, sad,
bored, angry, good/bad mood, worried, nervous

> ***Estamos** aburridos.*
> *–¿Cómo **estás** hoy, Mónica? –**Estoy** un poco **cansada**.*

– to refer to temporary situation.

> *La casa **está** sucia. (It is usually clean.)*
> *La sopa **está** caliente.*

El jefe **está** de mal humor hoy.

● In negative sentences, we place *no* before the verb.

> *Ana **no está** en casa.*   *Hoy **no estoy** de buen humor.*

Las tiendas **están** abiertas.   Las tiendas **están** cerradas.

● In questions, we usually place the subject after the verb

> *¿**Está** Juan en casa?*   *¿Dónde **está** Guatemala?*

▶ UNIT 56: Present of *estar* + gerund

42.1. Where are they? Complete the sentences with *estoy, estás, está...*

① Estoy _____ en México.

② ¿Dónde _____? _____ en Paraguay.

③ ¿Dónde _____? _____ en París.

④ ¿Dónde _____ en Cuzco? _____ en Perú.

CUZCO

ACIERTOS ...../7

42.2 Complete the sentences with *estoy, estás, está...* and the correct words.

① Estoy resfriado

② ¿Por qué _____?

③ 0—4 _____

④ _____

⑤ _____

⑥ ¿_____ Alberto?

⑦ Hoy _____

⑧ 2—0 ¿Por qué _____?

aburrida
agotado
contento
de buen humor
de mal humor
enfadado
~~resfriado~~
triste

ACIERTOS ...../8

42.3. Describe each drawing using *está* or *están* and the words from the box.

| ~~abierta~~ | apagada | cerrada | limpios | nublado | sucios |

① ② ③ ④ ⑤ ⑥

1. La ventana __está abierta__.
3. Los vasos _____.
5. La televisión _____.

2. La puerta _____.
4. El cielo _____.
6. Los platos _____.

ACIERTOS ...../6

42.4. Complete the dialogues with *estoy, estás, está...* in the affirmative or negative.

1. –¿Cómo __está__ usted, Elisa? –_____ muy bien, gracias.
2. –¿Cómo _____, Charo? –_____ bien. _____ enferma.
3. –¿_____ Luisa? –Sí, pero _____ en la cama.
4. El Machu Picchu _____ en México. _____ en Perú.
5. –¿_____ cansado, Virgilio? –No, _____ cansado. _____ aburrido.
6. –¿Dónde _____ mi chaqueta nueva? –_____ en el armario.
7. –¿Dónde _____ las Islas Galápagos? –_____ en el Pacífico.
8. La sopa _____ está caliente. Caliéntala.
9. ¿_____ en casa, Laura? –No, _____ en casa. _____ en la oficina.
10. –¿Dónde _____ tus padres? –_____ en Honduras.

ACIERTOS ...../22

42.5. Write questions with the present of *estar* and the given words in the correct order.

1. ¿dónde, Teresa? __¿Dónde está Teresa?__
2. ¿Luis, en la oficina? _____
3. ¿cómo, tus padres? _____
4. ¿la sopa, caliente? _____
5. ¿tus padres, en casa? _____
6. ¿dónde, tus hermanos? _____

ACIERTOS ...../6

43 soy alegre / estoy alegre
Contrasting *ser* and *estar*

Compare:

UNIT 41: Present indicative of *ser*

SER

● We use *ser* to speak about normal or permanent features or qualities about someone or something.

María **es muy activa**. (She is usually like this.)

Julián **es alegre**. (He is usually like this.)
El hielo **es frío**.

Sofía **es delgada**.
(She's always been thin.)

Rubén no **es muy elegante**.

UNIT 42: Present indicative of *estar*

ESTAR

● We use *estar* to speak about unusual or temporary characterstics or states about someone or something.

Hoy **está cansada**. (only today)

Hoy no **está alegre**. Está triste.
El café **está frío**.

┃ BUT: **Estar casado.**

● We use *estar* to indicate changes.

Estás muy delgado, Pedro.

● We use *estar* to stress the moment.
Rubén **está muy elegante** con ese traje.

● Some adjectives have different meanings with *ser* or *estar*:

Este perro **es muy malo**. (He is a naughty dog.)

ser malo = badly behaved or bad quality
ser aburrido = one who doesn't know how to have fun
ser bueno = well behaved or good quality
ser listo = intelligent
ser moreno = to have dark hair
ser rico = to have money
No me gusta este libro. **Es** muy malo.
   No quiero salir con Rubén. **Es** muy aburrido.
   El tío de Carlos **es** muy rico. Tiene fábricas.

Pepe **está malo**. (He is sick.)

estar malo = be sick
estar aburrido = has nothing to do for fun
estar bueno = tasty or recovered from illness
estar listo = ready
estar moreno = tan
estar rico = tasty
Felipe está en la cama. **Está** malo.
   Estamos aburridos. ¿Qué podemos hacer?
   Este cordero **está** muy rico.

● We use *ser* to indicate the place or moment of an event.

La boda **es** en la iglesia de Santa Marta, a las cinco.

● We use *estar* to indicate place or position of someone or something.

La iglesia de Santa Marta **está** en la Plaza de Córdoba.

▶ UNIT 56: Present of *estar* + gerund

43.1 **Circle the correct answer in each case.**

1. (*Soy*/*Estoy*)) cansado.
2. Este café (*es*/*está*) muy caliente.
3. Algunas rosas (*son*/*están*) blancas.
4. Esos cristales (*son*/*están*) sucios.
5. Este árbol (*es*/*está*) seco.
6. Ana y Sergio (*son*/*están*) casados.
7. Las margaritas (*son*/*están*) amarillas y blancas.
8. ¡Qué guapa (*eres*/*estás*) con ese sombrero, Lola!
9. Hoy no (*soy*/*estoy*) alegre.
10. Mis tíos (*son*/*están*) muy altos.

ACIERTOS
......./10

43.2 **Complete the sentences with forms of *ser* or *estar*.**

1. Las serpientes ___son___ peligrosas.
2. Este libro _____ muy interesante.
3. La nieve _____ blanca.
4. No os sentéis en esas sillas. _____ sucias.
5. Juan _____ muy guapo con uniforme.
6. La sopa _____ fría. Caliéntala un poco.
7. Los plátanos _____ amarillos.
8. ¡Qué guapo _____ Francisco! Tiene unos ojos grandísimos.
9. Flor y Pili _____ muy guapas con el nuevo peinado.
10. Esa camisa _____ de algodón.

ACIERTOS
......./10

43.3 **Complete the sentences with the present indicative of *ser* or *estar*.**

1. ¿Dónde ___es___ la fiesta?
2. El examen _____ a las diez.
3. ¿Dónde _____ mis gafas?
4. Mañana _____ mi cumpleaños.
5. El examen _____ en el aula 15.

6. El Teatro Real _____ en la Plaza de la Ópera.
7. ¿Dónde _____ la discoteca Futuro?
8. El examen _____ encima de la mesa.
9. El concierto _____ en el Teatro Real.
10. ¿Cuándo _____ la boda?

ACIERTOS
......./10

43.4 **Use forms of *ser* or *estar* to complete the sentences.**

① ¿Estás lista?

② Carlos _____ muy moreno.

③ Felipe _____ muy rico.

④ _____ malo.

⑤ Jorge _____ un poco aburrido.

⑥ Isabel _____ muy morena.

⑦ Esta paella _____ muy rica.

⑧ Ángel y Nieves _____ muy buenos.

⑨ _____ aburridos.

⑩ ¿Qué tal estás, Nacho? Bien gracias, Ya _____ bueno.

ACIERTOS
......./10

tengo, tienes, tiene...
Present indicative of *tener*

- *Tener*: present indicative

	tener
(yo)	**tengo**
(tú)	**tienes**
(usted)	**tiene**
(él, ella)	**tiene**
(nosotros, nosotras)	**tenemos**
(vosotros, vosotras)	**tenéis**
(ustedes)	**tienen**
(ellos, ellas)	**tienen**

*Adela y Jorge **no tienen** hijos.*

- We use *tener* to:

  – indicate possession.

  ¿***Tienes** dinero?*   ***Tengo** un ordenador nuevo.*   *Luis **no tiene** coche.*

  – ask for something (in questions).

  *–¿**Tienes** un lápiz? –Sí, pero lo necesito.*

  – speak about the family.

  *Cristina **tiene** siete hermanos.*   *–¿Cuántos hijos **tenéis**? –**No tenemos** hijos.*

  – describe people, objects, or places.

  *Enrique **tiene** los ojos verdes.*   *El piso **tiene** noventa metros cuadrados.*
  *Mi casa **no tiene** jardín.*   *Madrid **tiene** seis millones de habitantes.*

  – say our age.

  *–¿Cuántos años **tienes**? –Veinticinco.*   *Mis abuelos **tienen** noventa años.*

  – express some physical or emotional temporary states: hunger, thirst, cold, hot, fear, sleep, fever, flu, headache...

  ***Tienes** mala cara. ¿**Tienes** fiebre?*

- In negative sentences, we place *no* before the verb.
  ***No tengo** dinero.*   *Los niños **no tienen** sueño.*

- In questions, we usually place the subject after the verb.
  *¿Cuántos años **tiene** Pedro?*   *¿**Tienen** ustedes perro en casa?*

44 EXERCISES

44.1. Complete the sentences with *tengo*, *tienes*... in the affirmative or negative form.

	JULIO	PEPA Y JORGE		MARGARITA
EDAD	23	28	31	23
HERMANOS	---	una hermana	---	dos hermanos
HIJOS	---	3		---
COLOR DE OJOS	marrones	verdes	negros	marrones

1. MARGARITA: Jorge __tiene__ treinta y un años.
2. JULIO: Margarita y yo _____ veintitrés años.
3. PEPA: _____ veintiocho años. _____ los ojos marrones. Los _____ verdes.
4. JULIO: Jorge y yo _____ hermanos.
5. JORGE: Pepa _____ una hermana.
6. PEPA: Margarita _____ dos hermanos.
7. JORGE: Julio y Margarita _____ hijos. _____ los ojos marrones.
8. PEPA: Jorge y yo _____ tres hijos.

ACIERTOS ..../11

44.2. Complete the questions and the answers with *tengo, tienes* ... in the affirmative or negative.

1. ¿Cuántos años __tienes__?
2. ¿_____ hermanos?
3. ¿Cuántos años _____?
4. ¿_____ hijos?
5. ¿____ novia?
6. ¿Cuántos años _____?
7. ¿_____ piso?
8. ¿Cuántas habitaciones _____?
9. ¿_____ calefacción central?

1. _____ veintinueve.
2. Sí, _____ dos.
3. Veintiocho y veintiséis.
4. No, _____ hijos.
5. Sí. Se llama Laura.
6. Veinticinco.
7. Sí.
8. _____ cuatro en total.
9. No, _____.

ACIERTOS ..../14

44.3. Write sentences with *tengo, tienes*... and the words from the box.

calor	fiebre	frío	hambre	miedo	~~sed~~

① Tengo sed   ② _____   ③ _____   ④ _____   ⑤ _____   ⑥ ¿_____?

ACIERTOS ..../6

44.4. Write sentences with *tengo, tienes*...

1. usted / sueño — ¿Tiene usted sueño?
2. (tú) dinero — ¿_____?
3. (nosotros) no / coche — _____.
4. ustedes / hijos — ¿_____?
5. mis abuelos / doce nietos — _____.
6. usted / una casa grande — ¿_____?
7. (vosotras) muchos amigos ¿_____?
8. ustedes / perro — ¿_____?
9. (tú) un diccionario — ¿_____?
10. mi casa / no / ascensor — _____.
11. (yo) el pelo largo — _____.
12. (vosotros) hijos — ¿_____?

ACIERTOS ..../12

44.5. Write questions with the present of *tener* and the given words in the correct order.

1. ¿coche / ustedes? — ¿Tienen ustedes coche?
2. ¿cuántos años / Miguel? — _____
3. ¿tu casa / piscina? — _____
4. ¿hambre / ustedes? — _____
5. ¿Pedro / frío? — _____
6. ¿cuántos hijos / Rosa? — _____

ACIERTOS ..../6

97

45 Hay un vaso en la mesa.
Present indicative of *haber* (impersonal)

Hay un vaso en la mesa.

Hay cinco alumnos en clase.

No hay leche.

● *Hay* + countable nouns (*vaso, alumno...*)

hay	+ *un, una* + singular countable noun + *uno, una*	**Hay un pájaro** en el balcón. –¿**Hay un hotel** por aquí? –**Hay uno** en la calle Arenal.
hay	(+ *unos, unas; dos, tres...; muchos, pocos...*) + plural countable noun	**Hay naranjas** en la nevera. En mi calle **hay muchos árboles**.
hay	+ *dos, tres...* + *muchos, pocos...*	–¿**Hay muchos cines** en tu barrio? –**Hay tres**. –¿Compro plátanos? –No, hay **muchos**.
¿Cuántos, cuántas + plural countable noun + *hay*?		–¿**Cuántos chicos hay** en tu clase? –**Hay** nueve.

no hay (+ *ningún, ninguna*) + singular countable noun	**No hay ningún hotel** en esta calle. En Santa Marta **no hay aeropuerto**.
no hay (+ *muchos, muchas*) + plural countable noun + *muchos, muchas*	En mi calle **no hay árboles**. En mi barrio **no hay muchos bares**. –¿Cuántas plazas hay en tu barrio? –**No hay muchas**.

● *Hay* + uncountable nouns (*pan, agua...*)

(*no*) hay	(+ *mucho, poco...*) + uncountable noun + *mucho, poco*	**Hay agua** en el suelo. **No hay mucha mantequilla**. –¿**Hay** pan? –No **hay mucho**.
¿Cuánto, cuánta + uncountable noun + *hay*?		*¿Cuánta leche hay* en la nevera?

● We use *hay*:

– to indicate or ask about the existence of something or someone at a certain place.
> ¿**Hay una frutería** por aquí?
> –¿**Hay pan** (in house)? –Sí, **hay dos barras**.

– to ask about the situation of something or someone whose existence is unknown.
> ¿Dónde **hay un estanco**? (I don't know if there is a cigar store.)

Perdone, ¿dónde **hay** un buzón?

Hay uno en esa esquina.

▶ UNIT 46: Contrasting *haber* and *estar*   UNIT 77: Expressions with infinitive (1)

45 EXERCISES

45.1 **What is in the room? Look at the drawing and write sentences with *hay* in the affirmative or negative form.**

1. (*mesa*) Hay una mesa_____.
2. (*espejo*) No hay espejo_____.
3. (*alfombra*) _____.
4. (*sillas*) _____.
5. (*lámpara*) _____.

6. (*televisor*) _____.
7. (*reloj*) _____.
8. (*cuadros*) _____.
9. (*cojín*) _____.
10. (*sillón*) _____.

ACIERTOS ..../10

45.2 **Read the information about Ciudad Nueva and write sentences with *hay* in the affirmative or negative form.**

CIUDAD NUEVA	
1. colegios	5
2. cines	1
3. hospitales	no
4. polideportivos	1
5. parques	2
6. estaciones de ferrocarril	no
7. estaciones de autobús	1
8. hoteles	no
9. iglesias	2
10. bibliotecas	1

1. Hay cinco colegios_____.
2. _____.
3. _____.
4. _____.
5. _____.
6. _____.
7. _____.
8. _____.
9. _____.
10. _____.

ACIERTOS ..../10

45.3 **What is in the fridge? Look at the drawing and write sentences with *hay* in the affirmative or negative form.**

1. (*leche*) Hay leche_____.
2. (*agua*) _____.
3. (*mantequilla*) _____.
4. (*queso*) _____.
5. (*seis huevos*) _____.
6. (*uvas*) _____.
7. (*naranjas*) _____.
8. (*plátanos*) _____.
9. (*zumo de naranja*) _____.
10. (*yogures*) _____.

ACIERTOS ..../10

45.4 **Write sentences with *hay* in the affirmative or negative form.**

1. –¿Dónde (*buzón*) hay un buzón___? –(*uno*) Hay uno___ en la esquina.
2. En mi barrio (*no, metro*) _____.
3. –¿Dónde (*estanco*) _____? –(*uno*) _____ a cien metros.
4. –¿(*muchas tiendas*) _____ en tu barrio? –No, (*no, muchas*) _____.
5. –¿Cuántos (*huevos*) _____ en la nevera? –_____ ninguno.
6. –¿Cuánta (*leche*) _____? –(*un litro*) _____.
7. –¿(*cafetería*) _____ por aquí? –Sí, (*una*) _____ en la Plaza Mayor.
8. –¿Cuántos (*yogures*) _____ en la nevera? –(*tres*) _____.

ACIERTOS ..../15

99

Hay un cine. Está en la calle Mayor.
Contrasting *haber* and *estar*

Compare:

HAY	ESTAR
▶ UNIT 45: Present indicative of *haber* (impersonal) ▌	▶ UNIT 42: Present indicative of *estar* ▌

● We use *hay* to speak about the **existence** of something or someone unknown (new information).

Hay un señor que quiere hablar con usted.
(I don't know who the man is.)

Hay un restaurante nuevo en el barrio.
(I am not familiar with that restaurant.)

● We use *hay* to speak about the existence of an unspecific person or place.

Hay un cine en la calle Monterrey.
En Madrid **hay muchos museos.**

● We use *hay* to ask about the location of something or someone unknown.

Perdone, ¿dónde **hay** una farmacia?

¿Dónde hay una farmacia?
(I don't know of any pharmacies around here.)
¿Dónde hay un restaurante?

● We use *estar* to indicate the **location** of something or someone previously mentioned (known information).

Está en la recepción.

Está en la recepción.
(The man who I spoke about.)

Está en la calle Apodaca.
(The restaurant of which I spoke.)

● We use *estar* to speak about the location of something or someone unique or specific.

El cine América está en la calle Monterrey.
El Museo del Prado está en Madrid.

● We use *estar* to ask about the location of something known.

Oye, Marta, ¿dónde **está** la farmacia de tu tía?

¿Dónde está la farmacia de tu tía?
(I know your aunt has a pharmacy.)
¿Dónde está Casa Pepe?

BE CAREFUL! ▌

With *hay* we don't use *el/la/los/las* or *mi/tu/su/*...

    Hay el ~~Museo de Cera~~ en la Plaza de Colón.
    Hay un museo en la Plaza de Colón. or **El Museo de Cera** está en la Plaza de Colón.

    ¿Dónde hay ~~la parada de~~ autobús?
    ¿Dónde hay una parada de autobús? or **¿Dónde está la parada de autobús más próxima?**

    ~~¿Dónde **hay mis herramientas**?~~
    ¿Dónde hay herramientas? or **¿Dónde están mis herramientas?**
    (I don't know if there are any tools.) (I have tools, but I don't know where they are.)

hay + singular or plural	singular + *está*	plural + *están*
Hay un supermercado en el pueblo. En este pueblo **hay tres bares.**	**El supermercado está** en la plaza.	**Los bares están** en el centro.

46.1 ⟩ **Circle the correct answer in each case.**

1. (*Hay*/*Está*) un paquete para ti. (*Hay*/*Está*) en tu habitación.
2. ¿Cuántos alumnos (*hay/están*) en tu clase?
3. –¿(*Hay/Está*) pan? –Sí, (*hay/está*) en la mesa.
4. –¿(*Hay/Está*) algo para comer? –Sí, (*hay/está*) queso en la nevera.
5. ¿Qué (*hay/está*) en esa caja?
6. ¿(*Hay/Está*) una estación de metro por aquí?
7. La cafetería del hospital (*hay/está*) en el noveno piso.
8. En este edificio (*hay/están*) dos oficinas. (*Hay/Están*) en el primer piso.
9. (*Hay/Está*) un ratón en mi habitación. (*Hay/Está*) debajo de la cama.
10. (*Hay/Están*) muchos museos en Barcelona.

ACIERTOS ...../15

46.2 ⟩ **Choose the correct form and write sentences.**

| ¿Dónde | hay / está / están | una farmacia?
una parada de autobús?
la parada de autobús más próxima?
el Hospital Central?
las ruinas de Tikal?
un banco?
el Banco de Galicia?
los cines Luna? |

1. ¿Dónde hay una farmacia?
2. _____
3. _____
4. _____
5. _____
6. _____
7. _____
8. _____

ACIERTOS ...../8

46.3 ⟩ **Complete the sentences with *hay*, *está*, or *están*.**

1. __Hay__ diez alumnos en mi clase.
2. ¿Dónde _____ la casa de tu abuelo?
3. _____ un cine nuevo en mi barrio. _____ en la calle Casañé.
4. Perdone, ¿_____ la calle 67 por aquí?
5. Mis compañeros _____ en la cafetería.
6. ¿Dónde _____ la parada del 61?
7. _____ un departamento nuevo en la empresa. _____ en el piso cuarto.
8. –¿_____ leche? –Sí, _____ un litro. _____ en la nevera.
9. ¿Dónde _____ una parada de taxis?
10. En mi pueblo _____ dos piscinas. _____ en las afueras.
11. ¿Dónde _____ un buen restaurante?
12. ¿Dónde _____ el hotel La Montaña?
13. ¿_____ una papelería por aquí?
14. _____ unas cartas para usted. _____ en el salón.
15. En mi calle _____ un hotel. _____ cerca de mi casa.
16. ¿Dónde _____ un cenicero?
17. En Bogotá _____ un museo del oro.
18. ¿Dónde _____ mis llaves?
19. En Lima _____ muchos edificios antiguos. _____ todos en el centro.
20. En Ciudad de México _____ mucho tráfico en el centro.

ACIERTOS ...../28

47 *trabajo, trabajas...*
Present indicative: verbs ending in *–ar*

Perdone.
¿**Trabaja** usted aquí?

Llevas un uniforme muy bonito.

Trabaja and *llevas* are forms of the present indicative.

● Forming the present indicative: regular verbs ending in *–ar*

	trabaj-ar
(yo)	trabaj-**o**
(tú)	trabaj-**as**
(usted)	trabaj-**a**
(él, ella)	trabaj-**a**
(nosotros, nosotras)	trabaj-**amos**
(vosotros, vosotras)	trabaj-**áis**
(ustedes)	trabaj-**an**
(ellos, ellas)	trabaj-**an**

Negative sentences: ***No trabajo** los lunes.*

Questions: *¿Dónde **trabaja Héctor**?*

BE CAREFUL!

*dar: **doy**, das, da, da, damos, dais, dan, dan*

  *Soy profesor. **Doy** clases de Física.*

● The present indicative is used for:

– asking or giving information about the present.

  *–¿**Estudias** o **trabajas**? –**Estudio** Física.*
  *El hermano de Alicia **trabaja** en una empresa de informática.*
  *La película **dura** tres horas.*

– speaking about things we do habitually (every day, once a week, always, at times, never).

▶ UNIT 87: Adverbs and expressions of frequency

  *En mi casa **cenamos** muy temprano.*   *Cristina **lleva** siempre vaqueros.*
  *¿**Trabajas** los domingos?*   *Siempre **desayuno** cereales.*
  *Normalmente **pasamos** el fin de semana en el campo.*

– telling general or universal truths.

  *La Tierra **gira** alrededor del Sol.   Los chilenos **hablan** español.*

– describing actions that are happening at the moment of speaking.

  *¿Qué **pasa**?*   *Antonio **lleva** una corbata preciosa.*

¿Qué tocas?

Una obra de Mozart.

▶ UNIT 52: Present indicative: other uses

▶ UNIT 56: Present of *estar* + gerund

47 EXERCISES

47.1 Read the information and complete the sentences with the verbs from the box in the affirmative or negative.

arreglar	dar	estudiar	preparar	trabajar

	ARTURO	JOSÉ	PILAR	MARÍA	ANA	PEDRO
LUGAR DE TRABAJO	taller	hospital	instituto	instituto	Universidad de Sevilla	Universidad de Salamanca
OCUPACIÓN	arreglar coches	preparar comida	clases de Filosofía	clases de Francés	estudiante de Historia	estudiante de Economía

1. ARTURO: _Trabajo_ en un taller. _____ coches.
2. PILAR: María y yo _____ en un instituto. María _____ clases de Francés y yo _____ clases de Filosofía.
3. JOSÉ : _____ en un hospital. _____ comida para los enfermos.
4. PEDRO: Ana y yo _____; somos estudiantes. Ana _____ Historia y yo _____ Economía.

ACIERTOS ...../10

47.2 Complete the sentences with the correct form of the verbs in parentheses in the affirmative or negative.

1. –Yo (*cantar*) _____ en un grupo de *rock* y Ana y Eva (*tocar*) _tocan_ la guitarra.
2. Lalo y yo (*no, viajar*) _____ nunca en avión.
3. ¿(*hablar*) _____ usted español?
4. Mis padres (*pasar*) _____ el verano en Galicia.
5. –¿Quieres un cigarrillo? –Gracias. (*no, fumar*) _____ .
6. Yo solo (*escuchar*) _____ música clásica.
7. Los argentinos (*hablar*) _____ español.
8. ¿A qué hora (*cenar*) _____ ustedes?
9. –Siempre (*tú, llegar*) _____ tarde. –Lo siento.
10. Pepe (*llamar*) _____ a su novia todos los días.
11. Mi mujer y yo (*nadar*) _____ media hora todas las mañanas y en verano (*dar*) _____ largos paseos.
12. Luis y yo (*dar*) _____ clases de Matemáticas en un instituto.

ACIERTOS ...../14

47.3 Complete the questions and answers with the verbs in parentheses.

1. –¿A qué hora (*vosotros, cenar*) _cenáis_ ? –_Cenamos_ a las nueve.
2. –¿Dónde (*tú, pasar*) _____ los veranos? –_____ los veranos en Punta del Este.
3. –¿De qué (*tú, dar*) _____ clase? –_____ clases de Historia.
4. –¿Dónde (*tú, trabajar*) _____ ? –_____ en unos grandes almacenes.
5. –¿Qué (*coleccionar*) _____ usted? –_____ sellos.
6. –¿Qué (*vosotras, estudiar*) _____ ? –_____ español.
7. –¿Qué idiomas (*hablar*) _____ ustedes? –_____ español e italiano.

ACIERTOS ...../14

47.4 Complete the sentences with the verbs from the box in the affirmative or negative.

beber	llamar	llevar (2)	pasar

① Mira a Lucía. _____ un sombrero muy bonito.
② ¿Qué _____ ?
③ ¿Qué _____ en la cabeza?
④ ¿A quién _____ ?
⑤ ¿Qué _____ ?

ACIERTOS ...../5

47.5 Put the words in the correct order.

1. Hans / habla / español ¿ _Habla Hans español_ ?
2. tus padres / trabajan / dónde ¿_____?
3. da clases / Pedro / dónde ¿_____?
4. Carmen / estudia ¿_____?
5. tus amigos / viven / dónde ¿_____?
6. en casa / desayuna / Luis ¿_____?
7. Felipe / estudia / qué ¿_____?
8. llega / Toni / a qué hora ¿_____?

ACIERTOS ...../8

48 *como, comes...*
Present indicative: verbs ending in *–er*

No, gracias. **No como** carne.

¿**Conoces** a Susana?

Como and *conoces* are forms of the present indicative.

- Forming present indicative: regular verbs ending in *-er*

	com-er
(yo)	com-**o**
(tú)	com-**es**
(usted)	com-**e**
(él, ella)	com-**e**
(nosotros, nosotras)	com-**emos**
(vosotros, vosotras)	com-**éis**
(ustedes)	com-**en**
(ellos, ellas)	com-**en**

> Negative sentences: *Luisa **no come** carne.*
>
> Questions: *¿Qué **come** Juan?*

BE CAREFUL!

The **first person** (yo) of the following verbs is irregular:

coger ▸ *cojo*	poner *pongo*	conocer ▸ *conozco*	saber ▸ *sé*
hacer *hago*	traer ▸ *traigo*	parecer ▸ *parezco*	ver ▸ *veo*

Hago gimnasia todas las mañanas.

Te **conozco**. Tú eres Berta.

No **sé** alemán.
No **veo** nada.
Con esta ropa **parezco** más joven.

- Uses of the present indicative: ▸ UNIT 47: Present indicative: verbs ending in *–ar*

  –Speaking about the present.

  *Antonio **lee** muchas novelas policíacas.*   *Julia **sabe** mucha Historia.*

  –Speaking about what we do habitually.

  *–¿Qué **hacéis** los fines de semana? –**Hacemos** excursiones a la sierra.*

  –Speaking about general truths.

  *Los vegetarianos **no comen** carne.*   *Los gatos **ven** en la oscuridad.*

  –Speaking about what is happening at the moment of speaking.

  *–¿Qué **bebes**? –Leche.*   *¿**Ven** ustedes a Lina desde ahí?*

▸ UNIT 52: Present indicative: other uses

EXERCISES

48.1. **Complete the sentences with the correct form of the verbs in parentheses in the affirmative or negative.**

1. ¿A qué hora (*vosotros, comer*) coméis ?
2. (*nosotros, no, ver*) _____ mucho la tele. ¿Cuantas horas al día (*vosotros, ver*) _____ la tele?
3. Los leones (*no, comer*) _____ hierba.
4. ¿(*beber*)_____ usted alcohol?
5. ¿Qué periódico (*tú, leer*)_____?
6. –¿Qué (*vosotros, hacer*) _____ los fines de semana? –(*hacer*) _____ nada especial.
7. –¿(*tú, conocer*) _____ a Maricruz? –No, _____ la _____.
8. Mis padres (*hacer*)_____ un viaje todos los años.
9. (*yo, no, poner*) _____ sal a la carne.
10. Los canguros (*proceder*) _____ de Australia. (*comer*) _____ plantas.
11. ¿(*tú, saber*)_____ esquiar? –No, (*no, saber*)_____ .
12. Guillermo (*no, saber*)_____ hablar italiano.
13. Los pingüinos (*poner*)_____ un solo huevo. Las cigüeñas (*hacer*)_____ sus nidos en lugares altos.
14. Peter (*parecer*)_____ latino. Es muy moreno.
15. –¿(*tú, coger*) _____ el metro a menudo? –No, no lo _____ mucho. (*yo, traer*) _____ el coche todos los días. **ACIERTOS** /24

48.2. **Complete the questions and answers.**

1. –¿(*tú, saber*) Sabes conducir? –Sí, pero no _____ muy bien.
2. –¿Qué (*vosotros, beber*) _____ en las comidas? –Normalmente _____ agua.
3. –¿(*hacer*) _____ usted muchas fiestas? –No, solo _____ una en Navidad.
4. –¿(*saber*) _____ usted hablar inglés? –No, solo _____ hablar español.
5. –¿(*conocer*) _____ usted La Habana? –No, no la _____.
6. –¿(*yo, hacer*) _____ bien el café? –Sí, lo _____ bien.
7. –¿(*conocer*) _____ ustedes España? –Sí, la _____ muy bien.
8. –¿(*hacer*) _____ ustedes mucho deporte? –(*correr*) _____ un poco todos los días. **ACIERTOS** /16

48.3. **Complete with the verbs from the box in the affirmative or negative.**

| beber | comer | conocer | correr | hacer | leer | parecer | ~~ver~~ |

48.4. **Complete with the verbs from the box in the affirmative or negative.**

| comer | conocer | hacer (2) | poner | saber (2) | ver |

1. Sé/No sé conducir.
2. _____ gimnasia todos los días.
3. _____ hablar árabe.
4. Mis amigos _____ muchas fiestas.
5. _____ a muchos famosos.
6. _____ fruta todos los días.
7. _____ la radio por las mañanas.
8. _____ mucho la tele. **ACIERTOS** /8

49 *vivo, vives...*
Present indicative: verbs ending in *–ir*

¿Y dónde **vives** ahora?

Vivo en la calle Luna. Muy cerca de aquí.

Vives and *vivo* are forms of the present indicative.

● Forming the present indicative: regular verbs ending in *-ir*.

	viv-ir
(yo)	viv-**o**
(tú)	viv-**es**
(usted)	viv-**e**
(él, ella)	viv-**e**
(nosotros, nosotras)	viv-**imos**
(vosotros, vosotras)	viv-**ís**
(ustedes)	viv-**en**
(ellos, ellas)	viv-**en**

> Negative sentences: **No vivo** en España.
> Questions: ¿Dónde **vive Agustín**?

● Irregular forms:

– First person singular (*yo*) irregular.

conducir: **conduzco**, conduces, conduce, conduce, conducimos, conducís, conducen, conducen

traducir: **traduzco**, traduces, traduce, traduce, traducimos, traducís, traducen, traducen

salir: **salgo**, sales, sale, sale, salimos, salís, salen, salen

Conduzco *un autobús de pasajeros.*   **No salgo** *mucho por la noche.*

– All forms are irregular except nosotros/as and vosotros/as.

construir: **construyo, construyes, construye, construye,** construimos, construís, **construyen, construyen**

oír: **oigo, oyes, oye, oye,** oímos, oís, **oyen, oyen**

Tomás no **oye** nada.

– All forms are irregular.

ir: **voy, vas, va, va, vamos, vais, van, van**

¿Adónde **vas**?   **Voy** a casa.

● Uses of the present indicative:

– Speaking about the present.

*Hannah **traduce** libros de economía.*   *El padre de Raúl **construye** casas.*

– Speaking about what we do habitually.

***Voy** a clase de alemán dos veces a la semana.*

–Speaking about general truths.

*Algunas ballenas **viven** en aguas cálidas.*

– Speaking about what is happening at the moment of speaking.

*¿Qué dices? **No oigo**.*

49 EXERCISES

49.1 Complete the sentences with the correct form of the verbs in parentheses in the affirmative or negative.

1. ¿A qué hora (*abrir*) __abren__ las tiendas?
2. Cristina (*escribir*) _____ unas poesías muy bonitas.
3. Los osos polares (*vivir*)_____ en zonas frías.
4. Alberto (*no, conducir*) _____ muy bien.
5. Los sábados (*yo, salir*) _____ con mis amigos y los domingos (*yo, ir*) _____ a bailar.
6. Mi familia (*ir*) _____ a Punta del Este todos los veranos.
7. A veces (*yo, ir*) _____ de vacaciones en septiembre.
8. Soy traductor. (*traducir*) _____ libros del francés al español.
9. (*nosotros, ir*) _____ a España con frecuencia.
10. Clara y yo (*no, ir*) _____ nunca al teatro.
11. Soy constructor. (*construir*) _____ casas ecológicas.

ACIERTOS ...../12

49.2 Complete the questions and answers.

1. ¿Dónde (*vivir*) __vive__ usted?   _____ en Guayaquil.
2. ¿Dónde (*vivir*) _____ ustedes?   _____ en Mérida.
3. ¿Cómo (*tú, ir*) _____ a la oficina?   Normalmente _____ en metro.
4. ¿(*vosotros, salir*) _____ mucho?   No, solo _____ los fines de semana.
5. ¿Adónde (*tú, ir*) _____ los fines de semana?
6. ¿Cómo (*tú, conducir*) _____?   _____ muy bien.
7. ¿Adónde (*ir*) _____ usted en verano?   Normalmente _____ a la playa.
8. ¿(*vosotros, ir*) _____ mucho al cine?   _____ dos o tres veces al mes.
9. ¿(*oír, tú*)_____ a los niños?   No, no los _____ .
10. ¿(*salir, tú*) _____ mucho de noche?   Sí, _____ bastante.
11. ¿(*escribir*) _____ bien tu hermano?   Sí, _____ muy bien.

ACIERTOS ...../21

49.3 Complete with the verbs from the box in the affirmative or negative.

① ¿Adónde __vais__?

② Habla más alto. _____ bien.

③ Perdone, ¿adónde _____ este autobús?

④ _____ muy deprisa, Marisa.

conducir
ir (2)
oír

ACIERTOS ...../4

49.4 Answer the questions with the verbs from the box.

conducir	construir (2)	dirigir	escribir (2)	repartir	traducir

¿Qué hace....

1. ... un periodista? __Escribe__ artículos.
2. ... un cartero? _____ cartas.
3. ... una traductora? _____ libros.
4. ... un constructor? _____ casas.
5. ... una escritora? _____ libros.
6. ... un gerente? _____ empresas.
7. ... un camionero? _____ camiones.
8. ... un ingeniero? _____ carreteras y puentes.

ACIERTOS ...../8

49.5 Write true sentences, affirmative or negative, with the verbs from the box.

cerrar	conducir	escribir (2)	ir (2)	salir (2)	~~vivir~~

1. __Vivo / No vivo__ en un piso.
2. _____ poesías.
3. Los domingos _____ con mis amigos.
4. Mis amigos _____ todas las noches.
5. Mi familia _____ de vacaciones al extranjero.
6. _____ cartas a menudo.
7. _____ siempre con mucho ciudado.
8. En mi país, las farmacias _____ los domingos.

ACIERTOS ...../8

50 *pienso, quiero...*
Present indicative: irregular verbs (1)

Forming the present indicative: irregular verbs

- e → ie

	cerr-ar	quer-er	sent-ir
(yo)	cierr-o	quier-o	sient-o
(tú)	cierr-as	quier-es	sient-es
(usted)	cierr-a	quier-e	sient-e
(él, ella)	cierr-a	quier-e	sient-e
(nosotros, nosotras)	cerr-amos	quer-emos	sent-imos
(vosotros, vosotras)	cerr-áis	quer-éis	sent-ís
(ustedes)	cierr-an	quier-en	sient-en
(ellos, ellas)	cierr-an	quier-en	sient-en

No, gracias, **prefiero** un té.

¿**Quieres** un café?

Others: -ar: *calentar, empezar, fregar, pensar, regar.*

-er: *entender, perder.* Hans no **entiende** bien el español.

-ir: *mentir, preferir.* **Prefiero** salir mañana.

> **BE CAREFUL!**
> venir: ven**go**, vi**e**nes, vi**e**ne, vi**e**ne, venimos, venís, vi**e**nen, vi**e**nen
> tener: ten**go**, ti**e**nes, ti**e**ne, ti**e**ne, tenemos, tenéis, ti**e**nen, ti**e**nen
>
> –¿De dónde **vienes**? –**Vengo** de la academia.   ▶ UNIT 44: Present indicative of *tener*

- e → i

	med -ir
(yo)	mid-o
(tú)	mid-es
(usted)	mid-e
(él, ella)	mid-e
(nosotros, nosotras)	medim-os
(vosotros, vosotras)	med-ís
(ustedes)	mid-en
(ellos, ellas)	mid-en

Mido 1,75 m.

Others: *corregir, elegir, conseguir, freír, pedir, reír, repetir, seguir, servir, sonreír*

En este restaurante siempre **pido** pescado.   ¿Cuándo **corriges** los ejercicios?

> **BE CAREFUL!**
> decir: **digo**, dices, dice, dice, decimos, decís, dicen, dicen
> –¿Qué **dices**? –No **digo** nada.
> verbs ending in -*gir*: elijo, eliges, elige, elegimos, elegís, eligen
> verbs ending in -*guir*: sigo, sigues, sigue, seguimos, seguís, siguen

- Uses of the present indicative   ▶ UNIT 47: Present indicative: verbs ending in –*ar*

– Speaking about the present: *Ramón* **tiene** *tres hijos.*   *Susana* **miente** *mucho.*

– Speaking about what we do habitually: *Normalmente* **cerramos** *a las ocho.*

– Speaking about general truths: *Algunos cocodrilos* **miden** *seis metros.*

– Speaking about what is happening at the moment of speaking: *¿En qué* **piensas**?
  –¿De dónde **vienes**? –De casa.

50 EXERCISES

50.1 Complete the sentences in the correct form with the words in parentheses.

1. Antonio (*pensar*) ___piensa___ mucho en su futuro, (*querer*) _____ ser médico.
2. En verano (*yo, regar*) _____ las plantas todos los días.
3. La clase (*empezar*) _____ a las ocho.
4. Luis y Pili siempre (*perder*) _____ al golf.
5. Los bancos (*cerrar*) _____ a las dos.
6. Algunos alumnos (*venir*) _____ mucho a la biblioteca.
7. Antonia no (*mentir*) _____ nunca. Siempre (*decir*) _____ la verdad.
8. La pared (*medir*) _____ tres metros de ancho. ¿Cuánto (*medir*) _____ esos armarios?
9. A veces (*yo, decir*) _____ muchas tonterías.
10. ¿Quién (*dirigir*) _____ esta empresa?
11. Elena (*conseguir*) _____ todos sus deseos.
12. ¿A qué hora (*empezar*) _____ las noticias?
13. Mi profesora (*corregir*) _____ las redacciones muy pronto.
14. Álvaro no (*fregar*) _____ nunca los platos.
15. Siempre (*nosotros, perder*) _____ el autobús.
16. ¿A qué hora (*empezar*) _____ el concierto?

ACIERTOS ...... /19

50.2 Complete the questions and answers.

1. ¿Cuánto (*tú, medir*) ___mides___ ?   _____ 1,75 metros.
2. ¿Cuándo (*tú, regar*) _____ las plantas?   Las _____ una vez a la semana
3. ¿Cómo (*venir*) _____ Carlos a clase?   _____ en bici.
4. ¿(*preferir*) _____ usted carne o pescado?   _____ el pescado
5. ¿Qué (*decir*) _____ tus padres de las vacaciones? No _____ nada.
6. ¿A qué hora (*vosotros, empezar*) _____ a trabajar? _____ a las nueve.
7. ¿Quién (*fregar*) _____ los platos en tu casa? Los _____ yo.
8. ¿Qué (*tú, tener*) _____ en la mano?   _____ un bolígrafo.
9. ¿Qué (*tú, querer*) _____ ser de mayor?   _____ ser arquitecto.
10. ¿Qué (*pedir*) _____ Pedro?   _____ más dinero.
11. ¿Cómo (*tú, venir*) _____ a la academia?   _____ en autobús.

ACIERTOS ...... /22

50.3 Complete the sentences with the verbs from the box.

| decir | pensar | querer | tener | ~~venir~~ |

ACIERTOS ...... / 5

50.4 Put the words in the correct order.

1. Andrés / viene / de dónde ¿___De dónde viene Andrés___ ?
2. tus padres / piensan / qué ¿_____ ?
3. los bancos / cierran / a qué hora? ¿_____ ?
4. Li / entiende / español ¿_____ ?
5. Mercedes / miente / por qué ¿_____ ?
6. Sofía / viene / cuándo ¿_____ ?

ACIERTOS ...... / 6

51 *duermo, juego...*
Present indicative: irregular verbs (2)

Making the present indicative: irregular verbs (2)

● o → ue

	soñ-ar	pod-er	dorm-ir
(yo)	sueñ-o	pued-o	duerm-o
(tú)	sueñ-as	pued-es	duerm-es
(usted)	sueñ-a	pued-e	duerm-e
(él, ella)	sueñ-a	pued-e	duerm-e
(nosotros, nosotras)	soñ-amos	pod-emos	dorm-imos
(vosotros, vosotras)	soñ-áis	pod-éis	dorm-ís
(ustedes)	sueñ-an	pued-en	duerm-en
(ellos, ellas)	sueñ-an	pued-en	duerm-en

Solo **duermo** 5 horas al día.

Others: –ar: *comprobar, contar, costar, encontrar, probar, recordar, sonar, volar*
 –er: *morder, mover, volver, doler*
 –ir: *morir*

> No **encuentro** las gafas.
> Ese abrigo **cuesta** mucho.

> Este perro no **muerde**.
> Me **muero** de sueño.

● u → ue

	jug-ar
(yo)	jueg-o
(tú)	jueg-as
(usted)	jueg-a
(él, ella)	jueg-a
(nosotros, nosotras)	jug-amos
(vosotros, vosotras)	jug-áis
(ustedes)	jueg-an
(ellos, ellas)	jueg-an

¿A qué **jugáis**?

¡Al parchís!

● Uses of the present indicative

▶ UNIT 47: Present indicative: verbs ending in *–ar*

– To speak about the present:
 *¿Cuánto **cuesta** esta revista?* **No juego** muy bien al tenis.

– To speak about what we do habitually:
 ***Sueño** todas las noches.* *¿Cuántas horas **duermes** al día?*

– To speak about general truths:
 *Las gallinas **no vuelan**.*

– To speak about what is happening at the moment of speaking:
 *–¿Qué haces? –**Pruebo** la sopa.*

51 EXERCISES

51.1 Complete the sentences with the correct form of the verb in parentheses.

1. Elisa siempre (*probar*) __prueba__ la sopa antes de servirla.
2. ¿Nunca te (*doler*) _____ las muelas, Nati?
3. (*morir*) _____ muchas personas en la carretera.
4. Luis y Pili (*jugar*) _____ muy mal al golf.
5. Mi perro no (*dormir*) _____ nunca en el sofá.
6. Iliana (*soñar*) _____ con viajar a Italia.
7. Ahora mismo no (*yo, recordar*) _____ esa canción.
8. Ramiro (*encontrar*) _____ amigos por todas partes.
9. Estoy muy nerviosa. No (*poder*) _____ dormir.
10. Marga siempre (*aprobar*) _____ los exámenes.
11. ¿Por qué (*volver*) _____ tan tarde a casa, Rafa?
12. ¿Cuánto (*costar*) _____ esa camisa?
13. Mis hijos me (*contar*) _____ todos sus problemas.
14. ¿A qué velocidad (*volar*) _____ el Airbus?

SCORE ...... /14

51.2 Complete the questions and answers.

1. ¿Cuánto (*costar*) __cuesta__ ese reloj? | _____ unos 100 €
2. ¿Cuántas horas (*tú, dormir*) _____ al día? | _____ unas ocho horas.
3. ¿(*tú, soñar*) _____ con frecuencia? | _____ casi todas las noches.
4. ¿A qué hora (*tú, volver*) _____ por la noche? | _____ sobre la una.
5. ¿(*jugar*) _____ usted al tenis? | Sí, pero ahora _____ poco.
6. ¿(*morder*) _____ estos perros? | No, nunca _____.
7. ¿(*dormir*) _____ usted la siesta? | No, no la _____ nunca.
8. ¿(*yo, poder*) _____ ayudar en algo? | Sí, _____ poner la mesa.
9. ¿Dónde (*tú, colgar*) _____ las corbatas? | Las _____ en el armario.

SCORE ...... /18

51.3 Complete the sentences with the verbs from the box in the affirmative or negative.

| costar | encontrar | morder | ~~poder~~ | jugar |

SCORE ...... / 5

51.4 Put the words in the correct order.

1. Alfonso / recuerda / qué ¿ __Qué recuerda Alfonso__ ?
2. ese móvil / cuesta /cuánto ¿_____?
3. ustedes / juegan / a qué ¿_____?
4. Rufo / duerme / dónde ¿_____?
5. usted / sueña / mucho ¿_____?
6. ese reloj / suena / a las horas ¿_____?
7. las plantas / mueren / por qué ¿_____?
8. las gallinas / vuelan ¿_____?

SCORE ...... / 8

51.5 Write true sentences about yourself in the affirmative or negative.

1. (*Dormir*) __Duermo / No duermo__ ocho horas todos los días.
2. (*Soñar*) _____ todas las noches.
3. (*Doler*) _____ Me _____ la cabeza.
4. (*Jugar*) _____ al golf los fines de semana.
5. (*Recordar*) _____ mi infancia.
6. (*Volver*) _____ a casa tarde por la noche.

SCORE ...... / 6

111

52 *Mañana voy al médico.*
Present indicative: other uses

● Uses of the present indicative ▶ UNIT 47: Present indicative: verbs ending in –*ar*

● Other uses of the present indicative

– To speak about the near future when something is already agreed upon or scheduled; use with expressions such as *hoy, esta noche, mañana, la semana que viene...*

Luis **regresa** la semana que viene.

Mañana **voy** al médico.

Nos **vemos** el domingo.

El curso **termina** en diciembre.

¿Qué **haces** esta noche?

¿**Vamos** a la sierra el domingo?　No puedo. El domingo **como** con mis padres.

• These future actions are often connected to timetables.

La película **empieza** a las 10.

El avión **sale** a las 4.35.

¿Qué **hago**? ¿Lo **compro**?　No sé. Es un poco caro.　200€

– To ask for advice or an opinion

–¿**Invito** a Julio?

–Si tú quieres.

– To offer help

–¿Le **abro** la puerta?

–Gracias. Muy amable.

¿Te **llevo** los libros?

– To ask favors

¿Me **prestas** cincuenta euros?

¿Me **dejas** el diccionario?

¿Me **pasas** el agua, por favor?

– To make suggestions

–¿Por qué no le **pides** el coche a Jesús? –No me atrevo.

– ¿**Llamamos** a Nuria? –Sí, ¡venga!

–¿**Quedamos** el viernes? –Bueno.

52 EXERCISES

52.1 Today is Sunday. Look at Carlos's agenda for next week and complete his plans with the verbs from the box.

Agenda:
- LUNES: Consulta Dr. Prieto
- MARTES: reunión con Sr. Chávez
- MIÉRCOLES: Ópera
- JUEVES: Cenar con el director
- VIERNES: Visita fábrica en Tarragona
- SÁBADO: Tenis con Rodolfo
- DOMINGO: Salir con Laura

1. El lunes __voy al médico__.
2. El martes _____.
3. El miércoles _____.
4. El jueves _____.
5. El viernes _____.
6. El sábado _____.
7. El domingo _____.

| cenar |
| ir (2) |
| jugar |
| salir |
| tener |
| visitar |

52.2 Complete the sentences with the verbs from the box.

| acabar | casarse | dar | empezar | hacer | ir | irse(2) | llegar | regresar | salir | tener |

1. __Me voy__ (*yo*) _____ a Lisboa mañana.
2. Jorge y Elisa _____ el sábado.
3. Susana _____ una fiesta esta noche.
4. (*nosotros*) _____ al teatro el domingo.
5. Daniel _____ hoy de vacaciones a Asturias. El tren _____ a las 2.
6. La feria _____ el lunes y dura cuatro días.
7. Mis padres _____ hoy de Nicaragua.
8. Mañana (*yo*) _____ dos exámenes.
9. ¿Qué (*vosotros*) _____ este domingo?
10. Lucía _____ la carrera el año que viene.
11. ¿A qué hora _____ el vuelo de Sofía?

52.3 Complete the dialogues with the verbs from the box.

| ayudar | ~~cerrar~~ | cortar | dejar | jugar | lavar | llevar | poner | traer | ver |

1. ¿ _Cierro_ la ventana?
2. ¿Te _____ a casa?
3. ¿ _____ a las cartas?
4. ¿Nos ___ la cuenta, por favor?
5. ¿Donde lo ___?
6. ¿Le _____ el coche?
7. ¿Me ___, por favor?
8. ¿Por qué no te ___ el pelo?
9. ¿ ___ un vídeo?
10. ¿Me _____ el diccionario?

52.4 Complete the dialogues with the verbs from the box.

| ayudar | coger | comprar | decir | dejar (2) | hacer | ir | llevar | poner | ~~salir~~ |

1. –¿__Salimos__ a cenar esta noche? –Buena idea.
2. –¿Me _____ el coche? –Lo siento. Lo necesito.
3. –¿Qué me _____, la falda o los pantalones? –Ponte la falda. Es más elegante.
4. –¿Me _____ a preparar la cena? –Por supuesto. ¿Qué _____?
5. –¿ _____ al campo el domingo? –No puedo. Tengo que estudiar.
6. –¿Le _____ las bolsas? –Gracias, hijo.
7. –¿Por qué no se lo _____ a tus padres? –Me da vergüenza.
8. –¿Me _____ un bolígrafo? –Sí, toma.
9. –¿ _____ yo el teléfono? –Sí, cógelo.
10. –¿ _____ ya las entradas? –Sí, cómpralas.

53 *me levanto*
Verbs with *me, te, se...*

● Regular verbs with *se*: present indicative

▷ UNIT 50: Present indicative: irregular verbs (1)   UNIT 51: Present indicative: irregular verbs (2)

	levant-arse	atrev-erse	aburr-irse
(yo)	**me** levanto	**me** atrevo	**me** aburro
(tú)	**te** levantas	**te** atreves	**te** aburres
(usted)	**se** levanta	**se** atreve	**se** aburre
(él, ella)	**se** levanta	**se** atreve	**se** aburre
(nosotros, nosotras)	**nos** levantamos	**nos** atrevemos	**nos** aburrimos
(vosotros, vosotras)	**os** levantáis	**os** atrevéis	**os** aburrís
(ustedes)	**se** levantan	**se** atreven	**se** aburren
(ellos, ellas)	**se** levantan	**se** atreven	**se** aburren

*Ana **se levanta** a las siete.*

*¿**Te atreves** a venir al lago?*   *En verano no **nos aburrimos** nunca.*   *¿Cuándo **se casa** Tomás?*

● In negative sentences we place *no* before the pronoun.   *Los domingos **no** me levanto temprano.*

● Some irregular verbs with *se*: present indicative

– e → ie: div**e**rtirse: me div**ie**rto, te div**ie**rtes, se div**ie**rte, se div**ie**rte, nos divertimos, os divertís, se div**ie**rten, se div**ie**rten

   Others: *defenderse, despertarse, sentarse, sentirse*

– e → i: v**e**stirse: me v**i**sto, te v**i**stes, se v**i**ste, se v**i**ste, nos vestimos, os vestís, se v**i**sten, se v**i**sten

   Others: *despedirse, reírse*

– o → ue: ac**o**starse: me ac**ue**sto, te ac**ue**stas, se ac**ue**sta, se ac**ue**sta, nos acostamos, os acostáis, se ac**ue**stan, se ac**ue**stan

   Others: *acordarse, dormirse, encontrarse*

– ponerse: me **pongo**, te pones, se pone, se pone, nos ponemos, os ponéis, se ponen, se ponen

   *¿A qué hora **te acuestas**?*   *La niña de Ramón **se viste** sola.*   *Cuando pinto, **me pongo** ropa vieja.*

● Some verbs with *se* are used to indicate that the action or its effect falls:

– on the same person that does it.   – on a part of the body or on the clothes of that person.

*Luis **se lava** con agua fría.*

*Joaquina **se pinta** las uñas.*

Compare:

VERBS WITHOUT *me, te, se...*	VERBS WITH *me, te, se...*
● The action or the effect of the verb is received by someone or something else and not by who is doing the action.	● The action or the effect of the verb is received by the same person, body part, or clothes as the person doing the action.
Luis viste a los niños por la mañana.	*Luis se viste después de desayunar.*

53 EXERCISES

53.1. **Look at the drawings and complete the sentences with the verbs from the box.**

acostarse	bañarse	~~despertarse~~	ducharse	levantarse	vestirse

1. Arturo _se despierta_ a las ocho.
2. Ana y Luis _____ a las ocho y media.
3. Jaime _____ todas las mañanas.
4. Jaime _____ después de ducharse.
5. Ana y Luis _____ a las once y media.
6. Rosana _____ todas las noches.

SCORE ...... /6

53.2. **Complete the sentences with the verbs from the box in the affirmative or negative.**

aburrirse	afeitarse	atreverse	cansarse	defenderse	divertirse
enfadarse	lavarse (2)	mancharse	pintarse	ponerse	quedarse

1. Javi _se lava_ con un jabón especial.
2. Los domingos por la tarde (*nosotros*) _____ en casa.
3. Susana _____ los ojos algunas veces.
4. Ángel y yo _____ mucho en las fiestas.
5. Pepe es muy sucio. _____ mucho la ropa.
6. Alberto es muy tímido. _____ a hablar con Sarita.
7. A Iván no le gusta el cine; _____ mucho cuando va.
8. Mi hermana y yo _____ el pelo todos los días.
9. Los canguros _____ con las patas cuando los atacan.
10. Mi abuela _____ cuando sube escaleras.
11. (*yo*) _____ traje los domingos.
12. José _____ todavía. No tiene barba.
13. Lola _____ nunca. Es muy tranquila.

SCORE ...... /13

53.3. **Complete the questions and the answers with the verbs in parentheses.**

1. –¿A qué hora (*tú, levantarse*) _te levantas_____? –_____ a las siete.
2. –¿(*tú, ponerse*) _____ pijama para dormir? –No, _____ camisón.
3. –¿(*vosotros, bañarse*) _____ en el mar en verano? –No, pero _____ en la piscina.
4. –¿Qué (*vosotros, ponerse*) _____ los domingos? –_____ ropa normal: vaqueros y una camisa.
5. –¿Con qué (*afeitarse*) _____ usted? –_____ con maquinilla eléctrica.
6. –¿(*vestirse*) _____ usted antes o después de desayunar? –_____ después de desayunar.
7. –¿A qué hora (*levantarse*) _____ ustedes los domingos? –_____ temprano, sobre las nueve.
8. –¿Y a qué hora (*ustedes, acostarse*) _____? –_____ también temprano, sobre las diez.
9. –¿Cuándo (*vosotros, casarse*) _____? –_____ en julio.
10. ¿Por qué (*tú, enfadarse*) _____? –_____ porque siempre llegas tarde.

SCORE ...... /20

53.4. **Complete the sentences in the affirmative or negative, as appropriate for you.**

1. (*levantarse*) _(No) Me levanto_ temprano.
2. (*lavarse*) _____ el pelo todos los días.
3. (*pintarse*) _____ los labios.
4. (*ponerse*) _____ pijama para dormir.
5. (*acostarse*) _____ tarde por la noche.
6. (*reírse*) _____ mucho en las comedias.
7. (*aburrirse*) _____ en las fiestas.
8. (*cansarse*) _____ cuando corro.

SCORE ...... /8

Compare:

VERBS WITHOUT *me, te, se...*	REFLEXIVE VERBS WITH *me, te, se...*
● The action or the effect of the verb is received by **another person or object** that does the action.	● The action or the effect of the verb is received by **the same person** who does the action or a part of the body or clothes of that person.

Lavo **el pelo** a las clientas.

Me lavo el pelo todos los días.

Gonzalo **acuesta a los niños** a las nueve.

Gonzalo se acuesta a las once.

● Some verbs have a different meaning with *se*.

despedir = to fire from a job	*despedirse* = to say good-bye, to willingly leave your job
dormir = to sleep	*dormirse* = to fall asleep, to get bored
dejar = to lend	*dejarse* = to leave something behind
encontrar = to find, discover	*encontrarse* = to get together, to feel (good)
ir a un lugar = to go to a place, attend	*irse de un lugar* = to leave a place
llamar = to call, phone	*llamarse* = to be called (your name)
parecer = to seem	*parecerse* = to be similar

Te llama Jorge.

Ana **duerme** siete horas al día.
Voy a clase todos los días.
¿**Me dejas** este libro?
Emilio **parece** listo.
No **encontramos** las entradas.

¡Hola! **Me llamo Juana.**

Ana **se duerme** en la ópera.
¡Adiós! **Me voy** a clase.
¡Espera! **Te dejas** un libro.
Se parece a su madre.
Ayer **nos encontramos** con Pepa en el supermercado.
No **me encuentro** bien.

54 EXERCISES

54.1. Look at the drawings and complete the sentences with the verbs from the box.

 ① Raúl **lava** coches.

 ② Siempre _____ la camisa con los espaguetis.

 ③ María _____ a los niños a las ocho.

 ④ _____ a los niños todas las noches.

 ⑤ _____ los dientes antes de acostarme.

 ⑥ Lucas _____ mucho los cuadernos.

 ⑦ En verano _____ en el mar.

 ⑧ Los domingos _____ tarde.

acostar
bañar
bañarse
~~lavar~~
lavarse
levantarse
manchar
mancharse

SCORE ...... / 8

54.2. Complete the sentences with the verbs from the box.

1. Felipe __se aburre__ viendo la tele.
2. (yo) _____ las manos antes de las comidas.
3. Clara _____ a los niños después de desayunar y después _____ ella.
4. (yo) _____ muy tarde los sábados por la noche.
5. Alicia _____ la ropa a mano.
6. Juan _____ a sus hijos a las diez de la noche.
7. Miguel _____ mucho en el espejo.
8. Los payasos _____ a los niños.
9. Julián _____ mucho a las chicas.
10. (nosotros) _____ mucho en las fiestas.
11. Mi mujer _____ de las serpientes.
12. El perro de la vecina _____ a todo el mundo.

aburrir
~~aburrirse~~
acostar
acostarse
asustar
asustarse
divertir
divertirse
lavar
lavarse
mirarse
vestir
vestirse

SCORE ...... /13

54.3. Circle the correct answer in each case.

1. (Llamo / *Me llamo*) Andrés.
2. Tania siempre (despide / *se despide*) con un beso.
3. ¿A quién (pareces / te pareces), a tu padre o a tu madre?
4. (Vamos / Nos vamos) al cine dos veces al mes.
5. (Duermo / Me duermo) en clase de Filosofía.
6. Rita (parece / se parece) muy amable.
7. ¡Hasta luego! (Vamos / Nos vamos) al cine.
8. ¿(Llamamos / Nos llamamos) a Javi?
9. No (encuentro / me encuentro) mis gafas.
10. ¿Cuántas horas (duermes / te duermes) al día?
11. ¿(Encuentras / Te encuentras) bien?
12. Siempre (dejo / me dejo) las llaves en casa.
13. El lunes (voy / me voy) al dentista.
14. No (dejo / me dejo) nunca el coche a nadie.

SCORE ...... /14

54.4. Complete the sentences with the words from the box.

1. –¿Cómo __te llamas__? –Bárbara.
2. –¿_____ bien? –No, tengo fiebre.
3. ¿Dónde están las aspirinas? No las _____.
4. Juan _____ mucho a su padre.
5. Quiero hablar con Alicia, pero no _____ nunca.
6. Lola _____ enferma. Tiene muy mala cara.
7. Últimamente (yo) no _____ bien.
8. A Andrés no le gusta la música. _____ en los conciertos.

dormir
dormirse
encontrar
encontrarse
llamar
~~llamarse~~
parecer
parecerse

SCORE ...... / 8

117

55 ¿Te gusta la música?
Verbs with *me, te, le...*

¿Te gusta la música?

Sí, pero no me gusta el ruido.

- *Gustar, encantar*: present indicative

(a mí)	**me**			
(a ti)	**te**	gusta		
(a usted)	**le**	encanta	+	singular
(a él, ella)	**le**			
(a nosotros, nosotras)	**nos**			
(a vosotros, vosotras)	**os**	gustan		
(a ustedes)	**les**	encantan	+	plural
(a ellos, ellas)	**les**			

A mi hijo le encantan los pasteles.

¿Te gusta este traje?
Nos gustan la paella y el marisco.

¿Os gustan las naranjas?
A Ricardo no le gusta nada estudiar.

BE CAREFUL!

me, te... gusta + infinitive(s):

> ***Me gusta bailar.*** → *A Concha le gusta cantar y bailar.*
> *A Luis le ~~gustan~~ nadar y jugar al tenis.* → *A Luis le **gusta nadar y jugar** al tenis.*

a + noun / proper noun:

> ***A mis padres les** gusta mucho viajar.* → ***A Elsa** no **le** gusta cocinar.*

no + *me, te...* + *gusta, encanta...*

> ***No nos gusta** trabajar.*

- Other verbs with the same construction are: *apetecer, doler, importar, interesar...*

  ¿Te apetece dar un paseo?   *A Luisa **le duelen las muelas**.*
  ¿Te duele la cabeza?   ***Me duelen los pies**.*
  *No **me importa** madrugar.*   *¿Te interesan las matemáticas?*

- We use *a mí, a ti...* to:

  – give emphasis.

  > ***A nosotros** nos encanta la ópera.*

  – establish a contrast.

  > *–Me encanta el fútbol. –**A mí** no me gusta nada.*
  > *A Pedro le gusta Luisa, pero **a ella** no le gusta Pedro.*

  – make clear who we are referring to.

  > ¿Le gusta el pescado? → *¿**Le** gusta **a usted** el pescado?*
  > → *¿**Le** gusta **a él** el pescado?*
  > → *¿**Le** gusta **a ella** el pescado?*

- *Mucho, nada, más...* are usually placed between the verb and the subject.

  *Me **gusta mucho** bailar.*   *No me **interesan nada** las matemáticas.*
  *Me **duele mucho** la cabeza.*   *Me **gusta más** el queso.*

55 EXERCISES

55.1. Look at the table and complete the dialogues with *gustar* or *encantar* in the affirmative or negative.

	TORTILLA	QUESO	PAELLA	FABADA	CALAMARES	GAMBAS
NATI	☺	X	☺☺	X	☺	☺☺
GERARDO	X	X	☺☺	☺☺	X	☺☺
DON JESÚS	X	☺	X	☺☺	☺	X

☺ = gustar
☺☺ = encantar
X = no gustar

1. DON JESÚS: ¿ Te gusta la tortilla, Gerardo? GERARDO: No, _____.
2. GERARDO: A Nati _____ la tortilla.
3. NATI: ¿_____ el queso, don Jesús? DON JESÚS: Sí, _____.
4. DON JESÚS: A Nati y a Gerardo _____ el queso.
5. GERARDO: A Nati y a mí _____ la paella.
6. NATI: ¿_____ la fabada, don Jesús? DON JESÚS: Sí,_____.
7. DON JESÚS: ¿_____ los calamares, Nati? NATI: Sí, _____ mucho.
8. GERARDO: A mí _____ los calamares.
9. DON JESÚS: ¿_____ las gambas a Nati y a ti, Gerardo? GERARDO: Sí,_____.
10. NATI: ¿_____ a usted las gambas, don Jesús? DON JESÚS: No, _____.

SCORE ....../16

55.2. Complete the sentences with *gustar* or *encantar* in the affirmative or negative.

1. –¿ Te gusta (☺) bailar, Sara? –Sí, me encanta (☺☺). ¿Y a ti? – A mí no me gusta (x).
2. –¿_____ (☺) leer a Rubén y a ti? –A mí __ (_____☺☺), pero a Rubén _____ (x) mucho.
3. –¿_____ (☺) el pescado a tus hermanos? –A Julián _____ (☺), pero a Olga _____ (x).
4. A Nacho _____ (☺) Cristina, pero a Cristina _____ (x) Nacho.
5. –¿_____ (☺) viajar, Manuel? –Sí, mucho. ¿Y a vosotras? –_____ (☺☺).
6. – ¿Qué _____ (☺) a ustedes hacer en vacaciones? –_____ (☺) ir a la playa y descansar.
7. ¿_____ (☺) cocinar a tu hermana y a ti? –A mí (☺) _____, pero a mi hermana _____ (x).
8. –A nosotras_____ (☺☺) hacer deporte. ¿Y a ti, Norma? –_____ (☺) pasear y nadar.

SCORE ....../20

55.3. Complete the sentences with the following verbs: *apetecer, doler, importar, interesar*.

1. A mi abuela le duelen mucho las piernas.
2. –¿_____ salir esta noche, Luis? –No, estoy cansado.
3. Tengo que ir al dentista. _____ las muelas.
4. A José y a mí no _____ madrugar. ¿Quedamos a las ocho de la mañana?
5. Cuando llueve, a mi padre _____ la espalda.
6. –¿_____ a ustedes comer algo? –No, gracias. No tenemos hambre.
7. La informática es muy útil, pero a mí no _____ nada.
8. ¿Tienes una aspirina? _____ la cabeza.
9. A Belén _____ mucho las ciencias.
10. ¿_____ si me siento a tu lado?
11. –¿_____ a usted un gazpacho, Matías? –No, gracias. _____ el estómago.
12. A mis hermanos no _____ trabajar los domingos.
13. A nosotros _____ bastante la informática.

SCORE ....../14

119

56 *Estoy viendo las noticias.*
Present of *estar* + gerund

¿Qué **estás haciendo?**

Estoy viendo las noticias.

¡SShh! Isabel **está tocando** el piano.

Llévate el paraguas. **Está lloviendo.**

● Present of *estar* + gerund   ▶ UNIT 80: Gerund

(yo)	estoy	
(tú)	estás	
(usted)	está	estudiando
(él, ella)	está	
(nosotros, nosotras)	estamos	bebiendo
(vosotros, vosotras)	estáis	
(ustedes)	están	escribiendo
(ellos, ellas)	están	

Negative sentences: ***No estoy*** estudiando.

Questions: *¿Qué **está estudiando** María?*

▌ BUT: *¿Qué **están** ustedes **viendo**?*
          *¿Qué **están viendo** ustedes?*

● Making the gerund

– regular forms   verbs ending in *–ar*   → *–ando*:   trabajar→ trabajando
                   verbs ending in *–er / –ir* → *–iendo*:   comer → comiendo / vivir → viviendo

– some irregular forms
    decir → diciendo   vestir → vistiendo   dormir → durmiendo   leer → leyendo   oír → oyendo

● We use *estoy, estás…* + gerund:

– to speak about actions that are happening at the moment of speaking.
    *–¿Qué **estás haciendo**? –**Estoy escuchando** un disco de salsa.*
    *–¿Dónde está John? –**Está durmiendo** la siesta.*

estoy escuchando
está durmiendo
↓
————————————
right now

– to speak about a temporary situation not used with expressions of time such as *hoy, este mes, últimamente…*

    Luisa normalmente trabaja en España,
    *pero **este mes está trabajando** en Argentina.*
    ***Este año estamos estudiando** chino.*
    ***Últimamente estoy durmiendo** mucho.*

está trabajando
↓ ↓
————————
now
this month

estamos estudiando
↓ ↓
————————
now
this year

BE CAREFUL! ▌

Verbs with *se: lavarse, vestirse…*   ▶ UNIT 53: Verbs with *me, te, se…* ▌

me, te, se, nos, os, se + present of *estar* + gerund
    ***Me estoy** duchando.*   ***Se están** vistiendo.*

present of *estar* + gerund *–me, te, se, nos, os, se*
    *Estoy **duchándome**.*   *Están **vistiéndose**.*

¿Está Alfredo?

Sí, pero **se está** duchando.

56 EXERCISES

56.1. Look at the drawings and complete the dialogues with the verbs in the box.

| bailar | correr | ~~escribir~~ | estudiar | hacer | jugar | leer | llorar | llover | nevar | ver |

SCORE ____ / 11

56.2. Complete the sentences with the following verbs.

| acostarse | comer | dormir | escuchar (2) | estudiar |
| hablar | hacer (2) | jugar | ~~pasar~~ | preparar | vestirse |

1. –¿Dónde están tus padres? – __Están pasando__ unos días en Potosí.
2. –¿Dónde están los niños? – _____ en el parque.
3. –Date prisa, Pepa. –Espera un momento. _____.
4. –¿Con quién _____ Teresa? –Con una vecina.
5. Esta semana _____ mucho calor.
6. Mis hermanos _____ una fiesta.
7. Estoy cansado. Últimamente _____ muy poco.
8. Esta semana _____ mucho. Tenemos exámenes.
9. ¡Sssssssst! (*yo*) _____ las noticias.
10. –¿Por qué no come Cristina hoy con nosotros? – _____ en casa de una amiga.
11. –¿Dónde está Hans? – _____ un curso de español en Perú.
12. Esta semana estamos de fiesta y _____ muy tarde.
13. –¿Qué (*tú*) _____? –Música cubana.

SCORE ____ / 13

56.3. Answer the questions as in the example.

1. –¿Qué haces en el baño, Miguel? – __Me estoy afeitando. / Estoy afeitándome.__
2. –¿Dónde están los niños? – _____ en la piscina.
3. –¿Cómo lo estáis pasando? – _____ mucho.
4. –¿Dónde está Luisa? – _____ el pelo.
5. –¿Por qué no viene Rosa? –Un momento. _____.
6. –¿Dónde están Luis y Pedro? – _____. Estaban muy sucios.

| ~~afeitarse~~ |
| bañarse |
| divertirse |
| lavarse (2) |
| vestirse |

SCORE ____ / 6

56.4. Ask questions about now with the words given.

1. Carlos/ hacer/ qué ¿ __Qué está haciendo Carlos__ ?
2. Juan/ dibujar/ qué ¿_____?
3. Luisa/ dormir ¿_____?
4. ustedes/ qué / ver ¿_____?
5. Rodrigo/ leer/ qué ¿_____?
6. Fátima/ ducharse ¿_____?

SCORE ____ / 6

Compare:

PRESENT INDICATIVE	ESTAR + GERUND

PRESENT INDICATIVE

● We use the present indicative to speak about habitual actions.

Hago gimnasia todas las mañanas.

now

Hago gimnasia todas las mañanas.

*En mi casa **comemos** a las dos.*
*Olga **toca** la guitarra en un grupo.*

*En Acapulco **hace** calor en verano.*
***Trabajo** en Santiago.*
*Normalmente **pasamos** el verano en Lugo.*

● We use it to speak about general or universal truths.

*En Venezuela **llueve** mucho en invierno.*

ESTAR + GERUND

● We use *estar* + gerund to speak about short actions that are happening at the moment of speaking.

Estoy haciendo un rompecabezas.

now

Estoy haciendo un rompecabezas.

*¿Qué **estáis comiendo**?*
***Está tocando** una canción mexicana.*

● We use it to speak about temporary actions that are not usually used with expressions such as *esta semana, este mes, últimamente...*

*Este verano **está haciendo** frío.*
*Esta semana **estoy trabajando** en Iquique.*
***Estamos pasando** unos días en la costa.*

*No salgas. **Está lloviendo** mucho.*

● We don't usually use *estar* + gerund:

– with the verbs *ir* and *venir*.

***Vamos** a Viña todos los años.*
*Las cigüeñas **vienen** a España en primavera.*

*–¿Adónde **vais**? –**Vamos** a la playa*
*–¿De dónde **vienes**? –**Vengo** de una fiesta.*

– with the verbs *conocer, comprender, entender, querer, necesitar, amar, preferir, odiar, parecer, saber, tener, llevar.*

*Alicia **no lleva** nunca vaqueros.*
*Rodrigo **tiene** dos hermanos.*

*¿Qué **lleva** Jesús en la cabeza?*
*¿**Tienes** dinero? **Necesito** 50 euros.*

– with the verbs *ver* and *oír* (when they don't mean *mirar* or *escuchar*).

*Félix **no oye** nada por el oído izquierdo.*

*–¿**Oyes** algo? –Nada. Hablan muy bajo.*

▌ BUT: ***Estoy oyendo** la radio.* (I am listening)

● At times we can use the present indicative to speak about actions that are happening at the moment of speaking.

*–¿Qué **haces**? –Nada. **Leo** un rato.*

*–¿Qué **estás haciendo**? –**Estoy leyendo** el periódico.*

57 EXERCISES

57.1. Complete the sentences with some of the following verbs: *dar, estudiar, jugar, tocar, ver.*

Jorge y Santi son músicos.
Tocan en una orquesta.
Jorge _____ la batería y
Santi _____ la guitarra.
Ahora no _____.
_____ al ajedrez.

Daniela es profesora.
_____ clases de
Matemáticas. Ahora no
_____ clase.
_____ la tele en casa.

Cristina es estudiante.
_____ Medicina. Ahora
no _____. _____
al tenis con una amiga.

SCORE ...... / 11

57.2. Complete the sentences with the verb in the present indicative or *estar* + gerund.

1. En el desierto de Atacama (*no llover*) _no llueve_ nunca.
2. –¿(*tú, hablar*) _____ portugués? –Un poco.
3. Este invierno (*no hacer*) _____ mucho frío pero (*llover*) _____ mucho.
4. –¿Dónde (*tú, trabajar*) _____? –Soy abogado, pero este verano (*trabajar*)_____de camarero.
5. –¿Está Rosa? –Sí, pero (*dormir*) _____.
6. Los vegetarianos (*no comer*) _____ carne.
7. –¿(*tú, tocar*) _____ algún instrumento? –Sí, (*tocar*) _____ el violín.
8. –¿Qué (*cantar*) _____ Carlos? –Un tango.
9. (*yo, fumar*) _____ diez cigarrillos al día, aunque últimamente _____ menos.
10. Algunos bebés (*llorar*) _____ mucho.

SCORE / 14

57.3. Circle the correct answer in each case.

1. ¿Adónde (vais / *estáis yendo*)?
2. ¿(*Oyes / Estás oyendo*) algo?
3. ¿Qué (*quieres / estás queriendo*)?
4. Esta semana (*no estudio / no estoy estudiando*) mucho.
5. ¿En qué (*trabajas / estás trabajando*) ahora?
6. No (*entiendo / estoy entendiendo*). ¿Puedes repetir?
7. –¿Qué te pasa, Sara? (*Tienes / Estás teniendo*) mala cara. –Sí, (*vengo / estoy viniendo*) del dentista.
8. –¿Dónde están tus padres? –(*Viajan / Están viajando*) por América.
9. –¿Puedes ayudarme? –Lo siento. (*Veo / Estoy viendo*) una película.
10. Está muy oscuro. No (*veo / estoy viendo*) nada.

SCORE ...... / 11

57.4. Complete the sentences with the verb in the present indicative or *estar* + gerund.

1. –¿Adónde (*ir*) _vas_? –(*Ir*) _Voy_ a casa.
2. ¿(*tú, conocer*) _____ a esa chica?
3. ¿Qué (*tú, tener*) _____ en la mano?
4. –¿Qué (*tú, ver*) _____? –Un concurso.
5. No (*oír*) _____. Tengo que ir al médico.
6. –¿(*tú, saber*) _____ hablar español?
   –_____ un poco.
7. Ángela, ahora te (*yo, amar*)_____ más que nunca.
8. –Mira. Lola (*llevar*) _____ un vestido de lunares.
   –Sí, (*parecer*) _____ una bailaora.
9. –¿Qué (*querer*) _____ ustedes?
   –(*Necesitar*) _____ cucharas.
10. –¿(*tú, ver*) _____ algo?
   – No _____ nada. Está muy oscuro.
11. –¿Dónde está Juan? –No (*yo, saber*) _____.
12. –Tomás está en el salón. (*él, oír*) _____ la radio.

SCORE / 17

58 *trabajé, comí, viví*
Preterite: regular verbs

¿**Saliste** anoche?

No, **me quedé** en casa. **Vi** una película de terror.

Cervantes **nació** en Alcalá de Henares en 1547.

Saliste, me quedé, vi, and *nació* are forms of the preterite tense.

● Forming the preterite: regular verbs

	trabaj-ar	com-er	viv-ir
(yo)	trabaj-é	com-í	viv-í
(tú)	trabaj-aste	com-iste	viv-iste
(usted)	trabaj-ó	com-ió	viv-ió
(él, ella)	trabaj-ó	com-ió	viv-ió
(nosotros, nosotras)	trabaj-amos	com-imos	viv-imos
(vosotros, vosotras)	trabaj-asteis	com-isteis	viv-isteis
(ustedes)	trabaj-aron	com-ieron	viv-ieron
(ellos, ellas)	trabaj-aron	com-ieron	viv-ieron

BE CAREFUL!

d-ar: d-i, d-iste, d-io, d-io, d-imos, d-isteis, d-ieron, d-ieron

● We use the preterite to speak about past actions or situations. It tells us what happened at a specific past moment: *anoche, ayer, el jueves (pasado), la semana pasada, hace dos meses, en 1995...*

> *Anoche no salimos.*
> *Ayer vi a Luisa. Me **dio** un libro para ti.*
> *El domingo (pasado) vimos una película coreana.*
> *La semana pasada llovió todos los días.*
> *Mis padres **vivieron** en Quito **desde 1990 hasta 2001.***
> *La Primera Guerra Mundial **empezó** en **1914** y **acabó** en **1918.***
> *Alonso **regresó** de Inglaterra **hace dos años.***

– to ask about a past moment when something happened.

> –¿**Cuándo nacieron** tus hijos? –El primero en 1998, y el segundo en 2003.
> –¿**Cuándo acabaste** la carrera? –Hace dos años.

– in verbs with *se*: *lavarse, casarse...*

> *La semana pasada no **me lavé** el pelo.*
> *Bego y Jorge **se casaron** en enero de **2005.***
> *Ayer **nos quedamos** en casa a descansar.*

● In negative sentences, we place *no* in front of the verb.

> *Juan **no nació** en España.*　　　　　　*Ayer **no comí** en casa.*

● In questions, we usually place the subject after the verb.

> *¿Dónde **nació Juan**?*　　　　　　*¿Cuándo **se casaron ustedes**?*

58 EXERCISES

58.1 ▷ **Complete the sentences with the preterite and the verbs in parentheses.**

1. Pablo y Mar (*casarse*) <u>se casaron</u> hace tres meses.
2. ¿Qué (*ustedes, comer*) _____ ayer?
3. El domingo por la mañana (*yo, no salir*) _____. (*Levantarse*) _____ tarde, (*lavarse*) _____ el pelo, (*desayunar*) _____ y (*escribir*) _____ algunas cartas.
4. El año pasado (*nosotros, ver*) _____ a Mercedes Sosa en concierto.
5. Yolanda y Arturo (*vivir*) _____ en Argentina hasta 1998.
6. ¿Cuándo (*nacer*) _____ vuestro primer hijo?
7. –¿Qué os (*pasar*) _____ ayer? –(*No sonar*) _____ el despertador y (*llegar*) _____ tarde.
8. –¿Cuándo (*tú, conocer*) _____ a Gala? –La (*yo, conocer*) _____ en 1999, durante un viaje a Laos.
9. –¿A qué hora (*acabar*) _____ la fiesta anoche? –No lo sé. Yo (*acostarse*) _____ a las doce.
10. ¿Con quién (*tú, salir*) _____ el domingo?
11. Ayer mi hermano (*cumplir*) _____ 25 años.
12. Rubén y yo (*vivir*) _____ en Montevideo hace años.

SCORE ...... /20

58.2 ▷ **Complete the following questions.**

1. Ayer conocí a Donato.   ¿A quién <u>conociste</u> ayer?
2. El domingo dimos un paseo por el Malecón.   ¿Por dónde _____ un paseo el domingo?
3. De joven, viví seis meses en Chile.   ¿Dónde _____ de joven?
4. El año pasado trabajé en una academia.   ¿Dónde _____ el año pasado?
5. Anoche hablé con Alicia.   ¿Con quién _____ anoche?
6. La semana pasada comimos en un mesón.   ¿Dónde _____ la semana pasada?
7. El sábado pasamos el día con Araceli.   ¿Con quién _____ el día el sábado?
8. Di una fiesta hace una semana.   ¿Cuándo _____ una fiesta?

SCORE ...... /8

58.3 ▷ **Complete the sentences.**

1. Julián normalmente desayuna en casa, pero ayer _____ <u>desayunó</u> _____ en una cafetería.
2. Mis padres normalmente comen a las dos, pero ayer _____ a las tres.
3. Normalmente me levanto a las siete, pero ayer _____ a las diez.
4. Los sábados normalmente no trabajo, pero el sábado pasado _____.
5. Normalmente como con mi familia, pero ayer _____ solo.
6. Hans normalmente se acuesta temprano, pero anoche _____ tarde.
7. Antonio normalmente ve a Pili todos los días, pero ayer no la _____.
8. Andrés normalmente compra el periódico todos los días, pero ayer no lo _____.

SCORE ...... /8

58.4 ▷ **Write affirmative or negative sentences as appropriate for you.**

1. Ayer (*levantarse*) <u>(no) me levanté</u> temprano.
2. Ayer (*ver*) _____ la tele por la noche.
3. El sábado (*acostarse*) _____ tarde.
4. Ayer (*leer*) _____ el periódico.
5. El domingo pasado (*salir*) ___ con mis amigos.
6. El domingo pasado (*comer*) _____ en casa.
7. Ayer (*lavarse*) _____ el pelo.
8. Ayer (*dar*) _____ un paseo por la tarde.

SCORE ...... /8

58.5 ▷ **Put the words in the correct order.**

1. Sofía / nació / dónde ¿ _____ <u>Dónde nació Sofía</u> _____?
2. ustedes / comieron / ayer / dónde ¿ _____?
3. Gao / cumplió / ayer / cuántos años ¿ _____?
4. Rafa y Sole / se casaron / cuándo ¿ _____?
5. la fiesta / acabó / a qué hora ¿ _____?
6. tu primer hijo / nació / cuándo ¿ _____?

SCORE ...... /6

59 *estuve, fue*
Preterite: irregular verbs

Forming the preterite: irregular verbs

● Irregular in each person

		−e	(yo)
		−iste	(tú)
estar ▸	**estuv−**	−o	(usted)
hacer ▸	**hic− / hiz−**	−o	(él, ella)
tener ▸	**tuv−**	−imos	(nosotros, nosotras)
venir ▸	**vin−**	−isteis	(vosotros, vosotras)
		−ieron	(ustedes)
		−ieron	(ellos, ellas)

¿Qué **hiciste** el domingo?

Estuve en casa con unos amigos.

haber ▸ *hubo*   ▸ UNIT 105: Impersonal clauses

BE CAREFUL!

hacer: hice, hiciste, **hizo**, **hizo**, hicimos, hicisteis, hicieron, hicieron

> *El año pasado hice varios viajes a América del Sur.*
> *Los abuelos de Beatriz tuvieron diez hijos.*
> *El verano pasado hubo muchos incendios en Galicia.*

● Verbs *ir* and *ser* are the same in the preterite tense.

	ir, ser
(yo)	**fui**
(tú)	**fuiste**
(usted)	**fue**
(él, ella)	**fue**
(nosotros, nosotras)	**fuimos**
(vosotros, vosotras)	**fuisteis**
(ustedes)	**fueron**
(ellos, ellas)	**fueron**

¿Adónde **fuisteis** el verano pasado?

A Cuba. **Fueron** unas vacaciones fantásticas.

> *Alicia fue (ser) directora de un banco durante cuatro años.*
> *Antonio fue (ir) a Puerto Rico en 2001.*

● We use the preterite to speak about past actions or situations or to ask about a past moment when something happened.

   ▸ UNIT 58: Preterite: regular verbs

> *La semana pasada tuve gripe.*
> *¿Cuándo fuisteis a Egipto?*

– We use the preterite of *ser* to assess past facts or situations.

> *La civilización maya fue muy pacífica.*
> *Puskas fue un gran futbolista.*

59 EXERCISES

59.1 Complete the sentences with the preterite of the verbs in parentheses.

1. Alba (*venir*) _vino_ a España en 2006.
2. Unos amigos míos (*tener*) _____ un accidente el fin de semana pasado.
3. ¿Por qué no (*venir*) _____ Lucía y Paloma a la fiesta?
4. ¿Cuántos hijos (*tener*) _____ la abuela de Tere?
5. –¿Dónde (*vosotros, estar*) _____ anoche? –(*estar*) _____ en el teatro.
6. Ayer (*yo, ir*) _____ con Leandro a un concierto y (*yo, venir*) _____ tarde.
7. –¿Cuándo (*tener*) _____ usted su primer hijo? –En 1997.
8. –¿Qué (*ustedes, hacer*) _____ el domingo? –Nada especial. (*estar*) _____ en casa viendo la tele.
9. Anoche (*nosotros, tener*) _____ que dormir en casa de Alfredo.
10. –¿Por qué no (*venir*) _____ a cenar el lunes, Charo? –(*estar*) _____ en el hospital toda la noche.
11. Pilar (*tener*) _____ gripe la semana pasada.
12. ¿Quién (*hacer*) _____ la cena anoche?
13. ¿Cuánto tiempo (*estar*) _____ en Colombia, doña Leo?
14. El año pasado (*nosotros, hacer*) _____ un viaje por Brasil.
15. El verano pasado (*ser*) _____ muy caluroso.
16. El domingo (*haber*) _____ una fiesta en casa de Charo. (*ser*) _____ muy divertida.

SCORE ___/21

59.2 Complete these sentences about the history of Hispanoamerica. Use the verbs *hacer* and *ser*.

1. Cuauhtémoc _fue_ el último soberano azteca.
2. Hernán Cortés _____ gobernador de México.
3. Los aztecas _____ grandes escultores.
4. Los incas _____ muchas conquistas.
5. Manco Cápac I ____ el primer emperador inca.
6. Túpac Amaru I _____ el último emperador inca.
7. Los incas _____ grandes agricultores.
8. Los mayas _____ grandes constructores.

SCORE ___/8

59.3 Complete the conversations with the preterite of the corresponding verbs.

gustar	~~hacer~~	ir (3)	ser

1. –¿Qué _hiciste_ el verano pasado? –_____ a Chile.
   –¿Con quién _____? –Con un grupo de amigos. _____ en coche hasta Tierra del Fuego.
   –¿Os _____? –Sí, _____ un viaje muy interesante.

estar (2)	hacer	tener

2. –¿Dónde _____ ustedes en agosto?
   –_____ en Asturias. _____ mucha suerte. _____ muy buen tiempo.

estar	hacer	ir	ser	venir

3. –¿Qué _____ Pedro y tú el domingo?
   –Por la mañana _____ a una exposición. Por la tarde _____ unos amigos y _____ en casa. _____ un domingo muy tranquilo.

SCORE ___/15

59.4 Put the words in the correct order.

1. los padres de Ana / tuvieron / cuántos hijos ¿_Cuántos hijos tuvieron los padres de Ana_?
2. Adolfo / hizo / el domingo pasado / qué ¿_____?
3. Juan y Rosa / fueron / el verano pasado / adónde ¿_____?
4. Teresa / vino / cuándo ¿_____?
5. la civilización maya / fue / cómo ¿_____?
6. de la Cierva / fue / quién ¿_____?

SCORE ___/6

127

60 *he trabajado*
Present perfect (1)

Hoy **he tenido** un día agotador. Me **he levantado** temprano y **he dado** cuatro clases por la mañana. Por la tarde **he hecho** la compra...

He tenido, me he levantado, he dado, and *he hecho* are forms of the present perfect.

● Forming the present perfect: present indicative of *haber* + past participle of the corresponding verb.

	present simple of *haber*	+	participle of the main verb
(yo)	he		
(tú)	has		
(usted)	ha		trabajado
(él, ella)	ha		
(nosotros, nosotras)	hemos	+	comido
(vosotros, vosotras)	habéis		
(ustedes)	han		vivido
(ellos, ellas)	han		

● Making the participle
  – regular forms
    • verbs ending in −*ar* → -ado
      trabaj-**ar** ▸ trabaj-**ado**
    • verbs ending in −*er* / −*ir* → -ido
      com-**er** ▸ com-**ido**   viv-**ir** ▸ viv-**ido**
  – some irregular forms
    abrir ▸ **abierto**   escribir ▸ **escrito**
    ver ▸ **visto**   hacer ▸ **hecho**

● We use the present perfect to speak about past actions or situations that happened during a period of time that continues now: *hoy, este año/mes, esta mañana/tarde/semana...*

BE CAREFUL!

The participle never changes form.
  −Hoy **he** comid**o** paella. −Pues nosotras **hemos** comid**o** pescado.

Haber and the participle always go together.
  ~~He me levantado tarde.~~ → Me **he levantado** tarde.   ~~¿Qué ha Luisa comido?~~ → ¿Qué **ha comido** Luisa?

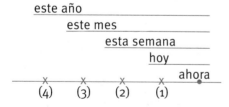

(1) **Hoy me he levantado** tarde. **He estado** en casa todo el día.
(2) Lara **ha salido** todas las noches **esta semana**.
(3) **Este mes hemos ido** al cine tres veces.
(4) **Este año** no **ha hecho** mucho frío.

– We can use the present perfect to speak about recent past actions or situations, with expressions such as *hace poco, hace un momento, hace un rato, hace cinco minutos...*
  He estado con Carlos **hace un momento.**
  Juego muy mal al golf. **He aprendido hace poco.**

– We usually use it to give recent news.
  −¿Qué **ha pasado?** −**Ha dimitido** el presidente.

¿Qué ha pasado?   Ha habido un accidente.

▶ UNIT 61: Present perfect (2)   UNIT 82: Participle

60 EXERCISES

60.1. **What has Betty done today? Use the verbs from the box.**

acostarse
cenar
ducharse
enviar
hacer
ir
jugar
~~levantarse~~

1. __Se ha levantado__ a las diez.
2. _____ *footing*.
3. _____.
4. unos correos electrónicos.
5. _____ al cine con una amiga.
6. _____ a los bolos.
7. _____ con unos amigos.
8. _____ a las doce.

SCORE __/8__

60.2. **Complete the sentences with the present perfect of the verbs in parentheses.**

1. Este verano (*nosotros, estar*) __hemos estado__ en Perú.
2. –¿(*tú, ver*) _____ a Cristina?
   –Sí, la (*yo, ver*) _____ hace un momento.
3. Hoy (*nosotros, trabajar*) _____ diez horas.
4. Este año (*llover*) mucho.
5. –¿Sabes usar este programa?
   –Regular. (*yo, empezar*) _____ a usarlo hace poco.
6. Mis padres (*estar*) _____ en la costa este invierno.
7. ¿Qué (*vosotros, hacer*) _____ este verano?
8. ¿(*tú, leer*) _____ algo interesante últimamente?
9. Hoy (*nosotras, comer*) _____ paella.
10. –¿Qué (*hacer*) _____ Martín este verano?
    –(*Quedarse*) _____ en Madrid. No tenía dinero.
11. Mis padres (*levantarse*) _____ muy pronto esta mañana.

SCORE __/13__

60.3. **Write the corresponding news for the headlines given. Use the verbs from the box.**

1. Fuga de 50 presos. __Se han escapado cincuenta presos__.
2. Fallece el Presidente. _____.
3. Dimite la ministra de Hacienda. _____.
4. Fin de la huelga del transporte. _____.
5. Choque de dos trenes. _____.
6. Sube la gasolina. _____.
7. Bajan los impuestos. _____.
8. Colo-Colo, campeón de Liga. _____.

acabar
bajar
chocar
dimitir
~~escaparse~~
ganar
morir
subir

SCORE __/8__

60.4. **Complete the sentences in the affirmative or negative as appropriate for you.**

1. Hoy (*levantarse*) __me he levantado / no me he levantado__ temprano.
2. Hoy (*escribir*) un poema.
3. (*lavarse*) _____ los dientes después de desayunar.
4. Esta semana (*ir*) _____ al cine.
5. Esta semana (*ver*) _____ mucho la tele.
6. Este año (*aprender*) _____ mucho español.

SCORE __/6__

61

he viajado mucho
Present perfect (2)

● We use the present perfect to speak about past activities or experiences, without saying when they ocurred. It tells what we have done in a time period up to now.

> He **tenido** una vida intensa.
> He **viajado** por todo el mundo.
> He **trabajado** en una fábrica.
> He **sido** actriz...

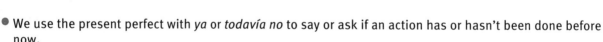

toda la vida ———→ ahora

América   Asia   fábrica   actriz

- In questions, it is usually used with *alguna vez* to ask about past experiences.

> *¿Has estado **alguna vez** en Argentina?*
> *¿Habéis bebido **alguna vez** chicha? Es una bebida de maíz.*

- We often use it with *nunca* to indicate lack of experiences.

> ***No hemos visto nunca** una ballena en el mar.*
> *Los padres de Ana **no han salido nunca** de España.*

No puedo entrar en casa.
He **perdido** la llave.

● We use the present perfect to speak of past actions with consequences in the present. It relays the causes of a present situation.

consequence	cause
–Llegas tarde.	–Lo siento. No **ha sonado** el despertador.
Estoy cansado.	**He trabajado** mucho.

● We use the present perfect with *ya* or *todavía no* to say or ask if an action has or hasn't been done before now.

- *Ya* → affirmative sentences:

> **Ya he terminado** el cuadro.
> (The painting is finished.)

- *Ya* → questions:

> *¿**Has acabado ya** el curso?*
> (I don't know if the course has finished or not at this moment.)

- *Todavía no* → negative sentences:

> *–¿Te ha gustado el libro que te presté? –**Todavía no lo he leído.***
> (Up to now, I haven't read the book yet.)

▶ UNIT 60: Present perfect (1)

61 EXERCISES

61.1. Look at the drawings. What has Ana Roldán done in her life? Use the words from the box.

conocer
escribir
~~estar~~
tener
trabajar
vivir

① Ha estado en Uruguay.

② _____

③ _____

④ _____

⑤ _____

⑥ _____

cinco hijos
Chile
hospital
libro
personajes famosos
~~Uruguay~~

61.2. Write sentences with these words.

1. Reinaldo / estar / nunca / en África ___Reinaldo no ha estado nunca en África___ .
2. ¿ustedes / comer / alguna vez / tortilla? ¿_____?
3. ¿(tú) / tener / alguna vez / un accidente? ¿_____?
4. ¿(vosotros) / enamorarse / alguna vez? ¿_____?
5. (yo) / nunca / ir / al teatro _____ .
6. ¿Rodolfo / trabajar / alguna vez en su vida? ¿_____?
7. mis padres / comer / nunca / comida peruana. _____ .
8. (nosotros) / beber / nunca / tequila _____ .

61.3. Join the consequences with the causes and complete the sentences.

consecuencias		causas
1. Juana no ve bien	a. trabajar mucho todo el día	
2. No puedo entrar en casa	b. perder las gafas	
3. No puedo pagar	c. comer demasiado	
4. Ana y Luisa están agotadas	d. olvidarse la cartera	
5. José no se siente bien.	e. perder las llaves	

1. ___Juana no ve bien porque ha perdido las gafas___ .
2. _____ .
3. _____ .
4. _____ .
5. _____ .

61.4. Write the questions and answers with *ya* or *todavía no.*

1. –La película / empezar ¿___Ha empezado ya la película___? –No, ___todavía no ha empezado___ .
2. –Rosa / llamar ¿_____? –Sí, _____ .
3. –tus padres / llegar ¿_____? –No, _____ .
4. –Tú / empezar ¿_____ las clases de informática? –No, _____ .
5. –Vosotros / hablar ¿_____ con Enrique? –Sí, _____ .
6. –Los niños / cenar ¿_____? –Sí, _____ .

61.5. Write affirmative or negative sentences according to your experiences.

1. viajar en avión ___(No) He viajado (nunca) en avión___
2. estar en Argentina _____
3. comer tortilla de patatas _____
4. ver películas españolas _____
5. visitar España _____
6. trabajar en una tienda _____
7. escribir un libro _____
8. plantar un árbol _____

62

he trabajado / trabajé
Contrasting present perfect and preterite

Compare:

PRESENT PERFECT	PRETERITE

PRESENT PERFECT

- We use the present perfect to speak about actions done in the immediate past: *hace poco, hace un rato, hace una hora...*

  > *¡**Hemos visto** a Antonio Banderas!*
  > *–¿Qué sabes de Pedro?*
  > *–**He hablado** con él hace un momento. Está bien.*

- We use the present perfect to speak about an action carried out at a time that forms part of the present: *hoy, esta mañana, este mes, este verano...*

  este año _____
  _____ este verano _____
  _____ hoy ____
  _____ ahora
  _____•_____

  > ***Hoy he tenido** dos exámenes.*
  > *–¿Qué **habéis hecho este verano**?*
  > *–**Hemos ido** a la playa. **Nos hemos divertido** mucho. Este año **he estado** algo enfermo.*

- We use the present perfect to speak about past experiences without indicating a specific time or moment.

  _____ ahora
  ——?——?——?————————•—

  > *¿**Has estado alguna vez** en Cuzco?*
  > *No **he viajado nunca** en avión.*
  > ***He trabajado** en un circo.*

  – We don't use the present perfect with expressions of past time.

  > *El año pasado ~~hemos estado~~ en Chile.* →
  > ***Hemos estado** en Chile.*

  > *He ~~corrido~~ un maratón ~~hace tres años~~.* →
  > ***He corrido** un maratón.*

- We use the present perfect with *ya* or *todavía no* to say or ask if an action has or hasn't been done before now.

  > *Ya **hemos visitado** Santiago.*
  > *¿**Has visitado** ya Santiago?*
  > *Todavía no **hemos visitado** Santiago.*

  – In questions, *ya* can be omitted.

  > *–¿**Habéis empezado** las clases?*

PRETERITE

- We use the preterite to speak about actions done in the past but some time ago: *hace una semana, hace un mes...*

  > ***Hace una semana vimos** a Antonio Banderas en el estreno de su última película.*

- We use the preterite to speak about an action carried out at a time that forms part of the past: *ayer, el mes pasado, aquel verano...*

  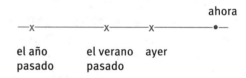

  el año   el verano   ayer
  pasado   pasado

  > ***Ayer tuve** dos exámenes.*
  > *–¿Qué **hicisteis el verano pasado**?*
  > *–**Fuimos** a la playa. **Nos divertimos** mucho. El año pasado **estuve** muy enfermo.*

- We use the preterite when we indicate the moment that the action took place.

  hace tres años   el mes pasado

  > ***Hace tres años estuvimos** en Cuzco.*
  > ***El mes pasado viajé** en avión por primera vez.*
  > ***Trabajé** en un circo **hace muchos años**.*

  > ***El año pasado estuvimos** en Chile.*

  > ***Corrí** un maratón **hace tres años**.*

  > ***Visitamos** Santiago el domingo pasado.*
  > *¿Cuándo **visitasteis** Santiago?*

  > *–Sí, las **empezamos hace una semana**.*

▶ UNIT 58: Preterite: regular verbs   UNIT 59: Preterite: irregular verbs

62 EXERCISES

62.1. **Circle the correct answer in each case.**

1. (*Hemos estado* / *Estuvimos*) con Rosa hace poco.
2. Hoy no (*he ido* / *fui*) a trabajar.
3. ¿Cuándo (*ha nacido* / *nació*) tu hijo mayor?
4. (*Hemos estado* / *Estuvimos*) en México el verano de 1998.
5. (*He llegado* / *Llegué*) hace cinco minutos.
6. Este invierno no (*ha nevado* / *nevó*) mucho.
7. (*He estado* / *Estuve*) con Carlos hace una semana.
8. ¡(*Hemos visto* / *Vimos*) a George Clooney!
9. Amalia y sus padres (*han venido* / *vinieron*) a España hace tres años.
10. Cuando nos casamos (*hemos hecho* / *hicimos*) un viaje por América Central.

SCORE /10

62.2. **Complete the sentences with the correct form of the present perfect or preterite.**

1. Mi hermana (*tener*) ___ha tenido___ un niño hace poco.
2. Rosana nos (*invitar*) _____ a su casa el fin de semana pasado.
3. –¿Qué (*ustedes, hacer*) _____ este verano? –En julio (*estar*) _____ en Cancún. Lo (*pasar*) _____ estupendamente.
4. Hoy no (*yo, ir*) _____ a clase.
5. El siglo pasado (*haber*) _____ dos guerras mundiales.
6. Lotta (*aprender*) _____ mucho español este año.
7. –¿Qué (*tú, hacer*) _____ ayer? –Nada, (*estar*) _____ en casa.
8. Este verano (*yo, bañarse*) _____ mucho en el mar.

SCORE /11

62.3. **Complete the sentences with the correct form of the present perfect or preterite.**

1. –¿(*vosotras, estar*) ___Habéis estado___ alguna vez en América del Sur? –Sí, hace cuatro años (*estar*) ___estuvimos___ en Uruguay.
2. ¿(*ustedes, montar*) _____ alguna vez a caballo?
3. –¿(*tú, comer*) _____ alguna vez paella? –Sí, la (*comer*) _____ cuando (*estar*) _____ en España.
4. Peter no (*estudiar*) _____ nunca español.
5. ¿(*tú, trabajar*) _____ alguna vez en una película?

SCORE /8

62.4. **Arnaldo and Maite are spending a weeks' vacation in Spain. Other tourists ask them questions. Complete the dialogue writing the questions and answers as in the example.**

1. *estar / Barcelona* ___¿Habéis estado ya en Barcelona?___ (*miércoles*) Sí, ___estuvimos el miércoles.___
2. *probar / el cocido* ¿_____? (*lunes*) Sí, _____.
3. *visitar / Museo del Prado* ¿_____? (*martes por la mañana*) Sí, _____.
4. *comprar / los regalos* ¿_____? No, _____.
5. *ir / a Sevilla* ¿_____? (*ayer*) Sí, _____.
6. *ver / una corrida de toros* ¿_____? No, _____.

SCORE /12

62.5. **Complete the sentences with the correct from of the present perfect or preterite.**

1. El partido todavía no (*terminar*) ___ha terminado___.
2. –¿Cuándo (*tú, ir*) _____ a México? –Hace dos años.
3. Javier (*correr*) _____ el maratón el domingo pasado.
4. –¿(*tú, ver*) _____ a Ana? –Sí, la (*ver*) _____ el sábado.
5. –¿_____ (*llegar*) ya el correo? –No, todavía no _____.
6. –¿(*cerrar*) _____ ya los bancos? –Sí, (*cerrar*) _____ hace dos horas.

SCORE /9

133

63 *trabajaba, comía, vivía*
Imperfect

*Cuando era joven, **trabajaba** en un laboratorio.*   *Los mayas **vivían** en Guatemala y en el sur de México.*

Trabajaba and *vivían* are forms of the imperfect past indicative.

● Forming the imperfect of regular verbs

	trabaj-ar	com-er	viv-ir
(yo)	trabaj-**aba**	com-**ía**	viv-**ía**
(tú)	trabaj-**abas**	com-**ías**	viv-**ías**
(usted)	trabaj-**aba**	com-**ía**	viv-**ía**
(él, ella)	trabaj-**aba**	com-**ía**	viv-**ía**
(nosotros, nosotras)	trabaj-**ábamos**	com-**íamos**	viv-**íamos**
(vosotros, vosotras)	trabaj-**abais**	com-**íais**	viv-**íais**
(ustedes)	trabaj-**aban**	com-**ían**	viv-**ían**
(ellos, ellas)	trabaj-**aban**	com-**ían**	viv-**ían**

● Irregular verbs

	ver	ser	ir
(yo)	**veía**	**era**	**iba**
(tú)	**veías**	**eras**	**ibas**
(usted)	**veía**	**era**	**iba**
(él, ella)	**veía**	**era**	**iba**
(nosotros, nosotras)	**veíamos**	**éramos**	**íbamos**
(vosotros, vosotras)	**veíais**	**erais**	**ibais**
(ustedes)	**veían**	**eran**	**iban**
(ellos, ellas)	**veían**	**eran**	**iban**

● We use the imperfect to speak about habitual past actions. It states what was usual in a past time period or what we usually did during a specific period of time in our lives: *cuando era joven, de pequeño, en aquella época, antes...*

>   *Los incas **cultivaban** maíz y papas.*   *Los mayas no **hablaban** español.*
>   *Cuando **era** joven, **trabajaba** mucho y **dormía** poco.*   *Antes **salía** mucho; ahora salgo menos.*

  – With the imperfect, we usually use expressions of frequency such as *siempre, a menudo, nunca, de vez en cuando, todos los días...*

>   *Cuando **vivía** en Buenos Aires, **iba** al teatro **todas las semanas**.*
>   *Cuando mi marido y yo **éramos** jóvenes, **íbamos** al campo **todos los fines de semana**.*
>   *De pequeña, **no salía nunca** sola.*

Yo vi al ladrón. **Era** alto, **tenía** el pelo corto y **llevaba** gafas de sol.

● We also use it to describe people, objects, or places in the past.

>   *Esta ciudad **era** más tranquila antes; no **había** tanta gente ni tanto tráfico.*
>   *El pteradonón **tenía** un pico muy grande, pero no **tenía** dientes.*

63 EXERCISES

63.1. **Complete the sentences with the imperfect of the verbs in parentheses.**

1. Cuando (*yo, ser*) __era__ pequeño, siempre (*rezar*) __rezaba__ antes de acostarme.
2. Cuando Martín y Pablo (*ser*) _____ jóvenes, (*llevar*) _____ camisas de flores y (*escuchar*) _____ música pop.
3. Cuando nos casamos, (*vivir*) _____ en un piso muy pequeño y Nuria (*trabajar*) _____ en una empresa de informática.
4. Loli (*ser*) _____ muy independiente de pequeña. (*Ducharse*) _____ sola, (*hacerse*) _____ la cama, (*prepararse*) _____ el desayuno e (*ir*) _____ sola al colegio.
5. –¿Qué (*tú, hacer*) _____ antes de casarte? –(*Estudiar*) _____ Derecho.
6. Cuando (*nosotros, vivir*) _____ en Ciudad de México, (*ir*) _____ a Acapulco todos los veranos.
7. –¿Qué (*querer*) _____ ser de pequeña, María? –(*Querer*) _____ ser astronauta.
8. Hace cincuenta años, pocas familias (*tener*) _____ televisión en España.
9. –¿Qué (*hacer*) _____ ustedes antes de venir a España? –(*ser*) _____ comerciantes.
10. –¿En qué parte de Perú (*vivir*) _____ usted? –(*vivir*) _____ en la selva, en Iquitos.
11. Cuando era pequeño, Ramón (*ir*) _____ unos días a la sierra todos los años.
12. Antes no me (*gustar*) _____ la fruta.

SCORE __/25

63.2. **Complete the sentences about the ancient civilizations in America.**

| adorar | beber | construir | criar | ~~hacer~~ | ser | tener | vivir |

1. Los aztecas __hacían__ sacrificios humanos.
2. Los mayas _____ un calendario de dieciocho meses.
3. Los aztecas _____ en el centro y sur de México.
4. Los incas _____ al sol.
5. Los aztecas _____ chocolate.
6. Los incas _____ llamas.
7. Los incas _____ las casas de adobe o de piedra.
8. Los caribes _____ cazadores y recolectores.

SCORE __/8

63.3. **Complete the text using the verbs in parentheses.**

Cuando era pequeño pasaba los veranos en el pueblo de mis abuelos. (*ser*) __Era__ un pueblo muy pequeño y muy pobre. Las casas (*ser*) _____ de adobe y (*tener*) _____ unas ventanas muy pequeñas.
La casa de mis abuelos (*estar*) _____ en las afueras del pueblo, cerca del río. (*tener*) _____ dos pisos y en la parte de atrás (*haber*) _____ un pequeño huerto con algunos frutales.

Mi abuelo (*no, ser*) _____ muy alto pero (*ser*) _____ fuerte. Como (*no, tener*) _____ casi pelo, siempre (*llevar*) _____ una boina negra. Mi abuela (*tener*) _____ el pelo y los ojos grises. Los dos me (*querer*) _____ mucho. Mi abuelo (*trabajar*) _____ en el campo; (*cultivar*) _____ trigo y uvas para hacer vino. Mi abuela le (*ayudar*) _____ y (*trabajar*) _____ en la casa.

Los veranos en el pueblo (*ser*) _____ muy divertidos. (*yo, tener*) _____ muchos amigos y (*salir*) _____ todas las tardes. Unas veces (*nosotros, jugar*) _____ al fútbol, otras (*bañarse*) _____ en el río. Cuando más (*nosotros, divertirse*) _____ era en las fiestas. Durante tres o cuatro días (*haber*) _____ baile todas las noches. Nosotros no (*bailar*) _____ mucho, pero nos (*gustar*) _____ la música y (*acostarse*) _____ tardísimo. (*ser*) _____ unos veranos maravillosos.

SCORE __/27

135

64 *trabajé / trabajaba*
Contrasting preterite and imperfect

Compare:

PRETERITE	IMPERFECT
• We use the preterite to speak about past actions or situations that occurred at a specific past moment.	• We use the imperfect to speak about habitual past actions.

La semana pasada **comí** con Luis.

De pequeña, **comía** mucho chocolate.

la semana pasada   ahora

———x———•———

de pequeña   ahora

———x–x–x–x———•———

*Cuando estuvimos en Río, **fuimos** una vez a la playa. En 2005 **viví** dos meses en Atenas.*

*Cuando **vivía** en Río, **iba** mucho a la playa. De pequeño **vivía** en un pueblo.*

– It tells us what was done or happened *ayer, el domingo (pasado), la semana pasada, hace un mes...*

– It tells us what was done or happening *normalmente, siempre, todos los días, los domingos...*

El domingo **fuimos** al campo.

Cuando era pequeño, **íbamos** al campo los domingos.

*Ayer **dimos** un paseo por el centro.*

*Anoche **salí** con un amigo.*

*Cuando vivíamos en Cádiz, **dábamos** un paseo todas las tardes.*
*De joven, **salía** todas las noches.*

• We use the preterite of *ser* to assess past facts or situations.

*Dalí **fue** un gran pintor.*
*Mi abuela María **fue** una gran mujer.*

• We use the imperfect of *ser* to give past descriptions.

***Era** alto y moreno.*
***Era** muy alta y **tenía** los ojos grises.*

64 EXERCISES

64.1 **Circle the correct answer in each case.**

1. Ayer no (*fui* / *iba*) a trabajar. (*Estuve* / *Estaba*) enfermo.
2. ¿(*Fuiste* / *Ibas*) mucho a la playa cuando (*viviste* / *vivías*) en Las Palmas?
3. El domingo pasado (*estuvimos* / *estábamos*) en la sierra.
4. Cuando (*fui* / *era*) joven, (*fui* / *iba*) mucho al cine.
5. ¿A qué hora (*llegaste* / *llegabas*) anoche?
6. ¿Qué (*hicisteis* / *hacías*) el sábado pasado?
7. Ana y Eva (*tenían* / *tuvieron*) un accidente el año pasado.
8. Cervantes (*nació* / *nacía*) en 1547 y (*murió* / *moría*) en 1616.
9. Cuando (*vivió* / *vivía*) sola, Paula siempre (*oyó* / *oía*) música en la cama.
10. Eva (*empezó* / *empezaba*) a trabajar cuando (*acabó* / *acababa*) la carrera.
11. La señora se (*cayó* / *caía*) al bajar del autobús.
12. Ayer (*teníamos* / *tuvimos*) mucha suerte. Nos (*tocó* / *tocaba*) la lotería.

SCORE ...... /19

64.2 **Complete the sentences with the imperfect or preterite.**

1. ¿Cuándo (*cumplir*) ____cumplió____ años tu hermano?
2. Roberto (*terminar*) _____ la carrera hace tres meses.
3. Rafael (*estar*) _____ más delgado cuando (*estudiar*) _____.
4. La Segunda Guerra Mundial (*acabar*) _____ en 1945.
5. Pedro (*conocer*) _____ a Laura en quinto de carrera y enseguida (*casarse*) _____.
6. Mi abuelo (*salir*) _____ del pueblo hace muchos años.
7. ¿En qué (*tú, trabajar*) _____ cuando (*tú, vivir*) _____ en Venezuela?
8. Cristina (*hablar*) _____ sueco cuando era pequeña.

SCORE ...... /11

64.3 **Complete the sentences with the imperfect or preterite.**

1. Ayer (*dar*) ____dimos____ un paseo por el campo.
2. Antes, todos los domingos (*dar*) _____ un paseo por el centro.
3. De joven (*yo, jugar*) _____ al fútbol todos los domingos.
4. ¿Qué (*vosotros, hacer*) _____ anoche?
5. Cuando vivíamos en Chile, normalmente (*ir*) _____ a Viña del Mar todos los fines de semana.
6. Cuando estuve en México, (*pasar*) _____ un fin de semana en Acapulco.

SCORE ...... /6

64.4 **Complete the dialogues with the verbs in parentheses.**

1. –¿Cuándo (*tú, conocer*) ____conociste____ a Maruja?
   –La (*conocer*) _____ cuando (*vivir*) _____ en Bogotá.
2. –El verano pasado (*nosotros, estar*) _____ en México.
   –¿Les (*gustar*) _____ mi país?
   –Sí, (*pasar*) _____ una semana en Ciudad de México y luego (*ir*) _____ al Yucatán.
3. –¿Qué (*usted, hacer*) _____ cuando (*vivir*) _____ en Ecuador?
   –(*ser*) _____ maestra.
   –¿Por qué (*venirse*) _____ a España?
   –(*no, tener*) _____ trabajo allí.

SCORE ...... /12

64.5 **Complete the sentences with the preterite or the imperfect of the verb *ser*.**

1. El siglo XX ____fue____ muy violento.
2. Mi abuelo _____ bajo y gordo.
3. Marconi _____ un gran inventor.
4. Los mayas _____ grandes constructores.
5. Picasso _____ un gran artista.
6. Mis padres tenían una casa en la sierra. _____ preciosa.
7. Andrea tenía dos hermanos. _____ altos y morenos.
8. De pequeño, yo _____ rubio.

SCORE ...... /8

65 trabajaré, comeré, viviré
Future: regular verbs

Mañana **lloverá** en el norte.

Llegaremos a Caracas a las cuatro y cuarto hora local.

Lloverá and *llegaremos* are forms of the future tense.

● Forming the future: regular verbs

	trabaj-ar	com-er	viv-ir
(yo)	trabajar-**é**	comer-**é**	vivir-**é**
(tú)	trabajar-**ás**	comer-**ás**	vivir-**ás**
(usted)	trabajar-**á**	comer-**á**	vivir-**á**
(él, ella)	trabajar-**á**	comer-**á**	vivir-**á**
(nosotros, nosotras)	trabajar-**emos**	comer-**emos**	vivir-**emos**
(vosotros, vosotras)	trabajar-**éis**	comer-**éis**	vivir-**éis**
(ustedes)	trabajar-**án**	comer-**án**	vivir-**án**
(ellos, ellas)	trabajar-**án**	comer-**án**	vivir-**án**

Verbs with *se*: sentirse → me sentiré, te sentirás, se sentirá, se sentirá, nos sentiremos, os sentiréis, se sentirán, se sentirán.

● We use the future to speak about future actions or situations. It tells us what will happen *mañana*, *dentro de (tres meses, dos días...)*, *la próxima semana*, *el año que viene*, etc.

El nuevo edificio **estará** *acabado dentro de seis meses.*

```
enero ---------- 6 meses ------ julio
ahora
————————•————————————x————————
  están construyendo      estará acabado
  un edificio             el edificio
```

Mañana **te sentirás** *mejor.*

– We usually use it with the following expressions:

> *luego, más tarde*
> *pronto*
> *el próximo (lunes)/ la próxima (semana)*
> *(el año/ la semana) que viene*
>
> *en el año 2050/ 3000...*
> *dentro de* + period of time

–*¿Has llamado a José?* –*No. Lo* **llamaré más tarde.**
No te preocupes. **Pronto encontrarás** *trabajo.*

–*¿Habéis escrito a la abuela?* –*No. Le* **escribiremos** *la semana que viene.*

El año que viene estudiaré *ruso.*
En el año 2025 acabaré *de pagar el piso.*
–*¿Han llegado los nuevos ordenadores?* –*No.* **Llegarán dentro de unos días.**

● We use the future to make predictions.

El fin de semana **nevará** *a partir de mil metros.*
Conocerá *a una persona maravillosa y* **se casarán.**
Llegaremos *a Marte en el siglo XXI.*

Vivirás muchos años y **tendrás** muchos hijos.

▶ **UNIT 101: Conditional clauses**   **UNIT 102: Time clauses**

65.1 **Complete the sentences with the future of the verbs in parentheses.**

1. Hoy no puedo ir. (*Ir*) ___Iré___ mañana.
2. –Nos vamos hoy a Panamá. –¿Y cuándo (*volver*) _____?
3. Hoy no te puedo llamar. Te (*llamar*) _____ el lunes.
4. –¿Habéis acabado la traducción? –No, la (*acabar*) _____ la semana que viene.
5. –¿Han arreglado ya el ordenador? –No, lo (*arreglar*) _____ cuando puedan.
6. –¿Has ido al dentista? –Todavía no. (*Ir*) _____ cuando tenga tiempo.
7. –¿Puedes prestarme tu bicicleta? –Sí, claro, pero ¿cuándo me la (*devolver*) _____?
8. Estas plantas están secas. Riégalas o (*morirse*)_____.
9. –¿Crees que (*yo, aprobar*) _____? –(*Aprobar*) _____ si estudias mucho.
10. Ahora no tenemos hambre. (*Comer*) _____ más tarde.
11. –Quiero una bicicleta. –Te (*yo, regalar*) _____ una para Reyes.
12. –Me gustaría ir a Cuba. –(*Ir*) _____ cuando podamos.

SCORE ..../ 13

65.2 **Complete the weather forecast for next weekend.**

El fin de semana (*ser*) ___será___ bastante frío. El sábado (*bajar*) _____ las temperaturas en todo el país y (*nevar*) _____ en zonas altas del norte. El domingo (*subir*) _____ un poco las temperaturas aunque (*seguir*) _____ haciendo frío. (*Llover*) _____ en el oeste y suroeste. En el centro (*soplar*) _____ fuertes vientos del norte.

SCORE ..../ 7

65.3 **Complete the horoscopes.**

ayudar	conocer	desaparecer	gastar	mejorar	pasar
recibir (2)	sentirse	ser (2)	verse	viajar	

1. Aries: ___Recibirá___ muchas invitaciones. _____ una semana muy divertida, aunque _____ un poco cansado y _____ más dinero de lo normal.

2. Tauro: _____ envuelto en problemas, aunque sus amigos le _____. Su salud _____ excelente.

3. Cáncer: _____ a algún país lejano y _____ a alguien importante. _____ su situación económica.

4. Escorpio: _____ todos sus problemas. _____ unos días muy felices con familia y amigos y _____ una sorpresa agradable.

SCORE ..../ 13

65.4 **Complete the conversation between a couple and a psychic.**

¿ ___Encontraremos___ trabajo pronto?

¿Y cuándo (*casarse*) _____?

¿(*ser*) _____ ricos?

¿(*viajar*) _____ mucho?

Sí, (*encontrar*) _____ trabajo dentro de unas semanas.

(*casarse*) _____ dentro de dos años y (*ser*) _____ muy felices.

No, pero uno de sus hijos (*ser*) _____ muy famoso y muy rico.

Sí, (*visitar*) _____ muchos países y (*vivir*) _____ varios años en otro país.

SCORE ..../ 10

66 *habrá, podré*
Future: irregular verbs

● Forming the future: irregular verbs

		–é	(yo)
		–ás	(tú)
		–á	(usted)
haber →	habr–	**–á**	(él, ella)
poder →	podr–	**–emos**	(nosotros, nosotras)
saber →	sabr–	**–éis**	(vosotros, vosotras)
		–án	(ustedes)
		–án	(ellos, ellas)

En el año 2050 **habrá** ciudades en la Luna.

		–é	(yo)
		–ás	(tú)
poner →	pon**d**r–	**–á**	(usted)
salir →	sal**d**r–	**–á**	(él, ella)
tener →	ten**d**r–	**–emos**	(nosotros, nosotras)
venir →	ven**d**r–	**–éis**	(vosotros, vosotras)
		–án	(ustedes)
		–án	(ellos, ellas)

¿Ha venido Amelia?   No, **vendrá** más tarde.

		–é	(yo)
		–ás	(tú)
		–á	(usted)
decir ▸	dir–	**–á**	(él, ella)
hacer ▸	har–	**–emos**	(nosotros, nosotras)
querer ▸	querr–	**–éis**	(vosotros, vosotras)
		–án	(ustedes
		–án	(ellos, ellas)

Les **diré** a mis padres que os he visto.
Les **hará** mucha ilusión.

● Uses of the future

– Future actions or situations: *Pondré la lavadora por la tarde.*
– Predictions: *En el futuro **podremos** vivir en la Luna.*   *Mañana **hará** buen tiempo en todo el país.*

● We also use the future to express opinions or hypotheses about the future.

*¿Crees que **vendrán** todos a la fiesta?*
*Estoy segura de que os **querréis** mucho y seréis muy felices.*
*Creo que la semana que viene **hará** buen tiempo.*

▶ UNIT 65: Future: regular verbs   UNIT 101: Conditional clauses

66.1 **Complete the sentences with the future of the verbs in the box.**

decir (2)	haber	hacer (3)	poner	saber	salir	~~tener~~	venir

1. Hoy no tengo dinero. Pero no te preocupes; lo ___tendré___ dentro de unos días.
2. –¿Has hecho la cama? –No, la _____ luego.
3. –¿Ha venido Sonia? –No, pero creo que _____ más tarde.
4. Mañana _____ tormentas en el centro del país y _____ bastante frío en el norte.
5. –¿Le has dicho a Pepe que no podemos ir a su fiesta? –No, se lo _____ mañana.
6. –¿Sabéis ya el resultado del examen? –No, pero lo _____ muy pronto.
7. –¿Ha salido ya Rocío? –No, _____ dentro de un rato.
8. –¿Has puesto el lavavajillas? –No, lo _____ esta noche después de cenar.
9. –¿Te han dicho las notas? –No, me las _____ esta tarde.
10. –¿Habéis hecho los ejercicios? –No, los _____ esta noche.

SCORE ...... / 11

66.2 **What will life be like in fifty years? Write sentences with the words given.**

1. Los robots / hacer / todos los trabajos físicos ___Los robots harán todos los trabajos físicos.___
2. (Nosotros) Poder / aprender / con ordenadores / en casa _____.
3. (Nosotros) Saber / curar / el cáncer _____.
4. No / haber / hambre _____.
5. Haber / ciudades satélite en el espacio _____.
6. Haber / menos enfermedades _____.
7. No / haber / guerras _____.
8. Todo el mundo / tener / un ordenador personal _____.
9. Haber / coches voladores _____.
10. (Nosotros) Poder / visitar la Luna _____.

SCORE ...... / 10

66.3 **Complete the sentences with the verbs in parentheses.**

1. Cuando tengas cincuenta años, tú también (tener) ___tendrás___ muchas arrugas.
2. –¿Crees que mañana (hacer) _____ buen tiempo? –No creo. Creo que (hacer) _____ frío.
3. –Supongo que (vosotros, venir) _____ todos el sábado. –No lo sé. Adela está un poco resfriada.
4. –¿Crees que (tú, poder) _____ ayudarme con la redacción? –Sí, creo que (poder) _____ ayudarte mañana.
5. –Susana quiere hacer una fiesta en su casa. ¿Qué crees que (decir) _____ sus padres?
   –Creo que (poner) _____ muchas dificultades.
6. Estoy seguro de que tus hijos te (querer) _____ siempre.

SCORE ...... / 9

66.4 **What are your predictions about the future? Write affirmative or negative sentences.**

1. (hacer) ___(No) Haré___ un viaje alrededor del mundo.
2. (tener) _____ muchos hijos.
3. (saber) _____ hablar español perfectamente.
4. (tener) _____ una vida muy larga.
5. (poder) _____ vivir sin trabajar.
6. (hacer) _____ algo importante.

SCORE ...... / 6

67 *voy a salir*
Present of *ir a* + infinitive

Voy a salir con unos amigos.

¿Qué vas a hacer esta noche?

● The present of the verb *ir* + *a* + infinitive of the main verb

(yo)	voy			
(tú)	vas			
(usted)	va			trabajar
(él, ella)	va	+	a +	comer
(nosotros, nosotras)	vamos			vivir
(vosotros, vosotras)	vais			
(ustedes)	van			
(ellos, ellas)	van			

> **BE CAREFUL!**
>
> Verbs with *se* → *Laura y Jaime **van a casarse** este verano.*
> *Laura y Jaime **se van a casar** este verano.*

● We use *voy, vas, va... a* + infinitive to:
  - speak about intentions or near future plans. It tells us what we are planning to do soon or *esta tarde, esta noche, mañana, este verano...*

    *Tengo sueño. **Voy a acostarme.***
    (I'm planning to do it right now.)

    *–¿Qué **vas a hacer** esta noche?*
    (What are your plans for tonight?)

    *–**Voy a ir** al cine.*
    (I intend to go to the movies.)

ahora	esta noche
tengo intención	de (ir al cine)

    *–¿**Van a cenar** en casa? –No, **vamos a salir**. **Vamos a ir** a un restaurante mexicano.*
    *¿Cuándo **vas a arreglar** la televisión?*
    *Hoy **no voy a dormir** la siesta.*

  - refer to something that, because of present circumstances, seems sure to happen.

    *Esa niña **va a caerse** de la silla.*
    *Escucha. **Va a hablar** el presidente.*

Llévate el paraguas.
Va a llover.

67 EXERCISES

67.1 **What are you going to do this evening? Write sentences with the expressions from the box.**

bañarse	~~jugar al tenis~~	pescar	recoger la habitación	trabajar en el jardín

1. Van a jugar al tenis.
2. _____
3. _____
4. _____
5. _____

67.2 **What are you going to do? Complete the sentences with the verbs from the box.**

acostarse	beber	comer	ducharse	encender	estudiar	~~lavar~~	ver

1. El coche está sucio. Lo _____ voy a lavar _____.
2. Tengo hambre. _____ algo.
3. Estamos cansados. _____.
4. Tengo sed. _____ algo.
5. Mañana tenemos un examen. _____ un poco.
6. _____ la calefacción. Tengo frío.
7. Estoy aburrido. _____ una película.
8. Estoy sucio. _____.

67.3 **Complete the dialogues with the verbs in parentheses.**

1. –¿Qué (hacer) _van a hacer_ ustedes este verano? –Los niños (pasar) _____ unos días en un campamento, y Celia y yo (ir) _____ a Marbella. –¿Y dónde (alojarse) _____? –En una casa. La (compartir) _____ con unos amigos.
2. –¿Cuándo (arreglar) _____ tu habitación, Marta? –Hoy no puedo. (Ir) _____ a la fiesta de Sandra. Es su cumpleaños. –¿Y qué le (regalar) _____? –No lo sé. Ahora le (comprar) _____ algo.
3. –¿Cuándo (tú, ver) _____ a Luchi? –El domingo. (Salir) _____ con ella y con Elena. –¿Adónde (ir) _____? –Al cine. (ver) _____ la última película de Almodóvar. –¿(Cenar) _____ fuera? –Sí, después del cine (ir) _____ a un nuevo restaurante argentino. Creo que es muy bueno.

67.4 **Look at the drawings and complete the sentences with the verbs from the box.**

aterrizar	caerse	casarse	chocar	empezar	escaparse	perder	~~tener~~

1. Vamos a tener un niño.
2. ¡Silencio! _____ la obra.
3. Mira. _____
4. ¡_____ el autobús!
5. ¡Esos barcos _____!
6. _____
7. _____
8. _____

68 haré / hago / voy a hacer
Contrasting different ways of expressing the future

Compare:

FUTURE

- We use the future:

  – to refer to something that will happen at a future time...

  –¿Cuándo queréis casaros?
  *–No tenemos prisa. Ya **nos casaremos**.* (At some moment in the future)

  *Algún día **iré** a China.* (At some moment in the future)

  – ... or that will probably happen in the future.

Este año probablemente **acabaré** mis estudios.

Este verano seguramente **iremos** a Marbella.
(When summer comes.)

– to make predictions.

Empezarás una nueva vida en otro país.

En el futuro los robots **harán** todo el trabajo.

VOY A + INFINITIVE

- We use *voy a* + infinitive:

  – to refer to current plans or intentions in the future.

  Vamos a casarnos este año.
  (They are our current plans.)

  *De mayor, **voy a ser** bombero.*
  (They are his current plans.)

El año que viene **voy a empezar** mis estudios de doctorado.

Vamos a ir a Marbella este verano
(They are current plans.)

– to refer to something that, because of present circumstances, seems sure to happen.

¡Callaos! **Van a empezar** las noticias.

¡Daos prisa! **Va a salir** el tren.

PRESENT INDICATIVE

- We use the present indicative:

  – to refer to something already agreed upon or scheduled in the future.

  *Luchi y Rodolfo **se casan** en enero.*
  (They already know when.)

  *En febrero **cumplo** veinticuatro años.* (I already know when.)

En julio **voy** al viaje de fin de carrera.

¡Me voy mañana a Marbella!
(Everything is agreed upon and scheduled.)

– to refer to something already agreed upon or scheduled in the future or that is part of a timetable.

La película **empieza** a las diez.

*–¿A qué hora **sales** esta noche?*
–A las ocho.

144

68 EXERCISES

68.1. Circle the correct form in each case.

1. ¡Daos prisa! (Va a salir / Saldrá) el tren.
2. Rocío (se casa / se casará) mañana.
3. El concierto (acaba / va a acabar) a la una.
4. ¡Cuidado! Te (caes / vas a caer).
5. Mañana no (trabajo / trabajaré). Es domingo.
6. Me (voy / iré) de vacaciones mañana.
7. ¿A qué hora (llegará / llega) el vuelo de La Habana?
8. ¡Mira! (Saldrá / Va a salir) el sol.

68.2. Complete the sentences with the future or with *voy, vas, va... a* + infinitive of the verbs in parentheses.

1. –¿Cuándo (*tú, arreglar*) __vas a arreglar__ la habitación? –No sé. La (*yo, arreglar*) __arreglaré__ más tarde.
2. ¿Qué (*ustedes, hacer*) _____ el domingo?
3. No se preocupen. (*Ser*) _____ ustedes muy felices y (*tener*) _____ muchos hijos.
4. ¡Cuidado con el perro! Te (*morder*) _____.
5. Te (*yo, llamar*) _____ cuando llegue a Santiago.
6. Esta noche no puedo salir. Me (*llamar*) _____ Osvaldo.
7. –¿(*yo, encontrar*) _____ trabajo pronto? –Sí, pero no (*tú, ganar*) _____ mucho.
8. ¿Adónde (*ustedes, ir*) _____ este verano?
9. Mira el cielo. (*Haber*) _____ una tormenta.
10. ¡Corre! (*nosotros, perder*) _____ el autobús.

68.3. Complete the sentences with the verbs from the box and help from the drawings.

cantar	caerse	empezar	~~salir~~	salir

Va a salir el sol. ① / El sábado _____ Shakira en el Calderón. ② / ¡_____! ③ / _____ el partido. ④ / El vuelo de Santiago _____ a las 20:15. ⑤

68.4. Complete the sentences with the future or the present indicative of the verbs in the box.

casarse	~~examinar~~	haber	ir	poder	regresar	salir	vivir

1. Estoy un poco nervioso. Me __examino__ mañana.
2. En el futuro _____ viajar por el espacio.
3. Algún día (yo) _____ junto al mar.
4. Alicia y Manuel _____ al médico esta tarde.
5. Esta noche _____ un buen partido en la tele.
6. –¿Cuándo _____ a Chile, Paco? –La semana que viene.
7. Seguramente Trini y yo _____ el año que viene.
8. ¿A qué hora _____ el tren de Carlos?

68.5. Complete the sentences with *voy, vas, va... a* + infinitive or the present indicative of the verbs in parentheses.

1. –¿Cuándo (*empezar*) __empiezan__ las clases? –El lunes que viene.
2. Daos prisa; es muy tarde. (*Cerrar*) _____ los restaurantes.
3. Ignacio y yo (*trabajar*) _____ en un restaurante este verano.
4. –¿Cuándo (*ser*) _____ el examen? –El día doce.
5. ¿A qué hora (*salir*) _____ tu avión mañana?
6. –¿Qué (*tú, hacer*) _____ mañana? –No sé. No tengo planes.
7. Perdone, ¿cuándo (*acabar*) _____ el concierto?
8. –¿Cuándo (*acabar*) _____ el cuadro, Miguel? –No sé. Pronto.

Abre la ventana.
Affirmative imperative: regular verbs

Abre la ventana. Hace calor.

Abrid el libro
en la página diez.

Pasen ustedes, por favor.

Abre, abrid, and *pasen* are affirmative forms of the imperative. We use them to give instructions, advice, permission, etc.

● Forming the affirmative imperative: regular verbs

trabaj-ar	com-er	viv-ir	
trabaj-**a**	com-**e**	viv-**e**	(tú)
trabaj-**e**	com-**a**	viv-**a**	(usted)
trabaj-**ad**	com-**ed**	viv-**id**	(vosotros, vosotras)
trabaj-**en**	com-**an**	viv-**an**	(ustedes)

BE CAREFUL!

Ver: ve, vea, ved, vean

– verbs ending in –*gar*: pagar	→	pa**ga**	pa**gue**	pa**gad**	pa**guen**
– verbs ending in –*ger*: escoger	→	esco**ge**	esco**ja**	esco**ged**	esco**jan**
– verbs ending in –*car*: practicar	→	practi**ca**	practi**que**	practi**cad**	practi**quen**
– verbs ending in –*zar*: cruzar	→	cru**za**	cru**ce**	cru**zad**	cru**cen**

● verb (+ personal pronoun)

    Escoge un libro.   ***Entrad.***
    Ahora ***habla tú**, Ismael.*   ***Pasen ustedes**, por favor.*

● We use the imperative to express:

    – orders and instructions: ***Envíe*** *esta carta, Sr. Aguayo, por favor.*
                                    Abra *con cuidado.*
                                    *¡Policía! ¡**Abran** la puerta!*
                                    Cruza *el puente y después **gira** a la izquierda.*

¡**Apaga**
la televisión
y **estudia**!

    – requests and invitations: ***Abre*** *la puerta, por favor.*
                                   Coged *un pastel. Están muy ricos.*

    – advice, suggestions, or warnings: ***Come*** *más. Estás muy delgado.*
                                       Trabaja *o tendrás problemas.*

    – giving permission: *–¿Puedo pasar? –Sí, por supuesto, **pasa**.*

69.1. Write the advice from the doctor. Use the verbs from the box.

andar	beber	comer	descansar	~~practicar~~

1. ____Practique____ algún deporte.
2. _____ después de las comidas.
3. _____ mucha fruta.
4. _____ mucha agua.
5. _____ dos kilómetros al día.

SCORE ...... / 5

69.2. What would you say in each case?

1. (a un amigo) Están llamando. (*Abrir*) ____Abre____ la puerta, por favor.
2. (a unos niños) (*Cruzar*)_____ por el paso de cebra.
3. (a unos amigos) La paella está muy rica. (*Comer*)_____ más.
4. (a un amigo) (*Hablar*)_____ más bajo. No soy sorda.
5. (a alguien de su familia) (*Bajar*)_____ la televisión. Está muy alta.
6. (a un amigo) −¿Puedo llamar por teléfono? −Sí, por supuesto. (*Llamar*) _____.
7. (a un niño) −¿Puedo comer otro pastel? −Sí, claro. (*Comer*)_____ todos los que quieras.
8. (a unos señores mayores) −¿Podemos pasar? −Sí, (*pasar*)_____ ustedes, por favor.
9. (a unos desconocidos) (*Cruzar*) _____ por aquí; es más seguro.
10. (a unos clientes) (*Pagar*) _____ en la caja, por favor.

SCORE ...... /10

69.3. Complete the following ads. Use the verbs in parentheses.

1. «Mes del ahorro en *Supermás*. (*Comprar*) ____Compre____ dos y (*pagar*) _____ uno.»
2. «(*Visitar*) _____ Andalucía. (*Recorrer*) _____ sus ciudades y sus pueblos. (*Descansar*) _____ en sus playas. (*Vivir*) _____ unos días mágicos.»
3. «Restaurante *Nuevo Mundo*. Algo nuevo para usted. (*Comer*) _____ en un ambiente especial y (*disfrutar*) _____ de un espectáculo inolvidable. (*Ver*) _____ las mejores actuaciones de América Latina.»
4. «¿Te gustaría hablar español? (*Estudiar*) _____ con el método *Naturalia* y (*aprender*) _____ español en diez meses.»
5. «¿No conoce usted América Latina? (*Enviar*) _____ una etiqueta de leche CAM a Radio Central. (*Participar*) _____ en nuestro concurso y (*ganar*) _____ un viaje a Perú para dos personas.»

SCORE ...... /14

70 *No abras la ventana.*
Negative imperatives: regular verbs

No abras la ventana, por favor. Tengo frío.

¡No toques eso! Es peligroso.

No abras and *no toques* are negative forms of the imperative.

● Forming the negative imperative: regular verbs

trabaj-ar	com-er	viv-ir	
no trabaj-**es**	no com-**as**	no viv-**as**	(tú)
no trabaj-**e**	no com-**a**	no viv-**a**	(usted)
no trabaj-**éis**	no com-**áis**	no viv-**áis**	(vosotros, vosotras)
no trabaj-**en**	no com-**an**	no viv-**an**	(ustedes)

BE CAREFUL!

> Ver: no ve**as**, no ve**a**, no ve**áis**, no ve**an**

– verbs ending in *–gar*: pagar	→no pa**gues**	no pa**gue**	no pa**guéis**	no pa**guen**
– verbs ending in *–ger*: escoger	→no esco**jas**	no esco**ja**	no esco**jáis**	no esco**ja**
– verbs ending in *–car*: practicar	→no practi**ques**	no practi**que**	no practi**quéis**	no practi**que**
– verbs ending in *–zar*: cruzar	→no cru**ces**	no cru**ce**	no cru**céis**	no cru**cen**

● We use the imperative to express:

– orders and instructions.

> **No habléis** en clase.   **No agite** la botella antes de abrirla.

– requests.

> **No abras** la ventana, por favor. Tengo frío.

– advice, suggestions, or warnings.

> **No coma** muchas grasas. Es malo para el corazón.
> **No bebáis** agua de esa fuente. No es potable.
> **No olviden** el paraguas. Puede llover.

– refusing permission.

> –Papá, ¿puedo coger el coche? –No, **no lo cojas**. Lo necesito yo.

70 EXERCISES

70.1. **Write the instructions from the driving school teacher. Use the verbs from the box.**

adelantar	aparcar	girar (2)	parar

1. ___No gire___ a la izquierda.
2. _____ a la derecha.
3. _____ aquí.

4. _____ aquí.
5. _____ aquí.

SCORE ...... /5

70.2. **What would this father say to his children in this situation?**

1. (Sus hijos están viendo una película violenta.)
   «___No veáis___ esa película.»
2. (Su hijo deja sus cosas en el salón.) «_____ tus cosas en el salón.»
3. (Sus hijos comen muchos caramelos.) «_____ tantos caramelos.»
4. (Su hijo está tocando la guitarra a las dos de la mañana.) «_____ la guitarra a estas horas.»
5. (Su hijo quiere regresar tarde.) «_____ muy tarde.»
6. (Sus hijos están discutiendo.) «_____.»
7. (Su hija está comiendo en el salón.) «_____ en el salón.»
8. (Su hijo bebe muchos refrescos.) «_____ tantos refrescos.»

SCORE ...... /8

70.3. **What would you say in each case?**

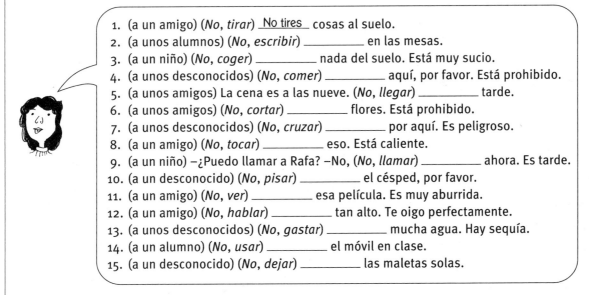

1. (a un amigo) (*No, tirar*) ___No tires___ cosas al suelo.
2. (a unos alumnos) (*No, escribir*) _____ en las mesas.
3. (a un niño) (*No, coger*) _____ nada del suelo. Está muy sucio.
4. (a unos desconocidos) (*No, comer*) _____ aquí, por favor. Está prohibido.
5. (a unos amigos) La cena es a las nueve. (*No, llegar*) _____ tarde.
6. (a unos amigos) (*No, cortar*) _____ flores. Está prohibido.
7. (a unos desconocidos) (*No, cruzar*) _____ por aquí. Es peligroso.
8. (a un amigo) (*No, tocar*) _____ eso. Está caliente.
9. (a un niño) −¿Puedo llamar a Rafa? −No, (*No, llamar*) _____ ahora. Es tarde.
10. (a un desconocido) (*No, pisar*) _____ el césped, por favor.
11. (a un amigo) (*No, ver*) _____ esa película. Es muy aburrida.
12. (a un amigo) (*No, hablar*) _____ tan alto. Te oigo perfectamente.
13. (a unos desconocidos) (*No, gastar*) _____ mucha agua. Hay sequía.
14. (a un alumno) (*No, usar*) _____ el móvil en clase.
15. (a un desconocido) (*No, dejar*) _____ las maletas solas.

SCORE ...... /15

71 *Cierra la ventana.*
Imperative: irregular verbs (1)

Cierra la ventana, por favor. Tengo frío.

Forming the imperative: some irregular verbs

- e → ie

cerr -ar		encend -er		
cierra	no cierres	enciende	no enciendas	(tú)
cierre	no cierres	encienda	no encienda	(usted)
cerrad	no cerréis	encended	no encendáis	(vosotros, vosotras)
cierren	no cierren	enciendan	no enciendan	(ustedes)

Others: -ar: *calentar, despertar, empezar, pensar, regar*
   -er: *defender, entender, perder*

> *No despiertes a Sonia. Está cansada.*
> *Riega las plantas todos los días.*

- e → i

ped -ir		
pide	no pidas	(tú)
pida	no pida	(usted)
pedid	no pidáis	(vosotros, vosotras)
pidan	no pidan	(ustedes)

Pide lo que quieras. Yo invito.

Others: *elegir, conseguir, corregir, freír, medir, repetir, seguir, servir, sonreír*

> *Corrige todos los ejercicios.*
> *No frías toda la carne. No tengo hambre.*
> *Sonreíd. Os voy a hacer una foto.*

BE CAREFUL!

verbs ending in -*gir*: elegir → elige, elija, elegid, elijan / no elijas, no elija, no elijáis, no elijan
verbs ending in -*guir*: seguir → sigue, siga, seguid, sigan / no sigas, no siga, no sigáis, no sigan

- Uses of the imperative ▶ UNIT 69: Affirmative imperative: regular verbs

  – orders and instructions:
    > *Corregid el ejercicio siete.*

  – requests and invitations:
    > *Enciende la luz, por favor.*   *Elige un libro. Te lo regalo.*

  – advice, suggestions, or warnings:
    > *No riegues mucho las plantas.*   *Sirve la sopa. Se va a enfriar.*

  – to give or refuse permission:
    > *–¿Puedo cerrar? Ya son las ocho. –Sí, cierra.*

71 EXERCISES

71.1 Complete the table.

EMPEZAR		DEFENDER		CONSEGUIR		
AFIRMATIVA	NEGATIVA	AFIRMATIVA	NEGATIVA	AFIRMATIVA	NEGATIVA	
empieza	no empieces	_____	_____	_____	_____	(tú)
_____	_____	_____	_____	_____	_____	(usted)
_____	_____	_____	_____	_____	_____	(vosotros, vosotras)
_____	_____	_____	_____	_____	_____	(ustedes)

SCORE ...../24

71.2 Complete the note with instructions to a friend. Use the verbs from the box.

1. _____Cierra_____ todas las ventanas cuando salgas.
2. _____ las plantas todos los días; una vez a la semana es suficiente.
3. _____ la llave del gas cuando acabes de cocinar.
4. _____ el pescado en la freidora, no en la sartén.
5. _____ el calentador una hora antes de ducharte.
6. _____ la calefacción; no hace frío.

cerrar (2)
encender (2)
freír
regar

SCORE ...../6

71.3 Complete the dialogues with the verbs from the box.

cerrar   despertar   pedir   ~~seguir~~   sonreír

71.4 What would you say in each case?

1. (a su familia) (*Empezar*) ____Empezad____ a comer. Yo llegaré un poco tarde.
2. (a un amigo) (*Elegir*) _____ un libro. Te lo regalo.
3. (a alguien de su familia) (*Encender*) _____ la luz. Está muy oscuro.
4. (a un camarero) No (*calentar*) _____ la leche. La quiero fría.
5. (a unos amigos) (*Sonreír*) _____. Os voy a hacer una foto.
6. (a unos alumnos) (*Corregir*) _____ el ejercicio.
7. (a un alumno) (*Cerrar*) _____ el libro.
8. (a un alumno) (*Repetir*) _____ lo que yo diga.
9. (a un amigo) (*Freír*) _____ más carne, por favor. Tengo mucha hambre.
10. (a un desconocido) (*Seguir*) _____ todo recto.
11. (a un niño) No (*pedir*) _____ nada a la gente. Es de mala educación.
12. (a un amigo) No (*despertar*) _____ a Carlos. Está cansado.

SCORE ...../12

71.5 Complete the ads.

1. Colchón Rex. (*Despertar*) __Despierte__ usted feliz y (*empezar*) _____ bien el día. (*Pensar*) _____ en su salud.
2. (*Elegir*) _____ Aerolatina, las líneas aéreas de Latinoamérica.
3. (*Sonreír*) _____ a la vida. No lo (*pensar*) _____ más. (*Seguir*) _____ la moda. Compre el nuevo Pestus y (*despertar*) _____ a nuevas sensaciones.

SCORE ...../8

72 No juegues aquí.
Imperative: irregular verbs (2)

Forming the imperative: other irregular verbs

● o → ue

soñ -ar		volv -er		
sueña	no sueñes	vuelve	no vuelvas	(tú)
sueñe	no sueñe	vuelva	no vuelva	(usted)
soñad	no soñéis	volved	no volváis	(vosotros, vosotras)
sueñen	no sueñen	vuelvan	no vuelvan	(ustedes)

Others: -ar: *comprobar, contar, encontrar, probar, recordar, volar*
    -er: *morder, mover*

Cuenta *hasta diez.*   **No muevan** *la mesa.*

● o → ue/u

dorm -ir		
duerme	no duermas	(tú)
duerma	no duerma	(usted)
dormid	no durmáis	(vosotros, vosotras)
duerman	no duerman	(ustedes)

«**Dormid** en esta habitación.
Es más fresca.»

No durmáis *fuera. Hace frío.*   **Duerma** *ocho horas todos los días.*

● u → ue

jug -ar		
juega	no juegues	(tú)
juegue	no juegue	(usted)
jugad	no juguéis	(vosotros, vosotras)
jueguen	no jueguen	(ustedes)

No **juegues** con el perro.
Es peligroso.

Juega *bien o perderás.*   **No juguéis** *en el salón.*

● Uses of the imperative ▶ UNIT 69: Affirmative imperative: regular verbs

– orders and instructions:

    ¡**Vuelve** *aquí inmediatamente!*   **Compruebe** *el cambio.*

– requests and invitations:

    Mueva *un poco la silla, por favor.*

– advice, suggestions, or warnings:

    No volváis *tarde. Hace frío.*   **Cuenta** *el dinero.*

– to give or refuse permission:

    –¿Podemos jugar aquí? –No, **no juguéis** *aquí.* **Jugad** *en el jardín.*

72.1 Complete the tables.

RECORDAR		MORDER		
AFIRMATIVA	NEGATIVA	AFIRMATIVA	NEGATIVA	
recuerda	no recuerdes	_____	_____	(tú)
_____	_____	_____	_____	(usted)
_____	_____	_____	_____	(vosotros, vosotras)
_____	_____	_____	_____	(ustedes)

SCORE ...... /16

72.2 Complete the dialogues with the verbs in the affirmative or negative.

colgar	jugar	morder	probar	~~volver~~

① ¡Vuelve pronto, Álvaro!

② _____ esta sopa, Ana.

③ ¡Niños! _____ en el salón.

④ _____ el abrigo en esa percha.

⑤ «Momo, _____ la silla.»

SCORE ...... /5

72.3 What would you say in each case?

1. (a un amigo) (*Recordar*) __Recuerda__ que mañana es mi cumpleaños.
2. (a una niña) No (*colgar*) _____ el abrigo en una silla
3. (a un alumno) (*Contar*) _____ hasta veinte en español.
4. (a unos niños) No (*jugar*) _____ con ese perro.
5. (a un alumno) (*Volver*) _____ a escribir esas frases
6. (a una amiga) (*Devolver*) _____me mis cedés, por favor.
7. (a una amiga) (*Probar*) _____ esta tarta.
8. (a un alumno) No (*dormir*) _____ en clase, por favor.
9. (a un alumno) (*Comprobar*) _____ las respuestas.
10. (a una amiga) (*Tostar*) _____ un poco más de pan, por favor.
11. (a unos amigos) No me (*contar*) _____ esa historia otra vez.
12. (a unos alumnos) No (*mover*) _____ las mesas.
13. (a unos alumnos) (*Recordar*) _____ que mañana hay un examen.
14. (a un hijo) No (*volver*) _____ tarde.

SCORE ...... /14

72.4 Complete the ads.

1. «(*Volar*) __Vuele__ con Aerolatina, las líneas aéreas de Latinoamérica. (*Comprobar*) _____ por qué somos el número uno»
2. «Usted es el rey. (*Dormir*) _____ en un colchón Rex y (*soñar*) _____ los mejores sueños.»
3. ¿Tienes problemas con el afeitado? (*Probar*) _____ Softy, la nueva crema para el afeitado. (*Volver*)_____ a tener la piel como un niño. (*Apostar*) _____ por un afeitado perfecto.
4. (*Probar*) _____ su suerte. (*Jugar*) _____ a la Lotería Nacional y (*soñar*) _____ con el futuro.

SCORE ...... /10

73 *Pon la mesa.*
Imperative: irregular verbs (3)

● Forming the imperative: other irregular verbs

	(tú)	(usted)	(vosotros, vosotras)	(ustedes)
– decir:	di	diga	decid	digan
	no digas	no diga	no digáis	no digan
– hacer:	haz	haga	haced	hagan
	no hagas	no haga	no hagáis	no hagan
– poner:	pon	ponga	poned	pongan
	no pongas	no ponga	no pongáis	no pongan

Enrique, Sofía,
poned la mesa.

Di algo. No estés callado.   **No digas** *tonterías.*
Haz la comida. Es tarde.   **No hagas** *ruido.*

– salir:	sal	salga	salid	salgan
	no salgas	no salga	no salgáis	no salgan
– tener:	ten	tenga	tened	tengan
	no tengas	no tenga	no tengáis	no tengan

Tenga cuidado. Este
cruce es peligroso.

¡Sal de aquí ahora mismo!   **No salgan.** *Hace mucho frío.*
No tengáis miedo. No pasa nada.

– venir:	ven	venga	venid	vengan
	no vengas	no venga	no vengáis	no vengan
– ser:	sé	sea	sed	sean
	no seas	no sea	no seáis	no sean
– ir:	ve	vaya	id	vayan
	no vayas	no vaya	no vayáis	no vayan

Venid aquí.   **No vengas** *ahora. Estoy ocupado.*
Sé amable, Lola.   **No seáis** *impacientes.*
Susana, **ve** *a comprar pan.*   **No vayáis** *a casa de Martín. No está.*

● Uses of the imperative

– orders and instructions:

   ¡Haz la cama ahora mismo!

   Salgan por la puerta número dos.

– requests and invitations:

   Ven a verme cuando quieras.

– advice, suggestions, or warnings:

   No vengáis tarde.

   Tienes mala cara. Ve al médico.

– to give or refuse permission:

   –¿Podemos ir a casa de Alicia? –No, **no vayáis** *ahora. Es muy tarde.*

▶ UNIT 69: Affirmative imperative: regular verbs

73.1 **Circle the correct form.**

1. No (*diga*/*digas*) eso a mis padres, Don Pablo.
2. (*Sed*/*sean*) buenos, chicos.
3. (*Pon*/*poned*) estos platos en el lavavajillas, Andrés.
4. No (*salgáis*/*salid*) todos a la vez, por favor.
5. (*Haga*/*Haz*) la comida, papá.
6. (*Ve*/*Id*) por una pizza, niños.
7. (*Sed*/*Seáis*) más puntuales la próxima vez, por favor.
8. (*Venga*/*Vengan*) al centro con nosotros. Les llevamos.
9. No (*pongas*/*pongáis*) la música tan fuerte, Ángel.
10. Nunca (*digas*/*diga*) mentiras.

73.2 **Complete the dialogues with the verbs from the box in the affirmative or negative.**

| decir | hacer (2) | poner (2) | salir | ser | tener | venir (2) |

① No hagan fotos.
② _____ tímido, pasa.
③ _____ ruido, por favor.
④ _____ con nosotros, vamos al cine.
⑤ La comida está lista. _____ la mesa.
⑥ _____ a mi oficina, Sr. Ruiz, por favor.
⑦ _____ atención. Tengo algo que deciros.
⑧ _____ todos a la calle.
⑨ _____ miedo. No es peligroso.
⑩ _____ gracias, Javi.

73.3 **Complete the sentences with the verbs in parentheses.**

1. (*Tener*) ____Tenga____ cuidado, don Antonio. Este cruce es peligroso.
2. No (*salir*) _____ ahora, niños. Está lloviendo.
3. ¡Arturo! ¡Elisa! (*Poner*) _____ la mesa. Vamos a comer.
4. No (*salir*) _____ con Alberto, Cristina. Es muy antipático.
5. Estoy aburrido. (*Poner*) _____ la televisión, José.
6. (*Decir*) _____ 'Gracias' al abuelo, Pepín.
7. –¿Puedo decir algo, Arturo? –No, no (*decir*) _____ nada, Ismael.
8. (*Ser*) _____ bueno, Julián, y (*hacer*) _____ lo que te digo.
9. (*Tener*) _____ cuidado en el agua, niños.
10. ¿Puedo ir a casa de Rosa? – No, no (*ir*) _____ ahora. Es muy tarde.
11. (*Hacer*) _____ una copia de esta carta, Sr. Vázquez.
12. No (*ser*) _____ impaciente, Jaime. Comemos dentro de diez minutos.
13. Chicos, no (*poner*) _____ la radio, por favor. Me duele la cabeza.
14. (*Venir*) _____ a mi fiesta, Sara. Lo vamos a pasar muy bien.
15. (*Ser*) _____ amables con Elvira, niños. Os quiere mucho.

74 Lávate.
Imperative of verbs with *se*

¡**Lávate** ahora mismo!

Quítese la camisa, por favor.

● Imperative: regular verbs with *se*

lav-arse		atrev-erse		sub-irse		
lávate	no te laves	atrévete	no te atrevas	súbete	no te subas	(tú)
lávese	no se lave	atrévase	no se atreva	súbase	no se suba	(usted)
lavaos	no os lavéis	atreveos	no os atreváis	subíos	no os subáis	(vosotros, vosotras)
lávense	no se laven	atrévanse	no se atrevan	súbanse	no se suban	(ustedes)

Son las ocho. **Levántate.** **No te atrevas** *a ir solo.* **No se suban** *a la estatua, por favor.*

● Some irregular verbs with *se*

– e → i: vestirse: ví**s**tete, ví**s**tase, vestíos, ví**s**tanse
   no te vi**s**tas, no se vi**s**ta, no os vi**s**táis, no se vi**s**tan
   Others: *despedirse, reírse*

– e → ie: despertarse: despi**é**rtate, despi**é**rtese, despertaos, despi**é**rtense
   no te despi**e**rtes, no se despi**e**rte, no os despertéis, no se despi**e**rten
   Others: *defenderse, divertirse, sentarse*

– o → ue: acostarse: ac**ué**state, ac**ué**stese, acostaos, ac**ué**stense
   no te ac**ue**stes, no se ac**ue**ste, no os acostéis, no se ac**ue**sten
   Others: *dormirse*

No te pongas ese sombrero. Es espantoso.

– ponerse: ponte, póngase, poneos, pónganse
   no te pongas, no se ponga, no os pongáis, no se pongan

– irse: vete, váyase, idos, váyanse
   no te vayas, no se vayan, no os vayáis, no se vayan

● Remember that some verbs with *se* are used to indicate that the action of the verb is received by the same person who does it, or by a body part or the clothes of that person.

Acuéstate.

Lávate las manos.

▶ UNIT 69: Affirmative imperative: regular verbs   UNIT 53: Verbs with *me, te, se...*

74.1. Complete the sentences with the verbs from the box in affirmative or negative.

abrocharse   bajarse   caerse   dormirse   levantarse   ~~ponerse~~   reírse   sentarse   subirse   vestirse

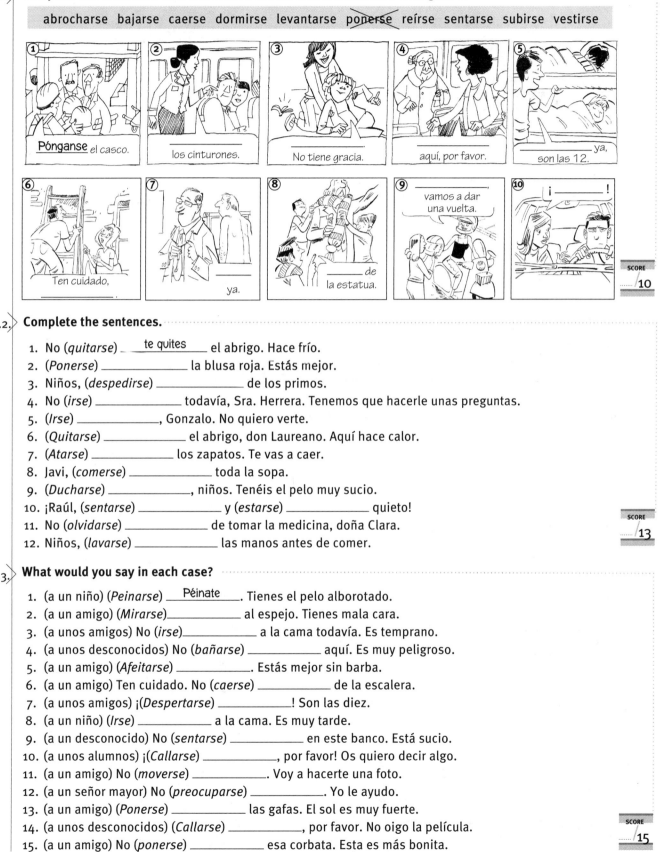

① <u>Pónganse</u> el casco.

② _____ los cinturones.

③ _____ No tiene gracia.

④ _____ aquí, por favor.

⑤ _____ ya, son las 12.

⑥ Ten cuidado, _____

⑦ _____ ya.

⑧ _____ de la estatua.

⑨ _____ vamos a dar una vuelta.

⑩ ¡ _____ !

SCORE ...... /10

74.2. Complete the sentences.

1. No (*quitarse*) ___te quites___ el abrigo. Hace frío.
2. (*Ponerse*) _____ la blusa roja. Estás mejor.
3. Niños, (*despedirse*) _____ de los primos.
4. No (*irse*) _____ todavía, Sra. Herrera. Tenemos que hacerle unas preguntas.
5. (*Irse*) _____, Gonzalo. No quiero verte.
6. (*Quitarse*) _____ el abrigo, don Laureano. Aquí hace calor.
7. (*Atarse*) _____ los zapatos. Te vas a caer.
8. Javi, (*comerse*) _____ toda la sopa.
9. (*Ducharse*) _____, niños. Tenéis el pelo muy sucio.
10. ¡Raúl, (*sentarse*) _____ y (*estarse*) _____ quieto!
11. No (*olvidarse*) _____ de tomar la medicina, doña Clara.
12. Niños, (*lavarse*) _____ las manos antes de comer.

SCORE ...... /13

74.3. What would you say in each case?

1. (a un niño) (*Peinarse*) ___Péinate___. Tienes el pelo alborotado.
2. (a un amigo) (*Mirarse*) _____ al espejo. Tienes mala cara.
3. (a unos amigos) No (*irse*) _____ a la cama todavía. Es temprano.
4. (a unos desconocidos) No (*bañarse*) _____ aquí. Es muy peligroso.
5. (a un amigo) (*Afeitarse*) _____. Estás mejor sin barba.
6. (a un amigo) Ten cuidado. No (*caerse*) _____ de la escalera.
7. (a unos amigos) ¡(*Despertarse*) _____! Son las diez.
8. (a un niño) (*Irse*) _____ a la cama. Es muy tarde.
9. (a un desconocido) No (*sentarse*) _____ en este banco. Está sucio.
10. (a unos alumnos) ¡(*Callarse*) _____, por favor! Os quiero decir algo.
11. (a un amigo) No (*moverse*) _____. Voy a hacerte una foto.
12. (a un señor mayor) No (*preocuparse*) _____. Yo le ayudo.
13. (a un amigo) (*Ponerse*) _____ las gafas. El sol es muy fuerte.
14. (a unos desconocidos) (*Callarse*) _____, por favor. No oigo la película.
15. (a un amigo) No (*ponerse*) _____ esa corbata. Esta es más bonita.

SCORE ...... /15

75 Cómprala. No la compres.
Imperative with object pronouns

● Direct object pronouns with the imperative

▶ **UNIT 29: Personal pronouns: direct object**

AFFIRMATIVE	NEGATIVE
verbo –me, –lo, –la, –nos, –los, –las	no + me, lo, la, nos, los, las + verb
mírame, míralo, mírala…	no me, lo, la… mires
míreme, mírelo, mírela…	no me, lo, la… mire
miradme, miradlo, miradla…	no me, lo, la… miréis
mírenme, mírenlo, mírenla…	no me, lo, la… miren

Mira esta lámpara. **Cómprala.** Es muy bonita.

No la compres. A mí no me gusta.

BE CAREFUL!

> mira, mire, miren → mírame, míreme, mírenme

Llámame mañana.

–¿Pongo la mesa? –No, **no la pongáis** todavía.

Mírame a los ojos.

–¿Puedo coger una hoja? –Sí, **cógela.**

No **me miréis**, por favor. Estoy horrorosa.

● Indirect object pronouns with the imperative   ▶ **UNIT 30: Personal pronouns: indirect object**

AFFIRMATIVE	NEGATIVE
verb –me, –le, –nos, –les	no + me, le, nos, les + verb
préstame, préstale…	no me, le… prestes
présteme, préstele…	no me, le… preste
prestadme, prestadle…	no me, le… prestéis
préstenme, préstenle…	no me, le… presten

Préstame tu diccionario.

No le prestes el tuyo, yo tengo dos.

BE CAREFUL!

> presta, preste, presten → préstame, présteme, préstenme

Arturo es muy antipático. **No le hables.**

Dame ese libro, por favor.

Pregúntale dónde vive.

Enseñadles el mapa.

Dinos la verdad.

– We usually use *le* or *les* in addition to the person we refer to when we mention the indirect object for the first time.

Pregúntale a Hans dónde vive.

Dale los bombones **a Elsa.**

● Uses of the imperative.   ▶ **UNIT 69: Affirmative imperative: regular verbs**

– orders and instructions:

¡Ciérralo!   **Agítelo** antes de abrir.

– requests and invitations:

Llámame esta noche, por favor.

– advice, suggestions, or warnings:

Pregúntale al doctor.   **No le digas** nada a Jesús.

– to give or refuse permission:

–¿Puedo usar el teléfono? –Sí, **úselo.**   –¿Puedo abrir la ventana? –No, **no la abras,** por favor. Estoy resfriado.

75 EXERCISES

75.1. Replace the underlined words with pronouns. Make the necessary changes.

1. Ama a tus padres. _____Ámalos_____ .
2. Comprad el periódico _____ .
3. No cojas mi bicicleta _____ .
4. Mira a Elvira _____ .
5. No mires a esos chicos _____ .
6. Llama a Carlos _____ .
7. Pregunta a tu madre _____ .
8. Venda la casa _____ .
9. No comáis la carne _____ .
10. No miren esas fotos _____ .
11. Pasa el agua _____ .
12. Compren el libro _____ .

75.2. Answer as in the examples.

1. –¿Hago la cena?
   –Sí, _____hazla_____ ya. Tengo hambre.
   –No, _no la hagas_ todavía. Es pronto.
2. –¿Apago la tele?
   –Sí, _____ ya. La película es muy aburrida.
   –No, _____ todavía. Quiero ver el final.
3. –¿Abrimos los regalos?
   –Sí, _____ ya.
   –No, _____ todavía. Esperad a mañana.
4. –¿Despierto a Andrés?
   –Sí, _____ ya. Es muy tarde.
   –No, _____ todavía. Déjale dormir.

5. –¿Frío las patatas?
   –Sí, _____ ya.
   –No, _____ todavía.
6. –¿Pongo el vídeo?
   –Sí, _____ ya.
   –No, _____ todavía. Voy al baño.
7. –¿Pagamos la cuenta?
   –Sí, _____ ya.
   –No, _____ todavía. Espera un poco.
8. –¿Llamamos a Antonio?
   –Sí, _____ .
   –No, _____ todavía. Es pronto.

SCORE /16

75.3. Write orders, instructions, suggestions, etc.

1. (tú) enseñar la casa / a ellos _____Enséñales la casa_____ .
2. (vosotros) no / decir nada / a los niños _No les digáis nada a los niños_ .
3. (ustedes) no / prestar el coche / a Luis _____ .
4. (tú) preguntar / a Alfredo _____ .
5. (tú) dar los regalos / a Rosa y Ana _____ .
6. (usted) no / preguntar nada / a nosotros _____ .
7. (usted) ayudar / a mí _____ .
8. (tú) pasar la sal / a mí _____ .
9. (vosotros) enseñar los cuadernos / a nosotros _____ .
10. (tú) no / prestar dinero / a Elsa _____ .

SCORE /10

75.4. Complete the recipe instructions with the verbs in parentheses and the correct pronoun if needed.

Tortilla de patatas

Para hacer tortilla de patatas (*pelar*) ___pele___ unas patatas y (*cortar*) ___córtelas___ en láminas finas. (*Echar*) _____ sal a las patatas y (*freír*) _____ en aceite muy caliente. (*Cortar*) _____ un poco de cebolla y (*freír*) _____ con las patatas. Luego (*batir*) _____ dos huevos y (*mezclar*) _____ con las patatas. (*Poner*) _____ la masa de patata y huevo en la sartén y (*freír*) _____ un par de minutos. (*Dar*) _____ la vuelta a la tortilla y, cuando esté dorada, (*poner*) _____ en un plato limpio.

SCORE /12

75.5. Complete the sentences with the verb in parentheses.

1. La luz está encendida. (*Apagar*) ___Apágala___ , por favor.
2. Estas cartas son urgentes. (*Enviar*) _____ hoy mismo, Srta. Utrera.
3. La radio está muy baja. (*Subir*) _____ . Quiero oír las noticias.
4. No sabemos hacer este ejercicio. (*Ayudar*) _____ , Jesús.
5. –¿Le pregunto a Jorge? –No, no (*preguntar*) _____ . No sabe nada.
6. Mario, (*hacer*) _____ un favor. (*Comprar*) _____ unos sellos cuando salgas.

SCORE /7

76 Viajar es estupendo.
Infinitive

Conducir es fácil.

Necesito descansar.

Conducir and *descansar* are infinitive forms. The infinitive of a verb is the form that is given in dictionaries. It expresses the meaning of the verb.

vivir v. Tener vida   **comer** v. Tomar alimento

- The infinitives end in *-ar, -er* or *-ir*.

trabaj-**ar** cant-**ar**	com-**er** beb-**er**	viv-**ir** re-**ír**

- The infinitive can be used with a noun.

    *Me encantan **los viajes**. = Me encanta **viajar**.*   *El tabaco es malo. = **Fumar** es malo.*

    *Quiero **comida**. = Quiero **comer**.*

  – The infinitive as a noun is singular and masculine.

    *Las compras son aburridas. = **Comprar** es **aburrido**.*

- The infinitive can be used:

  – on its own.   *–¿Qué hacéis los fines de semana? –**Pasear**.*

  – as a subject or object of a sentence.

    ***Escuchar** música es muy relajante.*   *Me encanta **viajar**.*

    *Juan no quiere **salir** el domingo. Prefiere **quedarse** en casa.*

  – after a preposition.

    *Llámame **antes de salir**.*   *Enrique conduce **sin mirar**.*

  – after other verbs. At times the two verbs go together, one after the other, and at times they are joined by a preposition.

    verb + infinitive   *No **puedo salir** esta noche.*

    verb + *a/con/de/en*... + infinitive   *He **empezado a estudiar** chino.*

  • Some verbs + infinitive: *decidir, encantar, esperar, gustar, necesitar, odiar, poder, preferir, querer, saber.*

    ***Espero aprobar**.*   ***Odio dormir** en hoteles.*   ***Necesitamos cambiar** dinero antes del viaje.*

  • Some verbs + preposition + infinitive:

    verb + *a* + infinitive: *aprender, ayudar, empezar, enseñar, ir, salir, venir...*

    *Estoy **aprendiendo a conducir**.*   *¿**Salimos a dar** una vuelta?*

    verb + *de* + infinitive: *acordarse, olvidarse, terminar...*

    *Lo siento. Me **olvidé de despertarte**.*

    verb + *con* + infinitive: *soñar.*

    *De pequeña, **soñaba con ser** bailarina.*

BE CAREFUL!

infinitive + pronoun: *Odio **levantarme** temprano. Espero **veros** pronto.*
    *No me acordé de ~~te~~ despertar. → No me acordé de **despertarte**.*

- To negate the infinitive, we put *no* before it.

    *Espero **no llegar** tarde.*

76.1 **Replace the underlined nouns with infinitives. Make the necessary changes.**

1. <u>Las mentiras</u> pueden ser dañinas. ___Mentir puede ser dañino___.
2. <u>La vida</u> es una lucha. _____.
3. <u>Los viajes</u> en avión son cansados. _____.
4. Necesitamos <u>una diversión</u>. _____.
5. <u>La bebida</u> trae problemas. _____.
6. Me gusta <u>el baile</u>. _____.
7. A veces son necesarios <u>los cambios</u>. _____.
8. Nos encantan <u>los juegos</u>. _____.

SCORE ___/8

76.2 **Complete the answers with the verbs from the box.**

cambiar   descansar   escuchar   hacer   ~~estudiar~~

① ¿Qué haces? — Estudiar.
② ¿Qué queréis? — ¡_____!
③ ¿Qué quiere? — _____ unas fotocopias.
④ ¿Qué haces ahí, Santi? — _____ música.
⑤ ¿Qué deseas? — _____ este billete.

SCORE ___/5

76.3 **Join the sentences as in the example. Make the necessary changes.**

1. He hablado con Raquel. Lo he conseguido. ___He conseguido hablar con Raquel___.
2. Trabajo los sábados. Lo odio. _____.
3. Conduzco deprisa. Me gusta. _____.
4. No digo nada. Lo prefiero. _____.
5. Como mucha verdura. Me encanta. _____.
6. No como carne de cerdo. No puedo. _____.
7. Bebo mucha agua. Lo necesito. _____.
8. No molesto. Espero. _____.
9. Trabajo de noche. No quiero. _____.
10. Me levanto pronto. Lo odio. _____.

SCORE ___/10

76.4 **Complete the sentences with the verbs from the box and *a, de, en,* or *con* if needed.**

1. ¿Cuándo empiezas ___a estudiar___ informática?
2. ¿Quieren ___tomar___ algo?
3. Julia y Arturo vienen _____ esta noche.
4. Mis padres me ayudan _____ el piso.
5. ¿Puedes _____ aquí un momento, por favor?
6. Prefiero _____ las entradas yo mismo.
7. Cuando era pequeño, Tomás soñaba _____ bombero.
8. ¿Por qué no me enseñas _____?
9. ¿Saben _____ español?
10. Fidel va _____ en un lago casi todos los domingos.
11. Rubén se olvidó _____ las fotos.
12. Un momento. Te ayudo _____ las maletas.

cenar
~~estudiar~~
hablar
hacer
nadar
pagar
pescar
reservar
ser
~~tomar~~
traer
venir

SCORE ___/12

77 voy a trabajar / tengo que trabajar
Expressions with infinitive (1)

● *ir a*

– We use *ir a* + infinitive to speak about immediate intentions.

   Voy a dar *una vuelta. ¿Viene alguien?*

– We use it to speak about plans or future intentions.

   El verano que viene **vamos a viajar** *por Perú.*

– We use it to make deductions or predictions about something that is about to happen or seems is going to happen.

   Callaos. **Va a empezar** *la película.*

   ¡Ten cuidado! Te **vas a hacer** *daño.*

Mira. **Va a salir** el sol.

● *tener que, haber que*

– We use *tener que* + infinitive to express an obligation or a personal need to do something imposed by the circumstances.

   Este domingo **tenemos que trabajar**. (Shops are open.)

   Ayer **tuve que quedarme** *en la oficina hasta las diez.* (There was a lot of work.)

– *No tener que* + infinitive indicates that it is not obligatory or necessary to do something.

   Mañana **no tengo que madrugar**. *Es fiesta.* (It isn't necessary get up early.)

Sara **tiene que levantarse** *a las cinco.*
(She has to get up at five o'clock.)

– We use *haber que* + infinitive to express an obligation or general need that is not personal. We use it only in the third person singular form: *hay, había, habrá...*

   Para viajar a Egipto **hay que tener** *un visado.* (It is obligatory for everyone.)

   No hay que hablar *alto. Podemos molestar.*

   Cuando yo era pequeño, **había que ser** *muy respetuoso con los mayores.*

● *poder*

– We use *poder* + infinitive to express permission or prohibition.

   ¿Puedo abrir *la ventana?*

   Aquí **no podemos aparcar**. *Está prohibido.*

– We use *se puede / no se puede* to indicate permission or prohibition in a general, not personal, way.

   En este museo **no se pueden hacer** *fotos.*

BE CAREFUL!

Pronoun + *ir a, tener que, poder* + infinitive	*ir a, tener que, poder* + infinitive–pronoun
Se *va a caer.*	*Va a caer***se**.
Lo *voy a comprar.*	*Voy a comprar***lo**.
Te *tengo que ver pronto.*	*Tengo que ver***te** *pronto.*
¿Me *puedes ayudar?*	*¿Puedes ayudar***me**?

77 EXERCISES

77.1 Use the corrrect form of *ir a* + the infinitives from the box.

1. ___Voy a apagar___ la tele. No hay nada interesante.
2. Encarna y Guille _____ una casa este verano.
3. _____ algo. Tengo hambre.
4. ¿Qué _____ con esas cerillas, Lola?
5. ¡Cuidado! _____ de la silla.
6. ¿No _____ Carmen con nosotros esta noche?
7. Ponte un jersey. _____ un resfriado.
8. Date prisa. _____ los invitados.

alquilar
~~apagar~~
caerse
cenar
coger
comer
hacer
llegar

77.2 Complete the sentences with the correct form of *tener que* or *no tener que*.

1. ___Tengo que___ hacerme unas gafas nuevas. Con estas no veo bien.
2. _____ ir a ver a Santi. Le va a gustar veros.
3. ¡Qué bien! Hoy _____ fregar los platos. Le toca a Ramón.
4. Esta noche _____ hacer yo la cena. No está Pablo.
5. Raúl _____ vender el coche. Necesita dinero.
6. No te preocupes. _____ conducir tú.
7. Cuando era pequeño, _____ andar tres kilómetros para ir al colegio.
8. ¿_____ trabajar mañana, Gerardo?
9. Ayer _____ ir a clase. Fue fiesta.
10. Mañana _____ madrugar. El avión sale a las 12.

SCORE __/10

77.3 Complete the sentences with the correct form of *haber que*.

1. Si hay un accidente, ___hay que___ llamar a una ambulancia.
2. En el futuro _____ hablar varios idiomas.
3. Ayer _____ llamar a un cerrajero para entrar en el piso.
4. Cuando yo iba al colegio, _____ llamar de usted a los profesores.
5. _____ ayudar a las personas mayores.

SCORE __/5

77.4 Replace the underlined expressions with the correct form of *tener que* or *haber que*. Make the necessary changes.

1. Es necesario que eche gasolina al coche. Casi no tiene. ___Tengo que echar gasolina al coche___.
2. Para ir a la universidad es necesario coger el autobús 53. _____.
3. Cuando éramos pequeños, era obligatorio no molestar a los adultos. _____.
4. No es necesario que lleve corbata en la oficina. _____.
5. Para viajar a algunos países es obligatorio vacunarse contra la fiebre amarilla. _____.
6. Si hay un incendio es necesario llamar a los bomberos. _____.
7. Es necesario que Raquel se vaya. Es muy tarde. _____.
8. No es necesario sacar al perro de noche. _____.

SCORE __/8

77.5 Complete the sentences with the correct form of *poder* and the verbs from the box in the affirmative or negative.

1. Lo siento. ___No se puede hacer___ fuego aquí. Está prohibido.
2. ¿_____ a casa? He acabado todo el trabajo.
3. _____ delante del hospital, Mila.
4. David, ¿nos _____ a casa?
5. ¿Sabes si _____ el móvil en la academia?
6. (yo) _____ esta noche. Tengo que estudiar
7. Os _____ en mi coche esta noche si queréis.
8. Silvia _____ con Miguel. Está comunicando.

aparcar
hablar
~~hacer~~
irse
llevar (2)
salir
usar

SCORE __/8

78 *Suelo comer en casa.*
Expressions with infinitive (2)

Suelo ir en metro
a la universidad.

Cuando era joven, **solía hacer**
mucho deporte.

Suelo and *solía* are forms of the verb *soler*.

● *soler*

– We use *soler* + infinitive to speak about habitual or frequent actions.

Solemos comer en casa. (We usually eat at home.)

¿Dónde **suelen pasar** las vacaciones? (Where do you usually go on vacation?)

No suelo trabajar por la tarde. (I usually don't work in the evening.)

– *Soler* is usually used in the present indicative and the imperfect.

	present indicative	imperfect
(yo)	suelo	solía
(tú)	sueles	solías
(usted)	suele	solía
(él, ella)	suele	solía
(nosotros, nosotras)	solemos	solíamos
(vosotros, vosotras)	soléis	solíais
(ustedes)	suelen	solían
(ellos, ellas)	suelen	solían

– In the present, *soler* indicates that the action or situation the verb refers to is habitual.

Renata **suele ir** en metro al trabajo. (She usually goes by metro. It is her habit.)

– In the imperfect, *soler* indicates that the action or situation the verb refers to was habitual in the past, but it isn't anymore.

De pequeño, **solía pasar** las vacaciones en Buenos Aires. (We don't go to Buenos Aires on vacation anymore.)

Cuando trabajábamos en Venezuela, **solíamos ir a pescar** todos los fines de semana. (We don't work in Venezuela or go fishing on the weekend anymore.)

BE CAREFUL!

pronoun + *soler* + infinitive	*soler* + infinitive-pronoun
Me suelo levantar tarde.	**Suelo levantarme** temprano.

78 EXERCISES

78.1 **What does Pilar do in the morning? Make sentences like the example with the verbs from the box.**

| comprar | desayunar | ducharse | empezar | ~~levantarse~~ | llegar | salir | tomar |

1. Pilar ___suele levantarse/se suele levantar___ a las siete.
2. _____ a las siete y diez.
3. _____ a las ocho menos veinte.
4. _____ al instituto a las ocho y veinte.
5. _____ las clases a las ocho y media.
6. _____ algo durante el recreo.
7. _____ del instituto a las dos y media.
8. _____ el periódico a las tres menos veinte.

SCORE ___/8

78.2 **What did Félix usually do on summer vacation?**

1. No madrugaba. Félix no ___solía madrugar___.
2. Se levantaba a las once. _____.
3. Se afeitaba por las mañanas. _____.
4. Desayunaba en una cafetería. _____.
5. Jugaba un poco al tenis. _____.
6. Comía en la piscina con amigos. _____.
7. Se echaba una siesta. _____.
8. Por la tarde jugaba a los bolos. _____.
9. Tomaba unas cervezas en un bar. _____.
10. Estaba en la discoteca hasta las tres. _____.
11. Se tomaba un vaso de leche. _____.
12. Se acostaba sobre las cuatro. _____.

SCORE ___/12

78.3 **Complete the sentences with the correct form of *soler* in the affirmative or negative.**

1. Hace unos años, (yo) ___solía___ jugar al tenis todos los fines de semana.
2. Julia _____ ir a la universidad en bicicleta, pero a veces va en metro.
3. Ahora no viajo mucho, pero antes de casarme _____ hacer dos o tres viajes al año.
4. _____ comer fuera, pero algunos domingos vamos a un restaurante.
5. ¿Qué (tú) _____ hacer en verano?
6. De pequeño _____ pasar las vacaciones con mis abuelos.
7. ¿ _____ ir a bailar cuando erais jóvenes?
8. _____ levantarme temprano, pero algunos días me levanto a las siete.

SCORE ___/8

78.4 **Replace the underlined expressions with the correct form of *soler* + infinitive.**

1. Raquel <u>normalmente va</u> a trabajar en el 115. ___Raquel suele ir a trabajar en el 115___.
2. <u>Normalmente vamos</u> a la sierra los fines de semana. _____.
3. Cuando vivíamos en Chile, <u>normalmente dábamos</u> un paseo después de cenar. _____.
4. En casa de mis abuelos <u>normalmente comen</u> paella los domingos. _____.
5. Cuando era pequeña <u>me bañaba a menudo</u> en el río de mi pueblo. _____.
6. ¿A qué hora <u>te levantas normalmente</u>? _____.
7. <u>Normalmente me acuesto</u> tarde los sábados. _____.

SCORE ___/7

El autobús acaba de irse.
Expressions with infinitive (3)

No gracias. **He dejado de tomar** café.

¡Mira! El autobús **acaba de irse.**

Dejar de and *acabar de* are expressions followed by an infinitive verb and have special meanings.

> **He dejado de tomar** café.
> (I stopped drinking coffee.)
>
> El autobús **acaba de irse.**
> (The bus has just left.)

● *dejar de, acabar de*

– We use *dejar de* + infinitive to indicate the interruption of a process.

> **Dejé de estudiar** griego hace dos años.
> (I stopped studying Greek two years ago.)
>
> **He dejado de salir** con Cristina.
> (I don't go out with Cristina anymore.)

• The negative form, *no dejar de* + infinitive, means "don't forget to" or "intend."

> Si vas a México, **no dejes de ver** las pirámides aztecas.
> (Don't forget to see the pyramids.)

– We use *acabar de* + infinitive to indicate that something has happened just before that moment. We generally use it in the present indicative and imperfect.

> **Acaba de llamarte** Luis.
> (Luis has just called you.)
>
> **Acababan de entrar** cuando empezó a llover.
> (They had just come in when it started raining)

● *volver a*

– We use *volver a* + infinitive to indicate the repetition of an action.

> **He vuelto a ver** a Teresa.
> (I have seen Teresa again.)
>
> **No vuelvas a hacer** eso o me enfado.
> (Don't do that again or I'll get mad.)
>
> **Se ha vuelto a estropear** el coche.
> (The car has broken down again.)

BE CAREFUL!

pronoun + *acabar de, dejar de, volver a* + infinitive	*acabar de, dejar de, volver a* + infinitive-pronoun
Se acaban de casar.	Acaban de casar**se**.
Me ha dejado de hablar.	Ha dejado de hablar**me**.
Se ha vuelto a caer.	Ha vuelto a caer**se**.

79.1. **Rewrite the sentences with *dejar de* / *no dejar de* in the correct form.**

1. Marisa ya no come carne. _____Marisa ha dejado de comer carne_____.
2. No olvides escribirnos cuando estés en Perú. _____.
3. La última vez que fumé fue hace seis meses. _____.
4. Marta ya no sale con Emilio. _____.
5. No olvidéis sacar la basura por la noche. _____.
6. No olviden llamarme cuando vengan a Sevilla. _____.
7. Ya no hace viento. _____.
8. Rocío ya no me quiere. _____.
9. Ya no monto en bicicleta. _____.
10. Mis padres ya no trabajan. _____.

SCORE ...... /10

79.2. **Rewrite the sentences with *acabar de* in the correct form.**

1. He visto a Ángel hace un momento. _____Acabo de ver a Ángel_____.
2. Habíamos comido hacía un momento cuando llegaron Susi y Toni. _____.
3. He regresado de clase hace un momento. _____.
4. Se fueron un momento antes de empezar la clase. _____ cuando empezó la clase.
5. El accidente ha ocurrido hace un momento. _____.
6. Cuando llegamos al hospital, hacía un momento que había nacido Irene. _____
_____.
7. He recogido el correo ahora mismo. _____.
8. Se ha estropeado el ordenador hace un momento. _____.
9. El concierto ha empezado hace un momento. _____.
10. El partido ha terminado ahora mismo. _____.

SCORE ...... /10

79.3. **Replace the underlined words with the correct form of *volver a*.**

1. He aprobado. No tengo que examinarme otra vez. _____No tengo que volver a examinarme_____.
2. ¡Por fin la televisión funciona de nuevo! _____.
3. No hemos visto otra vez a Lucía desde el verano. _____.
4. El año pasado alquilé otra vez la casa de la playa. _____.
5. Tenemos que hacer el trabajo de nuevo. _____.
6. ¿Cree que el coche se averiará otra vez? _____.
7. Gonzalo ha suspendido otra vez el examen del carné de conducir. _____.
8. ¿Han tenido carta de Guillermo otra vez? _____.
9. Ayer perdimos de nuevo. _____.
10. He leído *Cien años de soledad* de nuevo. _____.

SCORE ...... /10

79.4. **Put the words in the correct order.**

1. ha vuelto / averiar / se / a / el ordenador ___Ha vuelto a averiarse el ordenador / Se ha vuelto a
averiar el ordenador___.
2. duchar / de / me / acabo _____.
3. pagar / nos / han dejado / de _____.
4. no / vuelvas / te / caer / a _____.
5. ¿cuándo / lo / vas a acabar / pintar / de? _____.
6. me / escribir / de / no / dejes _____.
7. acaban / despedir / de / los _____.
8. No / ha vuelto / nos / llamar /a _____.

SCORE ...... /8

80 *trabajando, comiendo, viviendo*
Gerund

Mira, Arturo y Luis **montando** a caballo.

No hagas ruido. Está **durmiendo** Tere.

Montando and *durmiendo* are gerund verb forms. The gerund refers to doing the action indicated by the verb.

> *Mira, una foto de mi hijo **tocando** el piano.* (in the act of playing the piano)

- Forming the gerund

Regular verbs

verbs ending in –*ar*	trabaj-**ar** → trabaj-**ando**	
verbs ending in –*er*, –*ir*	com-**er** → com-**iendo**	viv-**ir** → viv-**iendo**

BUT:

vowel + -*er*/*ir*	le-**er** → le-**yendo**	o-**ír** → o-**yendo**	ir → **yendo**
	re-**ír** → r-**iendo**	fre-**ír** → fr-**iendo**	

Irregular verbs

e → i: decir → diciendo   Others: *corregir, pedir, repetir, seguir, sentir, venir, vestir(se)*

o → u: dormir → durmiendo   Others: *morir(se), poder*

verbs with *se*: atreverse → atreviéndose   ducharse → duchándose

- We use the gerund:

–to refer to doing an action.

> *Mira, Lucía y Andrés **jugando** al tenis.*

–with the verb *estar* to speak about something that is happening at this moment.

▶ **UNIT 56: Present of *estar* + gerund**

> *Mira, Pedro **está bailando** con Lola.*
>
> *–Juan, ¿puedes venir? –Lo siento. Ahora no puedo. **Estoy estudiando**.*

BE CAREFUL!

pronoun + *estar* + gerund	*estar* + gerund–pronoun
Me estoy duchando.	Estoy duchándo**me**.

- The gerund has only one form.

> **Luis** está **comiendo**.   **Luis y Ana** están **comiendo**.

Hay un hombre vendiendo fruta en la calle.

- *Hay/había...* + person, animal, or object + gerund.

> **Hay un perro ladrando** en la calle.
>
> **Había dos chicos esperando** a Ana.

80.1 **Write the gerund of the following verbs.**

1. beber ___bebiendo___
2. creer _____
3. repetir _____
4. pedir _____
5. vestirse _____
6. escribir _____
7. poder _____
8. decir _____
9. estudiar _____

80.2 **Complete the bottom of the drawings with the verbs from the box as in the example.**

| comer | bañarse | dormir | ~~esquiar~~ | hacer |

Elsa _esquiando_ en Bariloche.

Agustín _____ en Altea.

Mina _____ un helado en la Habana.

Don Ernesto _____ en una hamaca en Brasil.

Andrea _____ alpinismo en los Andes.

80.3 **Complete the sentences with the correct form of *estar* and the gerund of the verbs in parentheses.**

1. –¿Qué (*vosotros, hacer*) ___estáis haciendo___? –(*Cocinar*) _____ para la fiesta.
2. –¿Qué (*tú, hacer*) _____? –(*Esperar*) _____ a Luisa.
3. –¿Quién (*tocar*) _____ la guitarra? –Ernesto.
4. –¿Dónde (*llover*) _____? –_____ en el Norte.
5. –¿Qué (*tú, comer*) _____? –_____ un caramelo.
6. –¿De qué (*ellos, hablar*) _____? –_____ del examen.
7. –¿Quién (*ducharse*) _____? –Pedro.
8. –¿Qué (*Lucas, oír*) _____? –_____ un concierto.
9. –¿Qué (*decir*) _____ Rosa? –Nada importante.
10. –¿Quién (*morirse*)_____? –El abuelo de Andrés.

80.4 **Describe the scene with *hay* + the gerund form of the verbs from the box.**

| correr por el césped | escuchar música | jugar al fútbol | leer el periódico |
| ~~leer un libro~~ | montar en bici | tocar la guitarra | vender helados |

1. ___Hay___ un chico ___leyendo un libro___.
2. _____ un chica _____.
3. _____ unos chicos _____.
4. _____ un señor _____.
5. _____ una señora _____.
6. _____ dos chicas _____.
7. _____ un perro _____.
8. _____ un señor _____.

81 *Puedo hacerlo. Estoy haciéndolo.*
Object pronouns with infinitive and gerund

- Object pronouns with the **infinitive**   ▶ **UNIT 76: Infinitive**

  – With direct object pronouns: infinitive–*me/te/lo*...

    *Está enfadada con nosotros. No quiere ver**nos**.*   *No hay leche. He olvidado comprar**la**.*

  – With indirect object pronouns: infinitive–*me/te/le*/...

    *Venid aquí. Quiero deci**ros** algo.*

    *Me gustaría pregunta**rte** algo.*

  – With indirect and direct object pronouns: infinitive–*me/te/se*... –*lo/la/los/las*

    *La entrada es nuestra, pero no quiere dár**nosla**.*

  - There are two possibilities with some verbs.

	verb + infinitive–object pronoun	object pronoun + verb + infinitive
querer	*No quiere ver**nos**.*	*No **nos** quiere ver.*
poder	*Puedo hacer**lo**.*	***Lo** puedo hacer.*
ir a	*Vamos a comprar**lo**.*	***Lo** vamos a comprar.*
tener que	*Tienes que ayudar**la**.*	***La** tienes que ayudar.*
volver a	*He vuelto a ver**la**.*	***La** he vuelto a ver*
soler	*Suelo lavar**lo** los domingos.*	***Lo** suelo lavar los domingos.*

*¿Puedes **prestarme** un bolígrafo?*   *No, pero puedo **prestarte** un lápiz.*

- Object pronouns with the **gerund**   ▶ **UNIT 80: Gerund**

  – With direct object pronouns: gerund–*me/te/lo*...

    *–¿Qué hace con el regalo? –Está envolvién**dolo**.*

  – With indirect object pronouns: gerund–*me/te/le*...

    *¿Qué está dicién**dole**?*   *–¿Qué haces? –Estoy escribién**dole** a Laura.*

  – With indirect and direct object pronouns: gerund–*me/te/se*... –*lo/la/los/las*.

    *–¿Por qué tiene Susi la carta de Jaime? –Está leyén**domela**. Yo no veo bien.*

¿Qué está haciendo con la televisión?

*Está **arreglándola**.*

▌**BUT:**

Also: pronoun + *estar* + gerund
***Lo** está envolviendo.*   *¿Qué **te** está diciendo?*   ***Me lo** está leyendo.*

- The indirect object pronoun always goes before the direct object pronoun.

    ~~*Lo os*~~ *puede explicar.*→ ***Os lo** puede explicar.*   *Puedo explicar~~loos~~.* → *Puedo explicár**oslo**.*

    ~~*Lo se*~~ *estoy diciendo* → ***Se lo** estoy diciendo.*   *Estoy diciéndo~~lose~~.* → *Estoy diciéndo**selo**.*

BE CAREFUL!

dar → *dár**nosla***   *arreglando* → *arreglá**ndolo***   *prestar* → *prestá**rmelo***   *preguntando* → *preguntá**ndote***

▶ **UNIT 29: Personal pronouns: direct object**   **UNIT 30: Personal pronouns: indirect object**
  UNIT 31: Indirect and direct object pronouns

81 EXERCISES

81.1 Complete the sentences with the infinitives from the box and the correct pronouns.

ayudar	~~comprar~~	decir	dejar	devolver	escribir	preguntar	tirar	vender	ver

1. –¿Has comprado el periódico? –Se me ha olvidado _____ comprarlo _____.
2. Ese libro es mío, pero Carlos no quiere _____ devolvérmelo _____.
3. Sonia está enfadada con vosotros. No quiere _____.
4. Necesitamos dinero pero mi padre no quiere _____.
5. Estos zapatos están muy viejos. Voy a _____.
6. Ven aquí, Gabriel. Quiero _____ algo.
7. Ramón quiere comprarme ese cuadro, pero yo no quiero _____.
8. He tenido carta de Antón. Tengo que _____.
9. No sabemos hacer el ejercicio pero Hans no quiere _____.
10. No sabéis el secreto, pero no voy a _____.

SCORE ___/10

81.2 Rewrite the sentences changing the pronouns as in the examples.

1. Luis no quiere ayudarme. _____ Luis no me quiere ayudar _____.
2. Venid. Os quiero enseñar algo. _____ Quiero enseñaros algo _____.
3. Tengo un problema. Tenéis que ayudarme. _____.
4. ¿Te gusta este reloj? Voy a regalártelo. _____.
5. No tires ese sombrero. Me lo suelo poner en verano. _____.
6. No entendemos esto. ¿Nos puedes ayudar? _____.
7. ¿Os gusta ese cuadro? Os lo puedo vender barato. _____.
8. Li tiene una buena gramática. Me la va a dejar. _____.

SCORE ___/8

81.3 Replace the underlined words with pronouns and make the necessary changes.

1. Está limpiando las ventanas. _____ Está limpiándolas _____.
2. Estoy acabando la novela. _____.
3. Están preguntando al Sr. Oliva. _____.
4. Estamos lavando las camisas. _____.
5. Están haciendo la pregunta a Carla. _____.
6. Está lavando el pelo a su hijo. _____.
7. Está explicándome el problema. _____.
8. Están curando la pata al perro. _____.

SCORE ___/8

81.4 Rewrite the sentences from exercise 81.3, changing the pronouns as in the example.

1. Las está limpiando. _____.
2. _____.
3. _____.
4. _____.
5. _____.
6. _____.
7. _____.
8. _____.

SCORE ___/8

81.5 Order the words and put the accent marks where needed.

1. la sal / me / pasa _____ Pásame la sal _____.
2. la directora / nos / ver / quiere _____.
3. no tenemos pan / he olvidado / me / lo / comprar / de _____.
4. ¿me / ayudar / puedes? _____.
5. a Julio / se / pregunta / lo _____.
6. ¿quién / lo / está haciendo? _____.
7. me gustaría / a Sandra / lo / se / decir _____.
8. me / la pelota / pasa _____.

SCORE ___/8

82 trabajado, comido, vivido
Participle

La clase ha **terminado**.

El restaurante está **cerrado**.

Terminado and *cerrado* are forms of the participle.

● Forming the participle

– regular verbs

verbs ending in *–ar*	verbs ending in *–er/–ir*	
trabaj-*ar*→ trabaj-**ado**	com-**er** → com-**ido**	viv-**ir** → viv-**ido**
viaj-*ar* → viaj-**ado**	beb-**er** → beb-**ido**	sub-**ir** → sub-**ido**

– irregular verbs

abrir → **abierto**	poner, componer → **puesto, compuesto**
cubrir, descubrir → **cubierto, descubierto**	romper → **roto**
escribir → **escrito**	ver → **visto**
volver, devolver → **vuelto, devuelto**	morir → **muerto**
decir → **dicho**	hacer → **hecho**

● The participle is used with *haber* to form compound tenses. The participle never changes form.

▶ **UNIT 60: Present perfect (1)**

> Mis padres **han vuelto** hace un rato.
> ¿**Has estado** en Marruecos?
> Sonia **ha escrito** una novela.

– In verbs with *se*, the pronouns are placed before *haber*.

> Lidia no **se ha atrevido** a bañarse.
> ¿**Os habéis lavado**?

● The participle can also be used as an adjective. In this case it has the same form (masculine, feminine, singular, or plural) as the person, animal, or object it refers to.

> **Óscar** parece **cansado**.
> Leo es una **persona** muy **querida**.
> Habrá que cambiar **los cristales rotos**.
> Muchas **personas** estaban **heridas**.

82 EXERCISES

82.1 **Write the participle of the following verbs.**

1. decir ____dicho____
2. tener _____
3. abrir _____
4. asar _____

5. conocer _____
6. casar _____
7. caer _____
8. escribir _____

9. poner _____
10. volver _____
11. morir _____
12. acabar _____

SCORE
......./12

82.2 **Complete the sentences with the correct form of the participle from exercise 82.1.**

1. Se ha __acabado__ la gasolina.
2. ¿Está Juana _____?
3. ¿Qué te ha _____ Diana de mí?
4. ¿Dónde has _____ la nueva lámpara?
5. A mí me encanta el pollo _____.
6. Vargas Llosa ha _____ muchas novelas.

7. Mira. La peluquería ya está _____. Podemos entrar.
8. Mis amigos todavía no han _____ de las vacaciones.
9. Los barrenderos han recogido las hojas _____.
10. Paco siempre ha _____ mucha suerte.
11. ¿Has _____ ya a la nueva directora?
12. Hay que cortar las ramas _____.

SCORE
......./12

82.3 **Complete the text with the participles of the verbs from the box.**

alojar	asar	comprar	dedicar	desayunar	gustar
ir	levantarse	pedir	tener	~~venir~~	ver

Madrid, 12 de agosto

¡Hola Maribel!
Estoy en Madrid. He __venido__ con mi familia a pasar unos días. Es una ciudad tranquila en agosto. Estamos _____ en el hotel Asturias, junto a la Puerta del Sol. Hoy _____ hemos _____ pronto, hemos _____ en el mismo hotel y hemos _____ al Museo del Prado. Hemos _____ las salas _____ a Goya. Hemos _____ tiempo para visitar el Museo Thyssen, que también nos ha _____ mucho. Ahora mismo te estoy escribiendo desde un restaurante. Mi hermano y yo hemos _____ pollo _____ para cenar. Hace mucho calor. Te he _____ un regalo.
Besos y hasta pronto.

SCORE
......./13

82.4 **Rewrite the sentences with expressions with *estar* and the participle of the corresponding verbs.**

1. Se ha estropeado el ordenador. _El ordenador está estropeado._
2. Se ha parado el tren. _____.
3. Se han roto los cristales. _____.
4. Se ha averiado la impresora. _____.
5. Se rompió el móvil. _____.
6. Han detenido al sospechoso. _____.
7. Han cerrado las piscinas. _____.

SCORE
......./7

82.5 **Complete the sentences with the participle of the correct verb.**

abrir	aburrir	asustar	averiar	hacer	morir	~~pinchar~~	romper

1. Tengo que parar. Tenemos una rueda _pinchada_.
2. Óscar y Ana parecen un poco _____.
3. Todavía hay algunas farmacias _____.
4. El caballo tiene una pata _____.
5. Este móvil parece _____.
6. El perro está muy _____ por la tormenta.
7. Hay algunos peces _____ en el río.
8. ¿Están las camas _____?

SCORE
......./8

173

83 *Quiero a Marta. Le he dejado mi bici a Pedro.*
Direct and indirect objects

● The direct object

"Quiero a Marta."

In this sentence, Marta is the direct object: she is the person that is affected by the action of the verb.

Quiero mucho | a Marta.

– We use *a* before a direct object

• with people.

*Quiero mucho **a mis padres**.*   *¿Has visto **a Julia**?*

• with animals that we think of as people.

*Saca **a Toby** a pasear.*

• with verbs where animals are direct objects, but we usually use it with people as the direct object.

*Adoro **a mis hermanos**.*
*Felisa adora **a sus gatos**.*

*Lava **a Pancho**. Está muy sucio.*

– We don't use *a* before an indirect object

• with animals or objects.

*¿Viste **las jirafas** en el zoo?*   *He vendido **el coche**.*

• when we refer to an unspecific person.

*Necesitamos **una secretaria**.*   *Estoy buscando **una canguro** para mis hijos.*

Compare:

SOMEONE SPECIFIC	SOMEONE UNSPECIFIC
*No podemos traducir esto solos. Necesitamos **a Pedro**.*	*En mi empresa necesitan **un traductor**.*

• with the verb *haber* (impersonal).

*Hay **un señor** en la puerta.*

● The indirect object

"Le he dejado mi bici a Pedro."

He dejado | mi bici | a Pedro.

In this sentence, Pedro is the indirect object: he is the person who is **indirectly** affected by the verb.

– Before the indirect object, we always use *a*:

• People: *Le he hecho una pregunta **al profesor**.*
• Animals: *Hay que curarle la pata **a ese perro**.*
• Objects: *Echa sal **a la sopa**, por favor.*

83 EXERCISES

83.1. **Put *a* where and when it is necessary.**

1. Conozco Pedro desde niño. <u>Conozco a Pedro desde niño.</u>
2. Conozco Madrid desde niño. _____.
3. Felipe quiere mucho su perro. _____.
4. Pide otra cerveza, por favor. _____.
5. He visto Toledo muchas veces. _____.
6. ¿Has visto la nueva película de Almodóvar? _____.
7. Ayer vi Juan en la universidad. _____.
8. Quiero mucho mis hijos. _____.
9. Hay una señora esperándote. _____.
10. Tengo una duda. Necesito el profesor. _____.
11. No toques ese gato. _____.
12. No toques ese enchufe. _____.

SCORE ...... /12

83.2. **List whether the underlined words are OD (direct objects) or OI (indirect objects).**

1. Mi hermano ha comprado <u>una moto nueva</u> OD _____.
2. Han hecho <u>muchas preguntas</u> _____ al profesor _____.
3. Tenemos <u>mucha prisa</u> _____.
4. Blanca ha vendido <u>a Martina</u> _____ <u>su apartamento</u> _____.
5. Alberto quiere mucho <u>a Laura</u> _____.
6. Trae <u>a tus primos</u> _____ a la fiesta.
7. Dale <u>al camarero</u> _____ <u>una propina</u> _____.
8. Han entregado <u>los premios</u> _____ <u>a los actores</u> _____.
9. No digas <u>mentiras</u> _____.
10. Hay <u>un chico nuevo</u> _____ en clase.

SCORE ...... /14

83.3. **Circle the correct answer.**

1. Hay (*a* / Ø) un señor en recepción.
2. ¿Necesitan (*a* / Ø) una secretaria en tu oficina?
3. Préstale (*el* / *al*) coche (*a* / Ø) Héctor.
4. He visto (*a* / Ø) un ratón en la cocina.
5. Dale (*a* / Ø) un hueso (*el* / *al*) perro.
6. Estoy leyendo (*a* / Ø) un libro muy interesante.
7. Tengo que hacerle una pregunta (*el* / *al*) profesor.
8. Julia adora (*a* / Ø) su perro.

SCORE ...... /10

83.4. **Put *a* where and when it is necessary.**

1. Sus hermanos ayudan mucho Amalia. <u>Sus hermanos ayudan mucho a Amalia</u>.
2. Pide Juan la revista. _____.
3. Le he dado la noticia Julio. _____.
4. Les han dado mis padres las noticias. _____.
5. Necesito un coche nuevo. _____.
6. No des patadas las piedras. _____.
7. Di la verdad la profesora. _____.
8. ¿Quién le has dado tu boli? _____.
9. ¿Por qué no quieres ayudar Juan? _____.
10. Preséntale Ramón Rocío. _____.

SCORE ...... /10

175

84 *aquí, allí, arriba, abajo...*
Adverbs of place

Yo vivo **aquí** y Margarita
vive **enfrente**.

Aquí and *enfrente* are adverbs of place. They give information about the circumstances of place. They answer the questions *¿dónde?*, *¿adónde?*

> *Cuelga el cuadro* (where?) **ahí**.
> *Lleve este paquete* (to where?) **arriba**.

● *aquí, ahí, allí*

aquí → close to me	*ahí* → close to you	*allí* → far from you and me

Póngalo aquí, por favor.

Póngalo ahí, por favor.

Póngalo allí, por favor.

● *arriba, abajo...*
> –¿Vives **cerca**? –No, vivo muy **lejos**.   –¿Qué hay **arriba**? –Una sala de juegos.

arriba
abajo

enfrente

dentro
fuera

delante

detrás

lejos

cerca

encima

debajo

alrededor

● *Aquí, arriba...* usually go at the end of the sentence.
> *Este barrio tiene muchos parques* **alrededor**.   *Hay algo* **aquí**.

> **BUT:** They can also go at the beginning of a sentence to give emphasis.
> **Aquí** *hay un zapato. ¿Dónde está el otro?*

BE CAREFUL!

> When *aquí, arriba...* go at the beginning of a sentence, the subject goes after the verb.
> *Arriba ~~las habitaciones están~~.* → *Arriba* **están** *las habitaciones.* (The rooms are upstairs.)
> *Enfrente ~~Margarita vive~~.* → *Enfrente* **vive** *Margarita.* (Margarita lives in front of us.)

● It's common to use *aquí, ahí,* and *allí* with *arriba, abajo...*
> *Ponlo* **allí dentro**.   *Juan, ven* **aquí arriba**.

▶ UNIT 96: Prepositions (3)

84 EXERCISES

84.1. Complete with *aquí*, *ahí*, or *allí*.

1. Ven __aquí__, Bruno.
2. _____ hay agua.
3. _____ hay algo.
4. ¿Qué hay _____?

5. ¿Ves a Ana? Sí, está ____ arriba.
6. ¿Dónde pongo los platos? Ponlos ____ dentro.
7. Mira, ____ hay sombra.
8. Siéntate ____, a mi lado.

SCORE ...../8

84.2. Complete the sentences with the words from the box.

abajo   alrededor   debajo   delante   dentro   encima   enfrente   ~~fuera~~

1. Id a jugar __fuera__.
2. Prefiero dormir _____
3. Deje el paquete aquí _____
4. ¿Dónde está tu clase? Allí _____
5. Hay muchas montañas _____
6. ¿Quién se sienta _____?
7. Aquí ____ no nos mojamos.
8. ¿Dónde está Diana? Está _____.

SCORE ...../8

84.3. Order the words and complete the sentences.

1. mis padres / abajo / viven — Abajo __viven mis padres__.
2. cerca / Elena / vive — Elena _____.
3. la mesa / fuera / sacad — Sacad _____.
4. aquí / Benito / trabaja — Aquí _____.
5. lejos / mi oficina / está — Mi oficina _____.
6. abajo / yo / duermo — Yo _____.
7. delante / Bárbara / se sienta — Delante _____.
8. allí / la cafetería / está — Allí _____.
9. abajo / ahí / están / las tazas — Ahí _____.
10. está / allí / Gabriel — Allí _____.

SCORE ...../10

85 hoy, ayer, entonces, luego...
Adverbs of time (1)

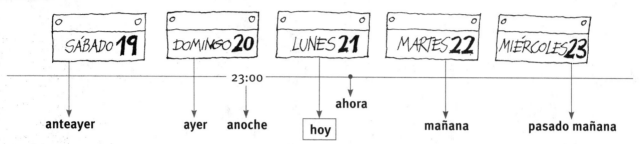

Anteayer, ayer, anoche... are adverbs of time. They give information about when something happens. They answer the question ¿cuándo?

> –¿Has visto a Rosa? –Sí. (when?) **Ayer** estuve con ella.
> –¿Cuándo me vas a devolver el libro que te dejé? –**Mañana** te lo devuelvo.
> –¿Me ayudas? –**Ahora** no puedo. Estoy ocupada.

● entonces, luego, después

– entonces (= at that moment) refers to the moment we were speaking about.

> Le pregunté por Paula y **entonces** (in that moment) me contó todo.

– luego (= after, later) and después (= later) refer to a moment later than we were speaking about.

> Ahora tengo clase. Nos vemos **luego**. (after the class)
> Me voy. **Después** te llamo. (I'll call you later.)

● pronto, temprano, tarde

– pronto
= in a short time, a short time later   Hemos corrido y hemos llegado **pronto**. (shortly after)
                                                           Lo sabréis **pronto**. (in a while)
= before the necessary or normal time   Es **pronto**. La clase no empieza hasta las ocho. (before the class started)

– temprano
= early hours in the morning or at night   Abel se levanta **temprano**, a las seis.
= before the necessary or normal time   Hoy quiero comer **temprano**. He quedado con Gonzalo a las tres. (before the usual lunch time)

– tarde
= late hours in the day or at night   Ayer cenamos muy **tarde**, a las doce.
= after the necessary or normal time   Habéis llegado **tarde**. El concierto ya ha empezado.
                                                          (after the concert's scheduled time to start)

Compare:

–¿Se ha ido María? –Sí, pero vuelve **pronto**. (shortly)	–Mamá, nos vamos. –Volved **temprano**. (get home early)

● Ahora, hoy... can go at the beginning or at the end of the sentence, or in the middle after the verb.

> **Anoche** no pude dormir. / No pude dormir **anoche**.
> **Ayer** estuve con Antón. / Estuve **ayer** con Antón. / Estuve con Antón **ayer**.

BE CAREFUL!

When ahora, hoy... go at the beginning of the sentence, the subject usually goes after the verb.

> Ayer ~~Pablo llegó~~. → Ayer **llegó Pablo**. (Pablo arrived yesterday.)

85.1. **Today is Saturday the 10th. Replace the underlined expressions with the words from the box.**

anoche	anteayer	ayer	hoy	mañana	~~pasado mañana~~

1. El lunes 12 voy al médico. _____Pasado mañana voy al médico_____.
2. El sábado 10 he quedado con Eloísa. _____.
3. El jueves 8 estuve en León. _____.
4. El domingo 11 vamos a hacer una excursión al campo. _____.
5. El viernes 9 por la noche salimos a cenar con unos amigos. _____.
6. El viernes 9 recibí una postal de Miguel. _____.

SCORE ...../ 6

85.2. **Order the words and complete the sentences.**

1. *pasado mañana / Emma / se marcha* → Pasado mañana _____se marcha Emma_____.
2. *mañana / el jefe / en la oficina / no estará* → El jefe _____.
3. *ayer / Olga / me llamó* → Ayer _____.
4. *pasado mañana / mis padres / llegan* → Pasado mañana _____.
5. *ahora / Concha / no está* → Ahora _____.
6. *y / entonces / el espectáculo / sonaron unas trompetas / empezó* → Sonaron unas trompetas _____
_____.

SCORE ...../ 6

85.3. **Circle the correct answer.**

1. No te preocupes. Estoy segura de que nos veremos (*temprano* / (*pronto*)).
2. Mañana nos tenemos que levantar (*temprano* / *tarde*). El avión sale a las siete.
3. Primero iremos a Mendoza y (*entonces* / *después*) a Bariloche.
4. Llamamos al timbre y (*entonces* / *después*) salió el marido de Tere.
5. Estoy acabando un trabajo, pero si quieres nos vemos (*entonces* / *luego*).
6. Habéis llegado (*tarde* / *temprano*). La película ya ha empezado.
7. Daos prisa. Los invitados van a llegar (*temprano* / *pronto*).
8. Primero habla con el jefe y (*después* / *entonces*) con Ángela.

SCORE ...../ 8

85.4. **Replace the underlined word with words from the box.**

después (2)	entonces (2)	luego	pronto (2)	tarde	temprano (2)

1. Tienen que hacer el proyecto en poco tiempo. → _____Tienen que hacer el proyecto pronto._____.
2. Mañana nos tenemos que levantar a primera hora del día. → _____.
3. Estaba hablando con Josefina y en ese momento llegó Roberto. → _____.
4. Ahora tengo trabajo. Te llamaré después del trabajo. → _____.
5. Era una hora avanzada de la noche, pero llamamos a una ambulancia y vino en muy poco tiempo. →
_____.
6. Hoy quiero cenar y acostarme antes de lo normal. Estoy cansado. → _____.
7. Ahora no tenemos hambre. Comeremos más tarde. → _____.
8. Apagaron las luces y en ese momento se oyó una voz. → _____.

SCORE ...../ 8

179

86 *ya, todavía*
Adverbs of time (2)

● *todavía, ya no*

– *Todavía* indicates that an action that started in the past continues into the present.

   ***Todavía** trabajo en el estudio de Mónica.*

¡Es increíble! Son las doce
y **todavía** está durmiendo.

– *Todavía* can go at the beginning or at the end of the sentence.

   *¿**Todavía** estás aquí?*

   *¿Estás aquí **todavía**?*

– *Ya no* indicates that something previously true is no longer true in the present.

   *Antes íbamos mucho a esquiar, pero **ya no** vamos nunca.*

   ***Ya no** trabajo en la academia. Ahora trabajo en la universidad.*

Compare:

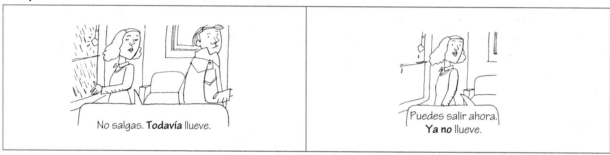

No salgas. **Todavía** llueve.

Puedes salir ahora.
Ya no llueve.

● *ya, todavía no*

– *Ya* indicates that the action or situation that we are referring to has been done previously. It can go before or after the verb.

   ***Ya** he terminado. Podemos marcharnos.*

   *He terminado **ya**. Me voy a casa.*

In interrogatives, it asks if the action or situation has previously been done. It often goes after the verb.

   *–¿Has hablado **ya** con Pedro? –Sí, hablé ayer.*

   *–¿Habéis acabado **ya** los ejercicios? –No, espere un momento, por favor.*

– *Todavía* with a negative verb indicates that the action or situation we are referring to hasn't been done previously. It can go before or after the verb.

   ***Todavía no** he acabado. Esperadme un momento.*

   *Mar **no** ha encontrado trabajo **todavía**.*

   *¿**Todavía no** te has vestido? Vamos a llegar tarde.*

Compare:

Todavía no
han comido.

Ya han comido.

86.1 **Circle the correct answer.**

1. Pablo y yo (*todavía* / (*ya no*)) salimos juntos. Lo dejamos hace tres meses.
2. Cuidado. La sopa (*todavía* / *ya no*) está caliente.
3. (*Todavía* / *Ya no*) trabajo con Pérez. Ahora trabajo en un banco.
4. –¿(*Todavía* / *Ya no*) vives en la calle Bolivia? –Sí, me gusta mucho el barrio.
5. Julián (*todavía* / *ya no*) estudia inglés. Ahora estudia chino.
6. ¿(*Todavía* / *Ya no*) fumas? Tienes que dejarlo. Es muy malo.
7. (*Todavía* / *Ya no*) vivo en esa calle. Me he mudado de piso.
8. (¿*Todavía* / *Ya no*) no te has duchado? ¿A qué esperas?

SCORE ...... /8

86.2 **Complete the sentences with *todavía* or *ya no*.**

1. No puedes irte. Todavía te necesito.
2. –¿Está Berta? –No, _____ vive aquí.
3. –¿Sigues jugando al tenis? –Sí, _____ juego de vez en cuando.
4. –¿Vas a la oficina? –No, _____ estoy de vacaciones.
5. –¿Ha dejado de fumar tu mujer? –Sí, _____ fuma.
6. Puedes irte. _____ te necesito.
7. –¿Me dejas la bicicleta, Manuel? –Lo siento, _____ tengo bicicleta. Se me rompió.
8. –¿Sigue estudiando griego? –Sí, _____ lo estudio. Me encanta.
9. No te vayas _____. –Tengo algo que decirte.
10. Julio y Álvaro _____ son amigos. Se han peleado.

SCORE ...... /10

86.3 **Complete the sentences with *ya* and *todavía no*.**

1. Estoy esperando a Lidia desde las seis, pero _____todavía no_____ ha llegado.
2. Venid. _____ han abierto las puertas.
3. –¿Qué quieres estudiar? –_____ lo sé.
4. –¿Sabes que Lorenzo se marcha a Chile? –Sí, _____ lo sé.
5. –¿Has leído _____ el fichero que te mandé? –No, _____ lo he abierto.
6. ¿_____ has pagado el alquiler? Se va a enfadar el casero.
7. –¿Ha vuelto _____ Pilar de México? –No, _____ ha vuelto.
8. _____ sé dónde está Viña. Me lo ha dicho Tomás.
9. Hace mal tiempo. _____ han abierto las piscinas.
10. ¿Habéis visto _____ la nueva película de Amenábar?

SCORE ...... /12

86.4 **Rewrite the sentences with *ya* or *todavía no*.**

1. La reunión empezó a las tres. Ha acabado. _Ya ha acabado la reunión_.
2. El partido empezó a las cinco. No ha acabado. _Todavía no ha acabado el partido_.
3. Hay una obra de García Lorca. La he visto. _____.
4. El jefe llamó hace un rato. No ha llegado. _____.
5. La impresora no funcionaba. La he arreglado. _____.
6. El gato estaba en el árbol. Lo han encontrado. _____.
7. Raúl está buscando trabajo. No ha encontrado. _____.
8. Tenía muchos ejercicios. Los he hecho. _____.
9. La película empezó hace una hora. No ha terminado. _____.
10. Julio ganó la partida. Ha acabado. _____.

SCORE ...... /10

87 *siempre, de vez en cuando, a veces...*
Adverbs and expressions of frequency

En el desierto de Atacama no llueve **nunca**.

Javier hace footing **todos los días**.

Nunca and *todos los días* are used to express the frequency that something happens or something is done. They answer the question *¿con qué frecuencia?*

> En mi casa comemos pescado (how often?) ***de vez en cuando***.

● Adverbs and expressions of frequency

siempre	normalmente casi siempre	a menudo frecuentemente	a veces de vez en cuando		casi nunca	nunca
100%	80%	60%	30%		5%	0%

– *Siempre, a veces...* can go before or after the verb, at the end of the sentence, or on their own.

> Luis **siempre estudia** por la noche.   ***A veces** trabajo por la tarde.*
> Luis estudia **siempre** por la noche.   *Trabajo **a veces** por la tarde.*
> Luis estudia por la noche **siempre**.   *Trabajo por la tarde **a veces**.*

– *Normalmente* can go at the beginning of the sentence.

> ***Normalmente**, los sábados salgo con mis amigos.*

– *Casi nunca, nunca*   ▶ UNIT 91: Negative adverbs

> nunca / casi nunca + verb in affirmative   ***Nunca voy** a la ópera.*
> verb in negative + *nunca / casi nunca*   ***No voy nunca** a la ópera.*

● Expressions of frequency with other constructions:

todos los días / meses / años...	*Me levanto temprano **todos los días**.*
todas las noches / semanas / tardes...	***Todas las noches** antes de acostarme leo un rato.*
(todos) los lunes / martes / fines de semana	*Voy a clase de guitarra **(todos) los martes**.*
una vez — *al día / mes / año...*	*Nos reunimos **una vez al mes**.*
dos / tres... veces — *a la semana*	*Limpiamos la casa **dos veces a la semana**.*
un día / dos días	*Como en casa de mis padres **un día a la semana**.*

– *Todos los días, una vez al año...* can go at the beginning or end of the sentence or on their own.

> ***Una vez a la semana** nos reunimos todos los amigos. / Nos reunimos todos los amigos **una vez a la semana**.*
> *–¿Vais mucho al cine? –**Una vez al mes**.*

● We often use *mucho* (= often) in questions to ask about the frequency in which something is done.

> *–¿Viaja **mucho** a México? –Dos o tres veces al año.*

87 EXERCISES

87.1 Complete with the expressions from the box. You can use more than one in some cases.

a menudo	casi nunca	de vez en cuando	frecuentemente
mucho	normalmente	nunca	siempre

1. _Casi nunca_ salgo con Teresa. Ahora vivimos muy lejos.
2. _____, suelo cenar en casa.
3. Me levanto _____ a las siete. Me gusta madrugar.
4. Vamos _____ al cine, dos o tres veces al mes.
5. _____ me acuesto antes de las doce. No puedo dormirme antes.
6. Mis padres hacen un viaje _____, una o dos veces al año.
7. –¿Ves _____ a Lola?
   –_____. La última vez fue hace dos meses.
8. Ernesto come _____ en casa. No le gustan los restaurantes.
9. Viajo _____ a Argentina. Tengo muchos amigos y me gusta verlos.
10. –¿Van _____ a la disco? –_____, una ves al mes o algo así.

SCORE ...... /12

87.2 Rewrite the sentences adding the expression in parentheses in the correct place. Make the necessary changes.

1. Voy ↑ al cine. (*nunca*)   No voy nunca al cine ___.
2. ↑ Salgo por la noche. (*nunca*)   _____.
3. Fernando ↑ viaja en coche. (*casi nunca*)   _____.
4. Vemos ↑ la televisión. (*casi nunca*)   _____.
5. Diana me llama ↑. (*nunca*)   _____.
6. ↑ Me regalan nada. (*nunca*)   _____.

SCORE ...... /6

87.3 Put the expressions from the box in order of frequency from more to less.

| todos los días |
| una vez a la semana |
| un día al mes |
| los lunes |
| cada dos días |
| dos veces al año |
| cada quince días |

⊕ 1. _____ todos los días _____
2. _____
3. _____ / _____
4. _____
5. _____
⊖ 6. _____

SCORE ...... /6

87.4 Rewrite the sentences with the correct expression of frequency.

1. [martes, martes, martes...] (*tenemos clases de español*) Tenemos clases de español todos los martes.
   _____.
2. [marzo **, abril **...] (*Elena tiene que ir al médico*) _____.
3. [2001, 2002, 2003...] (*pasamos unos días en Cancún*) _____.
4. [enero *, febrero *...] (*salimos a cenar con amigos*) _____
   _____.
5. [L M **X** J **V** S D] (*Miguel llama a Carla*) _____.
6. [L M **X** J V S D] (*voy al gimnasio*) _____.
7. [L***, M***...] (*Martín se lava los dientes*) _____.
8. [S D, S D, S D...] (*hacemos algún viaje*) _____.

SCORE ...... /8

88 muy, mucho, bastante...
Adverbs of quantity

*Nuria trabaja **mucho**.*

Julia y su hermano son **bastante** *diferentes.*

Es **demasiado** tarde.
El avión ya ha despegado.

Mucho, bastante, and *demasiado* are adverbs of quantity. They indicate different degress of intensity related to the words they refer to.

⊕ — muy / mucho — bastante — un poco — poco — nada — ⊖

demasiado = more than necessary or more than what is considered correct.

● *muy, bastante...* with adjectives and adverbs

muy		Fidel cocina **muy bien**.
bastante	+ adjetivo	Julia y su hermano son **bastante diferentes**.
un poco		Este ejercicio es **un poco difícil**.
poco	+ adverbio	Susana es **poco cariñosa**.
demasiado		Este hotel es **demasiado caro**.
nada		Gema no es **nada egoísta**.

> **BE CAREFUL!**
>
> With *nada* + adjective/adverb, the verb goes in the negative form.
>
> Alberto ~~es nada alto~~ → Alberto **no es nada alto**.
>
> *Un poco* has a positive meaning and is often used with adjectives that express negative qualities. *Poco* has a negative meaning and is often used with adjectives that express positive qualities.
>
> Soy **un poco tímida**. (I am shy.)   Soy **poco tímida**. (I am not shy.)
>
> ~~Felipe es un poco trabajador~~ → Felipe es **un poco vago**.

● *mucho, bastante...* with verbs

verbo +	mucho	Beatriz **trabaja mucho**.
	bastante	Ernesto **piensa bastante**.
	poco	Este tren **corre poco**.
	demasiado	Felipe **duerme demasiado**.
	nada	Juan **no come nada**.

> **BE CAREFUL!**
>
> With *nada* the verb goes in the negative form.
>
> Luis ~~estudia nada~~. → Luis **no estudia nada**.

● *muy, mucho*

– *Muy* is used with adjectives and adverbs.

Eres **muy amable**.   Es **muy tarde**. Tenemos que irnos.

– *Mucho* is used with verbs.

Sofía **trabaja mucho**.   Me **gusta mucho** la carne.
Andrés corre ~~muy~~. → Andrés corre **mucho**.   Leticia es ~~mucho~~ inteligente. → Leticia es **muy inteligente**.

88.1. Circle the correct form in each case.

1. Me encanta esta novela. Es extraordinaria. Es (*muy* / *poco*) buena.
2. No se puede oír nada. La música está (*algo* / *bastante*) alta.
3. Roberto no es (*poco* / *nada*) alegre. Nunca quiere salir.
4. Esther ha sido siempre (*poco* / *nada*) amable.
5. Este libro no es (*bastante* / *nada*) caro. Solo cuesta cinco euros.
6. Rubén es (*demasiado* / *poco*) sincero. A veces, es mejor no decir toda la verdad.
7. Silvia se lleva (*muy* / *demasiado*) bien con su hermana. Se ayudan mucho.
8. Es (*nada* / *bastante*) tarde. Deberíamos irnos.
9. Tomás es (*poco* / *un poco*) cariñoso. Nunca da un beso a nadie.
10. Ricardo está (*poco* / *un poco*) débil. Debería hacer algo de ejercicio.
11. Ayer estuve con Elisa y la encontré (*bastante* / *poco*) nerviosa. No paraba de hablar.

SCORE ...../11

88.2. Look at the drawings and complete the sentences with *bastante*, *demasiado*, *muy*, or *un poco*.

1. El traje le queda ____demasiado____ grande.
2. Catalina dibuja _____ bien.
3. Ernesto va _____ rápido.
4. Los zapatos son _____ pequeños.
5. El libro es _____ caro.

SCORE ...../5

88.3. Complete with *bastante*, *demasiado*, *mucho*, *nada*, or *poco*.

1. Ernesto estudia : ____mucho____ seis horas al día.
2. Este coche corre _____. No pasa de los ochenta kilómetros a la hora.
3. Víctor sale _____. No está nunca en casa y no estudia _____.
4. Suelo desayunar muy _____: un café con leche nada más.
5. Rosa y yo nos vemos _____, casi todas las semanas.
6. Tengo que tomarme algo. Me duele _____ la cabeza.
7. Nacho no ayuda _____ a sus padres.
8. María no estudia _____. Va a suspender todos los exámenes.

SCORE ...../9

88.4. Complete the sentences with the words from the box.

demasiado +++	muy/mucho ++	bastante +	poco –	nada – –

1. Ana es amable (++) ___Ana es muy amable___.
2. Jorge es simpático (– –) ___Jorge no es nada simpático___.
3. Nati corre (++) _____.
4. Guillermo trabaja (– –) _____.
5. Felipe sale (–) _____.
6. Este restaurante es caro (+++) _____.
7. Rosana es trabajadora (–) _____.
8. Víctor come (+++) _____.
9. Me gusta trabajar (--) _____.
10. Lola conduce bien (++) _____.

SCORE ...../10

88.5. Rewrite the sentences adding *muy* or *mucho*.

1. Esta novela es buena. ___Esta novela es muy buena___
2. Esther duerme. _____.
3. Mi casa está lejos. _____.
4. Raúl prepara bien la carne. _____.
5. Me parezco a mi madre. _____.
6. Hacer ejercicio es sano. _____.
7. Raúl llega siempre tarde. _____.
8. Eva gasta poco. _____.
9. A Antonio le gusta la música. _____.
10. Sara anda en vacaciones. _____.

SCORE ...../10

89 *bien, fácilmente*
Adverbs of manner

*Gema conduce **prudentemente**.*

*Serafín toca el piano muy **bien**.*

Prudentemente and *bien* are adverbs of manner. They express how something happens or how someone does something. They answer the question *¿cómo?*

> *Hans habla español* (how?) ***perfectamente**.*

> *Esteban es muy inteligente. Aprueba* (how?) ***fácilmente**.*

● Forming adverbs of manner

Feminine singular adjective + *–mente* → adverb

adjective	singular feminine	adverb
maravilloso	maravillosa →	maravillosa**mente**
fácil	fácil →	fácil**mente**
prudente	prudente →	prudente**mente**

> **BUT:**
>
> *bueno* → *bien*   *Es un conductor bueno. Conduce* (how?) ***bien**.*
> *malo* → *mal*   *Es un conductor malo. Conduce* (how?) ***mal**.*
> *deprisa*   *Julia siempre hace todo **deprisa**.*
> *despacio*   *Alberto camina muy **despacio**.*

– Some adverbs have the same form as the adjective and others have several forms.

adjective	adverb
alto (volumen) / bajo (volumen)	alto / bajo
rápido / lento	rápido, rápidamente / lento, lentamente

*No hables **alto**, por favor. Me duele la cabeza.*

*No me gusta ir con Blanca. Conduce muy **rápido**.*

● *así* = in this way

> *Hazlo **así** (in this way); es más fácil.*

● *Adverbs of manner* usually go after the verb.

> *Alba **vive alegremente**.*

> *Jesús **esquía mal**. Está aprendiendo.*

– They can also take other adverbs, such as *muy*, *bastante*...

> *Sara baila **bastante bien**.*

Compare:

ADJECTIVE	ADVERB
*Rosario es **una conductora prudente**.*	*Rosario **conduce prudentemente**.*
*Son unos **cantantes muy buenos**.*	***Cantan muy bien**.*

– In sentences where there are two or more adverbs with *–mente*, we add the ending to the last word only. The first adverb takes the feminine singular adjective form.

> *Lo hizo rápidamente y **eficazmente**.* → *Lo hizo **rápida** y **eficazmente**.*

BE CAREFUL!

With the ending *–mente*, if the adjective has an accent mark then the adverb does as well.

> *pru**de**nte → prudentemente*

> *fácil → fá**c**ilmente*

89 EXERCISES

89.1. **Write the adverbs of the following adjectives.**

1. elegante ___elegantemente___
2. difícil _____
3. astuto _____
4. fuerte _____
5. rápido _____
6. extraordinario _____
7. tranquilo _____
8. honrado _____
9. lento _____
10. serio _____

SCORE ...... /10

89.2. **Look at the drawings and complete the sentences with the adverbs from the box.**

1. Lorena conduce muy ___deprisa___.
2. Diana escucha _____.
3. Rubén canta muy _____.
4. Elisa habla muy _____.
5. Gerardo escribe muy _____.
6. Juan habla muy _____.

alto	atentamente
bajo	~~deprisa~~
despacio	mal

SCORE ...... /6

89.3. **Replace the underlined words with adverbs of manner.**

1. Hazlo <u>con tranquilidad</u>, Norma. ___Hazlo tranquilamente, Norma___.
2. Álvaro juega <u>con inteligencia</u>. _____.
3. Agustín actúa <u>de una forma irresponsable</u>. _____.
4. Ven <u>con rapidez</u>, Adela. _____.
5. Fran me llama <u>de manera continua</u>. _____.
6. Escribe <u>de este modo</u>, Luisa. _____.
7. Susana canta <u>de forma maravillosa</u>. _____.
8. Me golpeó <u>con fuerza</u>. _____.
9. Emilia nada <u>de una forma extraordinaria</u>. _____.
10. Mis hijos aprueban <u>con facilidad</u>. _____.
11. Se ganan la vida <u>con honradez</u>. _____.
12. La profesora de Matemáticas explica <u>con claridad</u>. _____.
13. Se bajó del árbol <u>con habilidad</u>. _____.

SCORE ...... /13

89.4. **Complete the sentences with the words from the box.**

1. Javier es un ___buen___ estudiante.
2. María es una cocinera _____.
3. Manuel resultó herido _____ en el accidente.
4. A veces Alejandro se porta _____ con sus amigos.
5. Adela es muy . No se interesa por nadie.
6. Mario canta muy _____. Tiene una voz muy bonita.
7. Un señor me cedió el asiento _____.
8. Noelia conoce Cuba _____.
9. Susana ha tenido un accidente muy _____.
10. Javi es un desastre. Conduce muy _____.
11. Es un disco muy _____. No me ha gustado nada.
12. Manuel es siempre muy _____ con sus tías.

| amable |
| amablemente |
| bien |
| ~~buen~~ |
| egoísta |
| egoístamente |
| exquisita |
| grave |
| gravemente |
| mal |
| malo |
| perfectamente |

SCORE ...... /12

89.5. **Replace the underlined words with adverbs of manner.**

1. Tatiana conduce <u>con lentitud</u> y <u>con cuidado</u>. ___Tatiana conduce lenta y cuidadosamente___.
2. Avelina trabaja <u>con tranquilidad</u> pero <u>con seriedad</u>. _____.
3. Javier camina <u>con lentitud</u> y <u>con pereza</u>. _____.
4. La carta está escrita <u>con limpieza</u> y <u>con corrección</u>. _____.

SCORE ...... /4

187

90 | *más rápido, mejor*
Comparison adverbs

No te oigo. Habla **más alto**, por favor.

No hay duda. Camila canta **mejor** que yo.

Más and *mejor* make the comparative forms of adverbs. They are used to indicate different degrees of intensity or to make comparisons between two people, animals, or things.

> *No te entiendo. Habla **más claro**, por favor.*
>
> *Susana dibuja **mejor que** yo.*

● Adverbs: forming the comparative

  – Superiority (+)

más + adverb (+ *que*)	
*Habla **más alto**, por favor.*	*El agua avanza **más rápido que** el fuego.*

  ◦ Irregular forms:

(+) bien → mejor (+ *que*)	*Hans habla español **mejor que** yo.*
(+) mal → peor (+ *que*)	*Vivimos **peor que** antes.*
(+) mucho → más (+ *que*)	*José Luis está trabajando **más que** nunca.*
(+) poco → menos	*Esteban corre **menos que** yo.*

  – Inferiority (–)

menos + adverb (+ *que*)
*Hoy hemos llegado **menos tarde que** ayer.*

  – equality (=)

tan + adverb (+ *como*)
*Este tren corre **tan rápido como** el AVE.*
*Noelia no dibuja **tan bien como** su madre.*

  ◦ Irregular forms:

(=) mucho → tanto (+ *como*)	*Trabajo **tanto como** tú.*

BE CAREFUL!

que/como + subject pronouns (*yo, tú, ...*)		
Ustedes hablan más ~~que mí~~.	→	*Ustedes hablan más **que yo**.*

The comparative form for inferiority is not used very often. The negative form for the comparative of equality is usually used in its place.

| *~~Félix suele llegar menos tarde que yo~~.* | → | *Félix **no** suele llegar **tan tarde** como yo.* |

90 EXERCISES

90.1. Complete the sentences with the comparative form of superiority or equality with the adverbs from the box.

1. No hables tan alto, por favor. Habla _____más bajo_____ .
2. Vas muy rápido. No vayas _____tan rápido_____ .
3. No vayas tan rápido. Ve _____ .
4. No trabajen tanto. Trabajen _____ .
5. Gritáis mucho. No gritéis _____ .
6. Os levantáis demasiado temprano. No os levantéis _____ .
7. –No puedo abrir la puerta. –Empuja _____ .
8. Este ejercicio está muy mal. Tienes que hacerlo _____ .
9. No seas alocada. Tienes que hacer las cosas _____ .
10. Siempre llegáis tarde. No tenéis que llegar _____ .

Box: ~~bajo~~ bien fuerte lento mucho poco ~~rápido~~ tarde temprano tranquilamente

SCORE ....../10

90.2. Write the comparisons according to what is indicated in parentheses.

1. Sofía vive cerca del cine. (+ *nosotros*) _Sofía vive más cerca del cine que nosotros_ .
2. Hoy hemos llegado tarde. (– *de costumbre*) _____ .
3. Susana corre mucho. (= *Eloísa*) _____ .
4. Julián cocina bien. (+ *Vicente*) _____ .
5. Arnaldo gasta mucho. (+ *Jesús*) _____ .
6. Jorge se levanta temprano. (= *yo*) _____ .
7. Sara y Eva conducen bien. (= *ustedes*) _____ .
8. Hablo poco. (+ *mi padre*) _____ .
9. Alonso habla inglés mal. (– *su hermana*) _____ .
10. Héctor come poco. (+ *antes*) _____ .

SCORE ....../10

90.3. Complete the sentences as indicated.

1. Hablo español bien, pero Li habla (+) _mejor que_ yo.
2. Antes vivíamos bien, pero ahora vivimos (+)_____ antes.
3. Ahora trabajo mucho, pero antes trabajaba (+)_____ ahora.
4. Jorge estudiaba mucho y ahora estudia (=)_____ antes.
5. Duermo mucho, pero María duerme (+)_____ yo.
6. Javier lee poco, pero Mario lee (+)_____ él.
7. Alberto habla mucho y su mujer habla (=) _____ él.
8. Enrique bebe poco, pero Manuel bebe (+) _____ él.

SCORE ....../8

90.4. Rewrite the sentences using the comparative form of equality.

1. Héctor corre menos rápido que tú. _Héctor no corre tan rápido como tú_ .
2. Lucas habla menos que yo. _____ .
3. Sonia se acuesta menos tarde que nosotros. _____ .
4. Silvia explica menos claro que Laura. _____ .
5. Camino menos lentamente que David. _____ .
6. Ernesto juega menos inteligentemente que Carlos. _____ .
7. Jorge ayuda menos que yo en casa. _____ .
8. Carlos come menos que antes. _____ .

SCORE ....../8

189

91 *no, nunca*
Negative adverbs

No, gracias.
No tomo café.

Josefina **nunca** tiene
tiempo para nada.

No and *nunca* are negative adverbs. They are used to contradict an action or situation.

- **no**

  – *No* is the most common negative adverb. It can be used on its own or with a verb.

    –*¿Vas a venir mañana?* –**No, no puedo**. *Lo siento.*
    –*¿Estás cansado?* –**No**.

  – Placement:

    • *No* (+ object pronoun) + verb

      No tengo *hambre.*
      Todavía **no he leído** *el periódico.*
      A Felipe **no le gusta** *levantarse tarde.*

    • *No* (+ object pronoun) + verb + negative element

      Ayer **no hice nada**.
      Ayer estuve en el Retiro, pero **no vi a nadie**.
      Tengo nada. → **No** *tengo nada.*

    • When the subject is *nadie* or *nada*, there are two possibilities.

Nadie, nada + verbo	**Nadie** me **quiere**.
	Nada es *imposible.*
No + verbo + *nadie, nada*	**No** me **quiere nadie**.
	No es *imposible* **nada**.

      Nadie no me vio. → **Nadie** *me vio.* / **No** *me vio* **nadie**.

- **nunca** ▶ UNIT 87 : Adverbs and expressions of frequency

  – *Nunca* can be alone in the sentence or with *no*.

    • *Nunca* (+ object pronoun) + verb

      Nunca se levantan *antes de las nueve.*

    • *No* (+ object pronoun) + verb + *nunca*

      –*¿***No has estado nunca** *en el Museo de América?* –*No,* **no lo he visitado nunca**.

      –*Comen nunca carne.* → **No** *comen* **nunca** *carne.* / **Nunca** *comen carne.*

91 EXERCISES

91.1. **Make the following sentences negative with *no*.**

1. Adela quiere ayudarnos. _____Adela no quiere ayudarnos_____.
2. ¿Por qué vienes mañana? _____.
3. A Sara le gusta vivir en Santiago. _____.
4. Me ha llamado Andrea. _____.
5. Me he duchado después del partido. _____.
6. Nos gusta la música rock. _____.
7. Esta mañana he desayunado. _____.
8. Prefiero trabajar. _____.
9. Hemos leído *Martín Fierro*. _____.
10. Roberto se acuesta tarde. _____.
11. El viernes pasado cenamos juntos. _____.
12. Salgo a correr frecuentemente. _____.
13. ¿Quieren tomar algo? _____.

SCORE ...... /13

91.2. **Complete the answers with the words in parentheses. Use *no* only if needed.**

1. –¿Conoces a alguien en la fiesta. –No, (*conozco, a nadie*) ___no conozco a nadie___.
2. –¿Ha llamado alguien? –No, (*ha llamado, nadie*) _____.
3. –¿Quién había en casa de Lucía? –(*había, nadie*) _____.
4. –¿Qué te han dicho del examen? –(*me han dicho, nada*) _____.
5. –¿Dónde está Alberto? –(*sabe, nadie*) ___ _____ dónde está.
6. –¿Qué le pasa a Carmina? –(*le pasa, nada*) _____.
7. –¿Qué quieres? –(*quiero, nada*) _____.
8. –¿Sabes algo de Jara? –No, (*sé, nada*) _____.
9. –¿Os ha visto alguien? –No, (*nos ha visto, nadie*) _____.
10. –¿No quieren ayudarte? –No, (*quiere ayudarme, nadie*) _____.

SCORE ...... /10

91.3. **Make sentences with the given words and *no* in the necessary cases. Write all the possibilities.**

1. Nadie / me vio. ___Nadie me vio. / No me vio nadie___.
2. Vi / nada. _____.
3. Pasa / nada. _____.
4. Nada / se ha roto. _____.
5. Nadie / lo quiere. _____.
6. He comprado / nada. _____.

SCORE ...... /6

91.4. **Rewrite the sentences adding *nunca* in the indicated place. Make all necessary changes.**

1. Bebo ↑ alcohol. ___No bebo nunca alcohol___.
2. ↑ Salimos los lunes. _____.
3. He visto ↑ un elefante. _____.
4. ↑ Desayuno antes de ducharme. _____.
5. ¿Has estado ↑ en Potosí? _____.
6. Sofía nos invita ↑. _____.
7. De pequeño, ↑ comía pescado. _____.
8. ↑ Te olvidaré. _____.
9. Voy ↑ al fútbol. _____.
10. Conduzco ↑ de noche. _____.
11. Viajo ↑ solo. _____.
12. Mi hermana ↑ me llama por teléfono. _____.

SCORE ...... /12

92
yo sí, yo no, yo también, yo tampoco
Expressing agreement or disagreement

● *también* and *tampoco*

– *También* and *tampoco,* with the following structures, are used to express **agreement** with another person's situation or opinion.

Yo, tú, usted, él, ella… Noun (Elena, José, mi hermana…) *A mí, a ti, a usted, a él, a ella…* *A + noun (Elena, José, mi hermana…)*	+	*también, tampoco*

– We use *también* at the end of an affirmative sentence.

   –*Juegas muy bien.* –**Tú también**.   –*A Pablo le gusta leer.* –*A **Elena** también*.

– We use *tampoco* at the end of a negative sentence.

   –*No hablo ruso.* –**Yo tampoco**.   –*A Marcos no le gusta viajar.* –**A Luisa tampoco**.

● *sí* and *no*

– *Sí* and *no,* with the following structures, can be used to express **disagreement** with another person's situation or opinion.

Yo, tú, usted, él, ella… Noun (Elena, José, mi hermana…) *A mí, a ti, a usted, a él, a ella…* *A + noun (Elena, José, mi hermana…)*	+	*sí, no*

– We use *no* in response to an affirmative sentence.

   –*Tengo calor.* –**Yo no**.
   –*A Sergio le encanta viajar.* –*Pues **a Gema no***.

– We use *sí* in response to a negative sentence.

   –*No estoy cansada.* –**Nosotros sí**.
   –*A Esteban no le gusta el deporte.* –*Pues **a Alba sí**. Mucho*.

● *Yo sí/no, a mí sí/no, yo también/tampoco,* and *a mí también/tampoco*
are also used in short answers to questions addressed to various people.

   –*¿Os ha gustado la película?* –**A mí sí**. –**A mí no**.

192

92 EXERCISES

92.1 **Express agreement. Complete the answers with *también* or *tampoco*.**

1. –Julia está contenta. –Yo _también_.
2. –No nos gusta el fútbol. –A nosotras _tampoco_.
3. –A Ramón no le gusta viajar en avión. –A su mujer _____.
4. –No sé conducir. –Yo _____. Tengo que aprender.
5. –Eres una persona encantadora. –Tú _____, Marisa.
6. –Estamos resfriadas. –Nosotras _____. Es que hace mucho frío.
7. –Erika habla español muy bien. –Ulrich _____.
8. –No tenemos entradas. –Laura y Sonia _____.
9. –A Miguel le gustaría visitar el Amazonas. –A mí _____. Debe de ser precioso.
10. –Elena nunca sale de noche. –Su hermano _____.

SCORE ...../10

92.2 **Express disagreement. Complete the sentences with *sí* or *no*.**

1. –Tengo sueño. –Yo _no_. Anoche dormí bien.
2. –Luis no sabe jugar al tenis. –Pues Ramón ___. Es bastante bueno.
3. –No me gusta el frío. –A nosotros ___. Es muy sano.
4. –Mañana no trabajo. –Yo ___. Trabajo todos los días.
5. –A Arturo le encanta estudiar. –Pues a Leo ___. Es un poco vago.
6. –No sé tocar ningún instrumento. –Yo ___. Sé tocar la guitarra.
7. –No tenemos suerte. Tú ___. Te ha tocado la lotería dos veces.
8. –No conozco España. –Nosotros ___. Estuvimos allí hace tres años.
9. –Me encanta madrugar. –Pues a mí ___.
10. –Milagros hace bien las tortillas. –Yo ___. Se me da mal la cocina.

SCORE ...../10

92.3 **Complete the dialogues expressing agreement or disagreement with the following key: = agreement, ≠ disagreement.**

1. –Me encanta el chile con carne. –(yo, ≠) _A mí no_. Es muy picante.
2. –Adrián conoce muy bien Guatemala. –(Charo, =) _____.
3. –Anoche no vi el partido. –(yo, =) _____. Me acosté pronto.
4. –Yo, de pequeña, era muy tímida. –(mi hermana, =) _____.
5. –No conozco a ese chico. –(nosotras, =) _____.
6. –Luis no sabe cocinar. –(Serafín, ≠) _____. Es un cocinero excelente.
7. –No comes mucho. –(tú, =) _____. Tienes que comer más.
8. –A Rosendo le encanta el rock. –(Diana, ≠) _____. Prefiere música más suave.
9. –Este año no tengo vacaciones. –(yo, ≠) _____, pero en septiembre.
10. –Cenamos fuera los sábados. –(nosotros, ≠) _____. Preferimos cenar en casa.

SCORE ...../10

92.4 **Complete the answers with agreement with the following key: (√) affirmative answer, (x) negative answer.**

1. –¿Sabéis jugar a las cartas? –(√) Yo _sí_.   –(x) Yo _no_.
2. –¿Tenéis coche? –(x) Yo _____.   –(x) Yo _____.
3. –¿Están cansados? –(√) Rosa _____.   –(√) David _____.
4. –¿Trabajáis mucho? –(x) Yo _____.   –(√) Yo _____.
5. –¿Os ha gustado el concierto?   –(x) A mí _____. –(x) A mí _____. –(√) A mí _____.
6. –¿Os gusta el dulce de leche?   –(x) A mí _____ pero (√) a Héctor _____.

SCORE ...../13

93 y, o, pero...
Conjunctions

Tengo dos hijas **y** un hijo.

No me gusta la carne, **pero** me encanta el pescado.

Y and *pero* are conjunctions. They are used to link and connect sentences or parts of sentences.

Trabajo en un banco. Estudio Económicas. → *Trabajo en un banco y estudio Económicas.*
*Tengo **dos hermanas.** Tengo **un hermano.*** → *Tengo dos hermanas **y** un hermano.*
Conozco a esa chica. No sé su nombre. → *Conozco a esa chica, **pero** no sé su nombre.*

● ***Y, ni*** link parts or similar ideas.

– *Y* links components or affirmative ideas.

Me gusta la carne. Me gusta el pescado. → *Me gustan la carne **y** el pescado.*
Gloria es mexicana. Rosario es mexicana. → *Gloria **y** Rosario son mexicanas.*

● *y* → *e* when the following word begins with *i–/hi–*.

*Sara **e Isabel** son madre **e hija**.*

● When there are more than two components, we place *y/e* before the last one.

*Fernando, Paco **y** María son españoles.*

– *Ni* links components or negative ideas.

No me gusta el té. No me gusta el café. → *No me gusta (ni) el té **ni** el café.*
Alberto no habla inglés. Alberto no habla francés. → *Alberto no habla (ni) inglés **ni** francés.*

● When the linked components go before the verb, we use *ni... ni* and the verb in the affirmative form.

Diana no habla inglés. Tere no habla inglés. → ***Ni** Diana **ni** Tere **hablan** inglés.*
Ni José ni Jorge ̶n̶o̶ quieren salir. → ***Ni** José **ni** Jorge **quieren** salir.*

● When there are more than two components, we place *ni* before each one of them.

***Ni** Ana, **ni** Laura **ni** Agustín quieren ver esta película.*

BE CAREFUL!

*Ángel **es alto**. Su hermana **es alta**.* → *Ángel y su hermana **son altos**.*
*A Sonia **le gusta** esquiar. A Rafa **le gusta** esquiar.* → *A Sonia y a Rafa **les gusta** esquiar.*
*A Andrés **le gusta** leer. A mí **me gusta** leer.* → *A Andrés y a mí **nos gusta** leer.*

● ***O*** links alternative components or indicates approximation.

*¿Quieres fruta **o** un dulce?*   *Había nueve **o** diez personas en la sala.*

– *o* → *u* when the following words begins with *o–/ho–*.

*No sé si siento amor **u** odio.*   *Había siete **u** ocho platos sobre la mesa.*

● ***Pero*** links contradicting components or ideas. It usually goes before the previous sentence and is separated by a comma (,).

*Enrique es **inteligente**. Enrique es **perezoso**.* → *Enrique es inteligente, **pero** perezoso.*
*Enrique **no estudia** mucho. Enrique **aprueba**.* → *Enrique no estudia mucho, **pero** aprueba.*

93 EXERCISES

93.1 Link the sentences with *y/e*, *ni*, or *ni... ni*. Make the necessary changes.

1. Keiko habla inglés. Keiko habla español. _____ Keiko habla inglés y español _____.
2. No hablo inglés. No hablo alemán. _____.
3. No me gusta la fruta. No me gustan las verduras. _____.
4. A Juan le gusta bailar. A Diana le gusta bailar. _____.
5. A Juan no le gusta el fútbol. A Diana no le gusta el fútbol. _____.
6. Héctor estudia idiomas. Héctor estudia informática. _____.
7. Luisa trabaja en la universidad. Luisa trabaja en una academia. _____.
8. Luis no tiene coche. Luis no sabe conducir. _____.
9. Mi hermano no quiere salir. Mi hermana no quiere salir. _____.
10. No me gusta la carne. No me gusta el pescado. _____.
11. A Luisa le gusta Ángel. A Andrea le gusta Ángel. _____.
12. Diana no habla alemán. Rocío no habla alemán. _____.

SCORE ..... /12

93.2 Complete the sentences with *o/u* or *y/e*.

1. ¿Es usted peruano _o_ boliviano?
2. ¿Tienes lápiz _____ papel?
3. No recuerdo si dijo septiembre _____ octubre.
4. Mis meses preferidos son julio _____ agosto.
5. No recuerdo si me dieron diez _____ once.
6. Solo conozco dos países europeos, Francia _____ Italia.
7. –¿Estudias _____ trabajas? –Estudio _____ trabajo.
8. Gabriel _____ Ignacio trabajan en la misma empresa.
9. Había veinte _____ veinticinco personas en la sala.
10. Ven mañana _____ otro día.

SCORE ..... /11

93.3 Link the sentences with *pero*.

1. Felipe es alto. No juega bien al baloncesto. _____ Felipe es alto, pero no juega bien al baloncesto _____.
2. Ese televisor es caro. Es muy bueno. _____.
3. Gana poco dinero. No necesita más. _____.
4. Juan es rico. Trabaja mucho. _____.
5. Salva juega bien al baloncesto. Corre poco. _____.
6. El pueblo es bonito. Está muy lejos. _____.
7. Ángela es inteligente. Es muy vaga. _____.
8. Puedo estudiar más. No quiero. _____.

SCORE ..... /8

93.4 Link the sentences about a group of friends with *y/e*, *ni*, *ni... ni*, or *pero*.

1. Raquel es española. Irene es española. _____ Raquel e Irene son españolas _____.
2. Raquel juega al baloncesto. No es muy alta. _____.
3. Pedro no es muy guapo. Pedro es muy simpático. _____.
4. A Pedro le gusta Raquel. A Raquel no le gusta Pedro. _____.
5. Raquel no trabaja. Pedro no trabaja. Irene no trabaja. _____.
6. A Raquel le gusta la música clásica. A Irene le gusta la música clásica. A Pedro le gusta la música clásica. _____.

SCORE ..... /6

195

Some prepositions are used to indicate temporary connections.

● *a* + hours

    *Te espero **a las cinco.***   *La fiesta acabó **a medianoche.***
    *Voy a ver a Amalia **a mediodía.***

● *por* + parts of the day

    *Ahora estoy trabajando **por las tardes.***

*Margarita se suele levantar **a las seis.***

> **BUT:**   ***por la / de** noche, **de** día, **de** madrugada, a las siete **de** la mañana.*

● *en* + months, seasons, years, and other periods of time such as Christmas, Easter week, or vacation.

    *Elisa y Armando se casan **en enero.***   *Mi cumpleaños es **en verano.***
    *Colón llegó a América **en 1492.***   *Vamos a hacer un viaje **en Semana Santa.***

> **BUT:**   ***de** + months and years in dates: Colón llegó a América el 12 **de** octubre **de** 1492.*

  – *en* + moment

    ***En este momento** no puedo atenderte.*

● ***Hasta*** indicates the last moment of an action or position.

    *Estaré en casa **hasta las ocho.***
    *Teresa vivió en Cuba **hasta 1987.***

    ●--------hasta------▶ x
    ahora   las ocho

  – We use it to say good-bye, to indicate when we will see each other again.

    *¡Adiós! **¡Hasta mañana!***

● ***Desde*** indicates the first moment of an action or situation.

    *Amanda no me llama **desde Navidad.***
    *No me siento bien **desde ayer.***

    x--------desde--------▶●
    Navidad   ahora

● ***De... a*** and ***desde... hasta*** indicate the first and last moment of an action or situation.

    *Lucía vivió en Panamá **de 1999 a 2001.***   *Trabajo sólo **de lunes a jueves.***
    *Natalia tiene clases **desde las cinco hasta las siete.***

  – With *de... a* time doesn't need an article.

    *Este dentista tiene consulta los viernes **de cinco a siete.***

● ***durante, antes de, después de***

    ***antes del** partido*   ***durante** el partido*   ***después del** partido*

    *Estuvieron hablando **durante** toda la película.*   *Dimos una vuelta **después de** la cena.*

● ***Dentro de*** + period of time refers to a future time period.

    *Te llamo **dentro de** dos días.*
    *Vuelvo **dentro de** cinco minutos.*

    ●---------dentro de dos días ------▶ x
    ahora
    martes   jueves

94.1. **Link the columns with the correct prepositions.**

1. Despiértame
2. Los domingos solo trabajo
3. Mi cumpleaños es el 31
4. Natalia nació
5. Podemos quedar
6. Lo siento. No puedo salir
7. Ana no puede estudiar
8. A veces vamos a esquiar
9. Llegaron a las dos
10. Solo puedo ir a la playa
11. Raquel regresó ayer
12. Siempre voy a España

a
de
e
por

a. vacaciones de verano.
b. navidades a ver a mi familia.
c. la mañana.
d. invierno a los Pirineos.
e. este momento.
f. la tarde, cuando estábamos comiendo.
g. las siete.
h. el año 1987.
i. mediodía para tomar algo.
j. madrugada.
k. octubre.
l. noche. Se duerme.

SCORE ...../12

94.2. **Complete the sentences with *a*, *hasta*, *de*, *desde*, or *dentro de*.**

1. Manuel vivió en Venezuela __de/desde__ 1993 __a/hasta__ 1998.
2. Trabajé en una empresa mexicana _____ el año pasado.
3. Patricia vive en Madrid _____ 2001.
4. Los bancos abren _____ ocho _____ dos.
5. Quiero ir a Bolivia _____ dos meses.
6. Anoche no me pude dormir _____ las tres.
7. Tengo mucho trabajo. No estoy libre _____ el jueves.
8. Olga lleva enferma _____ el lunes.
9. –¿Cuándo regresa Sebastián? –_____ unos días.
10. ¿Cuántos kilómetros hay _____ La Habana a Santiago?
11. Adiós. _____ el jueves.
12. Sandra vuelve siempre a casa _____ madrugada.

SCORE ...../14

94.3. **Complete the sentences with *de*, *desde*, *a*, *hasta*, *dentro de*, or *durante* and the expressions in parentheses.**

1. Darío estuvo con nosotros (*el principio*, *el fin del verano*) __Darío estuvo con nosotros desde el__ __principio hasta el fin del verano__.
2. Emilia vivió en Honduras (*1999–2002*) _____.
3. Eva y Mario se casan (*tres meses*) _____.
4. Trabajo en esta oficina (*el mes pasado*) _____.
5. Voy a un gimnasio (*siete*, *nueve*) _____.
6. Me voy. Ya no nos vemos (*la semana que viene*) _____.
7. Por favor, no hables con tus compañeros (*la clase*) _____.
8. Los domingos trabajamos (*diez / dos*) _____.

SCORE ...../8

94.4. **Complete the sentences with *antes de*, *durante*, or *después de* and the expressions from the box.**

1. Gabriel siempre está hablando __durante la clase__.
2. Estábamos agotados _____.
3. Mónica estaba muy nerviosa. _____.
4. Me quedé muy relajada _____.
5. Hay que tener los móviles apagados _____.
6. Tengo que acabar este trabajo _____.

la caminata por la sierra
el viernes
la entrevista
la ducha
los conciertos
~~la clase~~

SCORE ...../6

95 *a Tijuana, desde la playa...*
Prepositions (2)

Prepositions can also indicate a connection of movement or direction and place.

- **A** indicates destiny and distance.

    *–¿Adónde vas? –Voy **a la academia.***
    *¿Cuándo llegamos **a Tijuana?***
    *El pueblo está **a seis kilómetros.***

    a + el → *al: Voy **al** mercado. Necesitamos fruta.*

- **Hacia** indicates direction (= in direction toward).

    *Esta autopista va **hacia el sur.***

- **Hasta** indicates the ending point of a journey or route.

    *Corrimos **hasta la parada del autobús.***
    *Hicimos una marcha y llegamos **hasta Aranjuez.***

- **De, desde** indicate the place of origin or the starting point of a journey or a movement.

    *Han venido **de/desde la playa** en bicicleta.*
    *–¿De dónde vienes? –**De casa** de Eva. Está mejor.*

    de + el → *del: Regreso **del** instituto a las tres.*

    – We don't use *desde* when the important point is the place and not the movement.

    Venimos ~~desde~~ el cine. → *Venimos **del cine**. Hemos visto una película fabulosa.*

- **De/desde... a/hasta** indicate the starting and ending points of a movement.

    *Hay mucho camino **de/desde** la iglesia **a/hasta** el restaurante.*

- **En** indicates a position in a general sense.

en *la mesa*

en *la caja*

en *el jardín*

en *Ecuador*

    *Tengo sellos **en el cajón.***
    *Hay muchos árboles **en mi calle.***
    *Teresa vive **en el quinto piso.***
    *Entró **en la habitación** sin decir nada.*

> **BUT:** ***a** la derecha, **a** la izquierda, **al** norte/sur/este/oeste, **al** final.*
>
>   *Mi calle está **a la derecha** de la Gran Vía.*
>   *La casa está **al este** del río Arlanza.*
>   *Mi casa está **al final** de la calle.*

a la derecha
(de la Gran Vía)

- **Sobre** indicates a position over something or someone.

    *Hay muchos papeles **sobre el televisor.***
    *A veces pasan aviones **sobre la ciudad.***

- **Entre** indicates an intermediate place.

    *La farmacia está **entre el supermercado y el banco.***

95.1. **Circle the correct preposition in each case.**

1. Vengo (*hasta* / *de*) casa de Juana.
2. Ven (*a* / *hasta*) casa esta noche.
3. ¿Van a ir (*a* / *de*) Calpe este verano?
4. ¿Es usted (*de* / *desde*) Granada?
5. No mires (*a* / *hacia*) abajo. Te puedes marear.
6. (*Al* / *Del*) instituto (*a* / *hacia*) mi casa hay más de diez kilómetros.
7. ¡Ánimo! Tienes que llegar (*a* / *hacia*) la meta.
8. −¿(*A* / *Hasta*) dónde hay que llegar? −(*Hasta* / *Hacia*) el árbol que está en la esquina.
9. A mi madre le gustan las canciones (*de* / *desde*) su tierra.
10. Los bancos abren (*hasta* / *hacia*) las ocho de la tarde.

SCORE ...... / 12

95.2. **Complete with *a*, *hacia*, *hasta*, *de*, or *desde*. In some cases, there are two possibilities.**

1. ¿Nos puede llevar __a__ la estación?
2. ¿Vosotras podéis nadar _____ la orilla?
3. Este autobús no llega _____ el centro.
4. Para ver esa estrella hay que mirar _____ el este.
5. _____ Santiago _____ Lima hay una buena carretera.
6. El Ebro fluye _____ el este.
7. _____ aquí _____ casa de Lola hay solo dos kilómetros.
8. ¿Cuántos kilómetros hay _____ Valencia desde Murcia?
9. La farmacia está más adelante, _____ la izquierda.
10. −¿_____ dónde vienes? −_____ una conferencia sobre los mayas.
11. Hemos venido andando _____ la playa.
12. ¿Cómo se va _____ el estadio?
13. Segovia está _____ el norte de Madrid.
14. Mi habitación está _____ el final del pasillo.

SCORE ...... / 17

95.3. **Look at the drawings and complete the sentences with *de*, *a*, *sobre*, *en*, or *entre*.**

1. Hay una foto __sobre__ el piano.
2. Bibiana está _____ su madre y su padre.
3. Asunción está _____ Paraguay .
4. −¿Dónde están los niños? −_____ el jardín.
5. Tuerce por la primera _____ la izquierda.
6. Hay unas nubes _____ el pueblo.
7. Costa Rica está _____ Nicaragua y Panamá.
8. Solo hay dos alumnos _____ el aula.

SCORE ...... / 8

encima de la mesa, dentro de la caja...
Prepositions (3)

¿Dónde están los documentos?

Encima de la mesa.

Las llaves están **dentro del** cajón.

Encima de and dentro de are compound prepositions. They are used to indicate the postion of a person, animal, or object in relation to another person, animal, or object.

> ***Los documentos** están **encima de la mesa**.*

● **encima de, debajo de**

> *No dejéis nada **encima de las sillas**.*
> *Enrique guarda sus juguetes **debajo de la cama**.*

encima de la mesa   **debajo de** la mesa

● **dentro de, fuera de**

> *El abrigo está **dentro del armario**.*
> *Te has dejado la leche **fuera de la nevera**.*

dentro de la caja   **fuera de** la caja

● **cerca de, lejos de**

> *Rosa vive **cerca del centro**.*
> *El estadio está **lejos de aquí**.*

cerca de la parada   **lejos de** la parada

● **frente a / enfrente de**

> *Aurelio vive **enfrente de un parque**.*

frente al cine   **frente al** café
enfrente del cine   **enfrente del** café

● **junto a / al lado de**

> *Hay una papelería **junto a la academia**.*

junto a la librería   **junto a** la farmacia
al lado de la librería   **al lado de** la farmacia

● **alrededor de**

> *Hay muchas tiendas **alrededor de la plaza**.*

alrededor de la plaza

● **delante de, detrás de**

> *No me dejas ver. Estás siempre **delante del televisor**.*

detrás de Salvador   **delante de** Victoria

● prepositions + personal pronouns.   ▶ **UNIT 28: Personal pronouns: subject**

preposition + *mí, ti, usted, él, ella, nosotros, nosotras, vosotros, vosotras, ustedes, ellos, ellas*
> *¿Quién está **detrás de mí**?*

96.1. Look at the drawings and complete the sentences with the words from the box. Be careful with the articles.

alrededor de	encima de
debajo de	frente a
delante de	fuera de
dentro de	~~junto a~~
detrás a	lejos de

botella	la Tierra
cama	mesa
cine	museo
colegio	nevera
hospital	tienda

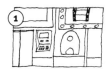   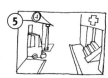

1. Hay un banco ___junto al cine___.
2. Hay muchos árboles _____.
3. Las zapatillas están _____.
4. Hay un parque _____.
5. La estación está _____.

6. Saturno está _____.
7. Hay una mosca _____.
8. Se han dejado la leche _____.
9. He dejado el coche _____.
10. Tengo una foto de mis hijos _____ la mesa.

SCORE ____/10

96.2. Complete the sentences with the prepositions from the box.

1. No podemos ir andando a la playa. Está ___lejos de___ aquí.
2. La cola es muy larga. Hay casi cien personas _____ nosotros.
3. Eduardo no se sienta nunca _____ Cristina.
4. No hace falta ir en coche. El cine está _____ mi casa.
5. Las tijeras están _____ uno de esos cajones.
6. Trae mala suerte pasar por _____ una escalera.
7. Por favor, no pongáis los pies _____ la mesa.
8. Hay una parada de autobús justo _____ mi casa.
9. Ponte _____ mí. Yo he llegado primero.
10. En las fiestas colocan puestos _____ la plaza.
11. Deja el paraguas _____ la casa.
12. Hay un quiosco de prensa _____ la cafetería.

alrededor de
cerca de
debajo de
delante de
dentro de
detrás de
encima de
enfrente de
frente a
fuera de
junto a
~~lejos de~~

SCORE ____/12

96.3. Order the words to make sentences. Be careful with the articles.

1. un bar / hay / el cine / frente a ___Hay un bar frente al cine___.
2. el suelo / los cables / debajo de / van _____.
3. una estación de metro / mi casa / hay / cerca de _____.
4. se sienta / junto a / Alfonso / mí _____.
5. el televisor / no pongas / encima de / nada _____.
6. te espero / el hotel / frente a _____.

SCORE ____/6

97
a Pedro, de Elvira, en autobús...
Prepositions (4)

● We use **a**:

– before the indirect object.

> *Le he regalado mi portátil **a Pedro**.*   *Tienes que dar la comida **a los gatos**.*

– before the direct object when it refers to people or personified animals, or with verbs that usually go with a direct object as a person.

> *Anoche vimos **a Elena** en el concierto.*   *Algunas personas quieren mucho **a sus perros**.*
> *Tengo que lavar **a Fifí**. Está sucísimo.*

▌**But:** We don't use *a* before the direct object when it refers to animals in general or as objects, when it refers to someone undetermined, or after the verbs *haber* and *tener*.

> *¿Has visto **las vacas** que hay en el establo?*   *Voy a fregar **los platos**.*
> *Necesito **un médico**.*   *Pedro tiene **tres hijos**.*
> *Hoy **hay poca gente** en el concierto.*

– to indicate the purpose with verbs of movement.

> *El fontanero ha venido **a arreglar** el baño.*

– to indicate the way, the manner, or the instrument with which something is done.

> *Hoy hemos comido calamares **a la romana**.*   *Estas sandalias están hechas **a mano**.*

● We use **de**:

*Este jarrón es **de porcelana**.*

– to indicate possession: *Este es el despacho **de Elvira**.*

– to indicate origin: *Esos señores son **de Costa Rica**.*

– to indicate the material of which something is made: *Me encantan las tartas **de chocolate**.*
> *Necesito una **caja de cartón**.*

– to indicate a subject or content: *Necesito una gramática **de español**. Tómate **un vaso de leche**.*
> *Hay que comprar **latas de sardinas**.*

– to indicate characteristics: *La chica **de la falda amarilla** es argentina.*   *Fernando tiene una **niña de diez años**.*

– to indicate purpose: *Necesito gafas de **sol**.* (glasses for sun protection.)

● We use **en**:

– with means of transportation.

> *El viaje al Machu Picchu se hace **en tren** y **en autobús**.*

– to indicate the way or manner of doing something, or with languages.

> *Me gusta trabajar **en silencio**.*   *No me hables **en ruso**. No te entiendo.*

▌**But:** **a** pie, **a** caballo: *Voy a trabajar **a pie**. Vivo muy cerca de la oficina.*

● We use **sobre**:

– to indicate approximation: *El cartero suele llegar **sobre las diez**.* (approximately)

– to indicate a subject or issue:

> *Mañana hay una conferencia **sobre la globalización**.*   *Estoy escribiendo un libro **sobre Miguel Ángel Asturias**.*

▶ UNIT 29: Personal pronouns: direct object   UNIT 30: Personal pronouns: indirect object
UNIT 103: Purpose clauses

97 EXERCISES

97.1. Insert *a* where necessary.

1. No he oído los niños todavía. _No he oído a los niños todavía_.
2. Todavía no he oído esa canción. _Todavía no he oído esa canción_.
3. ¿A qué hora has llamado Enrique? _____.
4. Quiero mucho mis padres. _____.
5. Begoña está regalando sus gatitos. _____.
6. ¿Has visto alguien de nuestro grupo? _____.
7. Tengo que saludar Bárbara. _____.
8. ¿Hay alguien en el aula? _____.
9. En mi oficina necesitan una secretaria. _____.
10. Le compré un regalo Fidel. _____.

SCORE ..... /10

97.2. Look at the drawings and complete the nouns with the words from the box and the correct preposition.

| atún | baño | chocolate | fútbol (2) | leche | oro | pana | queso | ~~sol~~ |

① gafas _de sol_   ② reloj _____   ③ cuarto _____   ④ campo _____   ⑤ galletas _____

⑥ pantalones _____   ⑦ botella _____   ⑧ bocadillo _____   ⑨ lata _____   ⑩ botas _____

SCORE ..... /10

97.3. Complete the sentences with the prepositions *a*, *de*, *en*, or *sobre*.

1. ¿Sabes escribir __a__ máquina?
2. Estrella va a clases _____ alemán.
3. Arístides es _____ Santo Domingo.
4. Mi abuelo siempre se hacía los trajes _____ medida.
5. Me encanta la tortilla _____ patatas.
6. Algunas ciudades tienen muchos problemas _____ tráfico.
7. No me siento _____ gusto con estos zapatos.
8. Han alquilado la casa _____ unos turistas.
9. ¿Cuándo vas _____ pintar la habitación?
10. Estoy leyendo un libro _____ los pueblos caribes.
11. Creo que Antonio y Marta se han casado _____ secreto.
12. Rocío siempre canta _____ inglés.

SCORE ..... /12

97.4. Complete the sentences with the prepositions *a*, *de*, *en,* or *sobre* and the words from the box.

1. Mañana tengo una entrevista _de trabajo_.
2. Me encanta pasear _____ por el campo.
3. Copiad los ejercicios _____.
4. Lorena siempre viene a la universidad _____.
5. John, ¿cuándo has empezado las clases _____?
6. ¿Quién es la chica _____?
7. Dijeron que vendrían _____.
8. He recibido una revista escrita _____.

| caballo |
| metro |
| las diez |
| el pelo largo |
| español |
| portugués |
| lápiz |
| ~~trabajo~~ |

SCORE ..... /8

para ti, por amor...
Prepositions (5)

- We use *para*:

  - to indicate destination or purpose.

    *Toma, un regalo **para ti**.*
    *He comprado unos altavoces **para el ordenador**.*

  - *para* + infinitive = purpose. ▶ UNIT 103: Purpose clauses

    *¿Tiene un cuchillo **para pelar** patatas?*

  - to indicate the end of a period of time.

    *He comprado unos pollos **para el domingo**.*
    *Necesitamos un apartamento **para este verano**.*

  - We use *para* + noun / personal pronun (object) to express an opinion.

    ***Para Julio**, su hermana es perfecta.* (Julio thinks that his sister is perfect.)
    ***Para mí**, eso no tiene importancia.* (I believe that it isn't important.)

Estas flores son **para usted**.

- We use *por*:

  - to indicate the cause of or the reason for an action.

    *Se suspendió el partido **por la lluvia**.*
    *Lo he hecho **por amor**.*

  - to indicate the means with which something is done.

    *Llámame **por teléfono** esta noche.*   *Envíale la factura **por fax**.*

  - to indicate an approximate place or transportation route.

    *Tiene que haber un banco **por aquí**.*   *Fuimos a Sevilla **por la autopista**.*

  - to indicate a price.

    *Hemos comprado un apartamento **por doscientos mil euros**.*

Gracias **por el reloj**.

- We use *con*:

  - to indicate company or accompaniment.

    *José sale **con Tina** los fines de semana.*   *¿Has probado el chile **con carne**?*

  - to indicate means.

    *Pagó las entradas **con la tarjeta de crédito**.*

- We use *sin*:

  - to indicate that something or someone is missing.

    *Me he acostumbrado a beber cerveza **sin alcohol**.*

- We use *contra*:

  - to indicate opposition.

    *Este domingo juega el Real Madrid **contra el River Plate**.*
    *Ayer fuimos a un manifestación **contra el paro**.*

98 EXERCISES

98.1 **Circle the correct preposition in each case.**

1. Te felicito (*para* / *por*) tu trabajo.
2. Hay que comprar comida (*para* / *por*) el domingo.
3. Me he comprado una camisa (*para* / *por*) treinta euros.
4. ¿(*Para* / *Por*) quién es esto?
5. Me han regañado (*para* / *por*) culpa tuya.
6. Enviadme un mensaje (*para* / *por*) email.
7. No pudimos salir (*para* / *por*) el frío.
8. No tengo las instrucciones (*para* / *por*) instalar el ordenador.

SCORE ...../8

98.2 **Link the sentences with the correct prepositions.**

1. Quiero un café		a. la pena de muerte.
2. No os podéis ir		b. escalera.
3. ¿Te gustan las patatas	**con**	c. tijeras.
4. No puedes cortar eso		d. carne?
5. No veo ese cartel	**contra**	e. lluvia.
6. Mañana hay una manifestación		f. leche.
7. No podemos pintar el techo	**sin**	g. permiso.
8. Es pesado conducir		h. gafas.

SCORE ...../8

98.3 **Complete the sentences with *por*, *para*, *sin*, *con*, or *contra*.**

1. Alfonso y Anselmo viven todavía __con__ sus padres.
2. No podrás encender el gas _____ cerillas.
3. Hay pocos remedios _____ el dolor de muelas.
4. Me encantaría inventar una máquina _____ tender la ropa.
5. ¿Te vienes _____migo al campo?
6. Puedes reservar las entradas _____ teléfono.
7. Carlota no se fue a México _____ sus padres.
8. Fernando invitó a Josefina _____ mi voluntad.
9. No entres _____ llamar.
10. He comprado unos libros _____ internet.

SCORE ...../10

98.4 **Complete the sentences with the prepositions and the nouns from the box.**

1. He recibido los documentos __por correo__.
2. Es difícil hacer esa traducción _____.
3. Necesitamos cortinas _____.
4. Hay que atravesar el río _____.
5. Me he dado un golpe _____.
6. Mándame el paquete _____.
7. Martina hace muchos gestos _____.
8. Hace frío. No salgas _____.
9. Están buscando una vacuna _____.
10. No pueden ir a comprar _____.

con		contra
para		por
	sin	

abrigo	el puente
avión	el sida
~~correo~~	la habitación
diccionario	los ojos
dinero	un martillo

SCORE ...../10

99 *Pienso en ti.*
Verbs with prepositions

¿Me **ayudas a recoger**?

Pienso en ti todos los días.

Ayudar and *pensar* need the prepositions *a* and *en* to link the next word.

Some verbs need a preposition to link to other verbs, to a noun, or a pronoun.

● verbs + prepositions

   – Some can go with an infinitive, a noun, or a pronoun.

     verb + preposition + infinitive → *¿Me **ayudas a limpiar** la casa?*
     verb + preposition + noun   → *Estamos **ayudando al padre** de Andrea.*
     verb + preposition + pronoun → *¿Quién me **ayuda a mí**?*

    ▶ **UNIT 34: Personal pronouns with prepositions**

   – Others go only with the infinitive.

     *Tengo que **acabar de pasar** esto a máquina esta noche.*

● Some verbs + *a*

   a + infinitive/noun/pronoun: *acostumbrarse, ayudar, dedicarse, enseñar, obligar*
   a + infinitive: *aprender, atreverse, comenzar, decidirse, negarse, volver, ir, venir*
   a + noun/pronoun: *parecerse*

     *Nos hemos **acostumbrado a las comidas** de Toni.*   *Tenéis que **venir a ver** nuestro piso.*
     *Tu hijo mayor **se parece a ti**.*

● Some verbs + *de*

   de + infinitive/noun/pronoun: *acordarse, arrepentirse, cansarse, olvidarse, reírse*
   de + infinitive/noun: *alegrarse*
   de + infinitive: *dejar, terminar, tratar*
   de + noun/pronoun: *desconfiar, disfrutar, divorciarse, enamorarse, sospechar*
   de + noun: *morir*

     *¿Te **acuerdas de Constantino**?*   *Javier siempre **trata de ser** amable.*
     *¿**Desconfías de nosotros**?*   *Dionisio **murió de un ataque** al corazón.*

● Some verbs + *con*

   con + infinitive/noun/pronoun: *conformarse, contentarse, soñar*
   con + noun/pronoun: *casarse, compararse, enfadarse*

     *Me **contento con ser feliz**.*   *Iván se va a **casar con una boliviana**.*

● Some verbs + *en*

   en + infinitive/noun/pronoun: *confiar*
   en + noun/pronoun: *creer, fijarse*

     Confío en no equivocarme mucho.   *¿Te **has fijado en ese hombre**?*

99.1 **Join the two columns with the correct prepositions.**

1. Valentín se dedica
2. Sara no cree
3. Siempre hemos soñado
4. Arturo se parece
5. Alba se ha enamorado
6. ¿Puedes ayudarme
7. Con Pablo te mueres
8. Confío

| a |
| con |
| de |
| en |

a. risa.
b. su madre.
c. mis amigos.
d. la existencia de extraterrestres.
e. llevar estas cajas?
f. su profesor.
g. exportar fruta.
h. visitar la isla de Pascua.

SCORE ...../ 8

99.2 **Complete the sentences with *a*, *de*, *en*, or *con*.**

1. ¿Confías _en_ nosotros?
2. Lina se ha divorciado _____ su marido.
3. ¿Te atreves _____ tirarte desde aquí?
4. Esther se ha enfadado _____ Amelia.
5. ¿Cuándo van a comenzar _____ pintar la casa?
6. Me alegro mucho _____ verte.
7. Tengo que aprender _____ conducir.
8. ¿Crees _____ las supersticiones?
9. La policía sospecha _____ la enfermera.
10. Bruno y Adela no se deciden _____ casarse.

SCORE ...../10

99.3 **Complete the sentences with *a*, *de*, *en*, *con*, and the expressions from the box.**

1. Esta noche vienen unos amigos _____a cenar_____.
2. ¡Qué dibujos más bonitos! ¿Quién te ha enseñado _____?
3. Yo me conformo _____.
4. Sonia se ha casado _____.
5. Ya me he acostumbrado _____.
6. Hay que disfrutar _____.
7. Sueño _____.
8. Esther está aprendiendo _____.
9. Lucio se arrepiente _____.
10. La hermana de Adrián murió _____.

cáncer
~~cenar~~
encontrar un buen empleo
ganar para vivir
hacer yoga
la vida
levantarme temprano
dibujar
su pasado
un italiano

SCORE ...../10

99.4 **Replace the words in parentheses with the correct form of the pronoun. Make all the necessary changes.**

1. Ayer me acordé de (*tú*) _ti_ en el concierto.
2. No confío en (*mi hermano*) _____.
3. No se quiere casar con (*yo*) _____.
4. No me gusta que se rían de (*mis amigos y yo*) _____.
5. Mis padres no desconfían de (*yo*) _____.
6. ¿Por qué se ha enfadado Tere con (*tú*) _____?
7. Elena siempre piensa en (*tú*) _____.
8. No te enfades con (*yo*) _____.

SCORE ...../ 8

100 *Creo que es muy caro.*
Subordinate clauses with *que*

Creo que es muy caro.

Recuerda que mañana es mi cumpleaños.

Some sentences are linked by means of *que*.

> Creo. Es muy caro. → Creo **que** es muy caro.

● Subordinate clauses with *que*

– When the object of a verb is a clause with a personal verb we use *que* before the linked clause.

> Recuerda **que tienes un examen.**
> Me parece **que tienes razón.**

decir			Dicen **que salís juntos.**
creer			Creo **que es muy tarde.**
pensar			Pienso **que tienes razón.**
ver	+ *que* + clause		No vi **que Luis estaba en clase.**
oír			Oí **que entraban en casa.**
saber			Sé **que tienes tres hijos.**
recordar			Recuerda **que tienes un examen.**
parecer			Parece **que va a llover.**

– In some cases the clauses are linked by *de* or *en* + *que*.

> Estamos seguros. Aprobarás. → Estamos seguros **de que** aprobarás.
> ¿Te has fijado? Está nevando. → ¿Te has fijado **en que** está nevando?

acordarse de			**¿Te acuerdas de que** mañana es fiesta?
avisar de			**Avisa** a Pedro **de que** están esperándolo.
convencer de			Pilar me **convenció de que** estaba equivocado.
olvidarse de	+ *que* + clause		**Olvídate de que** tienes amigos allí.
fijarse en			**¿Te has fijado en que** estamos de exámenes?
insistir en			**Insisto en que** ella tiene razón.
convencido de			Estoy **convencido de que** no son amigas.
seguro de			Estoy **seguro de que** no van a venir.

BE CAREFUL!

> Creo ~~de que~~ es temprano. → Creo **que** es temprano.
>
> Estoy seguro ~~que~~ Mariano tiene razón. → Estoy seguro **de que** Mariano tiene razón.

100 EXERCISES

100.1 **Put the words in order and use *que* in the correct place.**

1. no son / peruanos / creo _____ Creo que no son peruanos _____ .
2. aquí / estamos / no digas _____ .
3. somos / hermanas / saben _____ .
4. muy tarde / pensaba / era _____ .
5. veo / tienes / coche nuevo _____ .
6. novios / son / dicen _____ .
7. Rafa / cocina bien / sabemos _____ .
8. son / recuerda / los jefes _____ .
9. la verdad / sé / creo _____ .
10. están cansados / parece _____ .

100.2 **Circle the correct option.**

1. Dicen (*que* / *de que*) son amigos de Andrés.
2. Estoy convencido (*que* / *de que*) no me conocen.
3. Saben (*que* / *de que*) estoy casado.
4. No vi (*que* / *de que*) los niños estaban en el jardín.
5. Julio me avisó (*que* / *de que*) había mucho tráfico.
6. No insistas (*de que* / *en que*) tengo razón.
7. Están seguros (*que* / *de que*) los ayudaré.
8. Creen (*que* / *de que*) somos españoles.

100.3 **Complete the clauses with *de* or *en* + *que*.**

1. Marga se olvidó _____ de que _____ venía su familia.
2. Le convencieron _____ tenían razón.
3. En la empresa me avisaron _____ había un empleo libre.
4. No me fijé _____ no llevaba mucho dinero.
5. ¿Estás seguro _____ va a llover?
6. Nunca me acuerdo _____ no tienes coche.
7. José está convencido _____ hablo ruso.
8. Eusebio insiste _____ tengo un buen empleo.
9. Todos están seguros _____ podemos ganar el partido.

100.4 **Join the sentences with *que* and *de* or *en* if necessary.**

1. No vais a venir. Lo sé. _____ Sé que no vais a venir _____ .
2. No van a llamarnos. Estoy seguro. _____ .
3. Son extranjeros. Creo. _____ .
4. Mañana es mi cumpleaños. ¿Te acuerdas? ¿_____ ?
5. Va a nevar. Parece. _____ .
6. No tenías hambre. Pensaba. _____ .
7. Vais a ganar. Estamos convencidos. _____ .
8. No tienes razón. Insisto. _____ .
9. Hacen mucho ruido. Lo oigo. _____ .
10. Los bancos están cerrados. No me acordé. _____ .
11. Tenía la comida en la nevera. Se olvidó. _____ .
12. Tienen buena relación. Parece. _____ .

101 *Si ganan, serán campeones.*
Conditional clauses

¿Crees que van a ganar?

No sé; es posible. **Si ganan este partido**, serán campeones.

Si no llueve mañana, iré a la playa.

Si ganan este partido and *Si no llueve mañana* are conditional clauses. They express a condition so that another action or situation can take place.

(possible condition	⟶	consequence)
Si **ganan** este partido,		**serán** campeones.
Si no **llueve** mañana,		**iremos** a la playa.
Si **tienes** hambre,		**come** algo.

● Conditional clauses: possible conditions in the present or future

When we speak about a real situation and there is a possibility of something happening or coming true, we can use the following constructions.

condition	consequence
Si + present indicative	future simple, present indicative, or imperative
Si **acabo** la carrera este año,	**podré** trabajar en un bufete.
Si la **quiere,**	**se casará** con ella.
Si **te gusta** esa pluma,	te la **regalo.**
Si no **te gusta** la película,	**podemos** irnos.
Si **ves** a Luis,	**dile** que me llame.
Si **vienen** ustedes a Madrid,	**vengan** a visitarnos.

BE CAREFUL!

The conditional clause can go at the end of the sentence.

*Podemos irnos **si no te gusta la película**.*

● We usually use the future to indicate the consequence.

    *Si no nos damos prisa, **llegaremos** tarde.*

  – We use the present indicative

    • when the consequence is considered definite or very likely.

      *Si encuentro otro trabajo, **me cambio**.*   *Si discutís, **me voy**.*

    • to make a suggestion.

      *Si quieres salir, **podemos ir al cine**.*

  – We use the imperative when we express an order, a plea, or a request.

    *Si llaman de la oficina, **avísame**.* (I beg you to let me know.)

    *Si no quieren trabajar, **váyanse**.* (I order them to leave.)

101 EXERCISES

101.1. Complete the conditional with the expressions from the box in the affirmative or negative.

1. _____Si no vienes a clase_____, no aprenderás.
2. _____ mañana, haremos una excursión.
3. _____, beban algo.
4. _____, nos casamos.
5. _____, vete con Dolores al cine.
6. (yo) _____, ¿quién te llevará a la estación?
7. _____, ve al médico.
8. ¿Qué harás en el aeropuerto, _____?

encontrar piso
encontrarse mal
estar aburrida
hacer buen tiempo
poder conducir
tener que esperar
tener sed
~~venir a clase~~

SCORE
......../8

101.2. Complete the sentences with the consequences from the box in the affirmative or negative.

casarse	dar calambre	~~descansar~~	enfadarse	morirse
preocuparse		sentirse bien	tener que andar	

1. Tranquilos. Si os cansáis, _____descansad_____.
2. Si Elisa me dice que sí, _____.
3. Tienes que cuidar las plantas. Si no las riegas, _____.
4. Si perdemos el autobús, _____.
5. No he dormido mucho y si no duermo ocho horas, _____.
6. Si no visitamos a los Echevarría cuando vayamos a México, _____.
7. Tengo mucho trabajo, Alfonso. _____ si llego tarde.
8. ¡No toques eso! Si lo tocas, te _____.

SCORE
......../8

101.3. Join the conditions and consequences to make sentences with *si*.

condición	consecuencia
ganar el partido (*Ríos*)	pasar a la final (*él*)
no hacer buen tiempo	quedarse en casa (*ellos*)
no correr (*tú*)	perder el autobús (*tú*)
portarse bien (*vosotros*)	compraros un helado (*yo*)
no estar (*Alberto*)	volver más tarde (*nosotros*)
comerse esa fruta (*ustedes*)	ponerse malos (*ustedes*)
enfadarse (*tú*)	irse (*yo*)
querer ir al concierto (*tú*)	poder comprar las entradas por internet.

1. ___Si Ríos gana el partido, pasará a la final.___
2. _____
3. _____
4. _____
5. _____
6. _____
7. _____
8. _____

SCORE
......../8

101.4. Complete the dialogues with the verbs from the boxes.

1. –A lo mejor veo a Vera el domingo.
   –Si la __ves__, _____ le que me llame.
   –No te preocupes. Se lo _____ si la _____.

2. –Si _____ el domingo, _____ a la final.
   –No _____ si no _____ Salva.
   –Está lesionado. Si Salva no _____, no _____ jugar.

decir (2)

ver (2)

ganar (2)

jugar   pasar

poder

recuperarse

SCORE
......../10

211

102 *cuando era joven, antes de irme...*
Time clauses

Cuando era joven hacía mucho deporte.

Tengo que acabar este informe **antes de irme.**

Cuando era joven and *antes de irme* are time clauses. They give information about when the action or situation took place. They answer the question *¿cuándo?*

> *Quiero hablar con Ana (when?) **antes de comprar las entradas.***
> *Me duelen las muelas (when?) **cuando como carne.***

● *Antes de, después de*

antes de			*Quiero ver a Luis **antes de irme.***
	+	infinitive	
después de			*Podemos ir al cine **después de cenar.***

– We use *antes de*, *después de* + infinitive when the subject of the main clause and the time clause is the same.

> *(yo) Hablé con Marta **antes de** (yo) **invitar** a Sofía.*

● *Cuando, desde que, hasta que*

cuando			*Javi se enfada **cuando le grito.***
desde que	+	indicative	*La conozco **desde que era pequeña.***
hasta que			*Se quedaron **hasta que acabó la fiesta.***

– We use *cuando* + present indicative to refer to something habitual.

> *Mi abuela se pone muy contenta **cuando la llamo.***
> *Me duele la cabeza **cuando estudio.***

– We use *cuando, desde que* + imperfect to refer to a period of time in the past.

> *Cuando trabajaba **en Suiza, iba mucho a esquiar.***

– We use *desde que* + present indicative to refer to an action or situation that began in the past and continues in the present.

> *Estoy mucho mejor **desde que hago** ejercicio.*
> ***Desde que vivo** en España, he aprendido mucho español.*

– We use *cuando, hasta que, desde que* + preterite to refer to a moment in the past.

> *Ana me gusta **desde que la vi.***   *No nos fuimos **hasta que llegó Antonio.***
> *Nos fuimos **cuando empezó a llover.***   *Felipe está más **alegre desde que se casó.***

BE CAREFUL!

When the time clause has a subject, it usually goes after the verb.
> *Conozco a Ángel desde que me lo **presentó Susana.***

102.1 Rewrite the sentences with *antes de* or *después de* + infinitive as in the example.

1. Podemos ir a la bolera, pero cenaremos antes. ___Podemos ir a la bolera después de cenar___ .
2. Apaga la televisión y después acuéstate. _____ .
3. Cenaré, pero antes me voy a duchar. _____ .
4. Vicente vendrá a comer, pero antes llamará _____ .
5. Pagaremos, pero antes tomaremos café. _____ .
6. Acabaré estos ejercicios y después iré a la bolera. _____ .
7. Quiero hablar con Ana. Luego me iré. _____ .
8. No te vayas. Toma algo antes. _____ .

SCORE ...... /8

102.2 Join the sentences with *cuando*.

1. Llego a casa. Me ducho. ___Cuando llego a casa me ducho___ .
2. Salimos con Jorge. Nos divertimos mucho. _____ .
3. Llueve. Alicia se pone triste. _____ .
4. Llegó Juan. Empezamos la partida. _____ .
5. Hay tormenta. El perro se asusta. _____ .
6. Me levanto. Siempre me ducho. _____ .
7. Juego al parchís. Me aburro. _____ .
8. Vamos al centro. Cogemos el metro. _____ .

SCORE ...... /8

102.3 Circle the correct option.

1. Hans estudia español desde que (*fue* / (*era*)) niño.
2. Vivo en Madrid desde que (*nací* / *nacía*).
3. Ricardo está más contento desde que (*tiene* / *tuvo*) coche.
4. Cuando (*llega* / *llegó*) el verano, me pongo contento.
5. Cuando (*salimos* / *salíamos*) con Jorge, nos divertimos mucho.
6. No me sentí mejor hasta que (*comí* / *comía*) algo.
7. Cuando (*trabajé* / *trabajaba*) en el Mar del Norte, ganaba mucho dinero.
8. No empezamos a comer hasta que (*estuvimos* / *estábamos*) todos.

SCORE ...... /8

102.4 Complete the sentence with the correct form.

1. No nos fuimos (*hasta que, Rubén, llegar*) ___hasta que llegó Rubén___ .
2. Conozco a Luis (*desde que, ser, jóvenes*) _____ .
3. Me siento mejor (*desde que, comer, más*) _____ .
4. Iba mucho a bailar (*cuando, ser, joven*) _____ .
5. Me pongo triste (*cuando, llover*) _____ .
6. Nos acostamos (*cuando, la película, acabar*) _____ .
7. No me acosté (*hasta que, Rosa, llamar*) _____ .
8. Julián se casó (*cuando, acabar, la carrera*) _____ .
9. Hablo español mejor (*desde que, vivir, en España*) _____ .
10. Ana no salió (*hasta que, acabar, los ejercicios*) _____ .

SCORE ...... /10

102.5 Join the two sentences with the time clause given. Make the necessary changes.

1. Cenaremos. Iremos a dar un paseo. Después de ___cenar, iremos a dar un paseo.___
2. A veces me duele la cabeza. Me tomo una aspirina. Cuando _____ .
3. Vino Julián y empezamos a cenar. Hasta que _____ .
4. Tengo que acabar este trabajo. Luego me iré a la cama. Antes de _____ .
5. Fidel está a dieta. Está más delgado. Desde que _____ .
6. Piensa en lo que vas a decir. Después habla. Antes de _____ .

SCORE ...... /6

para estudiar...
Purpose clauses

Necesito tiempo **para estudiar**.

Lo he comprado
para abrir una tienda.

Para estudiar and *para abrir* are purpose clauses. They indicate why we do something—with what objective or reason.

> *Tengo que verte. Quiero contarte algo.* → *Tengo que verte **para contarte algo**.*
>
> *Se vistió deprisa. No quería llegar tarde.* → *Se vistió deprisa **para no llegar tarde***

– We also use purpose clauses to indicate the usefulness of an action or an object.

> *Estoy aprendiendo español **para poder viajar** por América del Sur.*
>
> *–¿Qué es un termómetro? –Es un instrumento **para medir la temperatura**.*
>
> *–¿Para qué compraste la tarta? –**Para** celebrar mi cumpleaños.*

¿Para qué sirve eso?

Para abrir
botellas.

● Purpose clauses

–*para* + infinitivo	*Anoche me llamó Juan **para quedar** el domingo.*
	*Es un aparato **para grabar** cedés.*

– When the objective or purpose is negative, we place *no* before the infinitive.

> *Me fui temprano **para no ver** a Julia.*

BE CAREFUL!

With verbs of movement such as *ir*, *venir*, *salir*, etc., we usually use *a* rather than *para*.
> *–¿Dónde está Lola? –**Ha salido a comprar** leche.*

103 EXERCISES

103.1 **Rewrite the sentences as in the example.**

1. Coge un paraguas o te mojarás. _____Coge un paraguas para no mojarte_____ .
2. Coge un taxi o no llegarás a tiempo. _____ .
3. Pon la radio o no oirás las noticias. _____ .
4. Daos prisa o llegaréis tarde. _____ .
5. Abrígate o cogerás un catarro. _____ .
6. Reservad las entradas o no veréis el concierto. _____ .
7. Salgan de noche o pasarán calor. _____ .
8. Tengo que ahorrar o no me compraré la moto. _____ .

103.2 **Complete the sentences with the verbs from the box.**

asegurar	~~alisar~~	apretar	calentar	freír	medir	orientarse	proyectar	poner	sacar

¿Para qué sirve...

1. ... una lima? _Para alisar_ metales.
2. ... una brújula? _____ en tierra.
3. ... un sacapuntas? _____ punta a los lápices.
4. ... un martillo? _____ clavos.
5. ... un destornillador? _____ tornillos.
6. ... una sartén? _____ alimentos.
7. ... un microondas? _____ alimentos.
8. ... una linterna? _____ luz.
9. ... un termómetro? _____ la temperatura.
10. ... un candado? _____ puertas o maletas.

103.3 **Complete the sentences with the verbs in parentheses and *a* or *para*.**

1. Vinieron a Madrid (*ver*)_____a/para ver_____ la final.
2. Fueron a Ecuador (*ver*) _____ las Galápagos.
3. Habla bajo (*no, despertar*) _____ a los niños.
4. Este verano vamos a pasar por Buenos Aires (*ver*) _____ a tu prima.
5. Llamé a Laura (*salir*) _____ con ella.
6. Están leyendo todos los anuncios (*alquilar*) _____ un piso.
7. Ayer salimos (*tomar*) _____ un poco el aire.
8. Voy a comprar unos huevos (*hacer*) _____ un flan.
9. Ha venido una vecina (*pedir*) _____ un poco de azúcar.

103.4 **Complete the sentences with *a* or *para* and the verbs from the box.**

comprar (2)	dar	enviar	hacer	~~hacerse~~	recibir	reservar	tomar	ver

¿Para/A qué va Adolfo a...

1. ... la óptica? _A/Para hacerse_ unas gafas.
2. ... la agencia de viajes? _____ un hotel.
3. ... la farmacia? _____ aspirina.
4. ... la copistería? _____ una fotocopia.
5. ... la pescadería? _____ marisco.
6. ... Correos? _____ un fax.
7. ... al bar? _____ una cerveza.
8. ... al parque? _____ un paseo.
9. ... al centro de la ciudad? _____ las tiendas.
10. ... a la estación? _____ a sus tíos.

104 *porque hace frío, por la niebla, por eso está en forma*
Reason and result clauses

● Reason clauses

Hoy no salimos **porque hace mucho frío**.

Porque hace mucho frío is a reason clause. It indicates the reason for an action or situation. It answers the question *¿por qué?*

(cause)

Hoy no salimos. (Why?) Hace mucho frío. → Hoy no salimos **porque hace mucho frío**.

porque	+	indicative	*Nos quedamos en casa **porque estábamos cansados**.*
por	+	noun	*Los aeropuertos están cerrados **por la niebla**.*

– *Es que* is used to give a cause as an explanation or pretext in an answer to a question or plea.

–*¿Por qué no viniste ayer?*

–**Es que** *tuve mucho trabajo.*

¿Por qué no me llevas a dar una vuelta en la moto?

Es que no tienes casco.

● Result clauses

Luis hace mucho ejercicio, **por eso está en forma**.

Por eso está en forma is a result clause. It indicates the consequence or the result of another action or situation.

(cause ⟶ consequence)

Luis hace mucho ejercicio. Está en forma. → *Luis hace mucho ejercicio, **por eso está en forma**.*

por eso	+	indicative
		*La semana pasada estuve muy ocupado, **por eso no te llamé**.*
		*No me gustó la fiesta y **por eso me fui**.*

104.1. **Join the sentences with *porque* or *por*.**

1. No se oye nada / hay mucho ruido. No se oye nada porque hay mucho ruido .
2. Menchu no salió / estaba lloviendo. _____ .
3. Llegaron tarde / el accidente. _____ .
4. No salieron / el frío. _____ .
5. Félix está cansado / trabaja mucho. _____ .
6. Han parado el partido / la lluvia. _____ .
7. Nicolás está nervioso / el examen. _____ .
8. Andrés no llamó / estaba ocupado. _____ .
9. Se divorciaron / no se querían. _____ .
10. No fueron de vacaciones / no tenían dinero. _____ .

SCORE /10

104.2. **Write the answers with *es que* and a phrase from the box.**

| está con gripe | está enfadada | estoy cansado | he cogido un taxi |
| no tengo mucha hambre | tengo que estudiar | tenía el móvil sin batería | tiene exámenes |

1. –¿Damos una vuelta? – Es que estoy cansado .
2. –Come más pollo. – _____ .
3. –¿Por qué no vamos al cine esta noche? – _____ .
4. –¿Por qué no me llamaste anoche? – _____ .
5. –¿Por qué no ha venido Anita? – _____ .
6. –Consuelo está nerviosa. – _____ .
7. –Mónica no ha venido a trabajar. – _____ .
8. –Llegas pronto, Alberto. – _____ .

SCORE /8

104.3. **Join the two sentences with *por eso*.**

1. No sonó el despertador / me levanté tarde. No sonó el despertador, por eso me levanté tarde .
2. Vienen mis abuelos / no me voy de viaje. _____ .
3. Hoy hay mucha gente / no voy de compras. _____ .
4. Estábamos aburridos / nos fuimos a dar una vuelta. _____ .
5. Era mi cumpleaños / los invité a cenar. _____ .
6. No me funcionaba el móvil / no pude llamarte. _____ .
7. La puerta de la jaula estaba abierta / se escaparon los pájaros. _____ .

SCORE /7

104.4. **Cicle the correct option.**

1. No escribí a Juan (porque / por eso) no tuve tiempo.
2. Mis padres se enfadaron (porque/por) las notas.
3. Hace frío, (porque/por eso) no salimos.
4. No me llamaste, (porque/por eso) no vine.
5. Sofía está nerviosa (porque/por) la boda.
6. Hice una fiesta (por/por eso) mi cumpleaños.
7. No comí más (porque/por eso) no tenía hambre.
8. Llegué tarde (porque/por) se estropeó el metro.

SCORE /8

104.5. **Join the sentences with *porque*, *por*, or *por eso*.**

1. Me dolía la cabeza / fui al médico. Me dolía la cabeza, por eso fui al médico .
2. Raquel está muy débil / la enfermedad. _____ .
3. Santiago no estudia / no tiene tiempo. _____ .
4. Es muy tarde / las tiendas están cerradas. _____ .
5. Me tomé una aspirina / me dolía la cabeza. _____ .
6. Llegaron tarde / había mucho tráfico. _____ .
7. Ana no sale de noche / sus padres. _____ .
8. Rocío no me invitó a la fiesta / no fui. _____ .

SCORE /8

105 *Hace frío.*
Impersonal clauses

Hoy **hace bastante frío.**

Es importante saber idiomas.

Hace bastante frío and *Es importante saber idiomas* are impersonal clauses: they don't refer to a specific person and don't have a subject.

Impersonal structures

● With the verb *ser*

– 3rd person singular + adjective + infinitive.

3rd person singular + adjective + infinitive	*Es fácil aprobar.*
	Era imposible entrar. Había mucha gente.
Infinitive + 3rd person singular + adjective	*Hablar español es útil.*
	Saber idiomas es importante.

• We use this structure to assess general situations.

Era inútil explicárselo. No lo entendían.   *Es injusto castigar a todos.*

• We use this structure with, among others, the following adjectives: *bueno, malo, mejor, peor, fácil, difícil, útil, inútil, justo, injusto, importante, imposible, necesario.*

Es mejor ir en tren.   *Ha sido difícil ganar.*

– 3rd person singular + time references: *temprano, pronto, tarde...*

Es tarde. Vámonos a casa.   *–¿Qué hora es? –Las ocho. Es temprano.*

● With the impersonal verb *haber* ▶   UNIT 45: Present indicative of *haber* (impersonal)

– hay, había, hubo... + noun

Hoy **hay niebla.**   *El año pasado* **hubo** *mucha* **nieve** *en la sierra.*

Ayer **había mucha gente.**   *Hay muchas* **nubes.** *Va a llover.*

– hay, había... + *que* + infinitive to refer to impersonal obligations or necessities.

▶ UNIT 77: Expressions with infinitive (1)

Hay que preparar *la comida.*

● With the verb *hacer*

– 3rd person singular of *hacer* + frío, calor, viento, sol, buen tiempo, mal tiempo

Ponte un jersey. **Hace frío.**   *Ayer* **hizo mucho calor.**

● With the 3rd person singular of verbs that indicate natural phenomena

En verano **amanece** *pronto.*
En el sur de España **llueve** *poco.*
No salgas ahora. **Está lloviendo.**

llueve

nieva

amanece

anochece

105.1. **Join the two sentences as in the example. Make the necessary changes.**

1. La gente se equivoca. Es fácil. _____Es fácil equivocarse_____ .
2. No hay que equivocarse. Es importante. _____Es importante no equivocarse_____ .
3. Hay que ser abiertos. Es mejor. _____ .
4. Hay que saber cocinar. Es útil. _____ .
5. Hay que hacer ejercicio. Es bueno. _____ .
6. No hay que ser egoísta. Es malo. _____ .
7. No se puede estudiar con tanto ruido. Es difícil. _____ .
8. No se puede salir con este tiempo. Es imposible. _____ .

SCORE ...../8

105.2. **Complete in the affirmative or negative according to your beliefs.**

1. conducir / fácil _____Conducir (no) es fácil_____ .
2. nadar / sano _____ .
3. comer poco / bueno _____ .
4. beber mucha agua / bueno _____ .
5. hablar una lengua extranjera bien / imposible _____ .
6. conocer otras culturas / importante _____ .

SCORE ...../6

105.3. **Rewrite the sentences with _hay que_.**

1. Es necesario saber idiomas. _____Hay que saber idiomas_____ .
2. Es obligatorio tener un visado para viajar a Egipto. _____ .
3. Es conveniente saber conducir. _____ .
4. Para aprender un idioma extranjero, es conveniente practicarlo. _____ .
5. En España es obligatorio tener 18 años para conducir un coche. _____ .

SCORE ...../5

105.4. **What's the weather like in Spain? Complete the sentences with the verbs from the box.**

1. En Galicia _____llueve / está lloviendo_____ .
2. En Asturias _____ .
3. En el País Vasco _____ .
4. En Cataluña _____ viento.
5. En Valencia _____ sol.
6. En Madrid _____ nubes.
7. En Castilla y León _____ niebla
8. En Extremadura _____ tormentas.
9. En Castilla-La Mancha _____ frío.
10. En Andalucía _____ calor.

| haber | hacer |
| llover | nevar |

SCORE ...../10

105.5. **Complete the sentences with the verbs from the box in the correct form.**

| amanecer | anochecer | haber (2) | hacer (2) | nevar | ser (3) |

1. Ayer _____hizo_____ bastante frío durante la noche.
2. No salí porque _____ pronto.
3. _____ que acostarse temprano. Mañana salimos a las siete.
4. –¿Qué hora es? –_____ temprano. Las seis y cuarto.
5. –¿A qué hora _____ en esta parte de México? –Pronto. A las cinco de la tarde.
6. Abre la ventana. _____ calor.
7. _____ temprano. Aún no _____ luz. En invierno _____ muy tarde.
8. Hoy _____ en la sierra. Las cumbres están blancas.

SCORE ...../10

médico, árbol, inglés
Accent marks (tilde)

El hermano de Ángel es **mé**dico.

The syllables **Án** in *Ángel* and **mé** in *médico* have an accent; it is more strongly pronounced than the rest of the word.

Some words indicate the accented syllable with a tilde (´): *árbol, café, hábil, médico*.

● Emphasis on words with more than one syllable

– Most words ending in a consonant, except *n*, or *s*: accent on the last syllable.
   español, hotel, salud, usted, amar, beber, reloj

– Most words ending in a vowel, *n,* or *s*: emphasis on the second-to-last syllable.
   casa, libro, restaurante, amas, aman, bebo, bebe

– For the words that don't follow these rules, we indicate the accent with a tilde.
   policía, café, ratón, inglés, fútbol, árbol, azúcar, lápiz, bolígrafo, médico, sábado

● One-syllable words

– Words with one syllable don't have a tilde.
   pan   tren   luz   sol   sal   dos

– However, in some cases we use the tilde to distinguish words written the same but with different meanings.

él (personal pronoun)	*Hans y Uta son alemanes. **Él** es de Hamburgo.*
el (article)	***El** coche de Andrés está mal aparcado.*
sí (affirmation)	***Sí**, quiero.*
si (conditional)	***Si** quieres, cómpratelo.*
mí (personal pronoun)	*¿Es para **mí**?*
mi (possessive)	*Es **mi** padre.*
tú (personal pronoun)	*Y **tú**, ¿dónde vives?*
tu (possessive)	*¿Quién es **tu** profesor?*
sé (verb *saber*)	***Sé** hablar español.*
se (personal pronoun)	***Se** levanta muy temprano.*
té (noun)	*No me gusta el **té**.*
te (personal pronoun)	*¿**Te** gusta el café?*

– We also use the tilde to distinguish the interrogatives and exclamatory expressions.
   ¿***Dónde** vives?*   *Esta es la casa **donde** nací.*
   ¡***Qué** frío!*   *Ese es el coche **que** quiero.*

106.1 **Underline the accented syllable.**

1. ba<u>lón</u>
2. cabeza
3. Sánchez
4. Madrid
5. Ecuador
6. Perú
7. Guatemala
8. enero
9. cama
10. mexicano
11. octubre
12. lloro
13. lloró
14. cárcel
15. azul
16. querer
17. capitán
18. balones
19. Chile
20. comes
21. hospital
22. España
23. argentino
24. portugués
25. viven

SCORE ...... /25

106.2 **Write the tilde above the accented syllable if necessary.**

1. me**lón**
2. fran**ces**
3. ale**ma**na
4. marro**qui**
5. ama**ri**llo
6. **ca**sa
7. **Pe**pe
8. Gon**za**lez
9. Pana**ma**
10. **A**frica
11. ale**man**
12. me**lo**nes
13. **la**piz
14. **la**pices
15. ac**triz**
16. **ut**il
17. **ar**boles
18. Bogo**ta**
19. **pa**jaro
20. Bra**sil**
21. vi**vis**
22. co**mi**
23. **vi**vo
24. A**me**rica
25. es**tas**

SCORE ...... /25

106.3 **Circle the correct answer.**

1. No (se/*sé*) nadar.
2. Esta carta es para (*mi*/*mí*).
3. ¿(*Tu*/*Tú*) fumas?
4. ¿(*Que*/*Qué*) quieres?
5. (*Si*/*Sí*), tienes razón.
6. Ese es (*mi*/*mí*) sombrero.
7. Lo siento, no (*te*/*té*) quiero.
8. ¿Es ese Pepe? Sí, es (*el*/*él*).
9. ¿Quién es (*tu*/*tú*) profesora?
10. Mario (*se*/*sé*) acuesta siempre muy tarde.

SCORE ...... /10

106.4 **Add the tilde wherever necessary.**

1. No sé nadar.
2. Felipe no se ducha por las mañanas.
3. ¿A que hora te levantas?
4. A mi no me gusta el te.
5. Es el coche de mi padre.
6. ¿Te gusta el zumo de piña?
7. ¡Que alto es Angel!
8. Si te gusta mi reloj, te lo regalo.
9. ¿Se acuerda de mi?
10. Es la chica que vive con Marisa.

SCORE ...... /10

107 *Arturo Sánchez*
Use of capital letters

A, S, C, M → capital letters

a, c, d → lowercase letters

● The following rules are used for beginning the word with a capital letter:

– the first word of a text and words that follow a period (.).

> *"En un lugar de La Mancha,..."*
> *–He visto a Jaime. Me ha dado recuerdos para ti. –¿Dónde lo has visto?*

– the first word after a colon (:) at the start of letters.

Querida Luisa: **E**spero que...

Muy Sres. míos: **C**omo les indiqué...

– proper nouns for people, places, or institutions.

Arturo Sánchez   **Museo del Prado**   **Bolivia**   **Ministerio de Educación**

If the proper noun has an article, the article is also capitalized.

Mi hermana vive en La Paz.   **El Escorial**   **Las Palmas**

– titles of status and their abbreviations.

el Rey   **el Papa**   **el Jefe de Gobierno**   **Sra. Allende**   **Dr. Blanco**

> **BUT:** We use lowercase when titles go with the proper noun or when there is no reference to a specific person or when the title is completely written out.
>
> **la reina Isabel II**   **Los reyes son personas privilegiadas.**
> **la señora Allende**

– The first letter of book titles, movies, paintings, newspapers, or magazines.

La vida es sueño   **Cien años de soledad**

– The names of historical events.

Segunda Guerra Mundial

– Most words formed by initials (acronyms).

ONU	**O**rganización de las **N**aciones **U**nidas
OEA	**O**rganización de **E**stados **A**mericanos
RAE	**R**eal **A**cademia **E**spañola
UE	**U**nión **E**uropea
UVI	**U**nidad de **V**igilancia **I**ntensiva
ONG	**O**rganización **N**o **G**ubernamental

BE CAREFUL!

When words begin with *ch* or *ll*, only the first letter is capitalized.
    Chile   **Ernesto Llamas**
Lowercase is used for days of the week and months.
    Nos vemos el domingo.   *Mi cumpleaños es en enero.*
Capital letters have a tilde in the necessary cases.
    Ayer estuve con Ángel.

107 EXERCISES

107.1 **Rewrite the sentences using capitals when necessary.**

1. mi padre nació en holanda. _____Mi padre nació en Holanda_____.
2. ayer fue dos de enero. fue el cumpleaños de manuel. _____.
3. hay una exposición sobre los incas en el museo de américa. la ha inaugurado el rey juan carlos.

   _____.
4. el martes estuve en la fundación san carlos con el señor arroyo. _____.
5. la ciudad de las columnas es un libro de alejo carpentier sobre la habana. _____.
6. ¿quién pintó la maja desnuda? _____.
7. muchas ong colaboran con la onu en países del tercer mundo. _____.
8. ¡qué impresionantes son las cataratas de iguazú! _____.

107.2 **Correct the mistakes with the use of capitals and lowercase.**

1. Gerardo nació El 23 de Enero. _____Gerardo nació el 23 de enero_____.
2. Queremos ir a CHina en Diciembre. _____.
3. ¿has leído El Siglo de las Luces? _____.
4. don Julio LLopis vivió muchos años en la Paz. _____.
5. ¿Cuándo fue la Guerra de la independencia? _____.
6. La Reina Sofía es Griega. _____.

SCORE /6

107.3 **Copy the text, correcting the mistakes with the use of capitals.**

querida Hermana:
LLevo una semana en Buenos aires. Estoy alojado en el hotel sur, en la avenida rivadavia, muy cerca del Centro.
Me gusta mucho la Ciudad. Ayer visité la casa rosada, donde vive el presidente del País. Esta noche voy a ir a escuchar Tangos al famoso barrio de La Boca. El Domingo próximo salgo para Chile.
¿cuándo llegas Tú?
besos

Querida hermana:
_____
_____
_____
_____
_____
_____
_____
_____
_____
_____

SCORE /19

107.4 **Join the names of organizations with their initials.**

1. Instituto Nacional del Libro Español   a. COI
2. Fondo Monetario Internacional → b. INLE
3. Objeto Volador No Identificado   c. OEA
4. Comité Olímpico Internacional   d. FMI
5. Síndrome de Inmunodeficiencia Adquirida   e. OVNI
6. Organización de las Naciones Unidas   f. ADN
7. Organización de los Estados Americanos   g. SIDA
8. Ácido Desoxirribonucleico.   h. ONU

SCORE /8

Index

Unit 1: Masculine, feminine (1). `1.1.` 1. F; *la periodista.* 2. M; *el cocinero.* 3. M; *el rey.* 4. F; *la estudiante.* 5. F; *la modelo.* 6. M; *el taxista.* 7. F; *la piloto.* 8. M; *el cantante.* 9. F; *la pianista.* 10. F; *la paciente.* `1.2.` 1. *señora.* 2. *directora.* 3. *fotógrafa.* 4. *artista.* 5. *actriz.* 6. *pintora.* 7. *abogada.* 8. *turista.* 9. *joven.* 10. *tenista.* 11. *reina.* 12. *alumna.* 13. *mujer.* 14. *dependienta.* 15. *doctora.* 16. *paciente.* 17. *mujer.* 18. *niña.* 19. *escritora.* 20. *princesa.* 21. *bailarina.* `1.3.` 1. *padre.* 2. *madre.* 3. *hermana.* 4. *hija.* 5. *hijo.* 6. *abuelo.* 7. *abuela.* 8. *tía.* 9. *tío.* 10. *hermano.*

Unit 2: Masculine, feminine (2). `2.1.` 1. *la ventana.* 2. *la pizarra.* 3. *el mapa.* 4. *la silla.* 5. *la mesa.* 6. *la foto.* 7. *el libro.* 8. *el bolígrafo.* 9. *el lapicero.* 10. *el cuaderno.* `2.2.` EL: *árbol; autobús; avión; cine; cumpleaños; día; hotel; idioma; lápiz; problema; programa; sofá; tren; viernes.* LA: *canción; ciudad; estación; habitación; leche; luz; llave; mano; moto; noche; nariz; radio; televisión; universidad.* `2.3.` *la gata; la yegua; la gallina; el perro; la leona; el toro.* `2.4.` 1. *la mariposa.* 2. *el gorila.* 3. *el pez.* 4. *el chimpancé.* 5. *la serpiente.* 6. *la jirafa.* `2.5.`.

Unit 3: Singular, plural. `3.1.` 1. *mujeres.* 2. *peces.* 3. *ventanas.* 4. *actrices.* 5. *habitaciones.* 6. *madres.* 7. *pantalones.* 8. *hoteles.* 9. *universidades.* 10. *televisiones.* 11. *niños.* 12. *hermanas.* 13. *leones.* 14. *días.* 15. *clases.* 16. *fotos.* 17. *vacas.* 18. *jueves.* 19. *actores.* 20. *estudiantes.* 21. *cumpleaños.* 22. *teléfonos.* 23. *casas.* 24. *flores.* 25. *vaqueros.* 26. *meses.* 27. *médicos.* 28. *países.* 29. *jugadores.* 30. *ladrones.* `3.2.` 1. *1 mesa; 2 botellas; 1 lámpara; 3 tijeras; 1 gafas; 2 postales; 4 libros; 3 lápices; 4 sillas; 2 vasos.* `3.3.` 1. *casas.* 2. *peces.* 3. *relojes.* 4. *paraguas.* 5. *pantalones.* 6. *autobuses.* `3.4.` 1. *tres hijos.* 2. *abuelos.* 3. *amigos.* 4. *hermanos.* 5. *padres.* 6. *compañeros.* 7. *bailarines.* 8. *profesores.* 9. *tíos.* 10. *alumnos.*

Unit 4: The indefinite article. `4.1.` 1. *una.* 2. *unas.* 3. *unos.* 4. *una.* 5. *unos.* 6. *un.* 7. *una.* 8. *unos.* 9. *una.* 10. *unas.* 11. *una.* 12. *un.* 13. *una.* 14. *unos.* 15. *un.* `4.2.` 1. *un deporte.* 2. *una ciudad.* 3. *un país.* 4. *una flor.* 5. *una fruta.* 6. *una isla.* 7. *un río.* // 1. *un futbolista.* 2. *una escritora.* 3. *un jugador de golf.* 4. *un cantante.* 5. *una tenista.* 6. *una actriz.* 7. *una cantante.* `4.3.` 1. *un coche.* 2. *unos niños.* 3. *un hacha.* 4. *unos libros.* 5. *una casa.* 6. *un gato.* 7. *unas vacas.* 8. *unas chicas.* 9. *una televisión.* 10. *unos árboles.* 11. *unas gafas.* 12. *un caballo.* `4.4.` 1. *Un.* 2. *un.* 3. *una.* 4. *un.* 5. *unos.* 6. *una.* 7. *un.* 8. *una.* 9. *unas.* 10. *unos.* 11. *unos.* 12. *unos.* 13. *unos.* 14. *un.* 15. *unas.* 16. *una.* 17. *una.* 18. *unas.*

Unit 5: Absence of the article. `5.1.` 1. *Eva es abogada.* 2. *José Luis es estudiante.* 3. *Carla es secretaria.* 4. *Félix es fotógrafo.* 5. *Mar es actriz.* 6. *Mario es fontanero.* 7. *Adrián es cocinero.* 8. *Eloísa es camarera.* 9. *Leonor es profesora.* 10. *Roberto es médico.* `5.2.` 1. *un cantante; mexicano.* 2. *una médica; argentina.* 3. *abogado; un abogado.* 4. *musulmán.* 5. *protestantes.* 6. *un actor.* 7. *un escritor; peruano.* 8. *estudiantes; socialistas.* 9. *bailarina.* 10. *un escritor.* 11. *suecas; unas suecas.* 12. *una flauta; un instrumento.* `5.3.` 1. Ø; Ø. 2. Ø; *unas.* 3. *un.* 4. Ø; *una.* 5. Ø. 6. Ø. 7. Ø. 8. Ø; Ø. 9. Ø. 10. Ø; *un.* 11. Ø; Ø. 12. Ø. 13. Ø. 14. *un.* 15. Ø.

Unit 6: The definite article. `6.1.` 1. *la.* 2. *el.* 3. *las.* 4. *el.* 5. *la.* 6. *el.* 7. *los.* 8. *el.* 9. *las.* 10. *los.* 11. *las.* 12. *el.* 13. *el.* 14. *la.* 15. *los.* `6.2.` 1. *El padre.* 2. *La madre.* 3. *El tío.* 4. *La tía.* 5. *Los abuelos.* 6. *Los hermanos.* 7. *La hermana.* 8. *El marido.* 9. *Las hijas.* 10. *La abuela.* `6.3.` 1. *el jardín.* 2. *la ventana.* 3. *el agua.* 4. *el diccionario.* 5. *la luz.* 6. *las tijeras.* `6.4.` 1. *Las.* 2. *la.* 3. *al.* 4. *El.* 5. *la; del.* 6. *La.* 7. *El.* 8. *Los.* 9. *Los.* 10. *las.* 11. *la.* 12. *del.* 13. *Las.* 14. *El.* 15. *del.*

Unit 7: Contrasting the indefinite and definite article. `7.1.` 1. *un;un; El; el; el; la.* 2. *un; una; El; la; la.* 3. *una; unos; Los; una; la; una.* 4. *un; el; del.* 5. *una; una; la; el; la; un.* 6. *unas; unas; las.* 7. *unos; una; los.* `7.2.` 1. *una.* 2. *una; El; un.* 3. *La.* 4. *un.* 5. *un; el.* 6. *una.* 7. *el.* 8. *un.* 9. *La.* 10. *El; una.* 11. *un.* 12. *el.* 13. *el.* 14. *La.* 15. *La; la.* `7.3.` 1. *unos.* 2. *el.* 3. *Una.* 4. *La.* 5. *los.* 6. *las.* 7. *unos.* 8. *unas.* 9. *unos.* 10. *el.* 11. *Un.* 12. *el.*

Unit 8: The definite article with proper nouns. `8.1.` 1. Ø. 2. Ø. 3. Ø; Ø. 4. *La.* 5. Ø. 6. *la.* 7. *El.* 8. Ø. 9. *La.* 10. Ø; Ø. `8.2.` 1. *El Hotel Central; la plaza de España.* 2. *El Museo Botero; la calle Mayor.* 3. *El Banco Nacional; el paseo del parque.* 4. *El Teatro Lorca; la avenida de América.* 5. *El Cine América; la plaza Real.* 6. *El Hospital; el paseo del Parque.* `8.3.` 1. *La Habana; Cuba.* 2. *(La) India; Asia.* 3. *El río Misisipi; Estados Unidos.* 4. *Las islas Galápagos; Ecuador.* 5. *Salvador; Guatemala; Honduras.* 6. *Los Ángeles; California.* 7. *El lago Titicaca; Perú; Bolivia.* 8. *El Amazonas; América del Sur.* 9. *Jamaica; el mar Caribe.* 10. *Puerto Rico; las islas Antillas.* 11. *La Pampa; Argentina.* 12. *Los Pirineos; España; Francia.* 13. *Alemania; Europa.* 14. *El Cairo; Egipto.* 15. *El Nilo.* `8.4.` 1. *el.* 2. Ø. 3. *la.* 3. *La; el.* 4. *La.* 5. Ø. 6. Ø; Ø. 7. *La.* 8. *El; la.* 9. *El; Ø.* 10. *El; Ø.*

Unit 9: The definite article with expressions of time. `9.1.` 1. *las tres y veinte.* 2. *la una y veinticinco.* 3. *las cuatro menos diez.* 4. *las dos.* 5. *las ocho y media.* 6. *las doce y cinco.* 7. *la una menos cuarto.* 8. *las diez y cuarto.* `9.2.` 1. *El.* 2. *los.* 3. *El.* 4. Ø. 5. Ø. 6. *Los.* 7. *El/Los.* 8. *el; el; El.* `9.3.` 1. Ø; Ø. 2. *el; Ø.* 3. *El; Ø.* 4. *el; Ø.* 5. *el.* 6. Ø; Ø; Ø. 7. *el; Ø.* 8. Ø. `9.4.` 1. *el; Ø.* 2. *El, Los.* 3. *la.* 4. *el; Ø; Ø.* 5. *el; las.* 6. Ø; Ø; Ø. 7. *las.* 8. *la; la.* 9. *el; Ø.* 10. *los.* 11. Ø. 12. *el.*

Unit 10: Other uses of the definite article. `10.1.` 1. *la guitarra.* 2. *el violín.* 3. *al ajedrez.* 4. *el piano.* 5. *al fútbol.* 6. *al tenis.* 7. *la trompeta.* 8. *las cartas.* `10.2.` *Las.* 2. Ø. 3. *El.* 4. *al.* 5. *las.* 6. Ø. 7. Ø. 8. Ø. 9. *La.* 10. *un.* 11. *una.* 12. *una.* 13. *la.* 14. Ø. 15. *el.* 16. Ø. 17. *la.* 18. Ø. 19. *el.* 20. Ø. `10.3.` 1. *la universidad.* 2. *la cárcel.* 3. *al hospital.* 4. *casa.* 5. *del lavabo.* 6. *la iglesia.* 7. *del colegio.* 8. *al cine.* 9. *el médico.* 10. *correos.*

Unit 11: Omitting the noun. `11.1.` 1. *los negros; los blancos.* 2. *Uno pequeño.* 3. *el negro; el marrón.* 4. *Los rojos; Los blancos.* 5. *La alta.* 6. *Uno entretenido.* 7. *las verdes; las rojas.* 8. *una limpia.* 9. *una buena.* 10. *uno portátil.* `11.2.` 1. *Las de la derecha.* 2. *El del pelo corto.* 3. *la de la izquierda.* 4. *Las de chocolate.* 5. *El del bigote.* 6. *Los de arriba.* 7. *el de Sandra Arenas.* 7. *el de Sevilla.* 9. *La de la falda larga.* 10. *El de los pantalones cortos.* `11.3.` 1. *las de.* 2. *la de.* 3. *uno.* 4. *unas.* 5. *los de.* 6. *al de.* 7. *Unos de.* 8. *unos.* 9. *el de.* 10. *una de.*

NOTE: In cases where the answer is in the second person (tú/usted; vosotros/ustedes), tú and vosotros are the answers given instead of both options.

Unit 12: Demonstrative adjectives. 12.1. 1. *Estas llaves.* 2. *Esa revista.* 3. *Aquella maleta.* 4. *Ese bolso.* 5. *Estas gafas.* 6. *Este paraguas.* 7. *Aquellos pisos.* 8. *Esas llaves.* 9. *Esta cartera.* 10. *Aquellos árboles.* 12.2. 1. *este.* 2. *ese/aquel.* 3. *Esta.* 4. *Aquel/Ese.* 5. *Este.* 6. *estas.* 7. *Aquella/Esa.* 8. *este.* 12.3. 1. *Este.* 2. *Este.* 3. *esta; Esta.* 4. *Esta.* 5. *estas.* 6. *Estos.* 7. *este.* 12.4. 1. *esto.* 2. *eso/aquello.* 3. *eso.* 4. *esto.* 5. *esto.*

Unit 13: Descriptive adjectives. 13.1. 1. *pequeño.* 2. *verdes; rubia; corto; rizado; simpática; alegre.* 3. *inteligentes.* 4. *blancas.* 5. *encantadora.* 6. *felices; enfadados.* 7. *roja; grises; blancos.* 8. *alto; fuerte; moreno; negros; guapo; antipático.* 9. *verde; amarilla.* 10. *simpáticos; trabajadores; amables.* 11. *jóvenes.* 12. *rápido; barato.* 13.2. 1. *rubias.* 2. *gordo.* 3. *alta.* 4. *tristes.* 5. *enferma.* 6. *alegre.* 7. *cansadas.* 8. *fuerte.* 9. *contentos.* 10. *feo.* 13.3. 1. *ojos azules.* 2. *flor roja.* 3. *idioma fácil.* 4. *buen profesor.* 5. *comida preferida.* 6. *día malo.* 7. *edificios antiguos.* 8. *ropa nueva.* 9. *color preferido.* 10. *mala noticia.* 11. *buena madre.* 12. *flores blancas.*

Unit 14: Adjectives of nationality. 14.1. 1. *brasileña; brasileños; brasileñas.* 2. *costarricense; costarricenses; costarricenses.* 3. *escocesa; escoceses; escocesas.* 4. *etíope; etíopes; etíopes.* 5. *francesa; franceses; francesas.* 6. *iraní; iranís/iraníes; iranís/iraníes.* 7. *japonesa; japoneses; japonesas.* 8. *mexicana; mexicanos; mexicanas.* 9. *nicaragüense; nicaragüenses; nicaragüenses.* 10. *sudanesa; sudaneses; sudanesas.* 11. *venezolana; venezolanos; venezolanas.* 12. *vietnamita; vietnamitas; vietnamitas.* 14.2. 1. *peruana.* 2. *chinas.* 3. *egipcios.* 4. *francesa.* 5. *belgas.* 6. *estadounidense.* 7. *italianas.* 8. *mexicanos.* 9. *india.* 10. *rusos.* 14.3. 1. *moneda japonesa.* 2. *moneda marroquí.* 3. *nombres escoceses.* 4. *escritor colombiano.* 5. *cantantes españoles.* 6. *ciudad francesa.* 7. *actriz estadounidense.* 8. *futbolistas brasileños.* 9. *ciudad belga.* 10. *un periódico argentino.* 11. *capital vietnamita.* 12. *ciudades canadienses.* 13. *bandera griega.* 14. *capital portuguesa.* 15. *bandera española.*

Unit 15: Comparative adjectives (1). 15.1. 1. *más guapo.* 2. *menos caprichoso.* 3. *más caro.* 4. *más antigua.* 5. *mejor.* 6. *menos poblado.* 7. *menos peligroso.* 8. *peor.* 9. *mayor.* 10. *más fácil.* 15.2. 1. *más alto que su hermano.* 2. *más pequeño que Argentina.* 3. *menos poblado que Ecuador.* 4. *menor que Clara.* 5. *más caras que los plátanos.* 6. *más largo que el Paraná.* 7. *más cara que esta radio.* 8. *más lentos que los Misima.* 9. *menos rápido que el león.* 15.3. 1. *menos antiguo.* 2. *más barata.* 3. *más pequeños.* 4. *más cómoda.* 5. *mejor.* 6. *menos dulces.* 7. *más entretenido.* 8. *menos cansado.* 9. *más larga.* 10. *más simpáticos.* 15.4. 1. *Soy más fuerte que tú.* 2. *más alto que vosotras.* 3. *mayores que nosotros.* 4. *menos rápido que yo.* 5. *menos inteligente que tú.*

Unit 16: Comparative adjectives (2). 16.1. 1. *es tan fácil como.* 2. *no es tan rápido como.* 3. *no es tan alto como.* 4. *es tan fuerte como.* 5. *no es tan grande como.* 6. *no es tan famoso como.* 7. *es tan bueno como.* 8. *es tan entretenido como.* 9. *no es tan peligrosa como.* 10. *no es tan malo como.* 11. *no es tan rápida como.* 12. *no es tan famosa como.* 16.2. 1. *no es tan joven como Alonso.* 2. *es tan alta como María.* 3. *no es tan caro como el Misima.* 4. *es tan caro como el Victorio.* 5. *no son tan baratas como las manzanas.* 6. *es tan rápido como Antonio.* 7. *no es tan alegre como Esther.* 8. *es tan inteligente como Margarita.* 9. *no es tan elegante como Fermín.* 10. *no es tan alto como Álvaro.* 16.3. 1. *tan listo como él.* 2. *tan elegantes como ella.* 3. *tan simpática.* 4. *tan amables como los peruanos.* 5. *tan cómoda.* 6. *tan amables cómo el.* 7. *tan viejo.* 8. *tan guapas como ella.* 16.4. 1. *no es tan guapo como yo.* 2. *no es tan alto como su padre.* 3. *no es tan cómoda como el sillón.* 4. *no es tan simpático como vosotras.* 5. *No eres tan trabajador como yo.*

Unit 17: Possessives (1). 17.1. 1. *tus.* 2. *Mis.* 3. *su.* 4. *Nuestra.* 5. *vuestros.* 6. *Mi.* 7. *tu.* 8. *sus.* 9. *Nuestros.* 10. *vuestra.* 11. *tu.* 17.2. 1. *tu.* 2. *nuestro.* 3. *sus.* 4. *su.* 5. *mi; mis.* 6. *vuestros.* 7. *tu.* 8. *tus.* 9. *su.* 10. *vuestra; vuestro.* 17.3. 1. *el.* 2. *los.* 3. *su.* 4. *los.* 5. *Mis.* 6. *la.* 7. *Su.* 8. *la.* 9. *las.* 10. *el.* 11. *una.* 12. *la.* 13. *los.* 14. *la.* 15. *Mi.*

Unit 18: Possessives (2). 18.1. 1. *mías.* 2. *mío.* 3. *suyo.* 4. *nuestros.* 5. *vuestros.* 6. *suyas.* 7. *tuyo/suyo.* 8. *suya.* 18.2. 1. *Las mías.* 2. *el nuestro.* 3. *El suyo.* 4. *el tuyo.* 5. *el nuestro.* 6. *el tuyo; El mío.* 7. *los tuyos; Los míos.* 8. *los suyos.* 9. *la mía.* 10. *Los nuestros / Los míos.* 11. *el mío.* 12. *La tuya; La mía.* 18.3. 1. *Un amigo mío.* 2. *Una amiga mía.* 3. *un primo vuestro.* 4. *amigo suyo.* 5. *prima nuestra.* 6. *tía tuya.* 7. *amigo nuestro.* 8. *unos familiares suyos.* 9. *dos amigas vuestras.* 10. *Dos tíos míos.* 11. *unos amigos tuyos.* 12. *un compañero suyo.*

Unit 19: Cardinal numbers (1). 19.1. 1. *veintiún.* 2. *Veintiuno.* 3. *Uno.* 4. *veintiuna.* 5. *veintiuna.* 6. *Una.* 7. *un.* 8. *veintiún.* 9. *Uno.* 10. *un.* 11. *un; veintiún.* 12. *veintiún.* 19.2. 1. *Diez de enero.* 2. *Quince de diciembre.* 3. *Veinticinco años.* 4. *Veintiocho de febrero.* 5. *Cinco de agosto.* 6. *Once alumnos.* 7. *Cuatro kilos.* 8. *Veintidós metros.* 9. *Veinte kilómetros.* 10. *Quince días.* 19.3. 1. *doce.* 2. *trece.* 3. *cuatro.* 4. *dieciséis.* 5. *cinco.* 6. *veinticuatro.* 7. *veinte.* 8. *veintisiete.* 9. *diez.* 10. *catorce.* 19.4. 1. *las tres y veinte.* 2. *la una y cuarto.* 3. *las nueve y media.* 4. *las seis menos cuarto.* 5. *las once menos veinticinco.* 6. *las ocho y cinco.* 7. *las nueve menos diez.* 8. *las tres menos cinco.* 9. *las doce menos veinte.* 10. *la una y veinticinco.* 19.5. 1. *nueve uno, tres cinco siete, ocho seis cero cuatro.* 2. *nueve seis, ocho dos seis, uno siete, tres cero.* 3. *nueve tres, tres dos siete, dos cero, uno cuatro.* 4. *ocho cero nueve, dos cero, dos siete, tres uno.* 5. *seis cero seis, cero nueve, tres cero, uno cinco.*

Unit 20: Cardinal numbers (2). 20.1. 1. *Treinta y uno.* 2. *Cuarenta y un.* 3. *Cincuenta y un.* 4. *Setenta y una.* 5. *Noventa y un.* 6. *Sesenta y un.* 7. *Ochenta y una.* 8. *Cuarenta y un.* 20.2. 1. *Treinta y cuatro metros.* 2. *Cuarenta y cinco kilómetros.* 3. *Treinta y seis meses.* 4. *Cuarenta y nueve kilos.* 5. *Cincuenta y tres años.* 6. *Noventa y dos kilos.* 7. *Ochenta y ocho centímetros.* 8. *Cuarenta días.* 9. *Cincuenta y siete euros.* 10. *Treinta y dos alumnos.* 11. *Cincuenta y cinco años.* 12. *Setenta y seis años.* 20.3. 1. *las dieciocho cincuenta y dos.* 2. *las nueve cincuenta.* 3. *las veinte cuarenta.* 4. *las doce treinta y siete.* 5. *las veintiuna treinta y cinco.* 6. *las dos cincuenta y nueve.* 7. *las diecinueve cuarenta y cinco.* 8. *las diecisiete cincuenta y cinco.* 9. *las ocho cuarenta y tres.* 10. *las trece treinta y ocho.* 20.4. 1. *noventa y tres, cinco, cuarenta y siete, ochenta y nueve, cero, dos.* 2. *noventa y dos, cuatro, cuarenta y siete, ochenta y nueve, cero, uno.* 3. *cinco, treinta y dos, cuarenta y cuatro, noventa y seis.* 4. *noventa y uno, cuatro, sesenta y cuatro, treinta y tres, cincuenta y ocho.* 5. *noventa y seis, tres, cincuenta y dos, sesenta y tres, sesenta y uno.* 6. *nueve, cincuenta y cinco, ochenta y ocho, setenta y nueve, cuarenta y uno.*

Unit 21: Cardinal numbers (3). 21.1. 1. *101.* 2. *3 017.* 3. *10 100.* 4. *13 508.* 5. *50 207.* 6. *100 001.* 7. *400 120.* 8. *1 100 000.* 9. *2 315 000.* 10. *1 300 000 000.* 21.2. 1. *cien.* 2. *ciento dos.* 3. *ciento ochenta y tres.* 4. *trescientos cuarenta y nueve.*

5. *mil setenta.* 6. *tres mil quinientos sesenta y uno.* 7. *sesenta y dos mil doscientos uno.* 8. *ciento quince mil cien.* 9. *cuatrocientos dieciséis mil doscientos cincuenta y dos.* 10. *novecientos treinta y tres mil trescientos cuarenta y cuatro.* 11. *un millón doscientos treinta y un mil setecientos cincuenta y ocho.* 12. *tres millones cincuenta mil novecientos cuarenta y siete.* 13. *veintidós millones ochocientos noventa y un mil seiscientos cuatro.* 14. *ciento un millones setecientos doce mil cuatrocientos trece.* 15. *doscientos millones treinta y cuatro mil veintisiete.* 16. *mil millones seiscientos quince mil ciento cinco.* 21.3. 1. *Doscientos cinco dólares.* 2. *Trescientos un euros.* 3. *Dos mil seiscientos doce yenes.* 4. *Ochenta y tres mil ciento noventa y cinco euros.* 5. *Mil cuatrocientas veintiuna coronas danesas.* 6. *Quinientos sesenta y ocho reales.* 7. *Ochocientas treinta y tres liras turcas.* 8. *Cuatrocientos setenta y un mil novecientos cincuenta pesos mexicanos.* 21.4. 1. *dos millones.* 2. *dos mil ochenta y cinco.* 3. *trescientas.* 4. *ciento veintiún.* 5. *mil doscientos setenta y cuatro.* 6. *ciento ocho.* 7. *quinientos.* 8. *trescientos diez.* 9. *doscientos cincuenta.* 10. *cien.* 21.5. 1. *Veintiuno de enero de mil ochocientos doce.* 2. *Dos de mayo de dos mil uno.* 3. *Veinticinco de octubre de mil novecientos cincuenta y cuatro.* 4. *Treinta y uno de diciembre de dos mil ocho.* 5. *Diez de julio de mil seiscientos trece.* 6. *Veintiocho de febrero de dos mil veinticinco.*

Unit 22: Ordinal numbers. 22.1. 1. *segundo.* 2. *once.* 3. *décima.* 4. *tercer.* 5. *doce.* 6. *primer.* 7. *catorce.* 8. *cuarta.* 9. *séptimo.* 10. *noveno.* 22.2. 1. *Juan Carlos primero.* 2. *Isabel primera.* 3. *Juan veintitrés.* 4. *Alfonso doce.* 5. *Luis quince.* 6. *Iván cuarto.* 7. *Margarita segunda.* 8. *Pío once.* 9. *Juana tercera.* 10. *Juan Pablo segundo.* 22.3. 1. *segundo.* 2. *primer.* 3. *quince; once.* 4. *primero.* 5. *tercero; quinta.* 6. *primeras.* 7. *quince.* 8. *primera; octavo.* 9. *segunda.* 10. *tercera, tercer.* 11. *dieciocho.* 12. *cuartas.* 13. *primeros.* 22.4. 1. *2.º* 2. *XV.* 3. *I.* 4. *4.º* 5. *II.* 6. *XXI.* 7. *VI.* 8. *I.*

Unit 23: Indefinite reference (1). 23.1. 1. *todo.* 2. *toda.* 3. *todas.* 4. *todas.* 5. *Todas.* 6. *todos.* 7. *todo.* 8. *todos.* 9. *toda.* 10. *toda.* 11. *Todas.* 12. *todos.* 23.2. 1. *Todas las cajas.* 2. *todo el queso.* 3. *Todos los niños.* 4. *Toda la leche.* 5. *Todas las tiendas.* 6. *todo el dinero.* 23.3. 1. *toda tu.* 2. *Todas sus.* 3. *todo su.* 4. *todos sus.* 5. *Todos nuestros.* 6. *todos sus.* 23.4. 1. *Todas.* 2. *todos.* 3. *toda.* 4. *todos.* 5. *toda.* 6. *todo.* 23.5. 1. *todo.* 2. *Todas.* 3. *Todos.* 4. *Todo el mundo.* 5. *Todo el mundo.* 6. *Todo.* 7. *Todos.* 8. *todas.* 9. *todos.* 10. *todo.*

Unit 24: Indefinite reference (2). 24.1. 1. *Una.* 2. *otra.* 3. *un.* 4. *Otra.* 5. *otros.* 6. *una* 7. *otras.* 8. *otra.* 24.2. 1. *unas.* 2. *otro.* 3. *otras.* 4. *unos.* 5. *unos.* 6. *unas.* 7. *otro.* 8. *otra.* 9. *otros.* 10. *otro.* 24.3. 1. *otros.* 2. *otras.* 3. *otro.* 4. *otros.* 5. *otra.* 6. *otro.* 7. *una; otra.* 8. *otro.* 9. *una.* 10. *otras.* 24.4. 1. *La otra.* 2. *El otro.* 3. *otro.* 4. *La otra.* 5. *otra.* 6. *La otra.*

Unit 25: Indefinite reference (3). 25.1. 1. *Sonia tiene muchos libros.* 2. *Alberto tiene pocos amigos.* 3. *Necesito muchos dólares.* 4. *Ayer dormimos muchas horas.* 5. *Bebo mucha agua al día.* 6. *Hemos comprado mucho aceite.* 7. *Quedan pocas patatas.* 8. *Luisa toma poco azúcar en el café.* 25.2. 1. *Trabaja demasiadas horas.* 2. *No duerme suficientes horas.* 3. *No bebe suficiente agua.* 4. *Como demasiados plátanos.* 5. *Bebe demasiado café.* 6. *Bebe suficiente agua.* 7. *Come demasiada carne.* 8. *No tenemos suficientes patatas.* 25.3. 1. *muchos coches.* 2. *poca agua.* 3. *mucha comida.* 4. *bastante gente.* 5. *muchos árboles.* 6. *poca gente.* 7. *mucho ruido.* 8. *mucha gente.* 9. *pocos árboles.* 10. *bastante dinero.* 25.4. 1. *mucha.* 2. *suficientes.* 3. *demasiadas.* 4. *suficiente.* 5. *poco.* 6. *mucha.* 25.5. 1. *poca.* 2. *un poco de.* 3. *un poco.* 4. *un poco de.* 5. *poco.* 6. *un poco de.* 7. *un poco de.*

Unit 26: Indefinite reference (4). 26.1. 1. *No hay nada.* 2. *Hay alguien.* 3. *Hay alguien.* 4. *No hay nadie.* 5. *Hay algo.* 6. *No hay nadie.* 7. *No hay nada.* 8. *Hay algo.* 26.2. 1. *alguien; algo.* 2. *Algo.* 3. *nada.* 4. *alguien.* 5. *Nadie.* 6. *alguien.* 7. *algo; nada.* 8. *nadie.* 9. *algo; nada.* 10. *alguien.* 11. *alguien.* 12. *algo; nada.* 26.3. 1. *Nadie me quiere.* 2. *No me quiere nadie.* 3. *No pasa nada.* 4. *Nada le gusta.* 5. *No tengo nada.* 6. *No sé nada.* 7. *No veo a nadie.* 8. *Nadie habla.* 26.4. 1. *algo de; nada de; algo de.* 2. *algo de; algo.* 3. *nada; algo de.* 4. *algo.* 5. *algo de; algo de.* 6. *nada de.* 26.5. 1. *algo de; nada.* 2. *algo de; algo.* 3. *nada de.* 4. *nada de; algo.* 5. *algo de.* 6. *algo de; algo.*

Unit 27: Comparisons with nouns. 27.1. 1. *más habitantes.* 2. *menos leche.* 3. *tanto arroz.* 4. *más libros.* 5. *tantas amigas.* 6. *tanto calor.* 7. *menos dinero.* 8. *tanta prisa.* 9. *más ropa.* 10. *más frío.* 27.2. 1. *menos dinero que Roberto.* 2. *tanta leche como Eloy.* 3. *más calor que ayer.* 4. *tantos habitantes como Mendoza.* 5. *más años que yo.* 6. *tantos estudiantes como ayer.* 7. *tanto frío como ayer.* 8. *tanta hambre como yo.* 9. *tantas corbatas como tú.* 10. *menos postales que vosotros.* 27.3. 1. *más.* 2. *tantos como tú.* 3. *menos.* 4. *tantos.* 5. *más.* 6. *menos.* 7. *más.* 8. *tanto como tú.* 9. *más.* 10. *menos.*

Unit 28: Personal pronouns: subject. 28.1. 1. *Ellas.* 2. *Nosotros.* 3. *Usted.* 4. *Yo.* 5. *Vosotros.* 6. *Ella.* 7. *Nosotras.* 8. *Tú.* 9. *Ustedes.* 10. *Él.* 11. *Ellos.* 12. *Ellas.* 28.2. 1. *ellos.* 2. *nosotros.* 3. *ellas.* 4. *vosotros.* 5. *ellos.* 6. *nosotros.* 7. *vosotros.* 8. *ellas.* 28.3. 1. *yo; Ella; yo.* 2. *Ella; él.* 3. *Ø; Ella; él.* 4. *yo; Ella; (yo).* 5. *Ø.* 28.4. 1. *tú; Ø.* 2. *Ø; Ø; tú; Ø.* 3. *ustedes; Ø.* 4. *Ø.* 5. *(Yo); vosotros/vosotras.* 6. *Ø.* 7. *(Yo).* 8. *(yo); vosotros.* 9. *(usted).* 10. *Ø.* 11. *Yo.* 12. *Ø.*

Unit 29: Personal pronouns: direct object. 29.1. 1. *lo.* 2. *las.* 3. *los.* 4. *lo.* 5. *la.* 6. *los.* 7. *la.* 8. *las.* 29.2. 1. *te.* 2. *los.* 3. *os.* 4. *la.* 5. *las.* 6. *os.* 7. *lo.* 8. *te.* 9. *la.* 10. *lo.* 29.3. 1. *lo.* 2. *la.* 3. *lo.* 4. *os.* 5. *las.* 6. *te.* 7. *los.* 8. *me.* 9. *los.* 10. *me.* 11. *los.* 12. *la.* 13. *te.* 14. *os.* 29.4. 1. *No te conozco.* 2. *No lo veo.* 3. *Yo os conozco.* 4. *Ella nos quiere.* 5. *Tú me necesitas.* 6. *No nos llaman.* 7. *Yo no la ayudo.* 8. *No lo encuentro.* 9. *No me quieren.* 10. *No os veo.*

Unit 30: Personal pronouns: indirect object. 30.1. 1. *te; Me.* 2. *Nos.* 3. *Le.* 4. *le.* 5. *Les.* 6. *os.* 7. *Le.* 30.2. 1. *No me han dicho nada.* 2. *No me ha dicho nada.* 3. *No nos ha dado nada.* 4. *No le han preguntado nada.* 5. *No te ha dicho nada.* 6. *No os/ nos han preguntado nada.* 7. *No me ha vendido nada.* 8. *No nos han dado nada.* 9. *No le han preguntado nada.* 10. *No les han regalado nada.* 11. *No le pasa nada.* 12. *No les pasa nada.* 30.3. 1. *A Rosa le ha dado una bufanda.* 2. *A don Antonio le ha dado una pluma.* 3. *A Lucas y Mar les ha dado unos bombones.* 4. *Astrid le ha dado un perfume.* 5. *Vicente e Isabel les ha dado unos reproductores de MP3.*

Unit 31: Indirect and direct object pronouns. 31.1. 1. *Se la he dado.* 2. *Se los han traído.* 3. *Se lo han alquilado.* 4. *Se lo han hecho.* 5. *Se las he escrito.* 6. *Se la ha vendido.* 7. *No se las has dado.* 8. *Se las habéis roto.* 9. *Se la han echado.* 10. *Se la han curado.* 31.2. 1. *Me; los.* 2. *Se; lo.* 3. *Nos; lo.* 4. *Te; las.* 5. *Se; lo.* 6. *Me; la.* 7. *Nos; lo.* 8. *Me; los.* 9. *Nos; lo.* 10. *Nos; la.* 31.3. 1. *no me lo ha dado.* 2. *nos lo ha prestado.* 3. *no se lo ha presentado.* 4. *me la ha enseñado.* 5. *nos la ha traído.* 6. *se los ha presentado.* 7. *no me los ha presentado.* 8. *no se lo ha vendido.* 9. *nos los ha enseñado.* 10. *te las ha traído.* 11. *se lo* *he cortado.* 12. *no se la he echado.* `31.4.` 1. *¿Se lo has dejado a Marta?; Sí, se lo he dejado.* 2. *¿Se los has dejado a Pablo?; No, no se los he dejado.* 3. *¿Se lo has alquilado a unos amigos?; Sí, se lo he alquilado.* 4. *¿Se los has dado al perro?; Sí, se los he dado.* 5. *¿Se la has presentado a tus padres?; No, no se la he presentado.*

Unit 32: Contrasting the personal pronouns. `32.1.` 1. *lo.* 2. *Lo.* 3. *la.* 4. *las.* 5. *Le; se; la; Se; la.* 6. *los.* 7. *Le.* 8. *Les; se; lo.* 9. *las.* 10. *la.* 11. *lo.* 12. *Les.* 13. *Le.* 14. *la.* 15. *le; Le.* `32.2.` 1. *I; Sí, la he visto.* 2. *I; No, ahora no lo necesito.* 3. *C.* 4. *I; No lo he visto.* 5. *I; Sra. Hernando, la llaman por teléfono.* 6. *C.* 7. *C.* 8. *I; Hoy no las he visto.* 9. *I; Sí, los conocí en una fiesta.* 10. *I; Los necesito.* `32.3.` 1. *la.* 2. *Le;* 3. *lo.* 4. *le.* 5. *Le, se; los.* 6. *la.* 7. *le.* 8. *les; le; le.* `32.4.` 1. *Le; se; lo.* 2. *lo.* 3. *Lo; lo.* 4. *Lo; se; lo.* 5. *lo; Le; la.* 6. *lo.* 7. *lo; la.* 8. *lo; lo.*

Unit 33: Reflexive pronouns. `33.1.` 1. *Me.* 2. *se.* 3. *Ø.* 4. *se.* 5. *Ø.* 6. *nos.* 7. *Ø.* 8. *os.* 9. *se.* 10. *te.* `33.2.` 1. *se.* 2. *se.* 3. *Ø.* 4. *te.* 5. *se.* 6. *nos.* 7. *Ø.* 8. *se.* 9. *Ø.* 10. *se.* 11. *Me.* 12. *Ø.* 13. *te.* 14. *os.* 15. *Ø.* `33.3.` 1. *Me.* 2. *os.* 3. *Ø.* 4. *Te.* 5. *Ø.* 6. *me.* 7. *Ø* 8. *te.* 9. *Ø.* 10. *Se.* 11. *te.* 12. *Ø.*

Unit 34: Personal pronouns with prepositions. `34.1.` 1. *ti.* 2. *ustedes.* 3. *-tigo.* 4. *vosotras.* 5. *vosotros.* 6. *nosotros.* 7. *usted.* 8. *nosotras.* 9. *mí.* 10. *-migo.* `34.2.` 1. *él.* 2. *ella.* 3. *él.* 4. *-tigo.* 5. *ellos.* 6. *nosotros/nosotras.* 7. *mí.* 8. *mí.* `34.3.` 1. *-migo.* 2. *tú.* 3. *ti.* 4. *-migo.* 5. *-tigo.* 6. *mí.* 7. *-migo.* 8. *-tigo.* `34.4.` 1. *yo.* 2. *ti.* 3. *mí.* 4. *yo.* 5. *conmigo.* 6. *mí.* 7. *mí.* 8. *yo.* 9. *ti.* 10. *tú.*

Unit 35: Relative pronouns. `35.1.` 1. *Tengo un perro que juega al fútbol.* 2. *Me gusta mucho el libro que estoy leyendo.* 3. *Conozco a unos actores que dan clase de teatro.* 4. *Estamos comiendo una paella que ha preparado Marisa.* 5. *No me gustó la película que vimos ayer.* 6. *Tengo un amigo que vive en Guatemala.* 7. *Usa el bolígrafo que está en la mesa.* 8. *Paco sale con una chica que es piloto.* 9. *Trabajo en una tienda que está en el centro de Madrid.* 10. *Tengo una tortuga que tiene doce años.* 11. *Alicia trabaja en una empresa que exporta guitarras.* 12. *Ayer se estropeó la lavadora que compré el año pasado.* 13. *Tengo una vecina que es enfermera.* `35.2.` 1. *Elisa es la chica que.* 2. *Miguel es el chico que.* 3. *Javier es el chico que.* 4. *Marisa es la chica que.* 5. *Julio es el chico que.* 6. *Marta es una chica que.* `35.3.` 1. *Un chico que conocí en el parque.* 2. *Una persona que no bebe alcohol.* 3. *Un cuadro que he pintado yo.* 4. *Unos obreros que están arreglando la calle.* 5. *Un chico que vive en el sexto.* 6. *Una persona que no cree en Dios.* 7. *Una persona que cuida niños.* 8. *Un animal que procede de los Andes.* 9. *Una persona que habla muchos idiomas.* `35.4.` 1. *donde.* 2. *que.* 3. *donde.* 4. *que.* 5. *donde.* 6. *que.* `35.5.` 1. *donde.* 2. *donde.* 3. *que.* 4. *que.* 5. *donde.* 6. *que.*

Unit 36: Interrogatives (1). `36.1.` 1. *Qué.* 2. *Quién.* 3. *Quiénes.* 4. *Qué.* 5. *Quién.* 6. *Qué.* 7. *Qué.* 8. *Quiénes.* 9. *Qué.* 10. *Quién.* 11. *Quiénes.* 12. *Quiénes.* 13. *Qué.* 14. *Quién.* 15. *Qué.* 16. *Quién.* `36.2.` 1. *Con quién.* 2. *De qué.* 3. *Qué.* 4. *De quién.* 5. *Con quién.* 6. *Quiénes.* 7. *Qué.* 8. *A quién.* 9. *Para quién.* 10. *Quién.* `36.3.` 1. *¿Qué tiene Julián en la mano?* 2. *¿De quién es este abrigo?* 3. *¿Para quién es ese anillo?* 4. *¿Qué pasó anoche?* 5. *¿De quién es esa bolsa?* 6. *¿Qué lleva en la cabeza Luis? / ¿Qué lleva Luis en la cabeza?* 7. *¿Con qué has abierto la puerta?* 8. *¿Quién está escribiendo una novela?* 9. *¿Quién vio el accidente?* 10. *¿De qué es la sopa?* `36.4.` 1. *¿A quién ha invitado Juan?* 2. *¿Qué ha comprado Luis?* 3. *¿Quién ha llamado?* 4. *¿Qué pasó ayer?* 5. *¿A quién va a ver Rosa?* 6. *¿De qué están hablando?* 7. *¿Con quién está estudiando Juan?* 8. *¿Qué tienen los niños?* 9. *¿Con quién está hablando Sofía?* 10. *¿Qué está buscando María?*

Unit 37: Interrogatives (2). `37.1.` 1. *Cuál de.* 2. *Cuál.* 3. *Cuál de.* 4. *Cuáles de.* 5. *Cuál de.* 6. *Cuál de.* 7. *Cuál.* 8. *Cuáles.* 9. *cuál de.* 10. *Cuáles.* `37.2.` 1. *Cuál de.* 2. *Cuál.* 3. *Cuáles.* 4. *Qué.* 5. *qué.* 6. *Cuál.* 7. *Cuál de.* 8. *qué.* 9. *Qué.* 10. *Cuáles.* 11. *Qué.* 12. *Qué.* 13. *cuál de.* 14. *Cuál.* 15. *Cuáles de.* `37.3.` 1. *Qué música / Qué tipo de música / Qué clase de música.* 2. *Cuál de tus hermanos.* 3. *Qué jersey.* 4. *Cuál de tus hermanas.* 5. *Qué coches / Qué tipo de coches / Qué clase de coches.* 6. *Cuál de tus tíos.* 7. *Qué queso / Qué tipo de queso / Qué clase de queso.* 8. *Qué cuadro.* 9. *Cuál de las entrenadoras.* 10. *Qué comida / Qué tipo de comida / Qué clase de comida.* `37.4.` 1. *¿Cuál de tus padres habla español?* 2. *¿A qué hora empieza la película?* 3. *¿Cuál de esas chicas es Sofía?* 4. *¿Qué escritor famoso nació en Alcalá?* 5. *¿En qué ciudad española está la Giralda?* 6. *¿Qué instrumento toca Mario?*

Unit 38: Interrogatives (3). `38.1.` 1. *Cuándo.* 2. *Adónde.* 3. *Adónde.* 4. *Cuándo.* 5. *Cuándo.* 6. *Dónde.* 7. *Dónde.* 8. *Dónde.* 9. *Cuándo.* 10. *dónde.* `38.2.` 1. *Cuánto.* 2. *Cuánto.* 3. *Cuántas.* 4. *Cuántos.* 5. *Cuánto.* 6. *Cuánta.* 7. *Cuánta.* 8. *Cuántas.* 9. *Cuánta.* 10. *Cuántos.* `38.3.` 1. *Cuánto.* 2. *Cuánto.* 3. *Cuántas.* 4. *Cuánto.* 5. *Cuántos.* 6. *Cuánto.* 7. *Cuántas.* 8. *Cuánto.* 9. *Cuánta.* 10. *Cuántos.* `38.4.` 1. *¿Adónde vais los domingos?* 2. *¿Dónde está mi bolígrafo?* 3. *¿Con cuántos hermanos vives?* 4. *¿Cuántas postales has recibido?* 5. *¿Cuánto vale este libro?* 6. *¿Dónde trabaja Sebastián?* 7. *¿Dónde vive Alicia?* 8. *¿De dónde es Peter?* 9. *¿Cuántas personas hay en la conferencia?* 10. *¿Cuándo se casa Rocío?* 11. *¿Para cuántos es esa paella?*

Unit 39: Interrogatives (4). `39.1.` 1. *Cómo / Qué tal.* 2. *Cómo.* 3. *Cómo.* 4. *Cómo / Qué tal.* 5. *Cómo / Qué tal.* 6. *Cómo.* `39.2.` 1. *Por qué; Porque.* 2. *Para qué.* 3. *Por qué; Porque.* 4. *Por qué; Porque.* 5. *Para qué.* 6. *Para qué.* `39.3.` 1. *¿Por qué no abres la ventana?* 2. *¿Por qué no compras un bocadillo?* 3. *¿Por qué no haces más ejercicio?* 4. *¿Por qué no te tomas una aspirina?* 5. *¿Por qué no estudias más?* 6. *¿Por qué no te pones las gafas?* 7. *¿Por qué no coges el metro?* 8. *¿Por qué no miras en Internet?* `39.4.` 1. *Cómo.* 2. *Cómo / Qué tal.* 3. *Cómo / Qué tal.* 4. *Por qué.* 5. *Por qué.* 6. *Cómo / Qué tal.* 7. *Para qué.* 8. *Por qué.* 9. *Cómo / Qué tal.* 10. *Para qué.* `39.5.` 1. *¿Cómo viste Juan? / ¿Qué tal viste Juan?* 2. *¿Cómo ves a Iván?* 3. *¿Por qué no viajas?* 4. *¿Para qué son esos pinceles?* 5. *¿Por qué no salen?* 6. *¿Cómo vas al trabajo?* 7. *¿Para qué necesitas dinero?* 8. *¿Por qué no viene Andrés?*

Unit 40: Exclamatories. `40.1.` 1. *¡Qué cara!* 2. *¡Qué largo!* 3. *¡Qué alto!* 4. *¡Qué baratos!* 5. *¡Qué guapa!* 6. *¡Qué sucios!* 7. *¡Qué caliente!* 8. *¡Qué grandes!* `40.2.` 1. *Qué mal.* 2. *Qué bien.* 3. *Qué rápido.* 4. *Qué tarde.* 5. *Qué calor.* 6. *Qué frío.* 7. *Qué hambre.* 8. *Qué sueño.* `40.3.` 1. *¡Qué camisa más/tan cara!* 2. *¡Qué coche más/tan largo!* 3. *¡Qué chico más/tan alto!* 4. *¡Qué relojes más/tan baratos!* 5. *¡Qué chica más/tan guapa!* 6. *¡Qué niños más/tan sucios!* 7. *¡Qué sopa más/tan caliente!* 8. *¡Qué sandías más/tan grandes!* `40.4.` 1. *¡Qué elegante es!* 2. *¡Qué calor hace hoy!* 3. *¡Qué bien habla Felipe!* 4. *¡Qué sed tengo!* 5. *¡Qué rápido conduce Arturo!* 6. *¡Qué cara está la vida!* 7. *¡Qué tacaña es Isabel!* 8. *¡Qué sucia está la calle!* 9. *¡Qué mal cocina Iliana!* 10. *¡Qué delgado está Ricardo!* 11. *¡Qué fácil era el ejercicio!* 12. *¡Qué lento es el camarero!*

Unit 41: Present indicative of ser. 41.1. 1. *sois; Somos.* 2. *es; Soy.* 3. *Somos.* 4. *Son; somos.* 5. *eres; Soy.* 6. *Son.* 41.2. 1. *eres;* *Soy.* 2. *son; Son.* 3. *sois; Somos.* 4. *Eres; soy.* 5. *es; Son.* 6. *es; Es.* 7. *Sois; somos.* 8. *es; Es.* 9. *sois; Somos.* 10. *son; Son.* 41.3. 1. *Elsa y Tomás son chilenos.* 2. *Juan y Elisa son de Zamora.* 3. *Yo soy alto y moreno.* 4. *Esa mesa es de cristal.* 5. *Mis padres son jóvenes.* 6. *Mi coche blanco.* 7. *Mi hermana y yo no somos morenos.* 8. *La fiesta es en mi casa.* 9. *La boda es a las cinco.* 10. *Ese libro es de Marta.* 11. *Hoy no es domingo.* 12. *En clase somos doce.* 41.4. 1. *somos / no somos.* 2. *somos / no somos.* 3. *es / no es.* 4. *soy / no soy.* 5. *es / no es.* 6. *es / no es.* 7. *es / no es.* 8. *son / no son.* 41.5. 1. *¿Qué día es hoy?* 2. *Sofía es estudiante.* 3. *¿Tus padres son de Granada?* 4. *Mis amigos son españoles.* 5. *Ana no es abogada.* 6. *¿Es Liebe belga?* 7. *¿De dónde son Julián y Rosa?* 8. *¿Cuándo es tu cumpleaños?*

Unit 42: Present indicative of estar. 42.1. 1. *Estoy.* 2. *estáis; Estamos.* 3. *estás; Estoy.* 4. *está; Está.* 42.2. 1. *Estoy resfriado.* 2. *está de buen humor.* 3. *Están tristes.* 4. *Estamos agotados.* 5. *Estoy aburrida.* 6. *Estás enfadado.* 7. *está de mal humor.* 8. *están contentos.* 42.3. 1. *está abierta.* 2. *está cerrada.* 3. *están sucios.* 4. *está nublado.* 5. *está apagada.* 6. *están limpios.* 42.4. 1. *está; Estoy.* 2. *estás; no estoy; estoy.* 3. *Está; está.* 4. *no está; Está.* 5. *Estás; no estoy; Estoy.* 6. *está; Está.* 7. *están; Están.* 8. *no está.* 9. *Estás; no estoy; Estoy.* 10. *están; Están.* 42.5. 1. *¿Dónde está Teresa?* 2. *¿Está Luis en la oficina?* 3. *¿Cómo están tus padres?* 4. *¿Está caliente la sopa?* 5. *¿Están tus padres en casa?* 6. *¿Dónde están tus hermanos?*

Unit 43: Contrasting ser and estar. 43.1. 1. *Estoy.* 2. *está.* 3. *son.* 4. *están.* 5. *está.* 6. *están.* 7. *son.* 8. *estás.* 9. *estoy.* 10. *son.* 43.2. 1. *son.* 2. *es.* 3. *es.* 4. *Están.* 5. *está.* 6. *está.* 7. *son.* 8. *es.* 9. *están.* 10. *es.* 43.3. 1. *es.* 2. *es.* 3. *están.* 4. *es.* 5. *es.* 6. *está.* 7. *está.* 8. *está.* 9. *es.* 10. *es.* 43.4. 1. *Estás.* 2. *está.* 3. *es.* 4. *Estoy.* 5. *es.* 6. *es.* 7. *está.* 8. *son.* 9. *Estamos.* 10. *estoy.*

Unit 44: Present indicative of tener. 44.1. 1. *tiene.* 2. *tenemos.* 3. *Tengo, No Tengo; tengo.* 4. *no tenemos.* 5. *tiene.* 6. *tiene.* 7. *no tienen; Tienen.* 8. *tenemos.* 44.2. 1. *tienes; Tengo.* 2. *Tienes; tengo.* 3. *tienen.* 4. *Tienes; no tengo.* 5. *Tienes.* 6. *tiene.* 7. *Tienes.* 8. *tiene; Tiene.* 9. *Tiene; no tiene.* 44.3. 1. *Tengo sed.* 2. *Tenemos hambre.* 3. *Tengo calor.* 4. *Tengo miedo.* 5. *Tienes fiebre* 6. *¿Tenéis frío?* 44.4. 1. *¿Tiene usted sueño?* 2. *¿Tienes dinero?* 3. *No tenemos coche.* 4. *¿Tienen ustedes hijos?* 5. *Mis abuelos tienen doce nietos.* 6. *¿Tiene usted una casa grande?* 7. *¿Tenéis muchos amigos?* 8. *¿Tienen ustedes perro?* 9. *¿Tienes un diccionario?* 10. *Mi casa no tiene ascensor.* 11. *Tengo el pelo largo.* 12. *¿Tenéis hijos?* 44.5. 1. *¿Tienen ustedes coches?* 2. *¿Cuántos años tiene Miguel?* 3. *¿Tiene piscina tu casa?* 4. *Tienen ustedes hambre* 5. *¿Tiene Pedro frío?* 6. *¿Cuántos hijos tiene Rosa?*

Unit 45: Present indicative of haber (impersonal). 45.1. 1. *Hay una mesa.* 2. *No hay espejo.* 3. *Hay una alfombra.* 4. *Hay tres sillas.* 5. *Hay una lámpara.* 6. *No hay televisor.* 7. *Hay un reloj.* 8. *Hay dos cuadros.* 9. *No hay ningún cojín. / No hay cojines.* 10. *Hay un sillón.* 45.2. 1. *Hay cinco colegios.* 2. *Hay un cine.* 3. *No hay ningún hospital. / No hay hospitales.* 4. *Hay un polideportivo.* 5. *Hay dos parques.* 6. *No hay ninguna estación de ferrocarril. / No hay estaciones de ferrocarril.* 7. *Hay una estación de autobús.* 8. *No hay ningún hotel. / No hay hoteles.* 9. *Hay dos iglesias.* 10. *Hay una biblioteca.* 45.3. 1. *Hay leche.* 2. *No hay agua.* 3. *Hay mantequilla.* 4. *Hay queso.* 5. *Hay seis huevos.* 6. *Hay uvas.* 7. *Hay naranjas.* 8. *No hay plátanos.* 9. *No hay zumo de naranja.* 10. *No hay yogures.* 45.4. 1. *hay un buzón; Hay uno.* 2. *no hay metro.* 3. *hay un estanco; Hay uno.* 4. *Hay muchas tiendas; no hay muchas.* 5. *huevos hay; No hay.* 6. *leche hay; Hay un litro.* 7. *Hay una cafetería; hay una.* 8. *yogures hay; Hay tres.*

Unit 46: Contrasting haber and estar. 46.1. 1. *Hay; Está.* 2. *hay.* 3. *Hay; está.* 4. *Hay; hay.* 5. *hay.* 6. *Hay.* 7. *está.* 8. *hay; Están.* 9. *Hay; Está.* 10. *Hay.* 46.2. 1. *¿Dónde hay una farmacia?* 2. *¿Dónde hay una parada de autobús?* 3. *¿Dónde está la parada de autobús más próxima?* 4. *¿Dónde está el Hospital Central?* 5. *¿Dónde están las ruinas de Tikal?* 6. *¿Dónde hay un banco?* 7. *¿Dónde está el Banco de Galicia?* 8. *¿Dónde están los cines Luna?* 46.3. 1. *Hay.* 2. *está.* 3. *Hay; Está.* 4. *está.* 5. *están.* 6. *está.* 7. *Hay; Está.* 8. *Hay; hay; Está.* 9. *hay.* 10. *hay; Están.* 11. *hay.* 12. *está.* 13. *Hay.* 14. *Hay; Están.* 15. *hay; Está.* 16. *hay.* 17. *hay.* 18. *están.* 19. *hay; Están.* 20. *hay.*

Unit 47: Present indicative: verbs ending in –ar. 47.1. 1. *Trabajo; Arreglo.* 2. *trabajamos; da; doy.* 3. *Trabajo, Preparo.* 4. *no trabajamos; estudia; estudio.* 47.2. 1. *canto; tocan.* 2. *no viajamos.* 3. *Habla.* 4. *pasan.* 5. *no fumo.* 6. *escucho.* 7. *hablan.* 8. *cenan.* 9. *llegas.* 10. *llama.* 11. *nadamos.* 12. *damos.* 47.3. 1. *cenáis; Cenamos.* 2. *pasas; Paso.* 3. *das; Doy.* 4. *trabajas; Trabajo.* 5. *colecciona; Colecciono.* 6. *estudiáis; Estudiamos.* 7. *hablan; Hablamos.* 47.4. 1. *Lleva.* 2. *pasa.* 3. *llevan.* 4. *llamas.* 5. *bebéis.* 47.5. 1. *¿Habla Hans español?* 2. *¿Dónde trabajan tus padres?* 3. *¿Dónde da clases Pedro?* 4. *¿Estudia Carmen?* 5. *¿Dónde viven tus amigos?* 6. *¿Desayuna Luis en casa?* 7. *¿Qué estudia Felipe?* 8. *¿A qué hora llega Toni?*

Unit 48: Present indicative: verbs ending in –er. 48.1. 1. *coméis.* 2. *no vemos; veis.* 3. *no comen.* 4. *Bebe.* 5. *lees.* 6. *hacéis; No hacemos.* 7. *Conoces; no; conozco.* 8. *hacen.* 9. *no pongo.* 10. *proceden; Comen.* 11. *sabes; no sé; Sabes.* 12. *no sabe.* 13. *ponen; hacen.* 14. *parece.* 15. *Coges; cojo; traigo.* 48.2. 1. *Sabes; sé.* 2. *bebéis; bebemos.* 3. *Hace; hago.* 4. *Sabe; sé.* 5. *Conoce; conozco.* 6. *Hago; haces.* 7. *Conocen; conocemos.* 8. *Hacen; Corremos.* 48.3. 1. *Ves;* 2. *comes.* 3. *corre.* 4. *parezco.* 5. *lees.* 6. *haces; No hago.* 7. *bebéis.* 8. *no te conozco.* 48.4. 1. *Sé / No sé.* 2. *Hago / No hago.* 3. *Sé / No sé.* 4. *hacen / no hacen.* 5. *Conozco / No conozco.* 6. *Como / No como.* 7. *Pongo / No pongo.* 8. *Veo / No veo.*

Unit 49: Present indicative: verbs ending in –ir. 49.1. 1. *abren.* 2. *escribe.* 3. *viven.* 4. *no conduce.* 5. *salgo; voy.* 6. *va.* 7. *voy.* 8. *Traduzco.* 9. *Vamos.* 10. *no vamos.* 11. *Construyo.* 49.2. 1. *vive; Vivo.* 2. *viven; Vivimos.* 3. *vas; voy.* 4. *Salís; salimos.* 5. *vas.* 6. *conduces; Conduzco.* 7. *va; voy.* 8. *Vais; Vamos.* 9. *Oyes; oigo.* 10. *Sales; salgo.* 11. *Escribe; escribe.* 49.3. 1. *vais.* 2. *No oigo.* 3. *va.* 4. *Conduces.* 49.4. 1. *Escribe.* 2. *Reparte.* 3. *Traduce.* 4. *Construye.* 5. *Escribe.* 6. *Dirige.* 7. *Conduce.* 8. *Construye.* 49.5. 1. *Vivo / No vivo* 2. *Escribo / No escribo.* 3. *Salgo / no salgo.* 4. *salen / no salen.* 5. *va / no va.* 6. *Escribo / No escribo.* 7. *Conduzco / No conduzco.* 8. *cierran / no cierran.*

Unit 50: Present indicative: irregular verbs (1). 50.1. 1. *quiere.* 2. *riego.* 3. *empieza.* 4. *pierden.* 5. *cierran.* 6. *vienen.* 7. *no miente; dice.* 8. *mide; miden.* 9. *digo.* 10. *dirige.* 11. *consigue.* 12. *empiezan.* 13. *corrige.* 14. *no friega.* 15. *perdemos.* 16. *empieza.* 50.2. 1. *mides; Mido.* 2. *riegas; riego.* 3. *viene; Viene.* 4. *Prefiere; Prefiero.* 5. *dicen; dicen.* 6. *empezáis; Empezamos.* 7. *friega; friego.* 8. *tienes; Tengo.* 9. *quieres; Quiero.* 10. *pide; Pide.* 11. *vienes; Vengo.* 50.3. 1. *vienes.* 2. *quieren.* 3. *dices.* 4. *Tengo.* 5. *piensas.* 50.4. 1. *¿De dónde viene Andrés?* 2. *¿Qué piensan tus padres?* 3. *¿A qué hora cierran* *los bancos?* 4. *¿Entiende Li español?* 5. *¿Por qué miente Mercedes?* 6. *¿Cuándo viene Sofía?*

Unit 51: Present indicative: irregular verbs (2). ⟨51.1.⟩ 1. *prueba.* 2. *duelen.* 3. *Mueren.* 4. *juegan.* 5. *no duerme.* 6. *sueña.* 7. *recuerdo.* 8. *encuentra.* 9. *No puedo.* 10. *aprueba.* 11. *vuelves.* 12. *cuesta.* 13. *cuentan.* 14. *vuela.* ⟨51.2.⟩ 1. *cuesta; Cuesta.* 2. *duermes; Duermo.* 3. *Sueñas; Sueño.* 4. *vuelves; Vuelvo.* 5. *Juega, juego.* 6. *Muerden, muerden.* 7. *Duerme; duermo.* 8. *Puedo; puedes.* 9. *cuelgas; cuelgo.* ⟨51.3.⟩ 1. *No puedo.* 2. *cuestan.* 3. *No encuentro.* 4. *No muerde.* 5. *jugáis.* ⟨51.4.⟩ 1. *¿Qué recuerda Alfonso?* 2. *¿Cuánto cuesta ese móvil?* 3. *¿A qué juegan ustedes?* 4. *¿Dónde duerme Rufo?* 5. *¿Sueña usted mucho?* 6. *¿Suena ese reloj a las horas?* 7. *¿Por qué mueren las plantas?* 8. *¿Vuelan las gallinas?* ⟨51.5.⟩ 1. *Duermo / No duermo.* 2. *Sueño / No sueño.* 3. *duele; no duele.* 4. *Juego / No juego.* 5. *Recuerdo / No recuerdo.* 6. *Vuelvo / No vuelvo.*

Unit 52: Present indicative: other uses. ⟨52.1.⟩ 1. *voy al médico.* 2. *tengo una reunión.* 3. *voy a la ópera.* 4. *ceno con el director.* 5. *visito una fábrica en Tarragona.* 6. *juego al tenis con Rodolfo.* 7. *salgo con Laura.* ⟨52.2.⟩ 1. *Me voy.* 2. *se casan.* 3. *da.* 4. *Vamos.* 5. *se va; sale.* 6. *empieza.* 7. *regresan.* 8. *tengo.* 9. *hacéis.* 10. *acaba.* 11. *llega.* ⟨52.3.⟩ 1. *Cierro.* 2. *llevo.* 3. *Jugamos.* 4. *trae.* 5. *pongo.* 6. *lavo.* 7. *ayudas.* 8. *cortas.* 9. *Vemos.* 10. *dejas.* ⟨52.4.⟩ 1. *Salimos.* 2. *dejas.* 3. *pongo.* 4. *ayudas; hago.* 5. *Vamos.* 6. *llevo.* 7. *dices.* 8. *dejas.* 9. *Cojo.* 10. *Compro.*

Unit 53: Verbs with *me, te, se...* ⟨53.1.⟩ 1. *se despierta.* 2. *se levantan.* 3. *se ducha.* 4. *se viste.* 5. *se acuestan.* 6. *se baña.* ⟨53.2.⟩ 1. *se lava.* 2. *nos quedamos.* 3. *se pinta.* 4. *nos divertimos.* 5. *Se mancha.* 6. *No se atreve.* 7. *se aburre.* 8. *nos lavamos.* 9. *se defienden.* 10. *se cansa.* 11. *me pongo.* 12. *no se afeita.* 13. *no se enfada.* ⟨53.3.⟩ 1. *te levantas; Me levanto.* 2. *Te pones; me pongo.* 3. *Os bañáis; nos bañamos.* 4. *os ponéis; Nos ponemos.* 5. *se afeita; Me afeito.* 6. *Se viste; Me visto.* 7. *se levantan; Nos levantamos.* 8. *se acuestan; Nos acostamos.* 9. *os casasteis; Nos casamos.* 10. *te enfadas; Me enfado.* ⟨53.4.⟩ 1. *Me levanto / No me levanto.* 2. *Me lavo / No me lavo.* 3. *Me pinto / No me pinto.* 4. *Me pongo / No me pongo.* 5. *Me acuesto / No me acuesto.* 6. *Me río / No me río.* 7. *Me aburro / No me aburro.* 8. *Me canso / No me canso.*

Unit 54: Contrasting verbs with or without *me, te, se...* ⟨54.1.⟩ 1. *lava.* 2. *me mancho.* 3. *Acuesta.* 4. *Baño.* 5. *Me lavo.* 6. *mancha.* 7. *nos bañamos.* 8. *me levanto.* ⟨54.2.⟩ 1. *se aburre.* 2. *Me lavo.* 3. *viste; se viste.* 4. *Me acuesto.* 5. *lava.* 6. *acuesta.* 7. *se mira.* 8. *divierten.* 9. *aburre.* 10. *nos divertimos.* 11. *se asusta.* 12. *asusta.* ⟨54.3.⟩ 1. *Me llamo.* 2. *se despide.* 3. *te pareces.* 4. *Vamos.* 5. *Me duermo.* 6. *parece.* 7. *Nos vamos.* 8. *Llamamos.* 9. *encuentro.* 10. *duermes.* 11. *Te encuentras.* 12. *me dejo.* 13. *voy.* 14. *dejo.* ⟨54.4.⟩ 1. *te llamas.* 2. *Te encuentras.* 3. *encuentro.* 4. *se parece.* 5. *llama.* 6. *parece.* 7. *duermo.* 8. *Se duerme.*

Unit 55: Verbs with *me, te, le...* ⟨55.1.⟩ 1. *Te gusta; no me gusta.* 2. *le gusta.* 3. *Le gusta; me gusta.* 4. *no les gusta.* 5. *nos encanta.* 6. *Le gusta; me encanta.* 7. *Te gustan; me gustan.* 8. *no me gustan.* 9. *Os gustan; nos encantan.* 10. *Le gustan; no me gustan.* ⟨55.2.⟩ 1. *Te gusta; me encanta; A mí no me gusta.* 2. *Os gusta; me encanta; a Rubén no le gusta.* 3. *Les gusta; le gusta; no le gusta.* 4. *le gusta; no le gusta.* 5. *Te gusta; A nosotras nos encanta.* 6. *les gusta; Nos gusta.* 7. *Os gusta; me gusta; a mi hermana no le gusta.* 8. *Nos encanta; A mí me gusta.* ⟨55.3.⟩ 1. *le duelen.* 2. *Te apetece.* 3. *Me duelen.* 4. *nos importa.* 5. *le duele.* 6. *Les apetece.* 7. *me interesa.* 8. *Me duele.* 9. *le gustan.* 10. *Te importa.* 11. *Le apetece; Me duele.* 12. *les apetece.* 13. *nos interesa.*

Unit 56: Present of *estar* + gerund. ⟨56.1.⟩ 1. *Estoy escribiendo.* 2. *Estamos jugando.* 3. *¿Está lloviendo?; está nevando.* 4. *está haciendo; Está leyendo.* 5. *Está estudiando; está viendo.* 6. *están llorando.* 7. *está bailando.* 8. *Estamos corriendo.* ⟨56.2.⟩ 1. *Están pasando.* 2. *Están jugando.* 3. *me estoy vistiendo.* 4. *está hablando.* 5. *está haciendo.* 6. *están preparando.* 7. *estoy durmiendo.* 8. *estamos estudiando.* 9. *Estoy escuchando.* 10. *Está comiendo.* 11. *Está haciendo.* 12. *nos estamos acostando.* 13. *estás escuchando.* ⟨56.3.⟩ 1. *Me estoy afeitando / Estoy afeitándome.* 2. *Se están bañando / Están bañándose.* 3. *Nos estamos divirtiendo / Estamos divirtiéndonos.* 4. *Se está lavando el pelo / Está lavándose el pelo.* 5. *Se está vistiendo / Está vistiéndose.* 6. *Se están lavando. / Están lavándose.* ⟨56.4.⟩ 1. *¿Qué está haciendo Carlos?* 2. *¿Qué está dibujando Juan?* 3. *¿Está durmiendo Luisa?* 4. *¿Qué están viendo ustedes?* 5. *¿Qué está leyendo Rodrigo?* 6. *¿Se está duchando Fátima? / ¿Está duchándose Fátima?*

Unit 57: Contrasting the present indicative of *estar* + gerund. ⟨57.1.⟩ 1. *Tocan; toca; toca; están tocando; Están jugando.* 2. *Da; está dando; Está viendo.* 3. *Estudia; está estudiando; Está jugando.* ⟨57.2.⟩ 1. *no llueve.* 2. *hablas.* 3. *no está haciendo; está lloviendo.* 4. *trabajas; estoy trabajando.* 5. *está durmiendo.* 6. *no comen.* 7. *Tocas; toco.* 8. *está cantando.* 9. *Fumo; fumo / estoy fumando.* 10. *lloran.* ⟨57.3.⟩ 1. *vais.* 2. *Oyes.* 3. *quieres.* 4. *estoy estudiando.* 5. *estás trabajando.* 6. *entiendo.* 7. *tienes; vengo.* 8. *Están viajando.* 9. *Estoy viendo.* 10. *veo.* ⟨57.4.⟩ 1. *vas; Voy.* 2. *Conoces.* 3. *tienes.* 4. *estás viendo.* 5. *oigo.* 6. *Sabes; Sé.* 7. *amo.* 8. *lleva; parece.* 9. *quieren; Necesitamos.* 10. *prefieres; Prefiero.* 11. *sé.* 12. *Está oyendo.*

Unit 58: Preterite regular verbs. ⟨58.1.⟩ 1. *se casaron.* 2. *comieron.* 3. *no salí; Me levanté; me lavé; desayuné; escribí.* 4. *vimos.* 5. *vivieron.* 6. *nació.* 7. *pasó; No sonó; llegamos.* 8. *conociste; conocí.* 9. *acabó; me acosté.* 10. *saliste.* 11. *cumplió.* 12. *vivimos.* ⟨58.2.⟩ 1. *conociste.* 2. *disteis.* 3. *viviste.* 4. *trabajaste.* 5. *hablaste.* 6. *comisteis.* 7. *pasasteis.* 8. *diste.* ⟨58.3.⟩ 1. *desayunó.* 2. *comieron.* 3. *me levanté.* 4. *trabajé.* 5. *comí.* 6. *se acostó.* 7. *vio.* 8. *compró.* ⟨58.4.⟩ 1. *(no) me levanté.* 2. *(no) vi.* 3. *(no) me acosté.* 4. *(no) leí.* 5. *(no) salí.* 6. *(no) comí.* 7. *(no) me lavé.* 8. *(no) di.* ⟨58.5.⟩ 1. *¿Dónde nació Sofía?* 2. *¿Dónde comieron ustedes ayer?.* 3. *¿Cuántos años cumplió Gao ayer?* 4. *¿Cuándo se casaron Rafa y Sole?* 5. *¿A qué hora acabó la fiesta?* 6. *¿Cuándo nació tu primer hijo?*

Unit 59. Preterite: irregular verbs. ⟨59.1.⟩ 1. *vino.* 2. *tuvieron.* 3. *vinieron.* 4. *tuvo.* 5. *estuvisteis; estuvimos.* 6. *fui; vine.* 7. *tuvo.* 8. *hicieron; Estuvimos.* 9. *tuvimos.* 10. *viniste; Estuve.* 11. *tuvo.* 12. *hizo.* 13. *estuvo.* 14. *hicimos.* 15. *fue.* 16. *hubo; Fue.* ⟨59.2.⟩ 1. *fue.* 2. *fue.* 3. *fueron.* 4. *hicieron.* 5. *fue.* 6. *fue.* 7. *fueron.* 8. *fueron.* ⟨59.3.⟩ 1. *hiciste; Fui; fuisteis; Fuimos; gustó; fue.* 2. *estuvieron; Estuvimos; Tuvimos; Hizo.* 3. *hicisteis; fuimos; vinieron; estuvimos; Fue.* ⟨59.4.⟩ 1. *¿Cuántos hijos tuvieron los padres de Ana?* 2. *¿Qué hizo Adolfo el domingo pasado?* 3. *¿Adónde fueron Juan y Rosa el verano pasado?* 4. *¿Cuándo vino Teresa?* 5. *¿Cómo fue la civilización maya?* 6. *¿Quién fue de la Cierva?*

Unit 60: Present perfect (1). ⟨60.1.⟩ 1. *Se ha levantado.* 2. *Ha hecho.* 3. *Se ha duchado.* 4. *Ha enviado.* 5. *Ha ido.* 6. *Ha jugado.* 7. *Ha cenado.* 8. *Se ha acostado.* ⟨60.2.⟩ 1. *hemos estado.* 2. *Has visto; he visto.* 3. *hemos trabajado.* 4. *ha llovido.*

5. *He empezado.* 6. *han estado.* 7. *habéis hecho.* 8. *Has leído.* 9. *hemos comido.* 10. *ha hecho; Se ha quedado.* 11. *se han levantado.* **60.3.** 1. *Se han escapado cincuenta presos.* 2. *Ha muerto el Presidente.* 3. *Ha dimitido la Ministra de Hacienda.* 4. *Ha acabado la huelga del transporte.* 5. *Han chocado dos trenes.* 6. *Ha subido la gasolina.* 7. *Han bajado los impuestos.* 8. *El Colo-Colo ha ganado la Liga.* **60.4.** 1. *no me he levantado / me he levantado.* 2. *no he escrito / he escrito.* 3. *no me he lavado / me ha lavado.* 4. *no me ido / he ido.* 5. *no he visto / he visto.* 6. *no he aprendido / he aprendido.*

Unit 61: Present perfect (2). **61.1.** 1. *Ha estado en Uruguay.* 2. *Ha escrito un libro.* 3. *Ha conocido a personajes famosos.* 4. *Ha vivido en Chile.* 5. *Ha trabajado en un hospital.* 6. *Ha tenido cinco hijos.* **61.2.** 1. *Reinaldo no ha estado nunca en África.* 2. *¿Han comido ustedes alguna vez tortilla?* 3. *¿Has tenido alguna vez un accidente?* 4. *¿Os habéis enamorado alguna vez?* 5. *No he ido nunca al teatro.* 6. *¿Ha trabajado alguna vez Rodolfo en su vida?* 7. *Mis padres nunca han comido comida peruana.* 8. *No hemos bebido nunca tequila.* **61.3.** 1. *Juana no ve bien porque ha perdido las gafas.* 2. *No puedo entrar en casa porque he perdido las llaves.* 3. *No puedo pagar porque me he olvidado la cartera.* 4. *Ana y Luisa están agotadas porque han trabajado mucho todo el día.* 5. *José no se siente bien porque ha comido demasiado.* **61.4.** 1. *¿Ha empezado ya la película?; todavía no ha empezado.* 2. *¿Ha llamado ya Rosa?; ya ha llamado.* 3. *¿Han llegado ya tus padres? todavía no han llegado.* 4. *¿Has empezado ya?; todavía no he empezado.* 5. *¿Habéis hablado ya?; ya hemos hablado.* 6. *¿Han cenado ya los niños?; ya han cenado.* **61.5.** 1. *He viajado en avión / No he viajado nunca en avión.* 2. *He estado en Argentina. / No he estado nunca en Argentina.* 3. *He comido tortilla de patatas / No he comido nunca tortilla de patatas.* 4. *He visto películas españolas / No he visto nunca películas españolas.* 5. *He visitado España / No he visitado España nunca.* 6. *He trabajado en una tienda / No he trabajado nunca en una tienda.* 7. *He escrito un libro / No he escrito nunca un libro.* 8. *He plantado un árbol / No he plantado nunca un árbol.*

Unit 62: Contrasting present perfect and preterite. **62.1.** 1. *Hemos estado.* 2. *he ido.* 3. *nació.* 4. *Estuvimos.* 5. *He llegado.* 6. *ha nevado.* 7. *Estuve.* 8. *Hemos visto.* 9. *vinieron.* 10. *hicimos.* **62.2.** 1. *ha tenido.* 2. *invitó.* 3. *han hecho. estuvimos; pasamos.* 4. *he ido.* 5. *hubo.* 6. *ha aprendido.* 7. *hiciste; estuve.* 8. *me he bañado.* **62.3.** 1. *Habéis estado, estuvimos.* 2. *Han montado.* 3. *Has comido; comí, estuve.* 4. *ha estudiado.* 5. *Has trabajado.* **62.4.** 1. *¿Habéis estado ya en Barcelona?; estuvimos el miércoles.* 2. *¿Habéis probado ya el cocido?; lo probamos el lunes.* 3. *¿Habéis visitado ya el Museo del Prado?; lo visitamos el martes por la mañana.* 4. *¿Habéis comprado ya los regalos?; todavía no los hemos comprado.* 5. *¿Habéis ido ya a Sevilla?; fuimos ayer.* 6. *Habéis visto ya una corrida de toros; No, todavía no hemos visto una corrida de toros.* **62.5.** 1. *ha terminado.* 2. *fuiste.* 3. *corrió.* 4. *Has visto; vi.* 5. *Ha llegado; ha llegado.* 6. *Han cerrado; cerraron.*

Unit 63: Imperfect. **63.1.** 1. *era; rezaba.* 2. *eran; llevaban; escuchaban.* 3. *vivíamos; trabajaba.* 4. *era; Se duchaba; se hacía; se preparaba; iba.* 5. *hacías; Estudiaba.* 6. *vivíamos; íbamos.* 7. *querías; Quería.* 8. *tenían.* 9. *hacían; Éramos.* 10. *vivía; Vivía.* 11. *iba.* 12. *gustaba.* **63.2.** 1. *hacían.* 2. *tenían.* 3. *vivían.* 4. *adoraban.* 5. *bebían.* 6. *criaban.* 7. *construían.* 8. *eran.* **63.3.** *Era; eran; tenían; estaba; Tenía; había; era; era; tenía; llevaba; tenía; querían; trabajaba; cultivaba; ayudaba; trabajaba; eran; Tenía; salía; jugábamos; nos bañábamos; nos divertíamos; había; bailábamos; gustaba; nos acostábamos; Eran.*

Unit 64: Contrasting preterite and imperfect. **64.1.** 1. *fui; Estaba.* 2. *Ibas; vivías.* 3. *estuvimos.* 4. *era; iba.* 5. *llegaste.* 6. *hicisteis.* 7. *tuvieron.* 8. *nació; murió.* 9. *vivía; oía.* 10. *empezó; acabó.* 11. *cayó.* 12. *tuvimos; tocó.* **64.2.** 1. *cumplió.* 2. *terminó.* 3. *estaba; estudiaba.* 4. *acabó.* 5. *conoció; se casaron.* 6. *salió.* 7. *trabajabas; vivías.* 8. *hablaba.* **64.3.** 1. *dimos.* 2. *dábamos.* 3. *jugaba.* 4. *hicisteis.* 5. *íbamos.* 6. *pasé.* **64.4.** 1. *conociste; conocí, vivía.* 2. *estuvimos; gustó; pasamos; fuimos.* 3. *hacía; vivía; Era; se vino; No tenía.* **64.5.** 1. *fue.* 2. *era.* 3. *fue.* 4. *eran.* 5. *fue.* 6. *Era.* 7. *Eran.* 8. *era.*

Unit 65: Future: regular verbs. **65.1.** 1. *Iré.* 2. *volveréis.* 3. *llamaré.* 4. *acabaremos.* 5. *arreglarán.* 6. *Iré.* 7. *devolverás.* 8. *se morirán.* 9. *aprobaré; Aprobarás.* 10. *Comeremos.* 11. *regalaré.* 12. *Iremos.* **65.2.** 1. *será; bajarán; nevará; subirán; seguirá; Lloverá; soplarán.* **65.3.** 1. *Recibirá; Será; se sentirá; gastará.* 2. *Se verá; ayudarán; será.* 3. *Viajará; conocerá; Mejorará.* 4. *Desaparecerán; Pasará; recibirá.* **65.4.** *Encontraremos; encontrarán; nos casaremos; Se casarán; serán; Seremos; será; Viajaremos; visitarán; vivirán.*

Unit 66: Future: irregular verbs. **66.1.** 1. *tendré.* 2. *haré.* 3. *vendrá* 4. *habrá; hará.* 5. *diré.* 6. *sabremos.* 7. *saldrá.* 8. *pondré.* 9. *dirán.* 10. *haré.* **66.2.** 1. *Los robots harán todos los trabajos físicos.* 2. *Podremos aprender con ordenadores en casa.* 3. *Sabremos curar el cáncer.* 4. *No habrá hambre.* 5. *Habrá ciudades satélite en el espacio.* 6. *Habrá menos enfermedades.* 7. *No habrá guerras.* 8. *Todo el mundo tendrá un ordenador.* 9. *Habrá coches voladores.* 10. *Podremos visitar la Luna.* **66.3.** 1. *tendrás.* 2. *hará; hará.* 3. *vendréis.* 4. *podrás; podré.* 5. *dirán; pondrán.* 6. *querrán.* **66.4.** 1. *(No) haré.* 2. *(No) Tendré.* 3. *(No) Sabré.* 4. *(No) Tendré.* 5. *(No) Podré.* 6. *(No) Haré.*

Unit 67: Present of *ir a* + infinitive. **67.1.** 1. *Van a jugar al tenis.* 2. *Van a bañarse.* 3. *Va a pescar.* 4. *Va a trabajar en el jardín.* 5. *Va a recoger la habitación.* **67.2.** 1. *voy a lavar.* 2. *Voy a comer.* 3. *Vamos a acostarnos.* 4. *Voy a beber.* 5. *Vamos a estudiar.* 6. *Voy a encender.* 7. *Voy a ver.* 8. *Voy a ducharme.* **67.3.** 1. *van a hacer; van a pasar; vamos a ir; van a alojarse; vamos a compartir.* 2. *vas a arreglar; Voy a ir; vas a regalar; voy a comprar.* 3. *vas a ver; Voy a salir; vais a ir; vamos a ver; Vais a cenar; vamos a ir.* **67.4.** 1. *Vamos a tener.* 2. *Va a empezar.* 3. *Va a aterrizar.* 4. *Vamos a perder.* 5. *Van a chocar.* 6. *Se van a casar.* 7. *Se van a escapar.* 8. *Se van a caer.*

Unit 68: Contrasting different ways of expressing the future. **68.1.** 1. *Va a salir.* 2. *se casa.* 3. *acaba.* 4. *vas a caer.* 5. *trabajo.* 6. *voy.* 7. *llega.* 8. *Va a salir.* **68.2.** 1. *vas a arreglar; arreglaré.* 2. *van a hacer.* 3. *Serán; tendrán.* 4. *va a morder.* 5. *llamaré.* 6. *va a llamar.* 7. *Encontraré; ganarás.* 8. *van a ir.* 9. *va a haber.* 10. *Vamos a perder.* **68.3.** 1. *Va a salir.* 2. *canta.* 3. *Va a caerse.* 4. *Va a empezar.* 5. *llega.* **68.4.** 1. *examino.* 2. *podremos.* 3. *viviré.* 4. *van.* 5. *hay* . 6. *regresa.* 7. *nos casaremos.* 8. *sale.* **68.5.** 1. *empiezan.* 2. *Van a cerrar.* 3. *vamos a trabajar.* 4. *es.* 5. *sale.* 6. *vas a hacer.* 7. *acaba.* 8. *vas a acabar.*

Unit 69: Affirmative imperative: regular verbs. **69.1.** 1. *Practique.* 2. *Descanse.* 3. *Coma.* 4. *Beba.* 5. *Ande.* **69.2.** 1. *Abre.* 2. *Cruzad.* 3. *Comed.* 4. *Habla.* 5. *Baja.* 6. *Llama.* 7. *Come.* 8. *pasen.* 9. *Crucen.* 10. *Paguen* **69.3.** 1. *Compre; pague.* 2. *Visite; Recorra; Descanse; Viva.* 3. *Coma; disfrute; Vea.* 4. *Estudia; aprende.* 5. *Envíe; Participe; gane.*

Unit 70: Negative imperative: regular verbs. `70.1.` 1. *No gire.* 2. *No gire.* 3. *No adelante.* 4. *No aparque.* 5. *No pare.* `70.2.` 1. *No veáis.* 2. *No dejes.* 3. *No comáis.* 4. *No toques.* 5. *No regreses.* 6. *No discutáis.* 7. *No comas.* 8. *No bebas.* `70.3.` 1. *No tires.* 2. *No escribáis. / No escriban.* 3. *No cojas.* 4. *No coman.* 5. *No lleguéis.* 6. *No cortéis.* 7. *No crucen.* 8. *No toques.* 9. *No llames.* 10. *No pise.* 11. *No veas.* 12. *No hables.* 13. *No gasten.* 14. *No uses. /No use.* 15. *No deje.*

Unit 71: Imperative: irregular verbs (1). `71.1.` 1. *empieza, no empieces; empiece, no empiece; empezad, no empecéis; empiecen, no empiecen.* 2. *defiende, no defiendas; defienda, no defienda; defended, no defendáis; defiendan, no defiendan.* 3. *consigue, no consigas; consiga, no consiga; conseguid, no consigáis; consigan, no consigan.* `71.2.` 1. *Cierra.* 2. *No riegues.* 3. *Cierra.* 4. *Fríe.* 5. *Enciende.* 6. *No enciendas.* `71.3.` 1. *Siga.* 2. *Cierra.* 3. *Sonrían.* 4. *No pidáis.* 5. *Despierta.* `71.4.` 1. *Empezad.* 2. *Elige.* 3. *Enciende.* 4. *No caliente.* 5. *Sonreíd.* 6. *Corregid/Corrijan.* 7. *Cierrra/Cierre.* 8. *Repite/Repita.* 9. *Fríe.* 10. *Siga.* 11. *No pidas.* 12. *No despiertes.* `71.5.` 1. *Despierte; empiece; Piense.* 2. *Elija.* 3. *Sonría; piense; Siga; despierte.*

Unit 72: Imperative: irregular verbs (2). `72.1.` 1. *recuerda, no recuerdes; recuerde, no recuerde; recordad, no recordéis; recuerden, no recuerden.* 2. *muerde, no muerdas; muerda, no muerda; morded, no mordáis; muerdan, no muerdan.* `72.2.` 1. *Vuelve.* 2. *Prueba.* 3. *No juguéis.* 4. *Cuelgue.* 5. *no muerdas.* `72.3.` 1. *Recuerda.* 2. *cuelgues.* 3. *Cuenta/Cuente.* 4. *juguéis.* 5. *Vuelve; Vuelva.* 6. *Devuélveme.* 7. *Prueba.* 8. *duermas/duerma.* 9. *Comprueba; Compruebe.* 10. *Tuesta.* 11. *contéis.* 12. *mováis/muevan.* 13. *Recordad/Recuerden.* 14. *vuelvas.* `72.4.` 1. *Vuele; Compruebe.* 2. *Duerma; sueñe.* 3. *Prueba; Vuelve; Apuesta.* 4. *Pruebe; Juegue; sueñe.*

Unit 73: Imperative: irregular verbs (3). `73.1.` 1. *diga.* 2. *Sed.* 3. *Pon.* 4. *No salgáis.* 5. *Haz.* 6. *Id.* 7. *Sed.* 8. *Vengan.* 9. *pongas.* 10. *digas.* `73.2.` 1. *No hagan.* 2. *No seas.* 3. *No hagan.* 4. *Ven.* 5. *Pon.* 6. *Venga.* 7. *Poned.* 8. *Salgan.* 9. *No tengas.* 10. *Di.* `73.3.` 1. *Tenga.* 2. *No salgáis.* 3. *Poned.* 4. *No salgas.* 5. *Pon.* 6. *Di.* 7. *no digas.* 8. *Sé; haz.* 9. *Tened.* 10. *no vayas.* 11. *Haga.* 12. *No seas.* 13. *No pongáis.* 14. *Ven.* 15. *Sed.*

Unit 74: Imperative of verbs with se. `74.1.` 1. *Pónganse.* 2. *Abróchense.* 3. *No te rías.* 4. *Siéntese.* 5. *Levantaos.* 6. *No te subas.* 7. *Vístase.* 8. *Bajaos.* 9. *Súbete.* 10. *¡No te duermas!* `74.2.` 1. *No te quites.* 2. *Ponte.* 3. *Despedíos.* 4. *No se vaya.* 5. *Vete.* 6. *Quítese.* 7. *Átate.* 8. *cómete.* 9. *Duchaos.* 10. *siéntate; estate.* 11. *No se olvide.* 12. *lavaos.* `74.3.` 1. *Péinate.* 2. *Mírate.* 3. *No os vayáis.* 4. *No se bañen.* 5. *Aféitate.* 6. *No te caigas.* 7. *Despertaos.* 8. *Vete.* 9. *No se siente.* 10. *Callaos/Cállense.* 11. *No te muevas.* 12. *No se preocupe.* 13. *Ponte.* 14. *Cállense.* 15. *No te pongas.*

Unit 75: Imperative with object pronouns. `75.1.` 1. *Ámalos.* 2. *Compradlo.* 3. *No la cojas.* 4. *Mírala.* 5. *No los mires.* 6. *Llámalo.* 7. *Pregúntale.* 8. *Véndala.* 9. *No la comáis.* 10. *No las miren.* 11. *Pásala.* 12. *Cómprenlo.* `75.2.` 1. *hazla; no la hagas.* 2. *apágala; no la apagues.* 3. *no abridlos; no los abráis.* 4. *despiértalo; no lo despiertes.* 5. *fríelas; no las frías.* 6. *ponlo; no lo pongas.* 7. *págala; no la pagues.* 8. *llámalo; no lo llames.* `75.3.` 1. *Enséñales la casa.* 2. *No les digáis nada a los niños.* 3. *No le presten el coche a Luis.* 4. *Pregúntale a Alfredo.* 5. *Dales los regalos a Rosa y Ana.* 6. *No nos pregunte nada* 7. *Ayúdeme.* 8. *Pásame la sal.* 9. *Enséñadnos los cuadernos.* 10. *No le prestes dinero a Elsa.* `75.4.` *pele; córtelas; Eche; fríalas; Corte; fríala; bata; mezclelos; Ponga; fríala; Dele; póngala.* `75.5.` 1. *Apágala.* 2. *Envíelas.* 3. *Súbela.* 4. *Ayúdanos.* 5. *no le preguntes.* 6. *hazme; Cómprame.*

Unit 76: Infinitive. `76.1.` 1. *Mentir puede ser dañino.* 2. *Vivir es una lucha.* 3. *Viajar en avión es cansado.* 4. *Necesitamos divertirnos.* 5. *Beber trae problemas.* 6. *Me gusta bailar.* 7. *A veces es necesario cambiar.* 8. *Nos encanta jugar.* `76.2.` 1. *Estudiar.* 2. *Descansar.* 3. *Hacer.* 4. *Escuchar.* 5. *Cambiar.* `76.3.` 1. *He conseguido hablar con Raquel.* 2. *Odio trabajar los sábados.* 3. *Me gusta conducir deprisa.* 4. *Prefiero no decir nada.* 5. *Me encanta comer verdura.* 6. *No puedo comer carne de cerdo.* 7. *Necesito beber mucha agua.* 8. *Espero no molestar.* 9. *No quiero trabajar de noche.* 10. *Odio levantarme pronto.* `76.4.` 1. *a estudiar.* 2. *tomar.* 3. *a cenar.* 4. *a pagar.* 5. *venir.* 6. *reservar.* 7. *con ser.* 8. *a nadar.* 9. *hablar.* 10. *a pescar.* 11. *de traer.* 12. *a hacer.*

Unit 77: Expressions with infinitive (1). `77.1.` 1. *Voy a apagar.* 2. *van a alquilar.* 3. *Voy a comer.* 4. *vas a hacer.* 5. *Vas a caerte.* 6. *va a cenar.* 7. *Vas a coger.* 8. *Van a llegar.* `77.2.` 1. *Tengo que.* 2. *Tenéis que.* 3. *no tengo que.* 4. *tengo que.* 5. *tiene que.* 6. *No tienes que.* 7. *tenía que.* 8. *Tienes que.* 9. *no tuve que.* 10. *tengo que.* `77.3.` 1. *hay que.* 2. *habrá que.* 3. *hubo que.* 4. *había que.* 5. *Hay que.* `77.4.` 1. *Tengo que echar gasolina al coche.* 2. *Para ir a la universidad hay que coger el autobús 53.* 3. *Cuando éramos pequeños, no había que molestar a los adultos.* 4. *No tengo que llevar corbata en la oficina.* 5. *Para viajar a algunos países hay que vacunarse contra la fiebre amarilla.* 6. *Si hay un incendio hay que llamar a los bomberos.* 7. *Raquel tiene que irse. Es muy tarde.* 8. *No tienes que sacar al perro de noche.* `77.5.` 1. *No se puede hacer.* 2. *Puedo irme.* 3. *No se puede aparcar.* 4. *puedes llevar.* 5. *se puede.* 6. *No puedo salir.* 7. *puedo llevar.* 8. *no puede hablar.*

Unit 78: Expressions with infinitive (2). `78.1.` 1. *suele levantarse / se suele levantar.* 2. *Suele ducharse / Se suele duchar.* 3. *Suele desayunar.* 4. *Suele llegar.* 5. *Suele empezar.* 6. *Suele tomar.* 7. *Suele salir.* 8. *Suele comprar.* `78.2.` 1. *solía madrugar.* 2. *Solía levantarse a las once.* 3. *Solía afeitarse / Se solía afeitar por las mañanas.* 4. *Solía desayunar en una cafetería.* 5. *Solía jugar un poco al tenis.* 6. *Solía comer en la piscina con amigos.* 7. *Solía echarse / Se solía echar una siesta.* 8. *Solía jugar a los bolos.* 9. *Solía tomar unas cervezas en un bar.* 10. *Solía estar en la discoteca hasta las tres.* 11. *Solía tomarse / Se solía tomar un vaso de leche.* 12. *Solía acostarse / Se solía acostar sobre las cuatro.* `78.3.` 1. *solía.* 2. *suele.* 3. *solía.* 4. *No solemos.* 5. *sueles.* 6. *solía.* 7. *Solíais.* 8. *No suelo.* `78.4.` 1. *Raquel suele ir a trabajar en el 115.* 2. *Solemos ir a la sierra los fines de semana.* 3. *Cuando vivíamos en Chile, solíamos dar un paseo después de cenar.* 4. *En casa de mis abuelos suelen comer paella los domingos.* 5. *Cuando era pequeña solía bañarme en el río de mi pueblo.* 6. *¿A qué hora sueles levantarte / te sueles levantar?* 7. *Suelo acostarme tarde los sábados.*

Unit 79: Expressions with infinitive (3). `79.1.` 1. *Marisa ha dejado de comer carne.* 2. *No dejes de escribirnos cuando estés en Perú.* 3. *Dejé de fumar hace seis meses.* 4. *Marta ha dejado de salir con Emilio.* 5. *No dejéis de sacar la basura por la noche.* 6. *No dejen de llamarme cuando vengan a Sevilla.* 7. *Ha dejado de hacer viento.* 8. *Rocío ha dejado de quererme.* 9. *He dejado de montar en bicicleta.* 10. *Mis padres han dejado de trabajar.* `79.2.` 1. *Acabo de ver a Ángel.* 2. *Acabábamos de comer cuando llegaron Susi y Toni.* 3. *Acabo de regresar de clase.* 4. *Se acababan de ir cuando empezó la clase.* 5. *Acaba* de ocurrir el accidente. 6. *Cuando llegamos al hospital, acababa de nacer Irene.* 7. *Acabo de recoger el correo.* 8. *Se acaba de estropear el ordenador.* 9. *Acaba de empezar el concierto.* 10. *Acaba de terminar el partido.* **79.3.** 1. *No tengo que volver a examinarme.* 2. *¡Por fin la televisión vuelve a funcionar!* 3. *No hemos vuelto a ver a Lucía desde el verano.* 4. *El año pasado volví a alquilar la casa de la playa.* 5. *Tenemos que volver a hacer el proyecto.* 6. *¿Cree que el coche se volverá a averiar?* 7. *Gonzalo ha vuelto a suspender el examen de conducir.* 8. *¿Han vuelto a tener carta de Guillermo?* 9. *Ayer volvimos a perder.* 10. *He vuelto a leer Cien años de soledad.* **79.4.** 1. *Ha vuelto a averiarse el ordenador. / Se ha vuelto a averiar el ordenador.* 2. *Acabo de ducharme. / Me acabo de duchar.* 3. *Han dejado de pagarnos. / Nos han dejado de pagar.* 4. *No vuelvas a caerte. / No te vuelvas a caer.* 5. *¿Cuándo vas a acabar de pintarlo? / ¿Cuándo lo vas a acabar de pintar?* 6. *No dejes de escribirme. / No me dejes de escribir.* 7. *Acaban de despedirlos. / Los acaban de despedir.* 8. *No ha vuelto a llamarnos. / No nos ha vuelto a llamar.*

Unit 80: Gerund. **80.1.** 1. *bebiendo.* 2. *creyendo.* 3. *repitiendo.* 4. *pidiendo.* 5. *vistiendo.* 6. *escribiendo.* 7. *pudiendo.* 8. *diciendo.* 9. *estudiando.* **80.2.** 1. *esquiando.* 2. *bañándose.* 3. *comiendo.* 4. *durmiendo.* 5. *haciendo.* **80.3.** 1. *estáis haciendo; Estamos cocinando.* 2. *estás haciendo; Estoy esperando.* 3. *está tocando.* 4. *está lloviendo; Está lloviendo.* 5. *estás comiendo; Estoy comiendo.* 6. *están hablando; Están hablando.* 7. *se está duchando.* 8. *está oyendo Lucas; Está oyendo.* 9. *está diciendo.* 10. *se está muriendo.* **80.4.** 1. *Hay; leyendo un libro.* 2. *Hay; montando en bici.* 3. *Hay; jugando al fútbol.* 4. *Hay; leyendo el periódico.* 5. *Hay; escuchando música.* 6. *Hay; tocando la guitarra.* 7. *Hay; corriendo por el césped.* 8. *Hay; vendiendo helados.*

Unit 81: Object pronouns with infinitive and gerund. **81.1.** 1. *comprarlo.* 2. *devolvérmelo.* 3. veros. 4. *dejárnoslo.* 5 tirarlos. 6 *preguntarte.* 7. *vendérselo.* 8. *escribirle.* 9. *ayudarnos.* 10. *decírselo.* **81.2.** 1. *Luis no me quiere ayudar.* 2. *Quiero enseñaros algo.* 3. *Me tenéis que ayudar.* 4. *Te lo voy a regalar.* 5. *Suelo ponérmelo en verano.* 6. *¿Puedes ayudarnos?* 7. *Puede vendéroslo barato.* 8. *Va a dejármela.* **81.3.** 1. *Está limpiándolas.* 2. *Estoy acabándola.* 3. *Están preguntándole.* 4. *Estamos lavándolas.* 5. *Están haciéndosela.* 6. *Están lavándoselo.* 7. *Están explicándomelo.* 8. *Están curándosela.* **81.4.** 1. *Las está limpiando.* 2. *La estoy acabando.* 3. *Le están preguntando.* 4. *Las estamos lavando.* 5. *Se la están haciendo.* 6. *Se lo están lavando.* 7. *Me lo están explicando.* 8. *Se la están curando.* **81.5.** 1. *Pásame la sal.* 2. *La directora quiere vernos.* 3. *Me he olvidado de comprarlo.* 4. *¿Puedes ayudarme?* 5. *Pregúntaselo a Julio.* 6. *¿Quién lo está haciendo?* 7. *Me gustaría decírselo a Sandra.* 8. *Pásame la pelota.*

Unit 82: Participle. **82.1.** 1. *dicho.* 2. *tenido.* 3. *abierto.* 4. *asado.* 5. *conocido.* 6. *casado.* 7. *caído.* 8. *escrito.* 9. *puesto.* 10. *vuelto.* 11. *muerto.* 12. *acabado.* **82.2.** 1. *acabado.* 2. *casada.* 3. *dicho.* 4. *puesto.* 5. *asado.* 6. *escrito.* 7. *abierta.* 8. *vuelto.* 9. *caídas.* 10. *tenido.* 11. *conocido.* 12. *muertas.* **82.3.** venido; alojados; nos; levantado; desayunado; ido; visto; dedicadas; tenido; gustado; pedido; asado; comprado. **82.4.** 1. *El ordenador está estropeado.* 2. *El tren está parado.* 3. *Los cristales están rotos.* 4. *La impresora está averiada.* 5. *El móvil está roto.* 6. *El sospechoso está detenido.* 7. *Las piscinas están cerradas.* **82.5.** 1. *pinchada.* 2. *aburridos.* 3. *abiertas.* 4. *rota.* 5. *averiado.* 6. *asustado.* 7. *muertos.* 8. *hechas.*

Unit 83: Direct and indirect objects. **83.1.** 1. *Conozco a Pedro desde niño.* 2. *Conozco Madrid desde niño.* 3. *Felipe quiere mucho a su perro.* 4. *Pide otra cerveza, por favor.* 5. *He visto Toledo muchas veces.* 6. *¿Has visto la nueva película de Almodóvar?* 7. *Ayer vi a Juan en la universidad.* 8. *Quiero mucho a mis hijos.* 9. *Hay una señora esperándote.* 10. *Tengo una duda. Necesito al profesor.* 11. *No toques a ese gato.* 12. *No toques ese enchufe.* **83.2.** 1. OD. 2. OD; OI. 3. OD. 4. OI; OD. 5. OD. 6. OD. 7. OI; OD. 8. OD; OI. 9. OD. 10. OD. **83.3.** 1. Ø. 2. Ø. 3. el; a. 4. Ø. 5. Ø; al. 6. Ø. 7. al. 8. a. **83.4.** 1. *Sus hermanos ayudan mucho a Amalia.* 2. *Pide a Juan la revista.* 3. *Le he dado la noticia a Julio.* 4. *Les han dado a mis padres las noticias.* 5. *Necesito un coche nuevo.* 6. *No des patadas a las piedras.* 7. *Di la verdad a la profesora.* 8. *¿A quién le has dado tu boli?* 9. *¿Por qué no quieres ayudar a Juan?* 10. *Preséntale a Ramón a Rocío.*

Unit 84: Adverbs of place. **84.1.** 1. *aquí.* 2. *Aquí.* 3. *Allí.* 4. *ahí.* 5. *allí.* 6. *ahí.* 7. *allí.* 8. *aquí.* **84.2.** 1. *fuera.* 2. *abajo.* 3. *encima.* 4. *enfrente.* 5. *alrededor.* 6. *delante.* 7. *debajo.* 8. *dentro.* **84.3.** 1. *viven mis padres.* 2. *vive cerca.* 3. *la mesa fuera.* 4. *trabaja Benito.* 5. *está lejos.* 6. *duermo abajo.* 7. *Delante se sienta Bárbara.* 8. *Allí está la cafetería.* 9. *Ahí abajo están las tazas.* 10. *Allí está Gabriel.*

Unit 85: Adverbs of time (1). **85.1.** 1. *Pasado mañana voy al médico.* 2. *Hoy he quedado con Eloísa.* 3. *Anteayer estuve en León.* 4. *Mañana vamos a hacer una merienda en el campo.* 5. *Anoche salimos a cenar con unos amigos.* 6. *Ayer recibí una postal de Miguel.* **85.2.** 1. *se marcha Emma.* 2. *no estará en la oficina mañana / no estará mañana en la oficina.* 3. *me llamó Olga.* 4. *llegan mis padres.* 5. *no está Concha.* 6. *y entonces empezó el espectáculo.* **85.3.** 1. *pronto.* 2. *temprano.* 3. *después.* 4. *entonces.* 5. *luego.* 6. *tarde.* 7. *pronto.* 8. *después.* **85.4.** 1. *pronto.* 2. *temprano.* 3. *entonces.* 4. *luego.* 5. *tarde; pronto.* 6. *temprano.* 7. *después.* 8. *entonces.*

Unit 86: Adverbs of time (2). **86.1.** 1. *ya no.* 2. *todavía.* 3. *Ya no.* 4. *Todavía.* 5. *ya no.* 6. *Todavía.* 7. *Ya no.* 8. *Todavía.* **86.2.** 1. *Todavía.* 2. *ya no.* 3. *todavía.* 4. *todavía.* 5. *ya no.* 6. *ya no.* 7. *ya no.* 8. *todavía.* 9. *todavía.* 10. *ya no.* **86.3.** 1. *todavía no.* 2. *Ya.* 3. *Todavía no.* 4. *ya.* 5. *ya; todavía no.* 6. *Todavía no.* 7. *ya; todavía no.* 8. *Ya.* 9. *Todavía no.* 10. *ya.* **86.4.** 1. *Ya ha acabado la reunión.* 2. *Todavía no ha acabado el partido.* 3. *Ya he visto la obra de García Lorca.* 4. *Todavía no ha llegado el jefe.* 5. *Ya he arreglado la impresora.* 6. *Ya han encontrado al gato.* 7. *Raúl todavía no ha encontrado trabajo.* 8. *Ya he hecho los ejercicios.* 9. *Todavía no ha acabado la película.* 10. *Ya ha acabado la partida.*

Unit 87: Adverbs and expressions of frequency. **87.1.** 1. *Casi nunca.* 2. *Normalmente.* 3. *siempre.* 4. *mucho / a menudo.* 5. *Nunca.* 6. *de vez en cuando.* 7. *mucho; casi nunca.* 8. *siempre.* 9. *mucho / a menudo / frecuentemente.* 10. *mucho; De vez en cuando.* **87.2.** 1. *No voy nunca al cine.* 2. *Nunca salgo por la noche.* 3. *Fernando casi nunca viaja en coche.* 4. *No vemos casi nunca la televisión.* 5. *Diana no me llama nunca.* 6. *Nunca me regalan nada.* **87.3.** 1. *todos los días.* 2. *cada dos días.* 3. *una vez a la semana / los lunes.* 4. *cada quince días.* 5. *un día al mes.* 6. *una vez al año.* **87.4.** 1. *Tenemos clases de español todos los martes.* 2. *Elena tiene que ir al médico dos veces al mes.* 3. *Pasamos unos días en Cancún todos los años.* 4. *Salimos a cenar con amigos una vez al mes.* 5. *Miguel llama a Carla tres veces por semana.* 6. *Voy al gimnasio una vez a la* semana. 7. *Martín se lava los dientes tres veces al día.* 8. *Todos los fines de semana hacemos algún viaje.*

Unit 88: Adverbs of quantity. 88.1. 1. *muy.* 2. *bastante.* 3. *nada.* 4. *poco.* 5. *nada.* 6. *demasiado.* 7. *muy.* 8. *bastante.* 9. *poco.* 10. *un poco.* 11. *bastante.* 88.2. 1. *demasiado.* 2. *muy/bastante.* 3. *un poco.* 4. *demasiado.* 5. *muy.* 88.3. 1. *mucho.* 2. *poco.* 3. *demasiado; nada.* 4. *poco.* 5. *bastante.* 6. *mucho.* 7. *mucho.* 8. *mucho.* 88.4. 1. *Ana es muy amable.* 2. *Jorge no es nada simpático.* 3. *Nati corre mucho.* 4. *Guillermo no trabaja nada.* 5. *Felipe sale poco.* 6. *Este restaurante es demasiado caro.* 7. *Rosana es poco trabajadora.* 8. *Víctor come demasiado.* 9. *No me gusta nada trabajar.* 10. *Lola conduce muy bien.* 88.5. 1. *Esta novela es muy buena.* 2. *Esther duerme mucho.* 3. *Mi casa está muy lejos.* 4. *Raúl prepara muy bien la carne.* 5. *Me parezco mucho a mi madre.* 6. *Hacer ejercicio es muy sano.* 7. *Raúl llega siempre muy tarde.* 8. *Eva gasta muy poco.* 9. *A Antonio le gusta mucho la música.* 10. *Sara anda mucho en vacaciones.*

Unit 89: Adverbs of manner. 89.1. 1. *elegantemente.* 2. *difícilmente.* 3. *astutamente.* 4. *fuertemente.* 5. *rápidamente.* 6. *extraordinariamente.* 7. *tranquilamente.* 8. *honradamente.* 9. *lentamente.* 10. *seriamente.* 89.2. 1. *deprisa.* 2. *atentamente.* 3. *mal.* 4. *alto.* 5. *despacio.* 6. *bajo.* 89.3. 1. *Hazlo tranquilamente, Norma.* 2. *Álvaro juega inteligentemente.* 3. *Agustín actúa irresponsablemente.* 4. *Ven rápidamente/rápido, Adela.* 5. *Fran me llama continuamente.* 6. *Escribe así, Luisa.* 7. *Susana canta maravillosamente.* 8. *Me golpeó fuerte/fuertemente.* 9. *Emilia nada extraordinariamente.* 10. *Mis hijos aprueban fácilmente.* 12. *Se ganan la vida honradamente.* 11. *La profesora de Matemáticas explica claro/claramente.* 12. *Se bajó del árbol hábilmente.* 89.4. 1. *buen.* 2. *exquisita.* 3. *gravemente.* 4. *egoístamente.* 5. *egoísta.* 6. *bien.* 7. *amablemente.* 8. *perfectamente.* 9. *grave.* 10. *mal.* 11. *malo.* 12. *amable.* 89.5. 1. *Tatiana conduce lenta y cuidadosamente.* 2. *Avelina trabaja tranquila pero seriamente.* 3. *Javier camina lenta y perezosamente.* 4. *La carta está escrita limpia y correctamente.*

Unit 90: Comparison adverbs. 90.1. 1. *más bajo.* 2. *tan rápido.* 3. *más despacio.* 4. *menos.* 5. *tanto.* 6. *tan temprano.* 7. *más fuerte.* 8. *mejor.* 9. *más tranquilamente.* 10. *tan tarde.* 90.2. 1. *Sofía vive más cerca del cine que nosotros.* 2. *Hoy hemos llegado menos tarde que de costumbre.* 3. *Susana corre tanto como Eloísa.* 4. *Julián cocina mejor que Vicente.* 5. *Arnaldo gasta más que Jesús.* 6. *Jorge se levanta tan temprano como yo.* 7. *Sara y Eva conducen tan bien como ustedes.* 8. *Hablo más que mi padre.* 9. *Alonso habla inglés peor que su hermana.* 10. *Héctor come menos que antes.* 90.3. 1. *mejor que.* 2. *mejor que.* 3. *más que.* 4. *tanto como.* 5. *más que.* 6. *más que.* 7. *tanto como.* 8. *más que.* 90.4. 1. *Héctor no corre tan rápido cómo tú.* 2. *Lucas no habla tanto como yo.* 3. *Sonia no se acuesta tan tarde como nosotros.* 4. *Silvia no explica tan claro como Laura.* 5. *Yo no camino tan lentamente como David.* 6. *Ernesto no juega tan inteligentemente como Carlos.* 7. *Jorge no ayuda en casa tanto como yo.* 8. *Carlos no come tanto como antes.*

Unit 91: Negative adverbs. 91.1. 1. *Adela no quiere ayudarnos.* 2. *¿Por qué no vienes mañana?* 3. *A Sara no le gusta vivir en Santiago.* 4. *No me ha llamado Andrea.* 5. *No me he duchado después del partido.* 6. *No nos gusta la música rock.* 7. *Esta mañana no he desayunado.* 8. *Prefiero no trabajar.* 9. *No hemos leído Martín Fierro.* 10. *Roberto no se acuesta tarde.* 11. *El viernes pasado no cenamos juntos.* 12. *No salgo a correr frecuentemente.* 13. *¿No quieren tomar algo?* 91.2. 1. *no conozco a nadie.* 2. *no ha llamado nadie.* 3. *No había nadie.* 4. *No me han dicho nada.* 5. *Nadie sabe.* 6. *No le pasa nada.* 7. *No quiero nada.* 8. *no sé nada.* 9. *no nos ha visto nadie.* 10. *nadie quiere ayudarme.* 91.3. 1. *Nadie me vio. / No me vio nadie.* 2. *No vi nada.* 3. *No pasa nada.* 4. *Nada se ha roto. / No se ha roto nada.* 5. *Nadie lo quiere. / No lo quiere nadie.* 6. *No he comprado nada.* 91.4. 1. *No bebo nunca alcohol.* 2. *Nunca salimos los lunes.* 3. *No he visto nunca un elefante.* 4. *Nunca desayuno antes de ducharme.* 5. *¿No has estado nunca en Potosí?* 6. *Sofía no nos invita nunca.* 7. *De pequeño, nunca comía pescado.* 8. *Nunca te olvidaré.* 9. *No voy nunca al fútbol.* 10. *No conduzco nunca de noche.* 11. *No viajo nunca solo.* 12. *Mi hermana nunca me llama por teléfono.*

Unit 92: Expressing agreement or disagreement. 92.1. 1. *también.* 2. *tampoco.* 3. *tampoco.* 4. *tampoco.* 5. *también.* 6. *también.* 7. *también.* 8. *tampoco.* 9. *también.* 10. *tampoco.* 92.2. 1. *no.* 2. *sí.* 3. *sí.* 4. *sí.* 5. *no.* 6. *sí.* 7. *sí.* 8. *sí.* 9. *no.* 10. *no.* 92.3. 1. *A mí no.* 2. *Charo también.* 3. *Yo tampoco.* 4. *Mi hermana también.* 5. *Nosotras tampoco.* 6. *Serafín sí.* 7. *Tú tampoco.* 8. *A Diana no.* 9. *Yo sí.* 10. *Nosotros no.* 92.4. 1. *sí; no.* 2. *no; tampoco.* 3. *sí; también.* 4. *no; sí.* 5. *no; tampoco; sí.* 6. *no; sí.*

Unit 93: Conjunctions. 93.1. 1. *Keiko habla inglés y español.* 2. *No hablo inglés ni alemán.* 3. *No me gustan la fruta ni las verduras.* 4. *A Juan y a Diana les gusta bailar.* 5. *Ni a Juan ni a Diana les gusta el fútbol.* 6. *Héctor estudia idiomas e informática.* 7. *Luisa trabaja en la universidad y en una academia.* 8. *Luis no tiene coche ni sabe conducir.* 9. *Ni mi hermano ni mi hermana quieren salir.* 10. *No me gusta la carne ni el pescado.* 11. *A Luisa y a Andrea les gusta Ángel.* 12. *Ni Diana ni Rocío hablan alemán.* 93.2. 1. *o.* 2. *y.* 3. *u.* 4. *y.* 5. *u.* 6. *e.* 7. *o; y.* 8. *e.* 9. *o.* 10. *u.* 93.3. 1. *Felipe es alto, pero no juega bien al baloncesto.* 2. *Ese televisor es muy caro pero (es) muy bueno.* 3. *Gana poco dinero, pero no necesita más.* 4. *Juan es rico, pero trabaja mucho.* 5. *Salva juega bien al baloncesto, pero corre poco.* 6. *El pueblo es bonito, pero está muy lejos.* 7. *Ángela es inteligente, pero (es) muy vaga.* 8. *Puedo estudiar más, pero no quiero.* 93.4. 1. *Raquel e Irene son españolas.* 2. *Raquel juega al baloncesto, pero no es muy alta.* 3. *Pedro no es muy guapo, pero es muy simpático.* 4. *A Pedro le gusta Raquel, pero a Raquel no le gusta Pedro.* 5. *Ni Raquel, ni Pedro ni Irene trabajan.* 6. *A Raquel, a Irene y a Pedro les gusta la música clásica.*

Unit 94: Prepositions (1). 94.1. 1. *Despiértame a las siete.* 2. *Los domingos sólo trabajo por la mañana.* 3. *Mi cumpleaños es el 31 de octubre.* 4. *Natalia nació en el año 1987.* 5. *Podemos quedar a mediodía para tomar algo.* 6. *Lo siento. No puedo salir en este momento.* 7. *Ana no puede estudiar de noche. Se duerme.* 8. *A veces vamos a esquiar en invierno a los Pirineos.* 9. *Llegaron a las dos de la tarde, cuando estábamos comiendo.* 10. *Solo puedo ir a la playa en vacaciones de verano.* 11. *Raquel regresó ayer de madrugada.* 12. *Siempre voy a España en Navidades a ver a mi familia.* 94.2. 1. *de/desde; a/hasta.* 2. *hasta.* 3. *desde.* 4. *de; a.* 5. *dentro de.* 6. *hasta.* 7. *hasta.* 8. *desde.* 9. *Dentro de.* 10. *de/desde.* 11. *Hasta.* 12. *de.* 94.3. 1. *Darío estuvo con nosotros desde el principio hasta el fin del verano.* 2. *Emilia vivió en Honduras de 1999 a 2002 / Emilia vivió en Honduras desde 1999 hasta 2002.* 3. *Eva y Mario se casan dentro de tres meses.* 4. *Trabajo en esta oficina desde el mes pasado.* 5. *Voy a un gimnasio de siete a nueve.* 6. *Me voy. Ya no nos vemos hasta la semana que* viene. 7. *durante la clase.* 8. *Los domingos trabajamos de diez a dos.* 94.4. 1. *durante la clase.* 2. *después de la caminata por la sierra.* 3. *antes de la entrevista.* 4. *después de la ducha.* 5. *durante los conciertos.* 6. *antes del viernes.*

Unit 95: Prepositions (2). 95.1. 1. *de.* 2. *a.* 3. *a.* 4. *de.* 5. *hacia.* 6. *Del; a.* 7. *a.* 8. *Hasta; Hasta.* 9. *de.* 10. *hasta.* 95.2. 1. *a.* 2. *hasta.* 3. *hasta/al.* 4. *hacia/al.* 5. *De/Desde; a/hasta.* 6. *hacia.* 7. *De/Desde; a/hasta.* 8. *hasta.* 9. *a.* 10. *De; de.* 11. *desde.* 12. *al.* 13. *al.* 14. *al.* 95.3. 1. *sobre.* 2. *entre.* 3. *en.* 4. *En.* 5. *a.* 6. *sobre.* 7. *entre.* 8. *en.*

Unit 96: Prepositions (3). 96.1. 1. *junto al cine.* 2. *alrededor del museo.* 3. *debajo de la cama.* 4. *detrás del colegio.* 5. *frente al hospital.* 6. *lejos de la Tierra.* 7. *dentro de la botella.* 8. *fuera de la nevera.* 9. *delante de la tienda.* 10. *encima de la mesa.* 96.2. 1. *lejos de.* 2. *delante de.* 3. *junto a.* 96.3. 1. *Hay un bar frente al cine.* 2. *Los cables van debajo del suelo.* 3. *Hay una estación de metro cerca de mi casa.* 4. *Alfonso se sienta junto a mí.* 5. *No pongas nada encima del televisor.* 6. *Te espero frente al hotel.* 4. *cerca de.* 5. *dentro de.* 6. *debajo de.* 7. *encima de.* 8. *enfrente de.* 9. *detrás de.* 10. *alrededor de.* 11. *fuera de.* 12. *frente a.*

Unit 97: Prepositions (4). 97.1. 1. *No he oído a los niños todavía.* 2. *Todavía no he oído esa canción.* 3. *¿A qué hora has llamado a Enrique?* 4. *Quiero mucho a mis padres.* 5. *Begoña está regalando sus gatitos.* 6. *¿Has visto a alguien de nuestro grupo?* 7. *Tengo que saludar a Bárbara.* 8. *¿Hay alguien en el aula?* 9. *En mi oficina necesitan una secretaria.* 10. *Le compré un regalo a Fidel.* 97.2. 1. *de sol.* 2. *de oro.* 3. *de baño.* 4. *de fútbol.* 5. *de chocolate.* 6. *de pana.* 7. *de leche.* 8. *de queso.* 9. *de atún.* 10. *de fútbol.* 97.3. 1. *a.* 2. *de.* 3. *de.* 4. *a.* 5. *de.* 6. *de.* 7. *a.* 8. *a.* 9. *a.* 10. *sobre.* 11. *en.* 12. *en.* 97.4. 1. *de trabajo.* 2. *a caballo.* 3. *a lápiz.* 4. *en metro.* 5. *de español.* 6. *del pelo largo.* 7. *sobre las diez.* 8. *en portugués.*

Unit 98: Prepositions (5). 98.1. 1. *por.* 2. *para.* 3. *por.* 4. *Para.* 5. *por.* 6. *por.* 7. *por.* 8. *para.* 98.2. 1. *Quiero un café con leche.* 2. *No os podéis ir sin permiso.* 3. *¿Te gustan las patatas con carne?* 4. *No puedes cortar eso sin tijeras.* 5. *No veo ese cartel sin gafas.* 6. *Mañana hay una manifestación contra la pena de muerte.* 7. *No podemos pintar el techo sin escalera.* 8. *Es pesado conducir con lluvia.* 98.3. 1. *con.* 2. *sin.* 3. *para.* 4. *para.* 5. *con.* 6. *por.* 7. *con.* 8. *contra.* 9. *sin.* 10. *por.* 98.4. 1. *por correo.* 2. *sin diccionario.* 3. *para la habitación.* 4. *por el puente.* 5. *con un martillo.* 6. *por avión.* 7. *con los ojos.* 8. *sin abrigo.* 9. *contra el sida.* 10. *sin dinero.*

Unit 99: Verbs with prepositions. 99.1. 1. *Valentín se dedica a exportar fruta.* 2. *Sara no cree en la existencia de extraterrestres.* 3. *Siempre hemos soñado con visitar la isla de Pascua.* 4. *Arturo se parece a su madre.* 5. *Alba se ha enamorado de su profesor.* 6. *¿Puedes ayudarme a llevar estas cajas?* 7. *Con Pablo te mueres de risa.* 8. *Confío en mis amigos.* 99.2. 1. *en.* 2. *de.* 3. *a.* 4. *con.* 5. *a.* 6. *de.* 7. *a.* 8. *en.* 9. *de.* 10. *a.* 99.3. 1. *a cenar.* 2. *a dibujar.* 3. *con ganar para vivir.* 4. *con un italiano.* 5. *a levantarme temprano.* 6. *de la vida.* 7. *con encontrar un buen empleo.* 8. *a hacer yoga.* 9. *de su pasado.* 10. *de cáncer.* 99.4. 1. *ti.* 2. *él.* 3. *conmigo.* 4. *nosotros.* 5. *mí.* 6. *contigo.* 7. *en ti.* 8. *conmigo.*

Unit 100: Subordinate clauses with *que*. 100.1. 1. *Creo que no son peruanos.* 2. *No digas que estamos aquí.* 3. *Saben que somos hermanas.* 4. *Pensaba que era muy tarde.* 5. *Veo que tienes coche nuevo.* 6. *Dicen que son novios.* 7. *Sabemos que Rafa cocina bien.* 8. *Recuerda que son los jefes.* 9. *Creo que sé la verdad.* 10. *Parece que están cansados.* 100.2. 1. *que.* 2. *de que.* 3. *que.* 4. *que.* 5. *de que.* 6. *en que.* 7. *de que.* 8. *que.* 100.3. 1. *de que.* 2. *de que.* 3. *de que.* 4. *en que.* 5. *de que.* 6. *de que.* 7. *de que.* 8. *en que.* 9. *de que.* 100.4. 1. *Sé que no vais a venir.* 2. *Estoy seguro de que no van a llamarnos.* 3. *Creo que son extranjeros.* 4. *Te acuerdas de que mañana es mi cumpleaños.* 5. *Parece que va a nevar.* 6. *Pensaba que no tenías hambre.* 7. *Estamos convencidos de que vais a ganar.* 8. *Insisto en que no tienes razón.* 9. *Oigo que hacen mucho ruido.* 10. *No me acordé de que los bancos están cerrados.* 11. *Se olvidó de que tenía la comida en la nevera.* 12. *Parece que tienen buena relación.*

Unit 101: Conditional clauses. 101.1. 1. *Si no vienes a clase.* 2. *Si hace buen tiempo.* 3. *Si tienen sed.* 4. *Si encontramos piso.* 5. *Si estás aburrida.* 6. *Si no puedo conducir.* 7. *Si te encuentras mal.* 8. *si tienes que esperar.* 101.2. 1. *descansad.* 2. *nos casamos.* 3. *se morirán.* 4. *tendremos que andar.* 5. *no me siento bien.* 6. *se enfadarán.* 7. *No te preocupes.* 8. *dará calambre.* 101.3. 1. *Si Ríos gana el partido, pasará a la final.* 2. *Si no hace buen tiempo, se quedarán en casa.* 3. *Si no corres, perderás el autobús.* 4. *Si os portáis bien, os compro/compraré un helado.* 5. *Si no está Alberto, volveremos más tarde.* 6. *Si se comen esa fruta, se pondrán malos.* 7. *Si te enfadas, me voy.* 8. *Si quieres ir al concierto, puedes comprar las entradas por Internet.* 101.4. 1. *ves; dile; diré; veo.* 2. *ganamos; pasaremos; ganaremos; juega; no se recupera; podrá.*

Unit 102. Time clauses. 102.1. 1. *Podemos ir a la bolera después de cenar.* 2. *Apaga la tele antes de acostarte.* 3. *Cenaré después de ducharme.* 4. *Vicente llamará antes de venir a comer; Vicente vendrá a comer después de llamar.* 5. *Pagaremos después de tomar café.* 6. *Acabaré estos ejercicios antes de ir a la bolera.* 7. *Quiero hablar con Ana antes de irme.* 8. *No te vayas antes de tomar algo.* 102.2. 1. *Cuando llego a casa, me ducho.* 2. *Cuando salimos con Jorge nos divertimos mucho.* 3. *Alicia se pone triste cuando llueve.* 4. *Cuando llegó Juan empezamos la partida.* 5. *El perro se asusta cuando hay tormenta.* 6. *Siempre me ducho cuando me levanto.* 7. *Cuando juego al parchís, me aburro.* 8. *Cuando vamos al centro, cogemos el Metro.* 102.3. 1. *era.* 2. *nací.* 3. *tiene.* 4. *llega.* 5. *salimos.* 6. *comí.* 7. *trabajaba.* 8. *estuvimos.* 102.4. 1. *hasta que llegó Rubén.* 2. *desde que éramos jóvenes.* 3. *desde que como más.* 4. *cuando era joven.* 5. *cuando llueve.* 6. *cuando acabó la película.* 7. *hasta que llamó Rosa.* 8. *cuando acabó la carrera.* 9. *desde que vivo en España.* 10. *hasta que acabó los ejercicios.* 102.5. 1. *cenar, iremos a dar un paseo.* 2. *me duele la cabeza, me tomo una aspirina.* 3. *no vino Julián no empezamos a cenar.* 4. *Antes de irme a la cama, tengo que acabar este trabajo.* 5. *Desde que Fidel está a dieta, está más delgado.* 6. *Antes de hablar, piensa en lo que vas a decir.*

Unit 103. Purpose clauses. 103.1. 1. *Coge un paraguas para no mojarte.* 2. *Coge un taxi para llegar a tiempo.* 3. *Pon la radio para oír las noticias.* 4. *Daos prisa para no llegar tarde.* 5. *Abrígate para no coger un catarro.* 6. *Reservad las entradas para ver el concierto.* 7. *Salgan de noche para no pasar calor.* 8. *Tengo que ahorrar para comprarme la moto.* 103.2. 1. *Para alisar.* 2. *Para orientarse.* 3. *Para sacar.* 4. *Para poner.* 5. *Para apretar.* 6. *Para freír.* 7. *Para calentar.* 8. *Para proyectar.* 9. *Para medir.* 10. *Para asegurar.* 103.3. 1. *a/para ver.* 2. *a/para ver.* 3. *para no despertar.* 4. *a/para ver.* 5. *para salir.* 6. *para alquilar.* 7. *a/para tomar.* 8. *para hacer.* 9. *a/para pedir.* 103.4. 1. *A/Para hacerse.* 2. *A/Para reservar.* 3. *A/Para comprar.* 4.

A/Para hacer. 5. *A/Para comprar.* 6. *A/para enviar.* 7. *A/Para tomar.* 8. *A/Para dar.* 9. *A/Para ver.* 10. *A/Para recibir.*

Unit 104. Reason and result clauses. 104.1. 1. *No se oye nada porque hay mucho ruido.* 2. *Menchu no salió porque estaba lloviendo.* 3. *Llegaron tarde por el accidente.* 4. *No salieron por el frío.* 5. *Félix está cansado porque trabaja mucho.* 6. *Han parado el partido por la lluvia.* 7. *Nicolás está nervioso por el examen.* 8. *Andrés no llamó porque estaba ocupado.* 9. *Se divorciaron porque no se querían.* 10. *No fueron de vacaciones porque no tenían dinero.* 104.2. 1. *Es que estoy cansado.* 2. *Es que no tengo mucha hambre.* 3. *Es que tengo que estudiar.* 4. *Es que tenía el móvil sin batería.* 5. *Es que está enfadada.* 6. *Es que tiene exámenes.* 7. *Es que está con gripe.* 8. *Es que he cogido un taxi.* 104.3. 1. *No sonó el despertador, por eso me levanté tarde.* 2. *Vienen mis abuelos, por eso no me voy de viaje.* 3. *Hoy hay mucha gente, por eso no voy de compras.* 4. *Estábamos aburridos, por eso nos fuimos a dar una vuelta.* 5. *Era mi cumpleaños, por eso los invité a cenar.* 6. *No me funcionaba el móvil, por eso no puede llamarte.* 7. *La puerta de la jaula estaba abierta, por eso se escaparon los pájaros.* 104.4. 1. *porque.* 2. *por.* 3. *por eso.* 4. *por eso.* 5. *por.* 6. *por.* 7. *porque.* 8. *porque.* 104.5. 1. *Me dolía la cabeza, por eso fui al médico.* 2. *Raquel está muy débil por la enfermedad.* 3. *Santiago no estudia porque no tiene tiempo.* 4. *Es muy tarde, por eso las tiendas están cerradas.* 5. *Me tomé una aspirina porque me dolía la cabeza.* 6. *Llegaron tarde porque había mucho tráfico.* 7. *Ana no sale de noche por sus padres.* 8. *Rocío no me invitó a la fiesta, por eso no fui.*

Unit 105: Impersonal clauses. 105.1. 1. *Es fácil equivocarse.* 2. *Es importante no equivocarse.* 3. *Es mejor ser abiertos.* 4. *Es útil saber cocinar.* 5. *Es bueno hacer ejercicio.* 6. *Es malo ser egoísta.* 7. *Es difícil estudiar con tanto ruido.* 8. *Es imposible salir con este tiempo.* 105.2. 1. *Conducir (no) es fácil.* 2. *Nadar (no) es sano.* 3. *Comer poco (no) es bueno.* 4. *Beber mucho agua (no) es bueno.* 5. *Hablar una lengua extranjera bien (no) es imposible.* 6. *Conocer otras culturas (no) es importante.* 105.3. 1. *Hay que saber idiomas.* 2. *Hay que tener un visado para viajar a Egipto.* 3. *Hay que saber conducir.* 4. *Para aprender un idioma extranjero hay que practicarlo.* 5. *Para conducir un coche en España hay que tener 18 años.* 105.4. 1. *llueve / está lloviendo.* 2. *nieva / está nevando.* 3. *llueve / está lloviendo.* 4. *hace viento.* 5. *hace.* 6. *hay.* 7. *hay.* 8. *hay.* 9. *hace.* 10. *hace.* 105.5. 1. *hizo.* 2. *era.* 3. *Hay.* 4. *Es.* 5. *anochece.* 6. *Hace.* 7. *Es; hay; amanece.* 8. *ha nevado.*

Unit 106: Accent marks (tilde). 106.1. 1. *balón.* 2. *cabeza.* 3. *Sánchez.* 4. *Madrid.* 5. *Ecuador.* 6. *Perú.* 7. *Guatemala.* 8. *enero.* 9. *cama.* 10. *mexicano.* 11. *octubre.* 12. *lloro.* 13. *lloró.* 14. *cárcel.* 15. *azul.* 16. *querer.* 17. *capitán.* 18. *balones.* 19. *Chile.* 20. *comes.* 21. *hospital.* 22. *España.* 23. *argentino.* 24. *portugués.* 25. *viven.* 106.2. 1. *melón.* 2. *francés.* 3. *alemana.* 4. *marroquí.* 5. *amarillo.* 6. *casa.* 7. *Pepe.* 8. *González.* 9. *Panamá.* 10. *África.* 11. *alemán.* 12. *melones.* 13. *lápiz.* 14. *lápices.* 15. *actriz.* 16. *útil.* 17. *árboles.* 18. *Bogotá.* 19. *pájaro.* 20. *Brasil.* 21. *vivís.* 22. *comí.* 23. *vivo.* 24. *América.* 25. *estás.* 106.3. 1. *sé.* 2. *mí.* 3. *Tú.* 4. *Qué.* 5. *Sí.* 6. *mi.* 7. *te.* 8. *él.* 9. *tu.* 10. *se.* 106.4. 1. *No sé nadar.* 2. *Felipe se ducha por las mañanas.* 3. *¿A qué hora te levantas?* 4. *A mí no me gusta el té.* 5. *Es el coche de mi padre.* 6. *¿Te gusta el zumo de piña?* 7. *¡Qué alto es Ángel!* 8. *Si te gusta mi reloj, te lo regalo.* 9. *¿Se acuerda de mí?* 10. *Es la chica que vive con Marisa.*

Unit 107: Use of capital letters. 107.1. 1. *Mi padre nació en Holanda.* 2. *Ayer fue dos de enero. Fue el cumpleaños de Manuel.* 3. *Hay una exposición sobre los incas en el Museo de América. La ha inaugurado el rey Juan Carlos.* 4. *El martes estuve en la Fundación San Carlos con el señor Arroyo.* 5. *La ciudad de las columnas es un libro de Alejo Carpentier sobre La Habana.* 6. *¿Quién pintó La maja desnuda?* 7. *Muchas ONG colaboran con la ONU en países del Tercer Mundo.* 8. *¡Qué impresionantes son las cataratas de Iguazú!* 107.2. 1. *Gerardo nació el 23 de enero.* 2. *Queremos ir a China en diciembre.* 3. *¿Has leído El siglo de las luces?* 4. *Don Julio Llopis vivió muchos años en La Paz.* 5. *¿Cuándo fue la Guerra de la Independencia?* 6. *La reina Sofía es griega.* 107.3. *Querida hermana: Llevo una semana en Buenos Aires. Estoy alojado en el hotel Sur, en la avenida Rivadavia, muy cerca del centro. Me gusta mucho la ciudad. Ayer visité la Casa Rosada, donde vive el presidente del país. Esta noche voy a ir a escuchar tangos al famoso barrio de La Boca. El domingo próximo salgo para Chile. ¿Cuándo llegas tú? Besos.* 107.4. 1. *Instituto Nacional del Libro Español (INLE).* 2. *Fondo Monetario Internacional (FMI).* 3. *Objeto Volador No Identificado (OVNI).* 4. *Comité Olímpico Internacional (COI).* 5. *Síndrome de Inmunodeficiencia Adquirida (SIDA).* 6. *Organización de las Naciones Unidas (ONU).* 7. *Organización de los Estados Americanos (OEA).* 8. *Ácido desoxirribonucleico (ADN).*

Glossary

SPANISH	ENGLISH
a bajo	downstairs
abogado	lawyer
abrigo	overcoat
abril	April
abrir (v)	open (v)
abrocharse (v)	fasten up (v)
abuela	grandmother
abuelo	grandfather
abuelos	grandparents
aburrido	bored, boring
aburrimiento	boredom
aburrir (v)	bore (v)
acabar (v)	finish (v)
academia	academy
accidente	accident
acción (película de)	action (film)
aceite	oil
aceptar (v)	accept (v)
acompañar (v)	accompany (v)
acostar/acostarse (v)	put to bed/go to bed (v)
acostumbrarse (v)	get used to (v)
actor	actor
actriz	actress
(de) acuerdo	all right
adelantar (v)	overtake (v), move forward (v)
además	furthermore
ADN (ácido desoxirribonucleico)	DNA (Deoxyribonucleic Acid)
adobe	adobe
adónde	where... (to)
adorar (v)	adore (v), worship (v)
afeitado	shave
afeitar/afeitarse	shave / have a shave (v)
afueras (las)	outskirts
agencia	agency
agosto	August
agotado (cansado)	exhausted
agricultor	farmer
agua	water
águila	eagle
ahí	there
ahora	now
ahorro	saving
ajedrez	chess
ala	wing
alarma	alarm
alborotado	excited
alcohol	alcohol
alegre	happy
alemán (nacionalidad)	German (nationality)
alemán (idioma)	German (language)
Alemania	Germany
alfabeto	alphabet
alfombra	rug
algo	something
algodón	cotton wool, cotton
alguien	someone, somebody
allí	there
alocado	irresponsible, thoughtless
alojarse (v)	stay (v)
alpinismo	mountaineering
alquilar (v)	rent (v)
alrededor (de)	around
alto (estatura)	tall
alto (sonido)	loud
alumna	pupil
alumno	pupil
amable	kind
amapola	poppy
amar (v)	love (v)
amarillo	yellow
Amazonas	The Amazon River, The Amazon Forest
ambiente	atmosphere
ambulancia	ambulance
América	The Americas
americano	American
amiga	friend
amigo	friend
amor	love
andar (v)	walk (v)
anillo	ring
animal	animal
anoche	last night
anteayer	the day before yesterday
antes (de)	before
antiguo	old, ancient
Antillas	The West Indies
antipático	unfriendly
año	year
apagar (v)	put out, switch off (v)
apagado (luces)	out (lights)
aparcar (v)	park (v)
apasionante	thrilling
apetecer (v)	feel like (v)
aprobar (v)	approve, pass (v)
aquel, aquella, aquello	that (one)
aquí	here
árabe (nacionalidad)	Arabian (nationality)
árabe (lengua)	Arabic (language)
árbol	tree
arena	sand
Argentina	Argentina
argentino	Argentinean
armario	wardrobe, cupboard
arquitecto	architect
arquitectura	architecture
arreglar (v)	mend (v)
arrepentirse (v)	regret, change your mind (v)
arriba	upstairs
arroz	rice
arruga	wrinkle
artista	artist
asar (v)	roast (v)
ascensor	lift, elevator
asesino	murderer
asiento	seat
asignatura	subject
aspirina	aspirin
astronauta	astronaut
astuto	cunning
asustar/asustar (se) (v)	scare / be scared (v)
atar/atarse (v)	tie / tie up (v)
atención	attention, care
ateo	atheist (n), atheistic (adj)
aterrizar (v)	land (v)
atrás	back
atravesar (v)	cross (v)
atreverse	dare (v)
atún	tuna fish
aula	classroom
aunque	although
autobús	bus
avanzado	advanced
ave	bird
averiarse (v)	break down (v)
avestruz	ostrich
avión	airplane
ayer	yesterday
ayuda	help
ayudar (v)	help (v)
azafata	flight attendant
azteca	Aztec
azúcar	sugar
azul	blue
b ailaora	flamenco dancer
bailar (v)	dance (v)
bailarín	dancer
baile	dance
bajar/bajarse (v)	go down / get off / download (v)
bajo (estatura)	short
bajo (sonido)	low
ballet	ballet
baloncesto	basketball
balonmano	handball
banco (negocio)	bank
banco (asiento)	bench
bandera	flag
bañar/bañarse (v)	bathe / take a bath (v)
baño	bath
bar	bar, pub
barato	cheap
barba	beard
barrendero	road-sweeper
barrio	neighbourhood
basura	rubbish
bata (casa)	dressing gown
bata (trabajo, escuela)	overall
batalla	battle
batería (coche)	battery (car)
batería (instrumento)	drum set (musical instrument)
bebé	baby
beber (v)	drink (v)
bebida	drink
belga	Belgian
beso	kiss
biblioteca	library
bici/bicicleta	bike/bicycle
bien	fine, well

bigote	moustache	casi	almost
billete (entrada)	ticket	castillo	castle
blanco	white	cataratas	cataracts
bocadillo	roll	católico	catholic
boda	wedding	cebolla	onion
boina	beret	cedé	compact disk
boliviano	Bolivian	ceder (dejar) (v)	give up (v)
bolívar (moneda)	bolivar	cena	dinner, supper
bolos	skittles	cenar (v)	dine, have supper (v)
bolsa	bag	cenicero	ashtray
bolso	handbag	centímetro	centimetre
bombero	fireman	central	central
bombón	chocolate	centro	centre
bonito	pretty	cerca (de)	near (to)
bota	boot	cerdo (carne de)	pork
botella	bottle	cerilla	match
botón	button	cerrado	closed, locked (with a key)
brasileño	Brazilian	cerrajero	locksmith
brújula	compass	cerrar (v)	close, lock (v)
buenas tardes	good afternoon, good evening	cerveza	beer
bueno (adj)	good (adj)	césped	lawn
bueno (adv)	well (adv)	chaqueta	cardigan, jacket
buenos días	good morning	chica	girl
bufanda	scarf	chico	boy
buscar (v)	look for, search for (v)	chile (picante)	chili
buzón	post box	chileno	Chilean
		chimpancé	chimpanzee
caballo	horse	chino (idioma)	Chinese (language)
caber (v)	fit (v)	chino (nacionalidad)	Chinese (nationality)
cabeza	head	chocar (v)	crash (v)
caerse (v)	fall down (v)	chocolate	chocolate
café	coffee	choque	crash
cafetería	cafeteria	cielo	sky
caja	box (container)	ciencia	science
cajón	drawer	cigarrillo	cigarette
calamares	squid	cigarro	cigar
calambre	electric shock	cigüeña	stork
calefacción	heating	cine	cinema
calendario	calendar	ciudad	city, town
calentar (v)	heat up (v)	civilización	civilization
caliente	hot	claridad	clarity, light
callarse (v)	be quiet (v)	claro (adv)	of course (adv)
calor	heat	clase	class
caluroso	hot	clásica (música)	classical
calle	street	clavo	nail
cama	bed	coche	car
cámara	camera	cocido	stew
camarera	waitress	cocina	kitchen
camarero	waiter	cocinar (v)	cook (v)
cambiar (v)	change (v)	cocinero	cook
cambio	change	coco	coconut
caminata	walk, trek	coger (v)	pick up, take (v)
camión	lorry, truck	COI (Comité Olímpico Internacional)	IOC (International Olympic Committee)
camionero	lorry-driver	cojín	cushion
camisa	shirt	cola (fila)	queue
campamento	camp	colchón	mattress
campeón	champion	colegio	school
campeonato	championship	coleccionar (v)	collect (v)
campo	field, countryside	colgar (v)	hang (v)
canadiense	Canadian	collar	necklace
cáncer	cancer	colocar (v)	put, place (v)
canción	song	colombiano	Colombian
candado	padlock	color	colour
canguro	kangaroo, babysitter	comedia	comedy
cansado	tired	comer (v)	eat, have lunch (v)
cantante	singer	comerciante	tradesman
cantar (v)	sing (v)	comida	food, meal
capital	capital	cómo	how
capitán	captain	cómodo	comfortable
capítulo	chapter	compañero	class/work mate
caprichoso	capricious, spoilt	compartir (v)	share (v)
cara	face	comprar (v)	buy (v)
caramelo	sweet	comprobar (v)	check (v)
cárcel	prison	comunicar (v)	communicate (v)
caribe (pueblo)	Caribbean	concierto	concert
cariñoso	affectionate	conducir (v)	drive (v)
carne	meat	conferencia	lecture
carné (identidad, conducir)	ID card, driving licence	confiar (v)	trust (v)
caro	expensive	conformarse (v)	be satisfied with (v)
carrera (universitaria)	degree course	conocer (v)	know (v)
carretera	road	conquista	conquest
carta	letter	conseguir (v)	achieve (v)
cartas (juego)	cards	construir (v)	build (v)
cartel	sign, poster	constructor	constructor, builder
cartera	postwoman	consulta	enquiry
cartero	postman	contar (1,2,3...) (v)	count (v)
casa	house	contar (una historia) (v)	tell (v)
casarse (v)	get married (v)	contento	happy
casco	crash-helmet	contestar (v)	answer (v)
casero (n)	landlord (n)	continuo	continuous

copiar (v)	copy (v)	diciembre	December
copistería	copy centre	dictar (v)	dictate (v)
corbata	tie	diente	tooth
corona (moneda)	crown (currency)	diferente	different
corrección	correction	difícil	difficult
corregir (v)	correct (v)	dificultad	difficulty
correo / correo electrónico	mail / e-mail	digital	digital
correo	the postal service	dimitir (v)	resign (v)
Correos	Post Office	dinero	money
correr (v)	run (v)	Dios	God
corrida (de toros)	bullfight	directora	headmistress (school)/manager
cortar/cortarse (v)	cut / cut yourself (v)		(company)
cortina	curtain	director	headmaster (school)/manager
corto	short		(company)
cosa	thing	dírham	dirham
costa	coast	disco	disk
costar (v)	cost (v)	discoteca	discotheque
costarricense	Costa Rican	disfrutar (v)	enjoy (v)
creer (v)	believe (v)	disquete	diskette
crema	cream	diversión	enjoyment
criar (v)	bring up (v)	divertido	funny
cristal	crystal/glass	divertirse (v)	have fun (v)
cruce	crossroads	divorciarse (v)	get divorced (v)
cruzar (v)	cross over (v)	doctor	doctor
cuaderno	exercise book	documento	document
cuadro	picture	dólar	dollar
cuando	when	doler (v)	hurt (v)
cuándo	when	domingo	Sunday
cuánto	how much	don	Mr.
cuarto (habitación)	room (bedroom)	doña	Mrs./Ms.
cuarto (hora)	quarter (time)	dónde	where
cuchara	spoon	dorado	golden
cucharada	spoonful	dormir/dormirse (v)	sleep / go to sleep (v)
cuero	leather	ducharse (v)	have a shower (v)
cuchillo	knife	duda	doubt
cuenta	account	dulce	sweet
¡Cuidado!	Look out!	dulce de leche	sweet spread
culpa	blame	durante	during
cumpleaños	birthday	durar (v)	last (v)
cumplir (años) (v)	have a birthday (v)		
curar (v)	heal/cure (v)	**e** char (v)	throw, throw out (v)
curso	course (of study), academic year	económico	economical
		edificio	building
d añino	harmful	editorial	publisher
dar	give	educación	education, upbringing
dar un paseo (v)	take a walk (v)	egipcio	Egyptian
darse bien/mal (v)	to be good / bad at (v)	egoísta	selfish
dato	piece of data / information	ejercicio (escrito)	exercise
decidirse (v)	make a decision (v)	ejercicio (físico)	exercise
decir	say (v), tell (v)	eléctrico	electrical
dedicar(se)	devote (v) / do for a living (v)	elegante	elegant
dedo	finger	elegir (v)	choose (v)
defender(se)	defend / defend yourself (v)	e-mail	e-mail
dejar (prestar)	lend (v)	emperador	emperor
(abandonar)	leave (v)	empezar (v)	begin, start (v)
(colocar)	place (v)	empleo	job
delante (de)	in front of	empresa	company
delgado	slim, thin	empujar (v)	push (v)
demasiado	too (much/many)	en	in, on, at
dentista	dentist	enamorarse (v)	fall in love (v)
dentro (de) (espacio)	in/inside (space) ...	encantado	delighted
dentro (de) (tiempo)	within (time)	encantador	delightful
departamento	department	encantar (v)	delight (v)
dependiente	shop assistant	encender (v)	switch on (electrical item) (v)
deporte	sport		light (gas, cigarette) (v)
deprisa	quickly	encendido	on (electrical item), lit (gas, cigarette)
derecha	right	enchufe	plug
Derecho (carrera)	Law (degree)	enciclopedia	encyclopaedia
desaparecer (v)	disappear (v)	encima	on top
desastre	disaster	encontrar (v)	find (v)
desayunar (v)	have breakfast (v)	enero	January
descansar (v)	rest (v)	enfadado	angry
desconfiar (v)	distrust (v)	enfadarse (v)	get angry (v)
desconocido	unknown	enfermedad	illness
desear (v)	wish (v)	enfermera	nurse
deseo	wish	enfermero	nurse
desierto	desert	enfermo	patient
desnudo	naked	enfrente	opposite (position)
despacho	office	enseguida	at once
despacio	slowly	enseñar (v)	teach (v), show
despedir/despedirse (v)	dismiss / say goodbye (v)	entender (v)	understand (v)
despertador	alarm clock	entenderse (v)	understand each other / one another
despertar/despertarse (v)	wake up (v)		(v)
después (de)	later/afterwards	entonces	then
destornillador	screw-driver	entrada	entrance
detener (v)	stop (v), arrest	entrada (billete)	ticket
devolver (v)	return (give back) (v)	entretenido	entertaining
día	day	entrevista	interview
dibujar (v)	draw (v)	enviar (v)	send (v)
dibujo	drawing	envuelto (implicado)	involved
diccionario	dictionary		

escalera	ladder	frase	phrase, sentence
escaparse (v)	get away / escape (v)	frecuencia (con)	frequency (with)
escocés	Scottish	freír (v)	fry (v)
escribir (v)	write (v)	fresa	strawberry
escritor	writer	frío	cold
escultor	sculptor	frontera	border
escuchar (v)	listen (to) (v)	fruta	fruit
eso	that	frutal	fruit tree
espacio	space	fuego	fire
español (nacionalidad)	Spanish (nationality)	fuera	outside
español (idioma)	Spanish (language)	fuerte	strong
especial	special	fuerza	strength
espectador	spectator	fuga	escape, leak (water, gas, etc.)
espejo	mirror	fumar (v)	smoke (v)
esperar (v)	wait, hope, expect (v)	funcionar (v)	work (machines) (v)
esposo	husband, spouse	fundación	foundation
esquí	ski	fútbol	football, soccer
esquiar (v)	ski (v)	futbolista	footballer
esquina	corner	futuro	future
estación	station		
estadio	stadium	**g**afas	glasses (spectacles)
estado	state	galleta	biscuit, cookie
estadounidense	from the United States, American	gallina	hen
estanco	tobacco shop	gallo	cockerel, rooster
estar (v)	be (v)	gambas	prawns
estatua	statue	ganador	winner
este, esta, esto	this	ganar (v)	win, earn (v)
estómago	stomach	gas	gas
estrella	star	gasolina	petrol
estropearse (v)	break down, wear out (v)	gastar (v)	spend (v)
estudiante	student	gato	cat
estudiar (v)	study (v)	gente	people
estupendamente	marvellously	gerente	manager
etiope	Ethiopian	gesto	gesture
euro	euro	gestoría	administrative representative's office
europeo	European	gimnasia	gymnastics
examen	exam	gimnasio	gymnasium
examinar (v)	examine (v)	girar (v)	turn (v)
excepto	except	gobernador	governor
existencia	existence	golf	golf
éxito	success	golpe	blow
explicar (v)	explain (v)	gordo	fat
exportar (v)	export (v)	gorila	gorilla
exposición	exhibition	gracia	wit
exquisito	exquisite	gracias	thanks
extraordinario	extraordinary	grado	degree
extraterrestre	alien	gramática	grammar
		gramo	gram
fabada	bean stew	grande	large (size), grand (importance)
fábrica	factory	grave	serious
fácil	easy	griego (nacionalidad)	Greek (nationality)
facilidad	ease	griego (idioma)	Greek (language)
falda	skirt	gripe	flu
fallecer (v)	die / pass away (v)	gris	grey
falso	false	gritar (v)	shout (v)
falta (necesidad)	need	grupo	group
familia	family	guante	glove
familiar	family (adj) familiar	guapo	handsome
famoso	famous	guardar (v)	keep, look after (v)
farmacia	pharmacy, chemist's	guerra	war
fax	fax machine, facsimile, fax	guerrero	warrior
febrero	February	guía (persona)	guide (person)
felicidad	happiness	guitarra	guitar
felicitar (v)	congratulate (v)	gustar (v)	like (v)
feliz	happy		
feo	ugly	**h**abilidad	skill
feria	fair	habitación	room, bedroom
ferrocarril	railway	haber (v)	have (v), there be
fichero (informático)	file	habitante	inhabitant
fiebre	temperature	hablar (v)	speak, talk (v)
fiebre amarilla	yellow fever	hace	ago
fiesta	party (event), public holiday	hacer (v)	make, do (v)
filosofía	philosophy	hacha	axe
fin	end	Hacienda	The Treasury, The Exchequer
final	final	hamaca	hammock
fin de semana	weekend	hambre	hunger (n), hungry (adj)
fino (delgado)	fine (thin)	hasta	until
física	physics	hay	there is/are
físico (adj)	physical	helado	ice cream
flor	flower	helado (adj)	frozen
fluir (v)	flow (v)	herido	wounded
FMI (Fondo monetario internacional)	IMF (International Monetary Fund)	hermana	sister
fontanero	plumber	hermano	brother
footing, futin	jogging	hermanos	brothers and sisters
forma	shape	hierba	grass
foto (fotografía)	photo	hija	daughter
fotocopia	photocopy	hijo	son
fotógrafo	photographer	hijos	children
francés (nacionalidad)	French (nationality)	historia (asignatura)	history
francés (idioma)	French (language)	historia (relato)	story

hoja	leaf
holandés	Dutch
hombre	man
honradez	honesty
honrado	honest
hora	time, hour
horrible	horrible
hospital	hospital
hotel	hotel
hoy	today
huelga	strike
huerto	market garden, orchard
hueso	bone
huevo	egg
humano	human
humor	mood
idioma	language
iglesia	church
igual	same
impaciente	impatient
importante	important
importar (v)	matter, import (v)
impresionante	impressive
impresora	printer
impuestos	taxes
inaugurar (v)	open (v)
inca	Inca
incendio	fire
incómodo	uncomfortable
independiente	independent
indio	Indian
infancia	childhood
informática	computing
ingeniero	engineer
inglés (nacionalidad)	English (nationality)
inglés (idioma)	English (language)
inolvidable	unforgettable
instituto (secundaria)	secondary/high/comprehensive school
instituto (institución)	school, institute
instrucciones	instructions
instrumento	instrument
inteligencia	intelligence
inteligente	intelligent
interior	indoor
internet	internet
inventar (v)	invent (v)
inventor	inventor
invierno	winter
invitación	invitation
invitar (v)	invite (v)
ir/irse (v)	go / go away (v)
iraní	Iranian
irresponsable	irresponsible
isla	island
italiano (nacionalidad)	Italian (nationality)
italiano (idioma)	Italian (language)
izquierda	left
jamón	ham
japonés (nacionalidad)	Japanese (nationality)
japonés (idioma)	Japanese (language)
jardín	garden
jefe	boss
jefe de estudios	director of studies
jersey	jersey
jirafa	giraffe
joven (adj)	young
joven (n)	young person
jueves	Thursday
jugador	player
jugar (v)	play (v)
julio	July
junio	June
junto (a)	beside, with
kilo	kilo
kilómetro	kilometre
labio	lip
ladrar (v)	bark (v)
ladrón	thief
lago	lake
lámina	print
lámpara	lamp
lana	wool
lapicero	pencil
lápiz	pencil
largo	long
lata	tin
latino	Latin
lavabo	washbasin
lavadora	washing-machine
lavarse (v)	have a wash (v)
lavavajillas	dishwasher
leche	milk
leer (v)	read (v)
lejano	far away
lejos	far
lentitud	slowness
lento	slow
león	lion
leona	lioness
letra (a, b, c...)	letter
levantarse (v)	get up (v)
libra (moneda)	pound (currency)
libre	free
libro	book
liga	league
lima	file
limpiarse (v)	clean yourself up (v)
limpieza	cleanliness
limpio	clean
líneas aéreas	airlines
linterna	torch, flashlight
lira (moneda)	lira (currency)
litro	litre
lunar	lunar
llama (animal)	llama
llamar / llamarse (v)	call / be called (v)
llave	key
llegar (v)	arrive (v)
llevar (v)	carry (v)
llevarse (bien/mal) (v)	get on well/badly with (v)
llorar (v)	cry (v)
llover (v)	rain (v)
lluvia	rain
lotería	lottery
lucha	struggle
luego	then, later
lugar	place
Luna	Moon
lunes	Monday
luz	light
madera	wood
madre	mother
madrugada	early morning, dawn
madrugar (v)	get up early (v)
mágico	magical
majo	nice
maleducado	rude
maleta	suitcase
malo	bad
mancha	stain, spot
manera	way
mango	handle
manifestación	demonstration
mantequilla	butter
mano	hand
manzana	apple
mañana (n)	morning
mañana (adv)	tomorrow
mapa	map
máquina	machine
mar	sea
maratón	marathon
maravilloso	marvellous
marcharse (v)	leave (v)
marear (v)	confuse (v)
margarita	daisy
marido	husband
mariposa	butterfly
marisco	shellfish, seafood
marrón	brown
marroquí	Moroccan
martes	Tuesday
martillo	hammer
marzo	March
más	more
matemáticas	mathematics
maya	Mayan
mayo	May
mayor	older, bigger
mayúscula (letra)	capital
mechero	cigarette lighter
media (hora)	half
media (medida)	half
Medicina	medicine
medicina (medicamento)	medicine, drug (medication)

médico	doctor
medida (traje a)	measure (made to)
medio	middle
mediodía	midday
medir (v)	measure (v)
mejor	better
mejorar (v)	improve (v)
melón	melon
(de) memoria	by heart
menos (hora)	to (with time)
menos	less
(a) menudo	often
mensaje	message
mentir (v)	lie (tell lies) (v)
mentira	lie
mes	month
mesa	table
mesón	inn
meta	target (fig.), finish line (race)
metro	metre
metro cuadrado	square metre
metro (transporte)	metro, underground
mexicano	Mexican
miedo	fear
miércoles	Wednesday
ministro	minister
minúscula (letra)	lower case
minuto	minute
mirar (v)	look (v)
moda	fashion
modelo	model
moderno	modern
modo	way
mojado	wet
mojarse (v)	get wet (v)
molestar (v)	disturb (v)
momento	moment
moneda	coin (tender), currency (monetary unit)
montaña	mountain
montar (en) (v)	ride (v)
montar (armar) (v)	organise (v)
morder (v)	bite (v)
moreno	dark (skin, hair)
morir (v)	die (v)
mosca	fly
moto	motorcycle
mover / moverse (v)	move (v)
móvil (teléfono)	mobile
mucho	a lot
mueble	furniture (piece of)
muela	molar
muerte	death
mujer	woman
mundial	world (adj)
mundo	world
museo	museum
música	music
músico	musician
musulmán	Muslim
muy	very
nacer (v)	be born (v)
nacional	national
nada	nothing
nadar (v)	swim (v)
nadie	nobody, no one
naranja	orange
nariz	nose
natación	swimming
Navidades	Christmas
negro	black
necesario	necessary
necesitar (v)	need (v)
nervioso	nervous
nevar (v)	snow (v)
nevera	refrigerator
nicaragüense	Nicaraguan
nido	nest
niebla	fog
nieto	grandchild
nieve	snow
niña	girl
niño	boy
no	no
noche	night
nombre	name
normal	normal
normalmente	normally
norte	north
norteamericano	North American
notas (calificaciones)	marks
noticia	news
novela	novel
novia	girlfriend, bride
noviembre	November
novio	boyfriend, groom
nube	cloud
nublado	cloudy
nuevo	new
(de) nuevo	again
número	number
nunca	never
obligatorio	compulsory, obligatory
oboe	oboe
obra (de teatro)	play (drama)
obrero	worker
octubre	October
ocupado	employed, busy
odiar (v)	hate (v)
oeste	west
oficina	office
ofrecer (v)	offer (v)
oír (v)	hear (v)
ojo	eye
oler (v)	smell (v)
olvidar(se) (v)	forget (v)
ONG (Organización No Gubernamental)	NGO (Non-Governmental Organisation)
ONU (Organización de Naciones Unidas)	UN (United Nations Organisation)
ópera	opera
óptica	optician's
ordenador	computer
ordenar (v)	tidy up (v)
organización	organisation
orilla	shore
oro	gold
orquesta	orchestra
oscuro	dark
oso	bear
OVNI	UFO (unidentified flying object)
paciente	patient
padre	father
padres	parents
paella	paella
país	country
pagar (v)	pay (v)
pan	bread
pana	corduroy
pantalones	trousers
pañuelo (de señora)	headscarf
papá	daddy
papel	paper
papelería	stationer's
paquete	packet, parcel
par	pair, even
parada	stop
parar / pararse (v)	stop (v)
paraguas	umbrella
parecer(se) (v)	seem, look like (v)
parque	park
parte	part
partido	match (football, etc.)
pasado	last
pasado mañana	the day after tomorrow
pasar (tiempo) (v)	spend (time) (v)
pasar (suceder) (v)	happen (v)
paseo	walk
pasillo	corridor
paso de cebra	zebra (pedestrian) crossing
pastel	cake
pata	leg
patada	kick
patata	potato
payaso	clown
pecera	fish bowl
pedir (v)	request, ask for (v)
peinar (v)	comb, brush (v)
pelar (v)	peel (v)
peligroso	dangerous
pelo	hair
pelota	ball
peluquería	hairdresser's
peluquero	hairdresser
pena (condena)	sentence
pendiente (adorno)	earring
peor	worse
pequeño	small
pera	pear

percha	coat-hook
perder (v)	lose (v)
perdonar (v)	forgive (v)
pereza	laziness
perfectamente	perfectly
perfume	perfume
periódico	newspaper
periodista	journalist
permiso	permission
pero	but
perra	bitch
perro	dog
persona	person
personaje	character
personal (adj)	personal
peruano	Peruvian
pesado (cansado)	boring
pescadería	fishmonger's
pescado	fish
pescar (v)	fish (v)
pesar (v)	weigh (v)
peso (moneda)	peso (currency)
pez	fish
pez de colores	goldfish
pianista	pianist
piano	piano
picante	spicy, hot
piedra	stone
piel	skin
pijama	pyjamas
piloto	pilot (airplane), driver
pincel	paintbrush
pinchar (v)	prick (v)
pingüino	penguin
pintar (v)	paint (v)
pintor	painter
piña	pineapple
Pirineos	Pyrenees
pisar (v)	step on (v)
piscina	swimming pool
piso	flat (apartment)
pizarra	blackboard
pizza	pizza
plan	plan
planta (piso)	floor
planta (vegetal)	plant
plantar (v)	plant (v)
plástico	plastic
plata	silver
plátano	banana
plato (comida)	dish
plato (utensilio)	plate
playa	beach
plaza	square
pluma (estilográfica)	fountain pen
poblado	settlement
pobre	poor
poco/a/os/as	little, few
poder	power
poema	poem
polar	polar
policía (agente)	policeman
policía (cuerpo)	police force
polideportivo	sports centre
políglota	polyglot
pollo	chicken
poner (v)	put (v)
ponerse (v)	put on (v)
pop	pop
por favor	please
por supuesto	of course
portarse (v)	behave yourself (v)
portátil	portable
portugués (nacionalidad)	Portuguese (nationality)
portugués (idioma)	Portuguese (language)
postal	postcard
potente	powerful
practicar (v)	practise (v)
precioso	precious
preferido	favourite
preferir (v)	prefer (v)
preguntar (v)	ask (v)
premio	prize, award
prensa	press
preocuparse (v)	worry (v)
preparar (v)	prepare (v)
presentar	present (v)
presidente	president (republic), prime minister (monarchy), chairman (company)
preso	prisoner
prestar (v)	lend (v)
Primer ministro	Prime minister
primo	cousin
princesa	princess
principal	main
príncipe	prince
principio	beginning
prisa (tener, darse)	hurry (be in a)
probar (v)	try, test, taste (v)
problema	problem
proceder (de) (v)	come from (v)
profesor	teacher (school), lecturer (univ)
prohibido	prohibited
propina	tip (restaurant)
protestante	protestant
próximo	next
pueblo	village
puente	bridge
puerta	door (building), gate (wall, fence)
puesto (de venta)	stall
puntual	punctual
pues	well (as interjection)
puro (tabaco)	cigar
qué	what
quedar (resto) (v)	remain (v)
quedar con (citar)	arrange to meet (v)
quedarse (v)	stay (v)
quemar / quemarse	burn / burn yourself (v)
querer	want (something), love (someone) (v)
queso	cheese
quién	who
(de) quién	who... from
quinto	fifth
quiosco	newsstand
quitarse (v)	take off (v)
radio	radio
rama	branch
rapidez	speed
rápido	quickly
raqueta	racket
rato	while (n)
ratón	mouse
real (moneda brasileña)	real
recepción	reception
recepcionista	receptionist
recibir (v)	receive (v)
recoger (v)	collect (v)
recolector	harvester
recomendar (v)	recommend (v)
recordar (v)	remind (v)
recorrer (v)	run (v)
recreo	playtime
recto	straight
recuerdo	memory
redacción	essay
refresco	soft drink
regalar (v)	give (as a gift) (v)
regalo	gift
regañar (v)	tell off (v)
regar (v)	water (v)
región	region
regresar (v)	return (v)
reírse (v)	laugh (v)
relajado	relaxed
reloj	clock, watch
remedio	remedy
repetir (v)	repeat (v)
reservar (v)	reserve (v)
resfriado	cold
respuesta	reply
restaurante	restaurant
resultado	result
resultar (v)	prove (v)
reunión	meeting
revista	magazine
rey	king
Reyes (fiestas)	Epiphany
rezar (v)	pray (v)
rico	rich
rico (sabroso)	tasty
río	river
risa	laughter
rizado	curly
robot	robot
rock (música)	rock (music)
rojo	red
romper, romperse (v)	break (v)
ropa	clothes

Spanish	English
rosa (n)	rose (n)
roto	broken
rubio	fair, blond
rueda	wheel
ruido	noise
ruso (nacionalidad)	Russian (nationality)
ruso (idioma)	Russian (language)
sábado	Saturday
saber (v)	know (v)
sacapuntas	pencil sharpener
sacar (v)	take out (v)
sacrificio	sacrifice
sal	salt
sala	living room
salir (v)	go out (v)
salón	lounge
salud	health
sandía	watermelon
sano	healthy
sartén	frying pan
sastrería	tailor's shop
satélite	satellite
seco	dry
secretaria	secretary
secreto	secret
sed	thirst (n)
sediento	thirsty (adj)
seguir (v)	follow (v)
seguramente	surely
selva	jungle
semana	week
sensación	sensation
sentarse (v)	sit down (v)
sentir, sentirse (v)	feel (v)
señor	sir
señora	madam
señorita	miss
separar (v)	separate (v)
septiembre	September
sequía	drought
ser (v)	be (v)
seriedad	seriousness
serpiente	snake
servicio	service
servir (usar) (v)	be used to/for (v)
sexto	sixth
SIDA (Síndrome de inmunodeficiencia adquirida)	AIDS (Acquired Immune Deficiency Syndrome)
siempre	always
(lo) siento	I'm sorry
sierra	mountains
siesta	siesta, nap
siglo	century
silla	chair
simpático	nice, friendly
situación	situation
soberano	sovereign
sobre (prep)	on (prep)
socialista	socialist
sol	sun
solo (adv)	only
solo (adj)	alone (adj)
sombra	shadow, shade
sombrero	hat
sonar (v)	sound (v)
soñar (v)	dream (v)
sonreír (v)	smile (v)
sopa	soup
soplar (v)	blow (v)
sordo	deaf
sorpresa	surprise
sortija	ring
sospechar (v)	suspect (v)
sospechoso	suspicious
suave	soft
subir (v)	go up (v)
sucio	dirty
sudanés	Sudanese
sueco (nacionalidad)	Swedish (nationality)
sueco (idioma)	Swedish (language)
suelo	land, floor, ground
sueño	dream
suerte	luck
suficiente	sufficient
superstición	superstition
sur	south
suroeste	southwest
suspender (v)	cancel (v)
tabaco	tobacco
también	also
tampoco	neither, either
tango	tango
tantos/as	so many
tarde (n)	afternoon, evening (n)
tarde (adv)	late (adv)
tarta	cake
taxi	taxi
taza	cup
teatro	theatre
techo	ceiling
té	tea
tela	cloth
teléfono	telephone
televisión	television
televisor	television set
temperatura	temperature
temprano	early
tender (v)	hang out (v)
tenedor	fork
tener (v)	have (v)
tenis	tennis
tenista	tennis-player
tequila	tequila
termómetro	thermometer
test	test
tía	aunt
tiempo	time
tiempo (meteorológico)	weather
tienda	shop
Tierra	Earth
tierra (país)	land (country)
tijeras	scissors
timbre	doorbell
tímido	shy
tío	uncle
tíos	aunts and uncles
tipo	type
tirar/ tirarse (v)	throw/ throw yourself (v)
titularse	qualify (v)
título	title (book), title
tocar (palpar) (v)	touch (v)
tocar (interpretar) (v)	play (v)
tocar (la lotería) (v)	win (v)
tocar (la vez) (v)	be (your turn) (v)
todavía	still
todo/a/os/as	all
tomar (v)	take, eat, drink (v)
tontería	nonsense
tónica	tonic water
torcer (v)	twist (v)
tormenta	storm
tornillo	screw
toro	bull
tortilla	omelette
tortuga	turtle
tostada	toast
tostar (v)	toast (v)
trabajador	worker
trabajar (v)	work (v)
trabajo	job, work
traducción	translation
traducir (v)	translate (v)
traductor	translator
traer (v)	bring (v)
tráfico	traffic
traje	suit
tranquilidad	peace and quiet
tranquilo	peaceful
transporte	transport
tren	train
trigo	corn, wheat
triste	sad
tulipán	tulip
turismo	tourism
turista	tourist
turístico	tourist
últimamente	lately
último	last
universidad	university
universitario	university student
unos/as (aproximadamente)	some (approximately)
urgente	urgent
usar (v)	use (v)
útil	useful
uva	grape
vacaciones	holidays

Spanish	English
vacío	empty
vacunarse	be vaccinated (v)
vago	lazy
valer (v)	be worth (v)
vaqueros	jeans
varios/as	several
vaso	glass
vecino	neighbour
vegetariano	vegetarian
vendedor	salesperson
vender (v)	sell (v)
venezolano	Venezuelan
venir (v)	come (v)
ventana	window
ver (v)	see (v)
veranear (v)	spend the summer (v)
verano	summer
verdad	truth
verde	green
verdura	vegetables
vestido	dress
vestir (v)	wear (v)
vez, a la vez	time, at the same time
viajar (v)	travel (v)
viaje	journey, trip
vida	life
vídeo	video
viejo	old
viento	wind
viernes	Friday
vietnamita (nacionalidad)	Vietnamese (nationality)
vietnamita (lengua)	Vietnamese (language)
vino	wine
violento	violent
violín	violin
visitar (v)	visit (v)
vivir (v)	live (v)
voluntad	will
volver (v)	return (v)
voz	voice
vuelo	flight
vuelta	return

Spanish	English
y	and
ya	already
yegua	mare
yen	yen
yoga	yoga
yogur	yoghurt

Spanish	English
z apatilla	slipper
zapatos	shoes
zona	area
zumo	fruit juice

English	Spanish
a cademy	academia
accept (v)	aceptar (v)
accident	accidente
accompany (v)	acompañar (v)
account	cuenta
achieve (v)	conseguir (v)
action (film)	acción (película de)
actor	actor
actress	actriz
administrative representative's office	gestoría
adobe	adobe
adore (v)	adorar (v)
advanced	avanzado
affectionate	cariñoso
afternoon	tarde (n)
afterwards	después (de)
again	(de) nuevo
agency	agencia
ago	hace
AIDS (Acquired Immune Deficiency Syndrome)	SIDA (Síndrome de inmunodeficiencia adquirida)
airlines	líneas aéreas
airplane	avión
alarm	alarma
alarm clock	despertador
alcohol	alcohol
alien	extraterrestre
all	todo/a/os/as
all right	(de) acuerdo
almost	casi
alone (adj)	solo (adj)
alphabet	alfabeto
already	ya
also	también
although	aunque
always	siempre
ambulance	ambulancia
American	americano
ancient	antiguo
and	y
angry	enfadado
animal	animal
answer (v)	contestar (v)
apple	manzana
approve (v)	aprobar (v)
April	abril
Arabian (nationality)	árabe (nacionalidad)
Arabic (language)	árabe (lengua)
architect	arquitecto
architecture	arquitectura
area	zona
Argentina	Argentina
Argentinean/Argentine	argentino
around	alrededor (de)
arrange to (v)	quedar con (citar)
arrive (v)	llegar (v)
artist	artista
ashtray	cenicero
ask (v)	preguntar (v)
ask for (v)	pedir (v)
aspirin	aspirina
astronaut	astronauta
at	en
at once	enseguida
atheist (n), atheistic (adj)	ateo
atmosphere	ambiente
attention, care	atención
August	agosto
aunt	tía
aunts and uncles	tíos
award	premio
axe	hacha
Aztec	azteca

English	Spanish
b aby	bebé
babysitter	canguro
back	atrás
bad	malo
bag	bolsa
ball	pelota
ballet	ballet
banana	plátano
bank	banco (negocio)
bar	bar
bark (v)	ladrar (v)
basketball	baloncesto
bath	baño
bathe (v)	bañar/bañarse (v)

battery (car)	batería (coche)	cancer	cáncer
battle	batalla	capital	capital
be (v)	ser, estar (v)	capital (letter)	mayúscula (letra)
be (your turn) (v)	tocar (la vez) (v)	captain	capitán
be born (v)	nacer (v)	car	coche
be quiet (v)	callarse (v)	caramel spread	dulce de leche
be satisfied with (v)	conformarse (v)	cards	cartas (juego)
be used to/for (v)	servir (usar) (v)	Caribbean	caribe (pueblo)
be vaccinated (v)	vacunarse	carry (v)	llevar (v)
be worth (v)	valer (v)	castle	castillo
beach	playa	cat	gato
bean stew	fabada	cataracts	cataratas
bear	oso	catholic	católico
beard	barba	ceiling	techo
bed	cama	center	centro
beer	cerveza	centimeter	centímetro
before	antes (de)	central	central
begin (v)	empezar (v)	century	siglo
beginning	principio	chair	silla
behave yourself (v)	portarse (v)	chairman (company)	presidente
Belgian	belga	champion	campeón
believe (v)	creer (v)	championship	campeonato
bench	banco (asiento)	change (n)	cambio
beret	boina	change (v)	cambiar (v)
beside	junto (a)	chapter	capítulo
better	mejor	character	personaje
bigger	mayor	cheap	barato
bike/bicycle	bici/bicicleta	check (v)	comprobar (v)
bird	ave	cheese	queso
birthday	cumpleaños	chess	ajedrez
bitch	perra	chicken	pollo
bite (v)	morder (v)	childhood	infancia
black	negro	children	hijos
blackboard	pizarra	Chilean	chileno
blame	culpa	chili	chile (picante)
blow (n)	golpe	chimpanzee	chimpancé
blow (v)	soplar (v)	Chinese (language)	chino (idioma)
blue	azul	Chinese (nationality)	chino (nacionalidad)
bolivar	bolívar (moneda)	chocolate	bombón, chocolate
Bolivian	boliviano	choose (v)	elegir (v)
bone	hueso	Christmas	Navidades
book (n)	libro	church	iglesia
boot	bota	cigar	cigarro, puro (tabaco)
border	frontera	cigarette	cigarrillo
bore (v)	aburrir (v)	cigarette lighter	mechero
bored, boring	aburrido	cinema	cine
boredom	aburrimiento	city	ciudad
boring	pesado (cansado)	civilization	civilización
boss	jefe	clarity	claridad
bottle	botella	class	clase
bowling	bolos	class/work mate	compañero
box (container)	caja	classical	clásica (música)
boy	chico, niño	classroom	aula
boyfriend	novio	clause	oración
branch	rama	clean	limpio
Brazilian	brasileño	clean up (v)	ordenar (v)
bread	pan	clean yourself up (v)	limpiarse (v)
break (v)	romper, romperse (v)	cleanliness	limpieza
break down (v)	averiarse, estropearse (v)	clock	reloj
bride	novia	close (v)	cerrar (v)
bridge	puente	close to	cerca (de)
bring (v)	traer (v)	closed	cerrado
bring up (v)	criar (v)	closet	armario
broken	roto	cloth	tela
brother	hermano	clothes	ropa
brothers and sisters	hermanos	cloud	nube
brown	marrón	cloudy	nublado
brush (v)	peinar (v)	clown	payaso
build (v)	construir (v)	coast	costa
building	edificio	coat hanger	percha
bull	toro	cock	gallo
bullfight	corrida (de toros)	coconut	coco
burn/ burn yourself (v)	quemar/ quemarse (v)	coffee	café
bus	autobús	coin (tender)	moneda
busy	ocupado	cold	frío
but	pero	cold	resfriado
butter	mantequilla	collect (v)	coleccionar (v)
butterfly	mariposa	collect (v)	recoger (v)
button	botón	Colombian	colombiano
buy (v)	comprar (v)	color	color
by heart	(de) memoria	comb (v)	peinar (v)
		come (v)	venir (v)
cafeteria	cafetería	come from (v)	proceder (de) (v)
cake	pastel, tarta	comedy	comedia
calendar	calendario	comfortable	cómodo
call / be called (v)	llamar / llamarse (v)	communicate (v)	comunicar (v)
camera	cámara	compact disk/CD	cedé
camp	campamento	company	empresa
Canadian	canadiense	compass	brújula
cancel (v)	suspender (v)	compulsory	obligatorio

computer	ordenador	distrust (v)	desconfiar (v)
computing	informática	disturb (v)	molestar (v)
concert	concierto	DNA (Deoxyribonucleic Acid)	ADN (ácido desoxirribonucleico)
confuse (v)	marear (v)	do (v)	hacer (v)
congratulate (v)	felicitar (v)	do / fasten up (v)	abrocharse (v)
conquest	conquista	doctor	doctor, médico
constructor, builder	constructor	document	documento
continuous	continuo	dog	perro
cook (n)	cocinero	dollar	dólar
cook (v)	cocinar (v)	door	puerta
cookie	galleta	doorbell	timbre
copy (v)	copiar (v)	doubt	duda
copy center	copistería	download (v)	bajarse (v)
corduroy	pana	downstairs	abajo
corner	esquina	draw (v)	dibujar (v)
correct (v)	corregir (v)	drawer	cajón
correction	corrección	drawing	dibujo
corridor	pasillo	dream (n)	sueño
cost (v)	costar (v)	dream (v)	soñar (v)
Costa Rican	costarricense	dress	vestido
cotton	algodón	dressing gown	bata (casa)
count (v)	contar (v)	drink (n)	bebida
country	país	drink (v)	tomar, beber (v)
countryside	campo	drive (v)	conducir (v)
cousin	primo	driver	piloto
crash (n)	choque	driver's license	carné (conducir)
crash (v)	chocar (v)	drought	sequía
cream	crema	drug	medicamento
cross (v)	cruzar (v)	drug store	farmacia
cross (v)	atravesar (v)	drum set (musical instrument)	batería (instrumento)
crossroads	cruce	dry	seco
crosswalk	paso de cebra	during	durante
crown (currency)	corona (moneda)	Dutch	holandés
cry (v)	llorar (v)		
crystal	cristal	eagle	águila
cunning	astuto	early	temprano
cup	taza	early morning	madrugada
cupboard	armario	earring	pendiente (adorno)
cure (v)	curar (v)	Earth	Tierra
curly	rizado	ease	facilidad
currency (monetary unit)	moneda	easy	fácil
curtain	cortina	eat (v)	tomar, comer (v)
cushion	cojín	economical	económico
cut / cut yourself (v)	cortar/cortarse (v)	education	educación
		egg	huevo
daddy	papá	Egyptian	egipcio
daisy	margarita	either	tampoco
dance (n)	baile	electric shock	calambre
dance (v)	bailar (v)	electrical	eléctrico
dancer	bailarín	elegant	elegante
dangerous	peligroso	e-mail	e-mail, correo electrónico
dare (v)	atreverse	emperor	emperador
dark	oscuro	empty	vacío
dark (skin, hair)	moreno	encyclopedia	enciclopedia
data	dato	end	fin
daughter	hija	engineer	ingeniero
dawn	madrugada	English (language)	inglés (idioma)
day	día	English (nationality)	inglés (nacionalidad)
deaf	sordo	enjoy (v)	disfrutar (v)
death	muerte	enjoyment	diversión
December	diciembre	enquiry	consulta
defend / defend yourself (v)	defender(se) (v)	entertaining	entretenido
degree	grado	entrance	entrada
degree course	carrera (universitaria)	Epiphany	Reyes (fiestas)
delight (v)	encantar (v)	escape (v)	escaparse (v)
delighted	encantado	escape (water, gas, etc.)	fuga
delightful	encantador	essay	redacción
demonstration	manifestación	Ethiopian	etiope
dentist	dentista	euro	euro
department	departamento	European	europeo
desert	desierto	even	par
devote(v)	dedicar(se) (v)	evening	tarde (n)
dictate (v)	dictar (v)	exam	examen
dictionary	diccionario	examine (v)	examinar (v)
die (v)	morir (v)	except	excepto
die (v)	fallecer (v)	excited	alborotado
different	diferente	exercise	ejercicio
difficult	difícil	exercise book	cuaderno
difficulty	dificultad	exhausted	agotado (cansado)
digital	digital	exhibition	exposición
dinner	cena	existence	existencia
director of studies	jefe de estudios	expect (v)	esperar (v)
dirham	dírham	expensive	caro
dirty	sucio	explain (v)	explicar (v)
disappear (v)	desaparecer (v)	export (v)	exportar (v)
disaster	desastre	exquisite	exquisito
dish	plato (comida)	extraordinary	extraordinario
dishwasher	lavavajillas	eye	ojo
disk	disco		
dismiss (v)	despedir (v)	face	cara

factory	fábrica	get married (v)	casarse (v)
fair (adj)	rubio	get off (v)	bajar (v)
fair (n)	feria	get up (v)	levantarse (v)
fall down (v)	caerse (v)	get up early (v)	madrugar (v)
fall in love (v)	enamorarse (v)	get used to (v)	acostumbrarse (v)
false	falso	get wet (v)	mojarse (v)
familiar	familiar	gift	regalo
family	familia	giraffe	jirafa
famous	famoso	girl	chica, niña
far	lejos	girlfriend	novia
far away	lejano	give	dar
farmer	agricultor	give (as a gift) (v)	regalar (v)
fashion	moda	give up (v)	ceder, dejar (v)
fat	gordo	glass	cristal
father	padre	glass	vaso
favorite	preferido	glasses (spectacles)	gafas
fax (machine)	fax	glove	guante
fear	miedo	go / go away (v)	ir/irse (v)
February	febrero	go down	bajar (v)
feel (v)	sentir, sentirse (v)	go out (v)	salir (v)
feel like (v)	apetecer (v)	go to bed (v)	acostar/acostarse (v)
few	poco/a/os/as	go up (v)	subir (v)
field	campo	God	Dios
fifth	quinto	gold	oro
file	lima, fichero (informático)	golden	dorado
final	final	goldfish	pez de colores
find (v)	encontrar (v)	golf	golf
fine (thin)	fino (delgado)	good (adj)	bueno (adj)
fine, well	bien	good afternoon	buenas tardes
finger	dedo	good evening	buenas tardes
finish (v)	acabar (v)	good morning	buenos días
finish line (race)	meta	gorilla	gorila
fire	fuego, incendio	governor	gobernador
firefighter	bombero	grade (of study)	curso
fish (n)	pescado, pez	gram	gramo
fish (v)	pescar (v)	grammar	gramática
fish bowl	pecera	grandchild	nieto
fishmonger's	pescadería	grandfather	abuelo
fit (v)	caber (v)	grandmother	abuela
flag	bandera	grandparents	abuelos
flamenco dancer	bailaora	grape	uva
flashlight	linterna	grass	césped, hierba
flat	piso	Greek (language)	griego (idioma)
flight	vuelo	Greek (nationality)	griego (nacionalidad)
flight attendant	azafata	green	verde
floor	planta (piso), suelo	grey	gris
floppy disk	disquete	groom	novio
flow (v)	fluir (v)	ground	suelo
flower	flor	group	grupo
flu	gripe	guide (person)	guía (persona)
fly	mosca	guitar	guitarra
fog	niebla	gymnasium	gimnasio
follow (v)	seguir (v)	gymnastics	gimnasia
food, meal	comida		
forget (v)	olvidar(se) (v)	hair	pelo
forgive (v)	perdonar (v)	hairdresser	peluquero
fork	tenedor	hairdresser's	peluquería
foundation	fundación	half	media
fountain pen	pluma (estilográfica)	hallway	pasillo
free	libre	ham	jamón
French (language)	francés (idioma)	hammer	martillo
French (nationality)	francés (nacionalidad)	hammock	hamaca
frequency (with)	frecuencia (con)	hand	mano
Friday	viernes	handbag	bolso
friend	amigo, amiga	handball	balonmano
from the United States, American	estadounidense	handle	mango
frozen	helado (adj)	handsome	guapo
fruit	fruta	hang (v)	colgar (v)
fruit juice	zumo	hang out clothes (v)	tender (v)
fruit tree	frutal	happen (v)	pasar (suceder) (v)
fry (v)	freír (v)	happiness	felicidad
frying pan	sartén	happy	alegre, contento, feliz
funny	divertido	harmful	dañino
furniture (piece of)	mueble	harvester	recolector
furthermore	además	hat	sombrero
future	futuro	hate (v)	odiar (v)
		have (v)	haber, tener (v)
game (football, etc.)	partido	have a birthday (v)	cumplir (años) (v)
garbage	basura	have a shave (v)	afeitar/afeitarse
garden	jardín	have breakfast (v)	desayunar (v)
gas	gas	have fun (v)	divertirse (v)
gate	puerta	have lunch (v)	comer (v)
German (language)	alemán (idioma)	have supper (v)	cenar (v)
German (nationality)	alemán (nacionalidad)	head	cabeza
Germany	Alemania	health	salud
gesture	gesto	healthy	sano
get along well/badly with (v)	llevarse (bien/mal) (v)	hear (v)	oír (v)
get angry (v)	enfadarse (v)	heat	calor
get away (v)	escaparse (v)	heat up (v)	calentar (v)
get divorced (v)	divorciarse (v)	heating	calefacción

helmet	casco	kitchen	cocina
help (n)	ayuda	knife	cuchillo
help (v)	ayudar (v)	know (v)	conocer, saber (v)
hen	gallina		
here	aquí	ladder	escalera
high school	instituto (secundaria)	lake	lago
history	historia (asignatura)	lamp	lámpara
honest	honrado	land	suelo
honesty	honradez	land (country)	tierra (país)
hope (v)	esperar (v)	land (v)	aterrizar (v)
horrible	horrible	landlord (n)	casero (n)
horse	caballo	language	idioma
hospital	hospital	large (size)	grande
hot	caliente, caluroso, picante	last (adj)	pasado, último
hotel	hotel	last (v)	durar (v)
hour	hora	last night	anoche
house	casa	late	tarde (adv)
how	cómo	lately	últimamente
how much	cuánto	later	después (de)
human	humano	Latin	latino
hunger	hambre	laugh (v)	reírse (v)
hungry	hambre	laughter	risa
hurry (be in a)	prisa (tener, darse)	Law (degree)	Derecho (carrera)
hurt (v)	doler (v)	lawn	césped
husband	esposo, marido	lawyer	abogado
		laziness	pereza
I'm sorry	(lo) siento	lazy	vago
ice cream	helado	leaf	hoja
ID card	carné (identidad)	league	liga
illness	enfermedad	leather	cuero
IMF (International Monetary Fund)	FMI (Fondo monetario internacional)	leave (v)	abandonar (v)
impatient	impaciente	leave (v)	marcharse (v)
important	importante	lecture	conferencia
impressive	impresionante	lecturer (univ)	profesor
improve (v)	mejorar (v)	left	izquierda
in	en	leg	pata
in front of	delante (de), enfrente	lend (v)	dejar, prestar (v)
in/inside (space) ...	dentro (de) (espacio)	less	menos
Inca	inca	letter	carta, letra (a, b, c...)
independent	independiente	library	biblioteca
Indian	indio	lie	mentira
indoor	interior	lie (tell lies) (v)	mentir (v)
information	dato, información	life	vida
inhabitant	habitante	lift (elevator)	ascensor
inn	mesón	light	luz
institute	instituto (institución)	light (gas, cigarette)	encendido
instructions	instrucciones	like (v)	gustar (v)
instrument	instrumento	line	cola (fila)
intelligence	inteligencia	lion	león
intelligent	inteligente	lioness	leona
internet	internet	lip	labio
intersection	cruce	lira (currency)	lira (moneda)
interview	entrevista	listen (to) (v)	escuchar (v)
invent (v)	inventar (v)	liter	litro
inventor	inventor	little	poco/a/os/as
invitation	invitación	live (v)	vivir (v)
invite (v)	invitar (v)	living room	sala
involved	envuelto, implicado	llama	llama (animal)
IOC (International Olympic Committee)	COI (Comité Olímpico Internacional)	lock (v)	cerrar (v)
Iranian	iraní	locked (with a key)	cerrado (con llave)
irresponsible	irresponsable	locksmith	cerrajero
IRS	Hacienda	long	largo
island	isla	look (v)	mirar (v)
Italian (language)	italiano (idioma)	look after (v)	guardar (v)
Italian (nationality)	italiano (nacionalidad)	look for (v)	buscar (v)
		look like (v)	parecer(se) (v)
jacket	chaqueta	Look out!	¡Cuidado!
January	enero	lose (v)	perder (v)
Japanese (language)	japonés (idioma)	lottery	lotería
Japanese (nationality)	japonés (nacionalidad)	loud	alto (sonido)
jeans	vaqueros	lounge	salón
jersey	jersey	love (n)	amor
job	empleo, trabajo	love (someone) (v)	querer
jogging	footing	love (v)	amar (v)
journalist	periodista	low	bajo (sonido)
journey	viaje	lower case	minúscula (letra)
July	julio	luck	suerte
June	junio	lunar	lunar
jungle	selva		
		machine	máquina
kangaroo	canguro	madam	señora
keep (v)	guardar (v)	magazine	revista
key	llave	magical	mágico
kick	patada	mail / e-mail	correo / correo electrónico
kilo	kilo	mailbox	buzón
kilometer	kilómetro	mailman	cartero
kind (adj)	amable	mailwoman	cartera
kind (n)	tipo	main	principal
king	rey	make (v)	hacer (v)
kiss	beso	make a decision (v)	decidirse (v)

252

English	Spanish	English	Spanish
man	hombre	night	noche
manager	gerente	night club	discoteca
manager (company)	director, directora	no	no
map	mapa	nobody	nadie
marathon	maratón	noise	ruido
March	marzo	nonsense	tontería
mare	yegua	normal	normal
marks	notas (calificaciones)	normally	normalmente
marvellous	maravilloso	north	norte
marvellously	estupendamente	North American	norteamericano
match	cerilla	nose	nariz
mathematics	matemáticas	nothing	nada
matter (v)	importar (v)	novel	novela
mattress	colchón	November	noviembre
May	mayo	now	ahora
Mayan	maya	number	número
measure (n)	medida	nurse	enfermera
measure (v)	medir (v)	nurse	enfermero
meat	carne		
medicine	medicina	oboe	oboe
meeting	reunión	October	octubre
melon	melón	of course	por supuesto, claro
memory	recuerdo	offer (v)	ofrecer (v)
message	mensaje	office	oficina, despacho
meter	metro	often	(a) menudo
metro	metro (transporte)	oil	aceite
Mexican	mexicano	old	viejo, antiguo
midday	mediodía	older	mayor
middle	medio	omelet	tortilla
milk	leche	on	en
minister	ministro	on (electrical item)	encendido
minute	minuto	on (prep)	sobre (prep)
mirror	espejo	on top	encima
miss	señorita	onion	cebolla
mobile	móvil (teléfono)	only	solo (adv)
model	modelo	open (v)	abrir, inaugurar (v)
modern	moderno	opera	ópera
molar	muela	optician's	óptica
moment	momento	orange	naranja
Monday	lunes	orchestra	orquesta
money	dinero	organization	organización
month	mes	organize (v)	montar (armar) (v)
mood	humor	ostrich	avestruz
Moon	Luna	out (lights)	apagado (luces)
more	más	outside	fuera
morning	mañana (n)	outskirts	afueras (las)
Moroccan	marroquí	overall	bata (trabajo, escuela)
mother	madre	overcoat	abrigo
motorcycle	moto	overtake (v)	adelantar (v)
mountain	montaña		
mountaineering	alpinismo	pack, package	paquete
mountains	sierra	padlock	candado
mouse	ratón	paella	paella
move (v)	mover / moverse (v)	paint (v)	pintar (v)
move forward (v)	adelantar (v)	paintbrush	pincel
movies	cine	painter	pintor
Mr.	don	pair	par
Mrs./Ms.	doña	pajamas	pijama
murderer	asesino	pants	pantalones
museum	museo	paper	papel
music	música	parents	padres
musician	músico	park	parque
Muslim	musulmán	park (v)	aparcar (v)
mustache	bigote	part	parte
		party (event), public holiday	fiesta
nail	clavo	pass away (v)	fallecer (v)
naked	desnudo	patient	enfermo
name	nombre	patient	paciente
nap	siesta	pay (v)	pagar (v)
national	nacional	peace and quiet	tranquilidad
near	cerca (de)	peaceful	tranquilo
necessary	necesario	pear	pera
necklace	collar	pedestrian crossing	paso de cebra
need	falta (necesidad)	peel (v)	pelar (v)
need (v)	necesitar (v)	pencil	lapicero, lápiz
neighborhood	barrio	pencil sharpener	sacapuntas
neighbour	vecino	penguin	pingüino
neither	tampoco	people	gente
nervous	nervioso	perfectly	perfectamente
nest	nido	perfume	perfume
never	nunca	permission	permiso
new	nuevo	person	persona
news	noticia	personal	personal (adj)
newspaper	periódico	Peruvian	peruano
newsstand	quiosco	peso (currency)	peso (moneda)
next	próximo	petrol	gasolina
NGO (Non-Governmental Organization)	ONG (Organización No Gubernamental)	pharmacy	farmacia
Nicaraguan	nicaragüense	philosophy	filosofía
nice	majo	photo	foto (fotografía)
nice, friendly	simpático	photocopy	fotocopia

photographer	fotógrafo	read (v)	leer (v)
phrase	frase	real	real (moneda brasileña)
physical	físico (adj)	receive (v)	recibir (v)
physics	física	reception	recepción
pianist	pianista	receptionist	recepcionista
piano	piano	recommend (v)	recomendar (v)
pick up(v)	coger (v)	red	rojo
picture	cuadro	refrigerator	nevera
pilot (airplane)	piloto	region	región
pineapple	piña	regret (v)	arrepentirse (v)
pizza	pizza	relaxed	relajado
place	lugar	remain (v)	quedar (resto) (v)
place (v)	colocar (v)	remedy	remedio
plan	plan	remind (v)	recordar (v)
plant	planta (vegetal)	rent (v)	alquilar (v)
plant (v)	plantar (v)	repair (v)	arreglar (v)
plastic	plástico	repeat (v)	repetir (v)
plate	plato (utensilio)	reply	respuesta
play (drama)	obra (de teatro)	request (v)	pedir (v)
play (v)	jugar, tocar (un instrumento) (v)	reserve (v)	reservar (v)
player	jugador	resign (v)	dimitir (v)
playtime	recreo	rest (v)	descansar (v)
please	por favor	restaurant	restaurante
plug	enchufe	result	resultado
plumber	fontanero	return	vuelta
poem	poema	return (give back) (v)	devolver (v)
polar	polar	return (v)	regresar (v)
police force	policía (cuerpo)	return (v)	volver (v)
policeman	policía (agente)	rice	arroz
polyglot	políglota	rich	rico
poor	pobre	ride (v)	montar (en) (v)
pop	pop	right	derecha
poppy	amapola	ring	anillo
pork	cerdo (carne de)	ring	sortija
portable	portátil	river	río
Portuguese (language)	portugués (idioma)	road	carretera
Portuguese (nationality)	portugués (nacionalidad)	road-sweeper	barrendero
Post Office	Correos	roast (v)	asar (v)
postcard	postal	robot	robot
poster	cartel	rock (music)	rock (música)
potato	patata	room	habitación
pound (currency)	libra (moneda)	room (bedroom)	cuarto (habitación)
power	poder	rose (n)	rosa (n)
powerful	potente	rude	maleducado
practise (v)	practicar (v)	rug	alfombra
pray (v)	rezar (v)	run (v)	correr, recorrer (v)
precious	precioso	Russian (language)	ruso (idioma)
prefer (v)	preferir (v)	Russian (nationality)	ruso (nacionalidad)
prepare (v)	preparar (v)		
present (v)	presentar	**s**acrifice	sacrificio
president (republic)	presidente	sad	triste
press	prensa	salesperson	vendedor
pretty	bonito	salt	sal
prick (v)	pinchar (v)	same	igual
Prime minister	Primer ministro	sand	arena
prime minister (monarchy)	presidente	satellite	satélite
prince	príncipe	Saturday	sábado
princess	princesa	save (v)	guardar (v)
principal (school)	director, directora	saving	ahorro
print	lámina	say (v)	decir (v)
printer	impresora	say goodbye (v)	despedirse (v)
prison	cárcel	scare / be scared (v)	asustar/asustar (se) (v)
prisoner	preso	scarf	bufanda, pañuelo
prize	premio	school	colegio, instituto (institución)
problem	problema	science	ciencia
prohibited	prohibido	scissors	tijeras
protestant	protestante	Scottish	escocés
prove (v)	resultar (v)	screw	tornillo
pub	bar	screwdriver	destornillador
publisher	editorial	sculptor	escultor
punctual	puntual	sea	mar
pupil	alumno, alumna	seafood	marisco
push (v)	empujar (v)	search for (v)	buscar (v)
put (v)	poner (v)	seat	asiento
put on (v)	ponerse (v)	secret	secreto
put out (v)	apagar (v)	secretary	secretaria
put to bed (v)	acostar/acostarse (v)	see (v)	ver (v)
put, place (v)	colocar (v)	seem (v)	parecer(se) (v)
Pyrenees	Pirineos	selfish	egoísta
		sell (v)	vender (v)
qualify (v)	titularse	send (v)	enviar (v)
quarter (time)	cuarto (hora)	sensation	sensación
quickly	deprisa	sentence	frase, oración, pena, condena
quickly	rápido	separate (v)	separar (v)
		September	septiembre
racket	raqueta	serious	grave
radio	radio	seriousness	seriedad
railway	ferrocarril	service	servicio
rain	lluvia	settlement	poblado
rain (v)	llover (v)	several	varios/as

shade	sombra	station	estación
shadow	sombra	stationery shop	papelería
shape	forma	statue	estatua
share (v)	compartir (v)	stay (v)	quedarse, alojarse (v)
shave	afeitado	step on (v)	pisar (v)
shellfish	marisco	stew	cocido
shirt	camisa	still	todavía
shoes	zapatos	stomach	estómago
shop	tienda	stone	piedra
shop assistant	dependiente	stop (n)	parada
shore	orilla	stop (v)	parar, pararse, detenerse (v)
short	corto, bajo (estatura)	stork	cigüeña
shout (v)	gritar (v)	storm	tormenta
show (v)	enseñar, mostrar (v)	story	historia (relato)
shrimp	gambas	straight	recto
shy	tímido	strawberry	fresa
siesta	siesta	street	calle
sign (n)	cartel	strength	fuerza
silver	plata	strike	huelga
sing (v)	cantar (v)	strong	fuerte
singer	cantante	struggle	lucha
sink	lavabo	student	estudiante
sir	señor	study (v)	estudiar (v)
sister	hermana	sub sandwich	bocadillo
sit down (v)	sentarse (v)	subject	asignatura
situation	situación	subway	metro (transporte)
sixth	sexto	success	éxito
ski (n)	esquí	Sudanese	sudanés
ski (v)	esquiar (v)	sufficient	suficiente
skill	habilidad	sugar	azúcar
skin	piel	suit	traje
skirt	falda	suitcase	maleta
sky	cielo	summer	verano
sleep / go to sleep (v)	dormir/dormirse (v)	sun	sol
slim	delgado	Sunday	domingo
slippers	zapatillas	superstition	superstición
slow	lento	supper	cena
slowly	despacio	surely	seguramente
slowness	lentitud	surprise	sorpresa
small	pequeño	suspect (v)	sospechar (v)
smell (v)	oler (v)	suspicious	sospechoso
smile (v)	sonreír (v)	Swedish (language)	sueco (idioma)
smoke (v)	fumar (v)	Swedish (nationality)	sueco (nacionalidad)
snake	serpiente	sweet (adj)	dulce
snow (n)	nieve	sweet (n)	caramelo
snow (v)	nevar (v)	swim (v)	nadar (v)
so many	tantos/as	swimming	natación
soccer	fútbol	swimming pool	piscina
soccer player	futbolista	switch off (v)	apagar (v)
socialist	socialista		
soft	suave	table	mesa
soft drink	refresco	tailor's	sastrería
some (approximately)	unos/as (aproximadamente)	take a shower (v)	ducharse (v)
somebody	alguien	take a walk (v)	dar un paseo (v)
someone	alguien	take off (v)	quitarse (v)
something	algo	take out (v)	sacar (v)
son	hijo	talk (v)	hablar (v)
song	canción	tall	alto (estatura)
sound (v)	sonar (v)	tango	tango
soup	sopa	target (fig)	meta
south	sur	taste (v)	probar (v)
southwest	suroeste	tasty	rico (sabroso)
sovereign	soberano	taxes	impuestos
space	espacio	taxi	taxi
Spanish (language)	español (idioma)	tea	té
Spanish (nationality)	español (nacionalidad)	teach (v)	enseñar (v)
speak (v)	hablar (v)	teacher (school)	profesor
special	especial	telephone	teléfono
spectator	espectador	television	televisión
speed	rapidez	television set	televisor
spend (time) (v)	pasar (tiempo) (v)	tell (v)	decir, contar (v)
spend (v)	gastar (v)	tell off (v)	regañar (v)
spend the summer (v)	veranear (v)	temperature	temperatura, fiebre
spicy	picante	tennis	tenis
spoilt	caprichoso	tennis player	tenista
spoon	cuchara	tequila	tequila
spoonful	cucharada	test	test
sport	deporte	thanks	gracias
sports center	polideportivo	that	aquel, aquella, aquello, eso
spot	mancha	The Amazon River, The Amazon Forest	Amazonas
square	plaza	The Americas	América
square meter	metro cuadrado	the day after tomorrow	pasado mañana
squid	calamares	the day before yesterday	anteayer
stadium	estadio	the postal service	correo
stain	mancha	The West Indies	Antillas
stall	puesto (de venta)	theater	teatro
stand	puesto (de venta)	then	entonces, luego
star	estrella	there	ahí, allí
start (v)	empezar (v)	there be	haber (v)
state	estado	there is/are	hay

255

thermometer	termómetro
thief	ladrón
thin	delgado
thing	cosa
thirst	sed
thirsty	sediento
this	este, esta, esto
thoughtless	alocado
thrilling	apasionante
throw (out) (v)	echar (v)
throw/ throw yourself (v)	tirar/ tirarse (v)
Thursday	jueves
ticket	billete, entrada
tidy up (v)	ordenar (v)
tie	corbata
tie / tie up (v)	atar/atarse (v)
time	tiempo, hora
time, at the same time	vez, a la vez
tin	lata
tip (restaurant)	propina
tired	cansado
title (book), title	título
to	menos (hora)
to be good / bad at (v)	darse bien/mal (v)
toast	tostada
toast (v)	tostar (v)
tobacco	tabaco
tobacco shop	estanco
today	hoy
tomorrow	mañana (adv)
tonic water	tónica
too (much/many)	demasiado
tooth	diente
touch (v)	tocar (palpar) (v)
tourism	turismo
tourist	turista
tourist	turístico
town	ciudad
tradesman	comerciante
traffic	tráfico
train	tren
translate (v)	traducir (v)
translation	traducción
translator	traductor
transport	transporte
trash	basura
travel (v)	viajar (v)
tree	árbol
trip	viaje
truck	camión
truck driver	camionero
trust (v)	confiar (v)
truth	verdad
try (v)	probar (v)
Tuesday	martes
tulip	tulipán
tuna fish	atún
turn (v)	girar (v)
turn on (electrical item) (v)	encender (v)
turtle	tortuga
twist (v)	torcer (v)
type	tipo
UFO (unidentified flying object)	OVNI
ugly	feo
umbrella	paraguas
UN (United Nations Organization)	ONU (Organización de Naciones Unidas)
uncle	tío
uncomfortable	incómodo
understand (v)	entender (v)
understand each other / one another	entenderse (v)
unforgettable	inolvidable
unfriendly	antipático
university	universidad
university student	universitario
unknown	desconocido
until	hasta
upstairs	arriba
urgent	urgente
use (v)	usar (v)
useful	útil
vacation	vacaciones
vegetable garden	huerto
vegetables	verdura
vegetarian	vegetariano
Venezuelan	venezolano
very	muy
video	vídeo
Vietnamese (language)	vietnamita (lengua)
Vietnamese (nationality)	vietnamita (nacionalidad)
village	pueblo
violent	violento
violin	violín
visit (v)	visitar (v)
voice	voz
wait (v)	esperar (v)
waiter	camarero
waitress	camarera
wake up (v)	despertar/despertarse (v)
walk	caminata
walk (n)	paseo
walk (v)	andar (v)
want (something) (v)	querer
war	guerra
warrior	guerrero
wash oneself (v)	lavarse (v)
washing machine	lavadora
watch	reloj
water (n)	agua
water (v)	regar (v)
watermelon	sandía
way	manera, modo
wear (v)	vestir (v)
wear out (v)	estropearse (v)
weather	tiempo (meteorológico)
wedding	boda
Wednesday	miércoles
week	semana
weekend	fin de semana
weigh (v)	pesar (v)
well (adv)	bueno (adv)
west	oeste
wet	mojado
what	qué
wheat	trigo
wheel	rueda
when	cuando, cuándo
where	donde, dónde
where... (to)	adónde
while (n)	rato
white	blanco
who	quién
who... from	(de) quién
will	voluntad
win (v)	tocar (la lotería) (v)
win, earn (v)	ganar (v)
wind	viento
window	ventana
wine	vino
wing	ala
winner	ganador
winter	invierno
wish	deseo
wish (v)	desear (v)
wit	gracia
within (time)	dentro (de) (tiempo)
woman	mujer
wood	madera
wool	lana
work (machines) (v)	funcionar (v)
work (n)	trabajo
work (v)	trabajar (v)
worker	obrero
worker	trabajador
world (adj)	mundial
world (n)	mundo
worry (v)	preocuparse (v)
worse	peor
wounded	herido
wrinkle	arruga
write (v)	escribir (v)
writer	escritor
year	año
yellow	amarillo
yellow fever	fiebre amarilla
yen	yen
yesterday	ayer
yoga	yoga
yoghurt	yogur
young	joven (adj)
young person	joven (n)